...A Doesn't Tell Us

VOL. 2

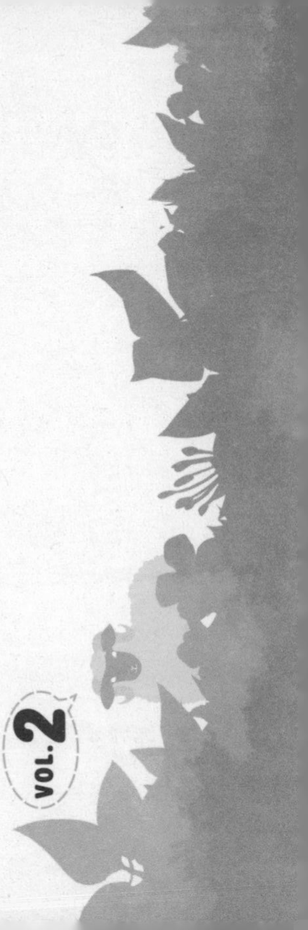

STORY

Animals Reformed and Cultured to be Humanoids, or Arcoids for short, are animals that transformed into human girls. Youko and her fellow Arcoids are having a good time learning how to belong in human society while at the Animalium research facility in Shikoku, Japan.

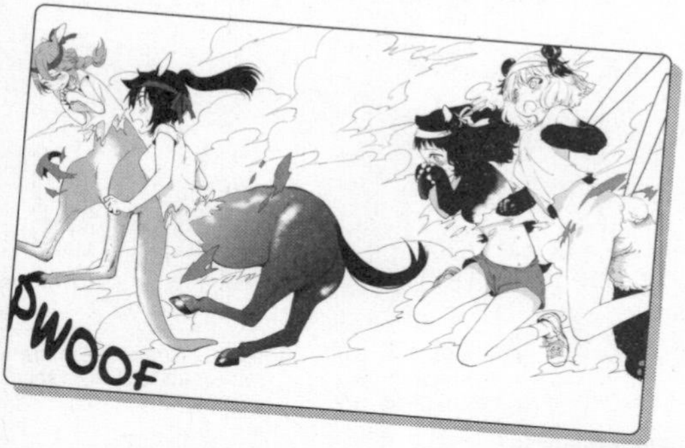
PWOOF

CHARACTERS

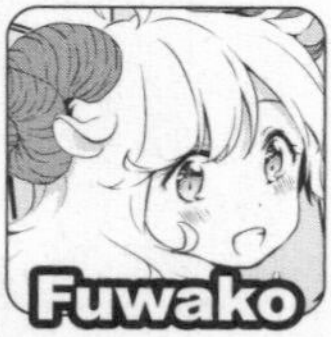
Fuwako

(Artiodactyla: Bovidae: Ovis)
Australian Merino

A sheep who was once kept for wool production, the laid-back Fuwako is in love with her own fleece.

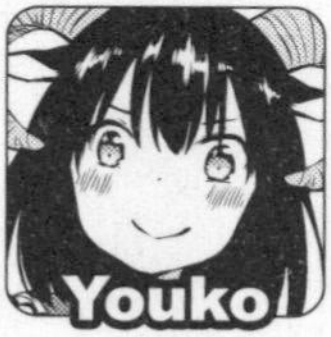
Youko

(Artiodactyla: Bovidae: Ovis)
Bighorn Sheep

Originally a wild sheep. Very capable; she used to help out at a ranch. Her species is known for their large horns.

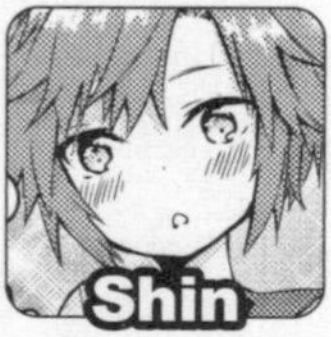
Shin

(Carnivora: Canidae: Canis)
Eastern Timber Wolf

A wolf that used to live with her family in a zoo. Completely in love with Usamii.

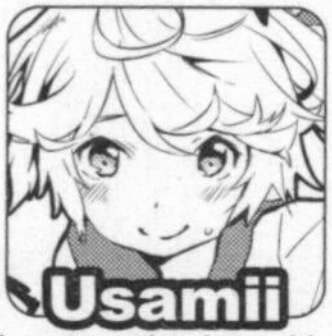
Usamii

(Lagomorpha: Leporidae: Oryctolagus)
Holland Lop Bunny

An inquisitive dwarf bunny with lop ears, her emotions immediately show on her face.

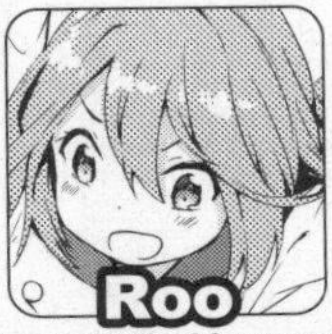

Roo

(Diprotodontia: Macropodidae: Macropus)
Red Kangaroo

A marsupial who leaps with her hind legs and tail.

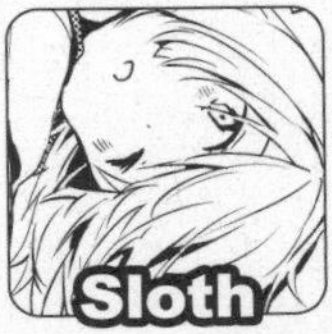

Sloth

(Pilosa: Bradypodidae: Bradypus)
Three-Toed Sloth

She is an energy-saving creature that moves slowly.

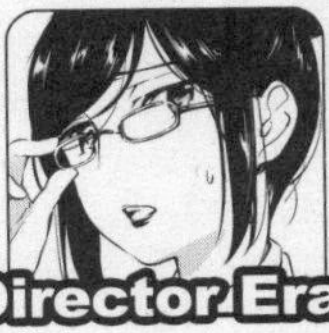

Director Erai

(Primates: Hominidae: Homo)
Homo Sapiens

She is the Director of Animalium and teaches Youko's class. Single.

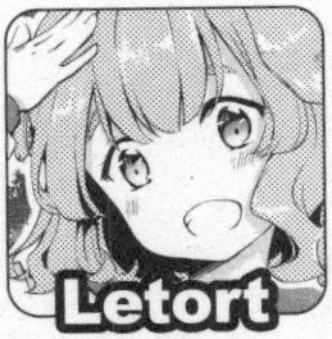

Letort

(Carnivora: Canidae: Canis)
Golden Retriever

She loves to work with other people. She gives tours to the new students.

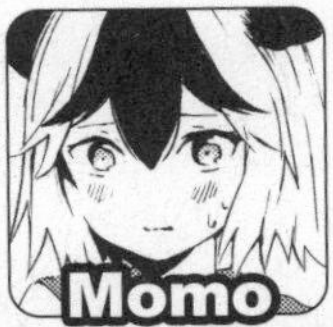

Momo

(Diprotodontia: Petauridae: Petaurus)
Sugar Glider

She gets lonely easily. Her species uses the membranes between their legs to glide.

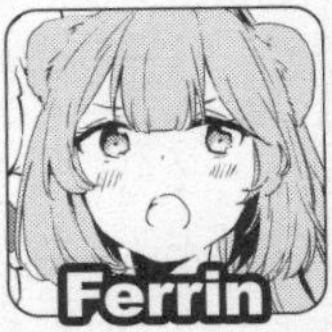

Ferrin

(Carnivora: Mustelidae: Mustela)
Ferret

Domesticated from the European polecat, she loves to play.

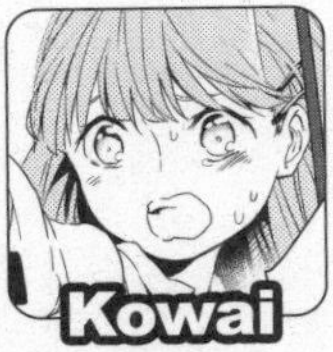

Kowai

(Primates: Hominidae: Homo)
Homo Sapiens

Assigned to teach the Wild Animal Class despite being timid. She has a problem with saying no.

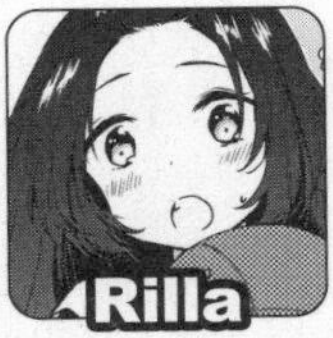

Rilla

(Primates: Hominidae: Gorilla)
Western Lowland Gorilla

She makes sounds and uses gestures to communicate with other gorillas.

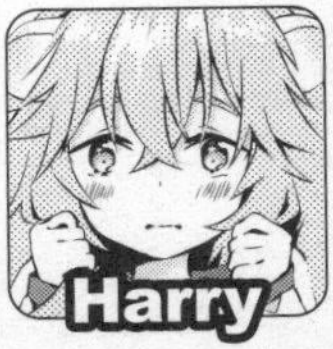

Harry

(Eulipotyphla: Erinaceidae: Atelerix
Four-Toed Hedgehog

Her body is covered in spikes that protect her from predators. Dorm leader for the domestic Arcoids.

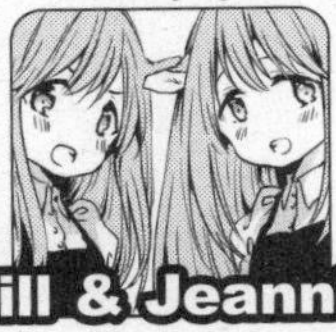

Jill & Jeannie

(Artiodactyla: Bovidae: Bos)
Jersey Cow

Julietta's twin daughters.

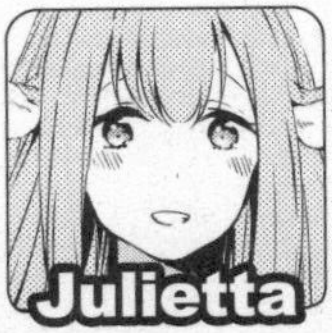

Julietta

(Artiodactyla: Bovidae: Bos)
Jersey Cow

She is the manager of Jersey Café.

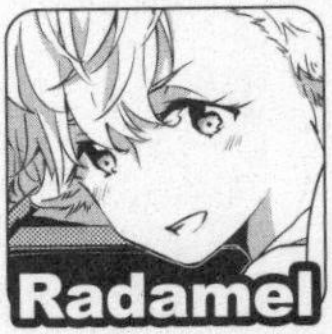

Radamel

(Artiodactyla: Camelidae: Camelus
Dromedary

Her body can adapt to hot and dry conditions.

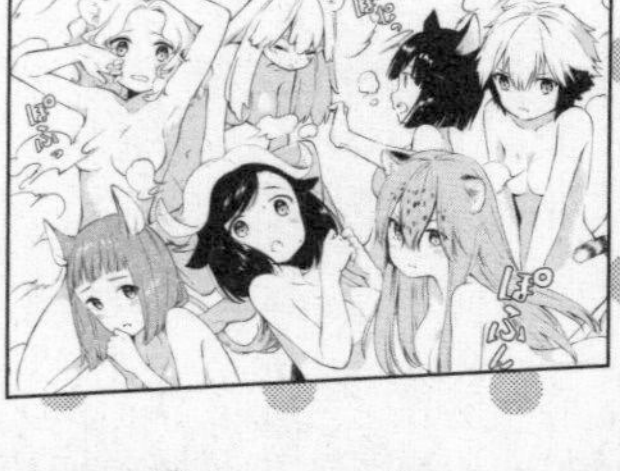
ぽふっ
ぽふん
ぽふ

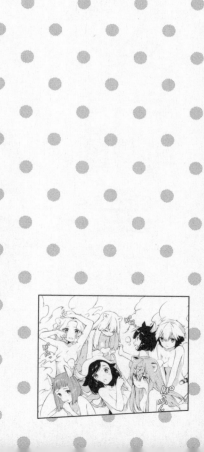

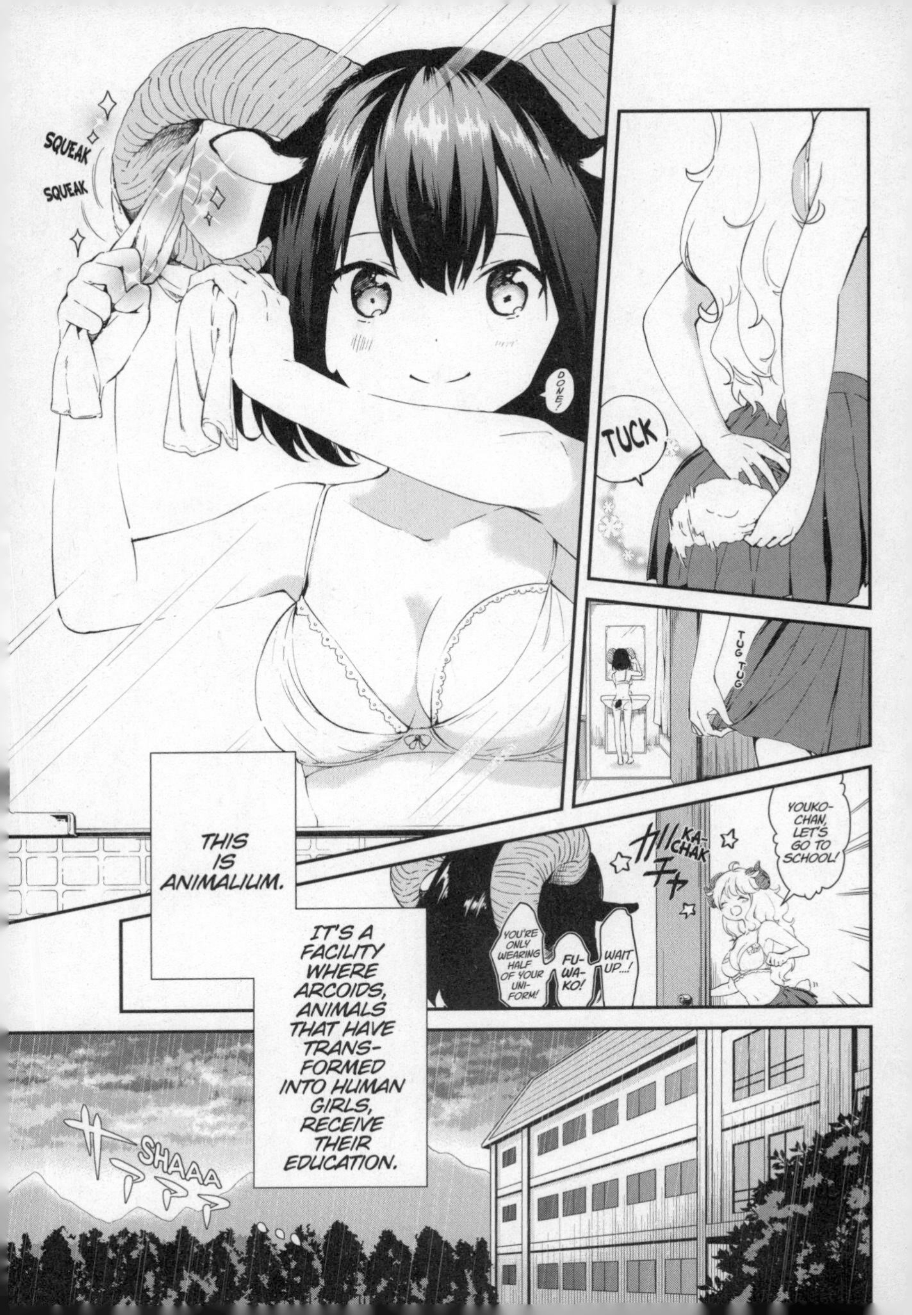

TUCK
TUG TUG
SQUEAK
SQUEAK
DONE!
KA-CHAK
YOUKO-CHAN, LET'S GO TO SCHOOL!
THIS IS ANIMALIUM.
WAIT UP...!
FU-WA-KO!
YOU'RE ONLY WEARING HALF OF YOUR UNI-FORM!
IT'S A FACILITY WHERE ARCOIDS, ANIMALS THAT HAVE TRANS-FORMED INTO HUMAN GIRLS, RECEIVE THEIR EDUCATION.
SHAAA

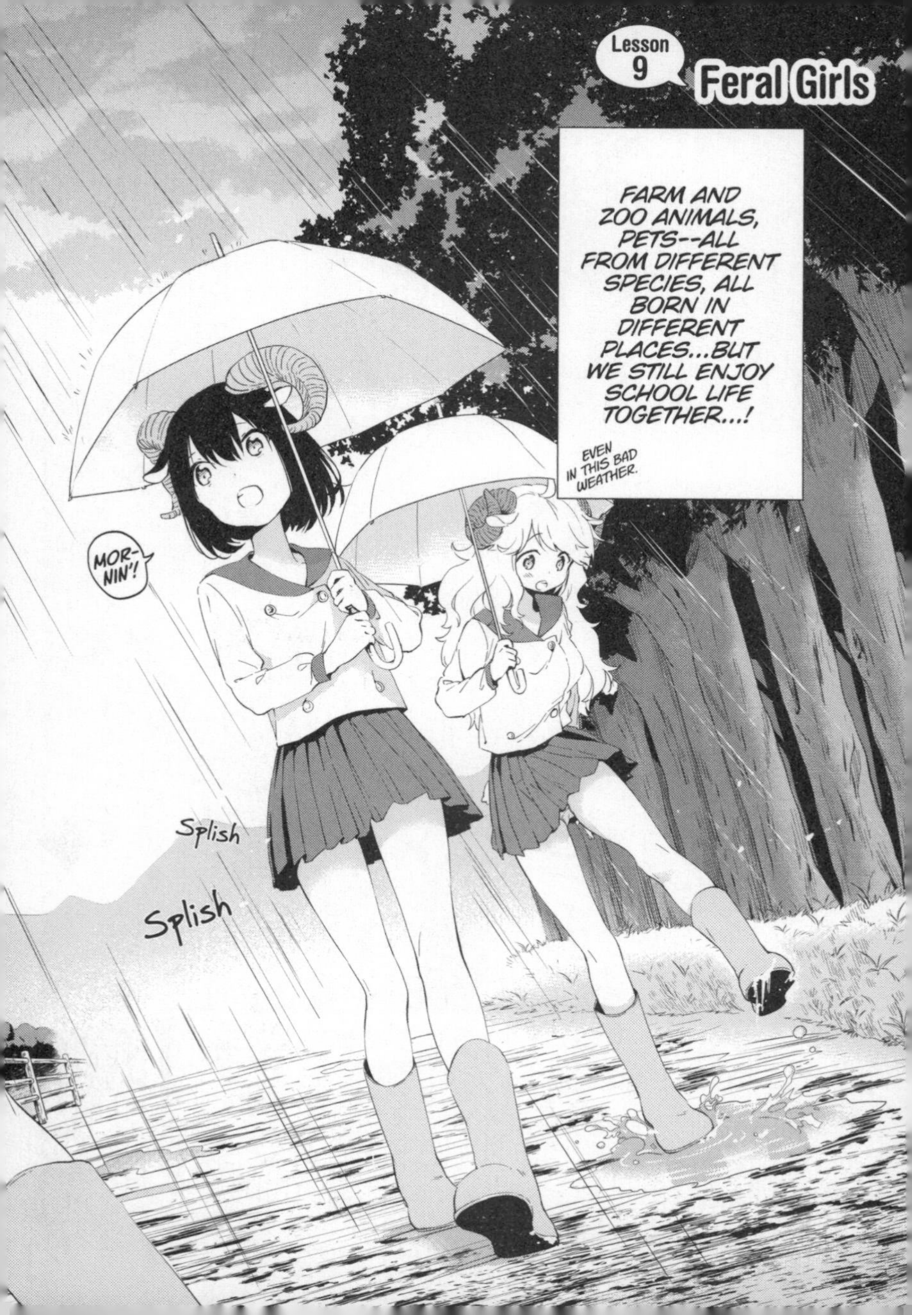
Lesson 9
Feral Girls
FARM AND ZOO ANIMALS, PETS--ALL FROM DIFFERENT SPECIES, ALL BORN IN DIFFERENT PLACES...BUT WE STILL ENJOY SCHOOL LIFE TOGETHER...!
EVEN IN THIS BAD WEATHER.
MOR-NIN'!
Splish
Splish

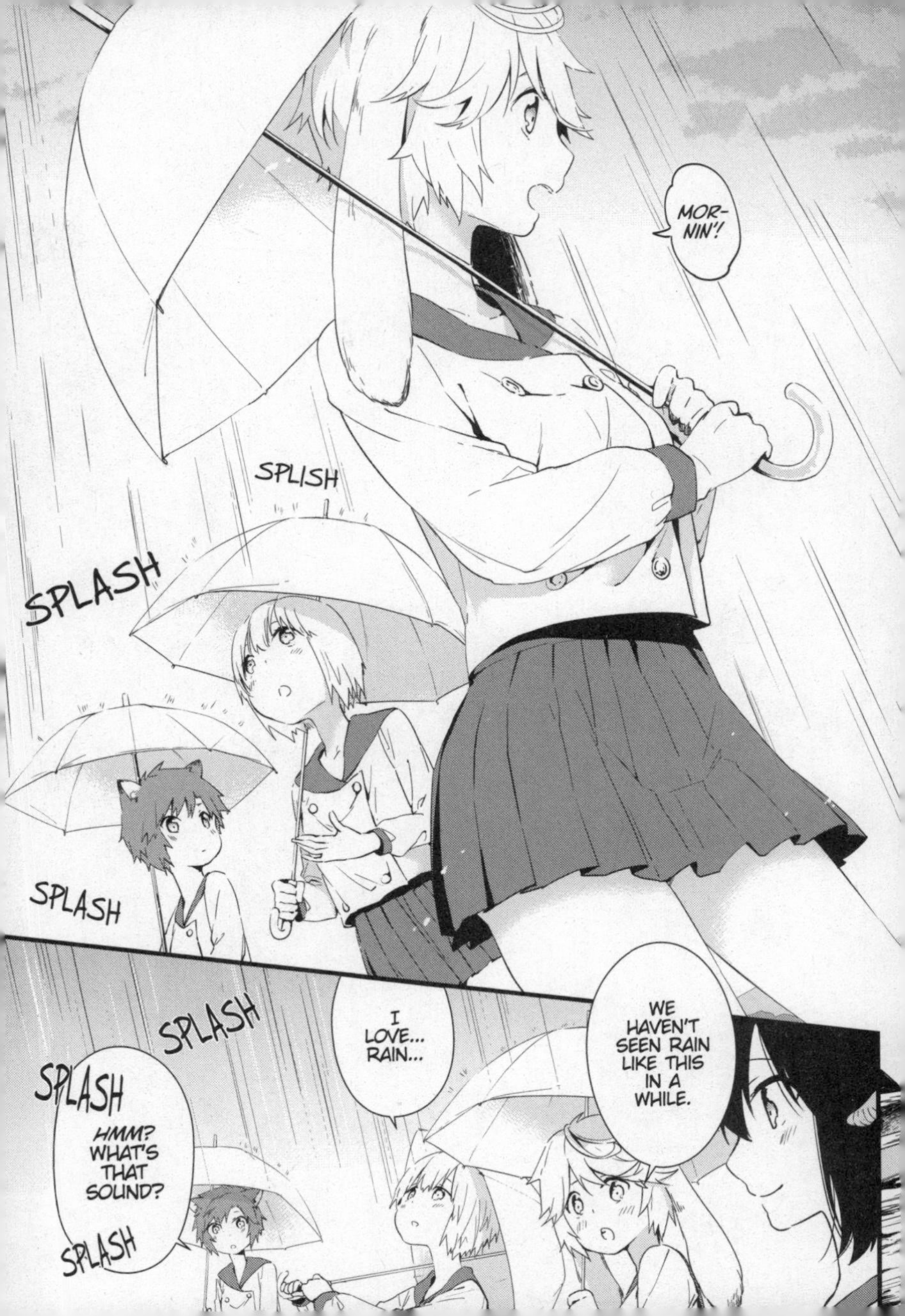
MOR-NIN'!
SPLISH
SPLASH
SPLASH
WE HAVEN'T SEEN RAIN LIKE THIS IN A WHILE.
I LOVE... RAIN...
SPLASH
SPLASH
HMM? WHAT'S THAT SOUND?
SPLASH

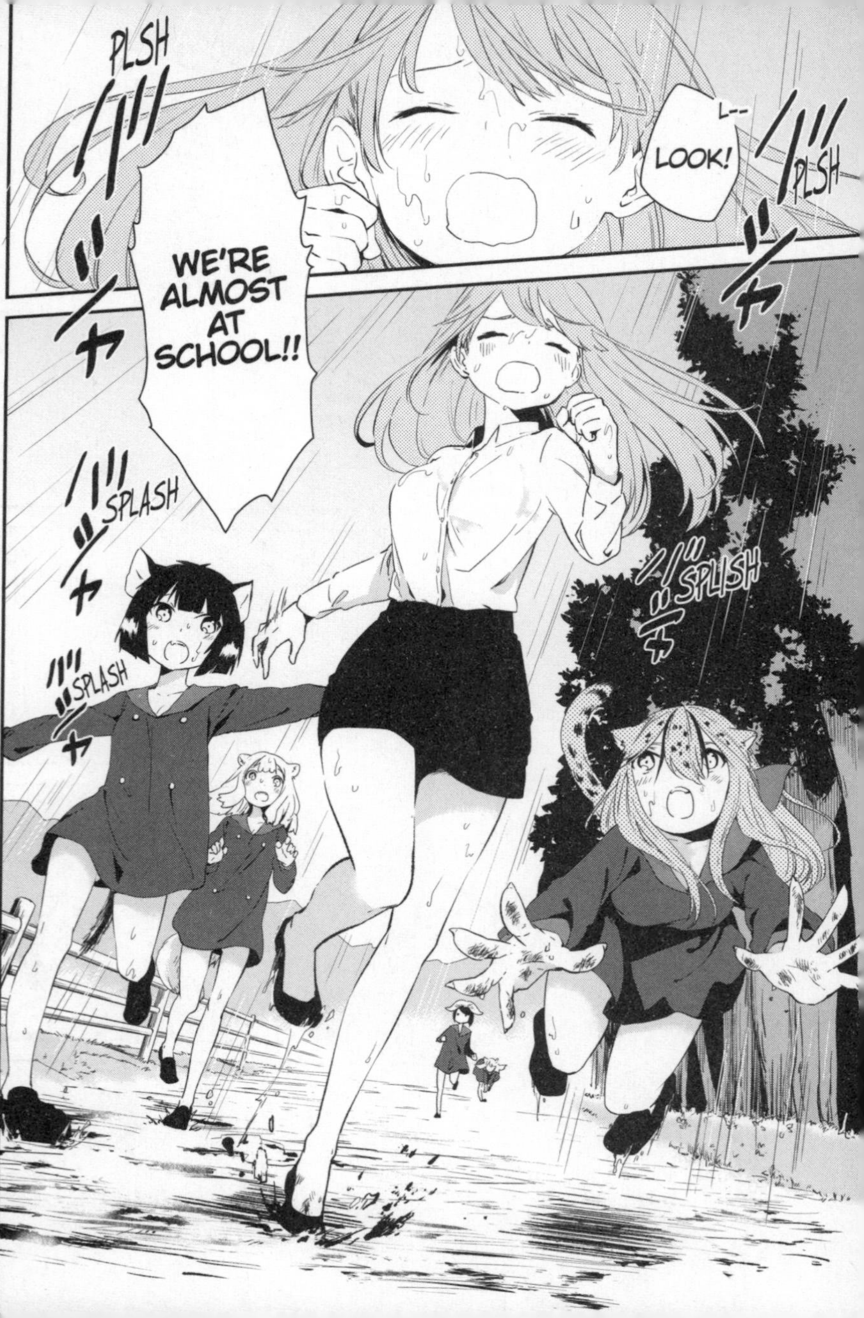
PLSH
LOOK!
PLSH
WE'RE ALMOST AT SCHOOL!!
SPLISH
SPLASH
SPLASH

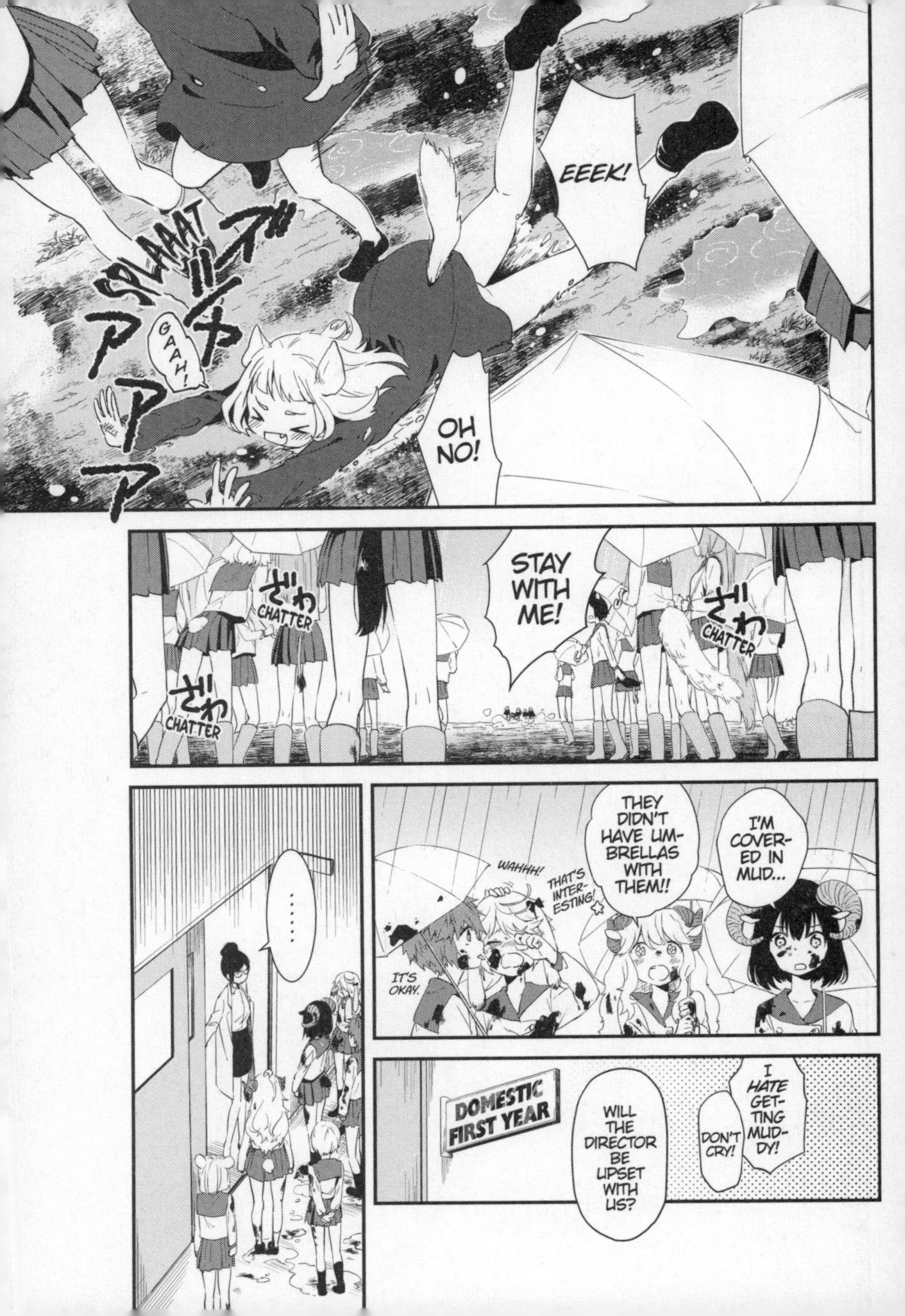
EEEK!
SPLAAAT
ベチャア
GAAH!
OH NO!
STAY WITH ME!
ざわ
CHATTER
ざわ
CHATTER
ざわ
CHATTER
I'M COVERED IN MUD...
THEY DIDN'T HAVE UMBRELLAS WITH THEM!!
THAT'S INTERESTING!
WAHHH!
IT'S OKAY.
I HATE GETTING MUDDY!
DON'T CRY!
WILL THE DIRECTOR BE UPSET WITH US?
DOMESTIC FIRST YEAR
......

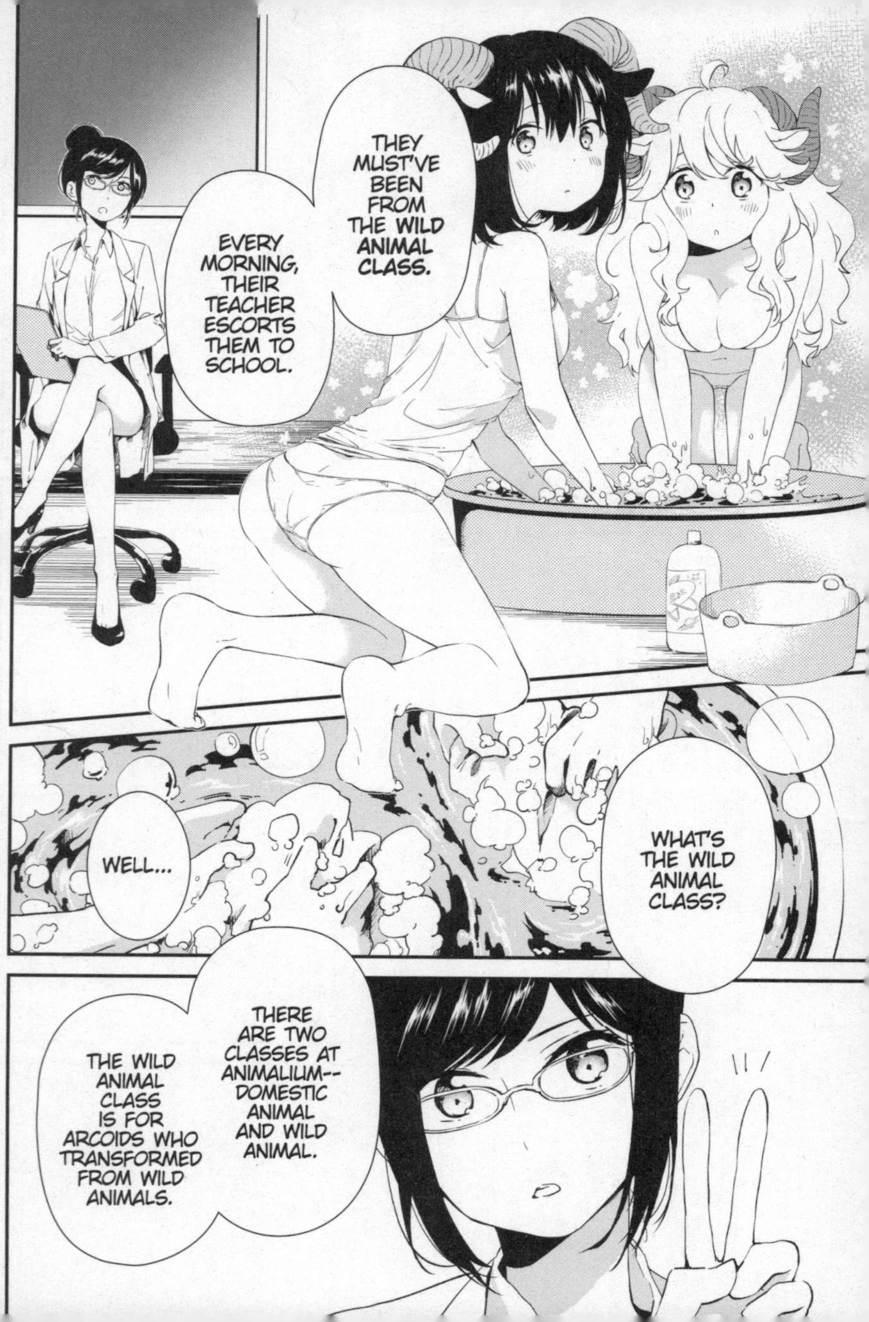
THEY MUST'VE BEEN FROM THE WILD ANIMAL CLASS.
EVERY MORNING, THEIR TEACHER ESCORTS THEM TO SCHOOL.
WHAT'S THE WILD ANIMAL CLASS?
WELL...
THERE ARE TWO CLASSES AT ANIMALIUM-- DOMESTIC ANIMAL AND WILD ANIMAL.
THE WILD ANIMAL CLASS IS FOR ARCOIDS WHO TRANSFORMED FROM WILD ANIMALS.

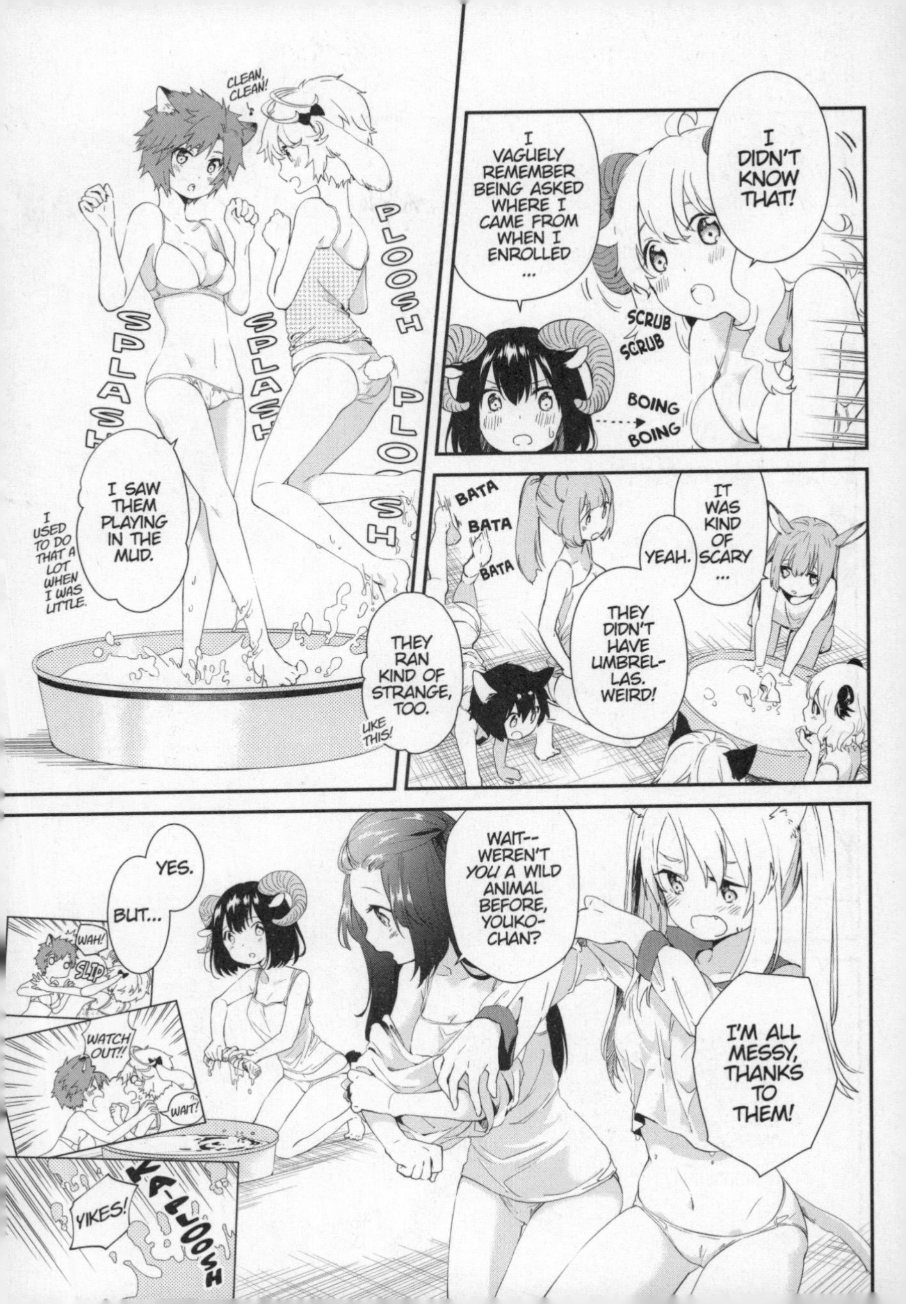
I DIDN'T KNOW THAT!
I VAGUELY REMEMBER BEING ASKED WHERE I CAME FROM WHEN I ENROLLED ...
SCRUB SCRUB
BOING BOING
IT WAS KIND OF SCARY ...
YEAH.
BATA BATA BATA
THEY DIDN'T HAVE UMBREL-LAS. WEIRD!
THEY RAN KIND OF STRANGE, TOO.
LIKE THIS!
CLEAN, CLEAN!
PLOOSH PLOOSH
SPLASH SPLASH
I SAW THEM PLAYING IN THE MUD.
I USED TO DO THAT A LOT WHEN I WAS LITTLE.
I'M ALL MESSY, THANKS TO THEM!
WAIT-- WEREN'T YOU A WILD ANIMAL BEFORE, YOUKO-CHAN?
YES.
BUT...
WAH!
SLIP
WATCH OUT!!
WAIT!
KA-PLOOSH
YIKES!

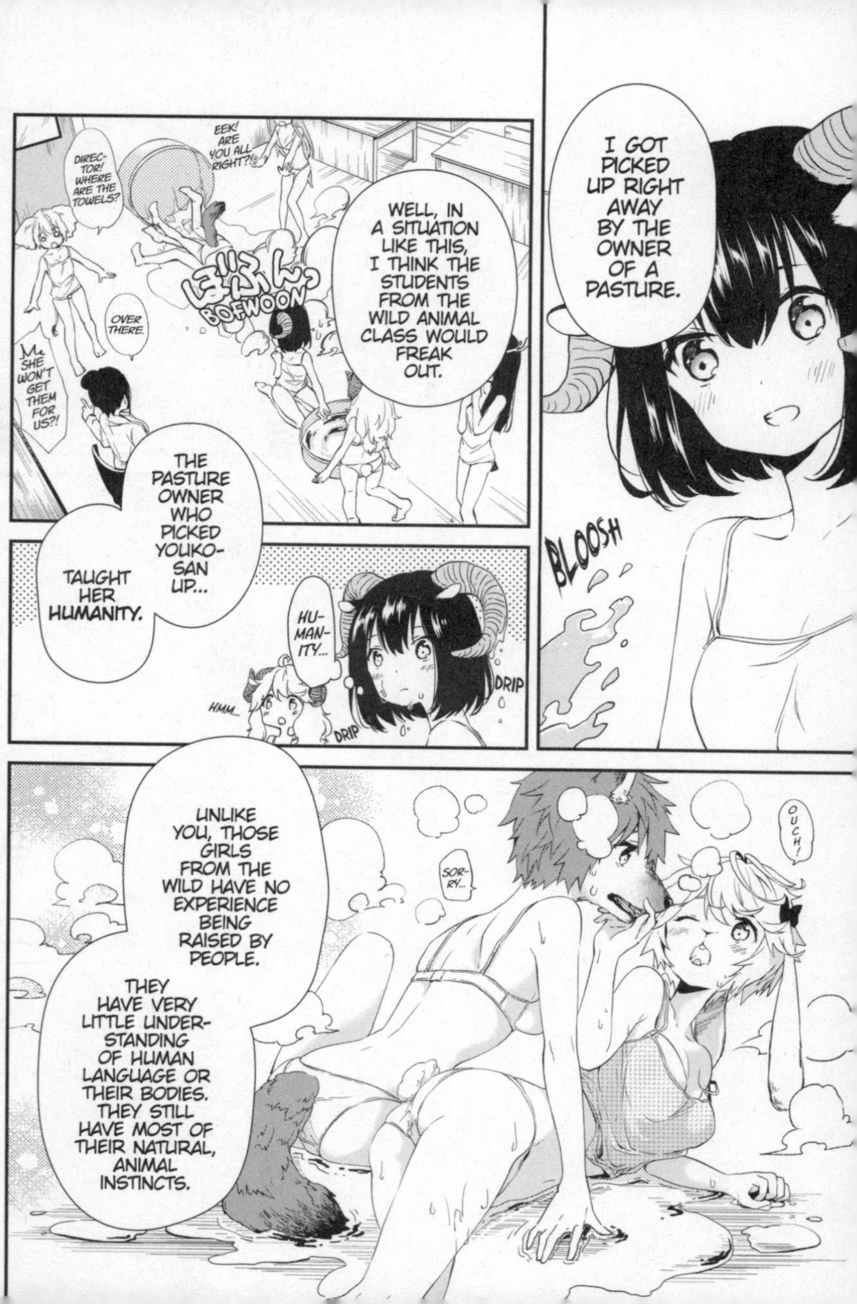

I GOT PICKED UP RIGHT AWAY BY THE OWNER OF A PASTURE.
BLOOSH
WELL, IN A SITUATION LIKE THIS, I THINK THE STUDENTS FROM THE WILD ANIMAL CLASS WOULD FREAK OUT.
EEK! ARE YOU ALL RIGHT?!
DIRECTOR! WHERE ARE THE TOWELS?
ぼふんっ
BOFWOON
OVER THERE.
SHE WON'T GET THEM FOR US?!
THE PASTURE OWNER WHO PICKED YOUKO-SAN UP...
TAUGHT HER HUMANITY.
HU-MAN-ITY...
DRIP
HMM...
DRIP
UNLIKE YOU, THOSE GIRLS FROM THE WILD HAVE NO EXPERIENCE BEING RAISED BY PEOPLE.
OUCH!
SORRY...
THEY HAVE VERY LITTLE UNDER-STANDING OF HUMAN LANGUAGE OR THEIR BODIES. THEY STILL HAVE MOST OF THEIR NATURAL, ANIMAL INSTINCTS.

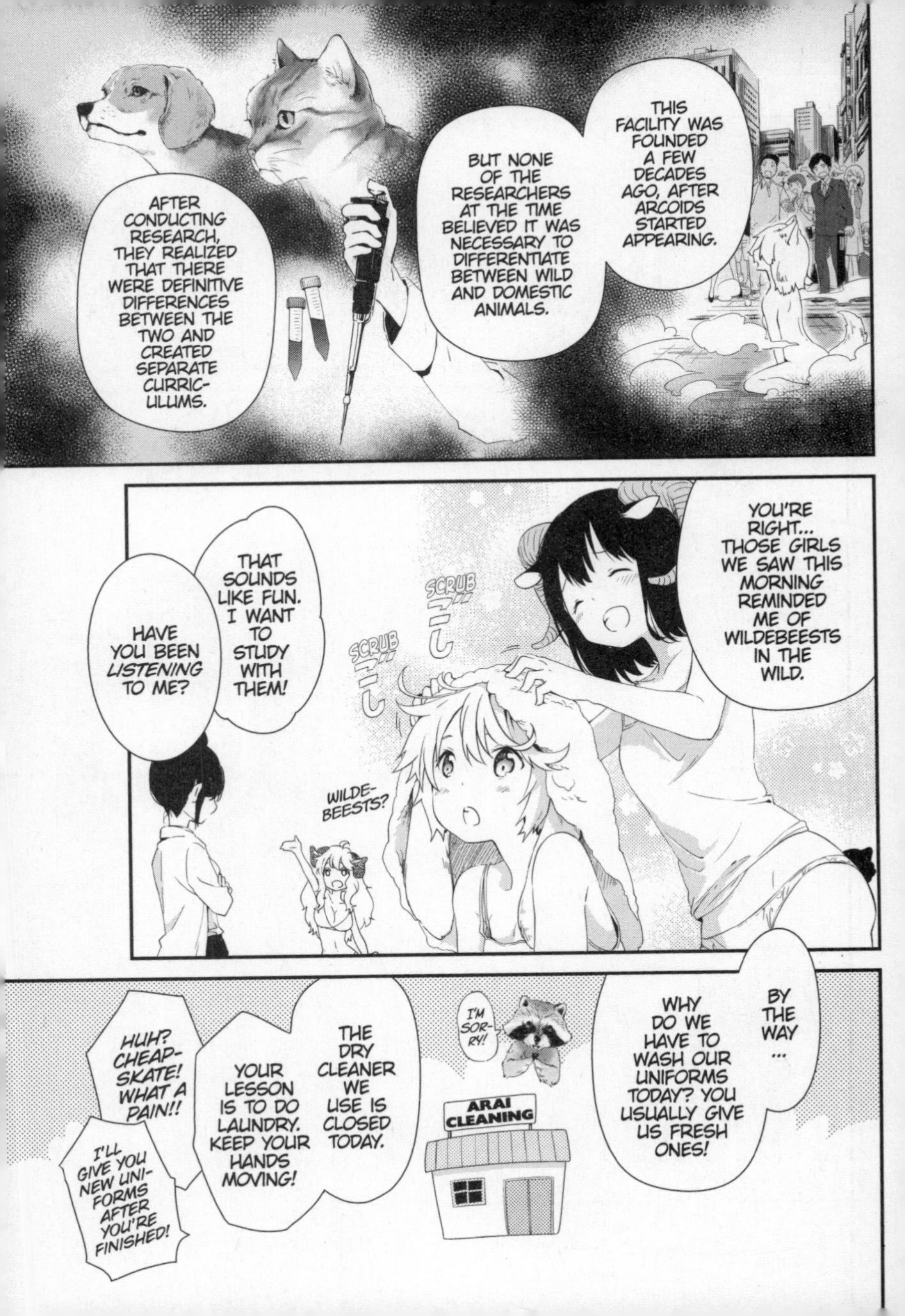
THIS FACILITY WAS FOUNDED A FEW DECADES AGO, AFTER ARCOIDS STARTED APPEARING.
BUT NONE OF THE RESEARCHERS AT THE TIME BELIEVED IT WAS NECESSARY TO DIFFERENTIATE BETWEEN WILD AND DOMESTIC ANIMALS.
AFTER CONDUCTING RESEARCH, THEY REALIZED THAT THERE WERE DEFINITIVE DIFFERENCES BETWEEN THE TWO AND CREATED SEPARATE CURRIC-ULUMS.
YOU'RE RIGHT... THOSE GIRLS WE SAW THIS MORNING REMINDED ME OF WILDEBEESTS IN THE WILD.
SCRUB
SCRUB
WILDE-BEESTS?
THAT SOUNDS LIKE FUN. I WANT TO STUDY WITH THEM!
HAVE YOU BEEN *LISTENING* TO ME?
BY THE WAY...
WHY DO WE HAVE TO WASH OUR UNIFORMS TODAY? YOU USUALLY GIVE US FRESH ONES!
I'M SOR-RY!
ARAI CLEANING
THE DRY CLEANER WE USE IS CLOSED TODAY.
YOUR LESSON IS TO DO LAUNDRY. KEEP YOUR HANDS MOVING!
HUH? CHEAP-SKATE! WHAT A PAIN!!
I'LL GIVE YOU NEW UNI-FORMS AFTER YOU'RE FINISHED!

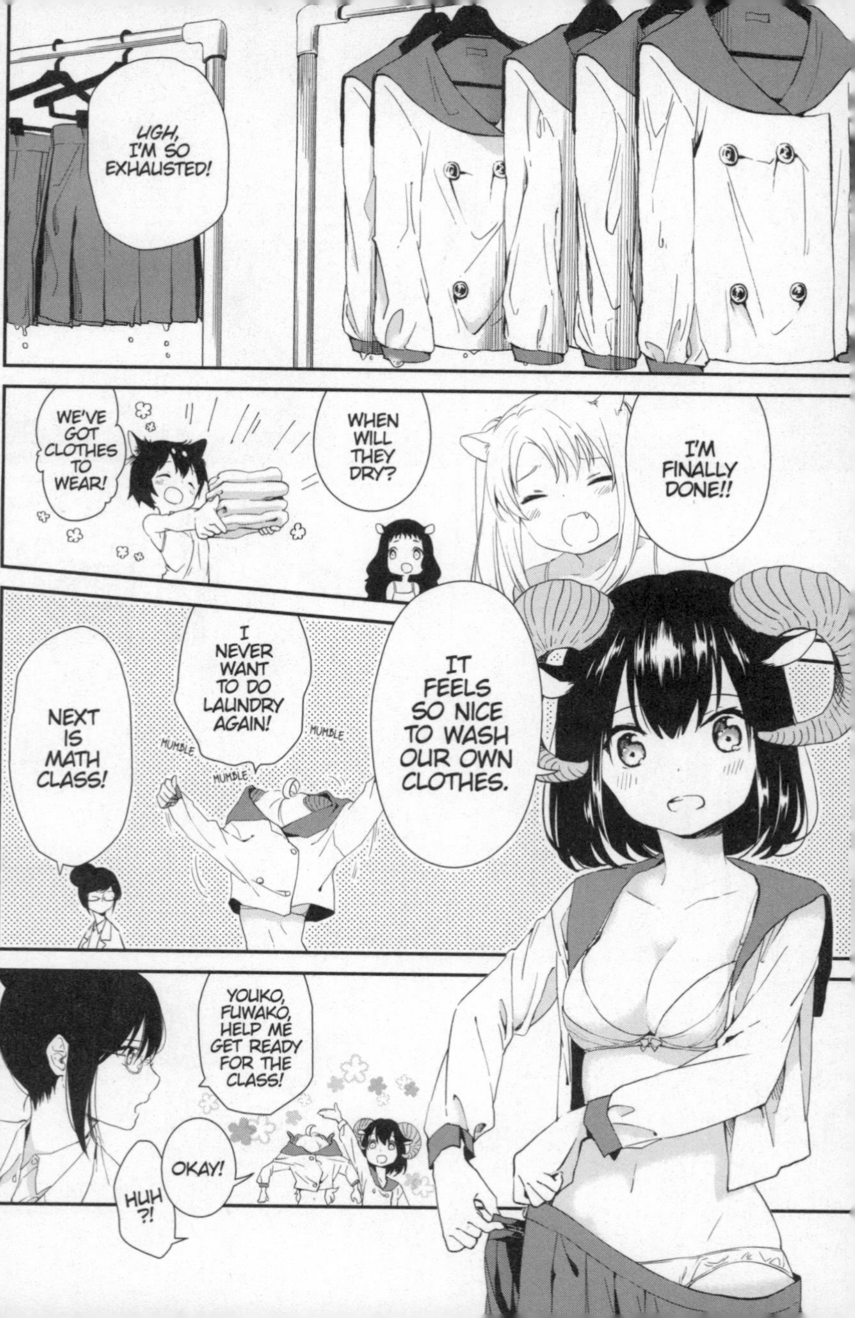
UGH, I'M SO EXHAUSTED!
I'M FINALLY DONE!!
WHEN WILL THEY DRY?
WE'VE GOT CLOTHES TO WEAR!
IT FEELS SO NICE TO WASH OUR OWN CLOTHES.
I NEVER WANT TO DO LAUNDRY AGAIN!
MUMBLE
MUMBLE
MUMBLE
NEXT IS MATH CLASS!
YOUKO, FUWAKO, HELP ME GET READY FOR THE CLASS!
OKAY!
HUH ?!

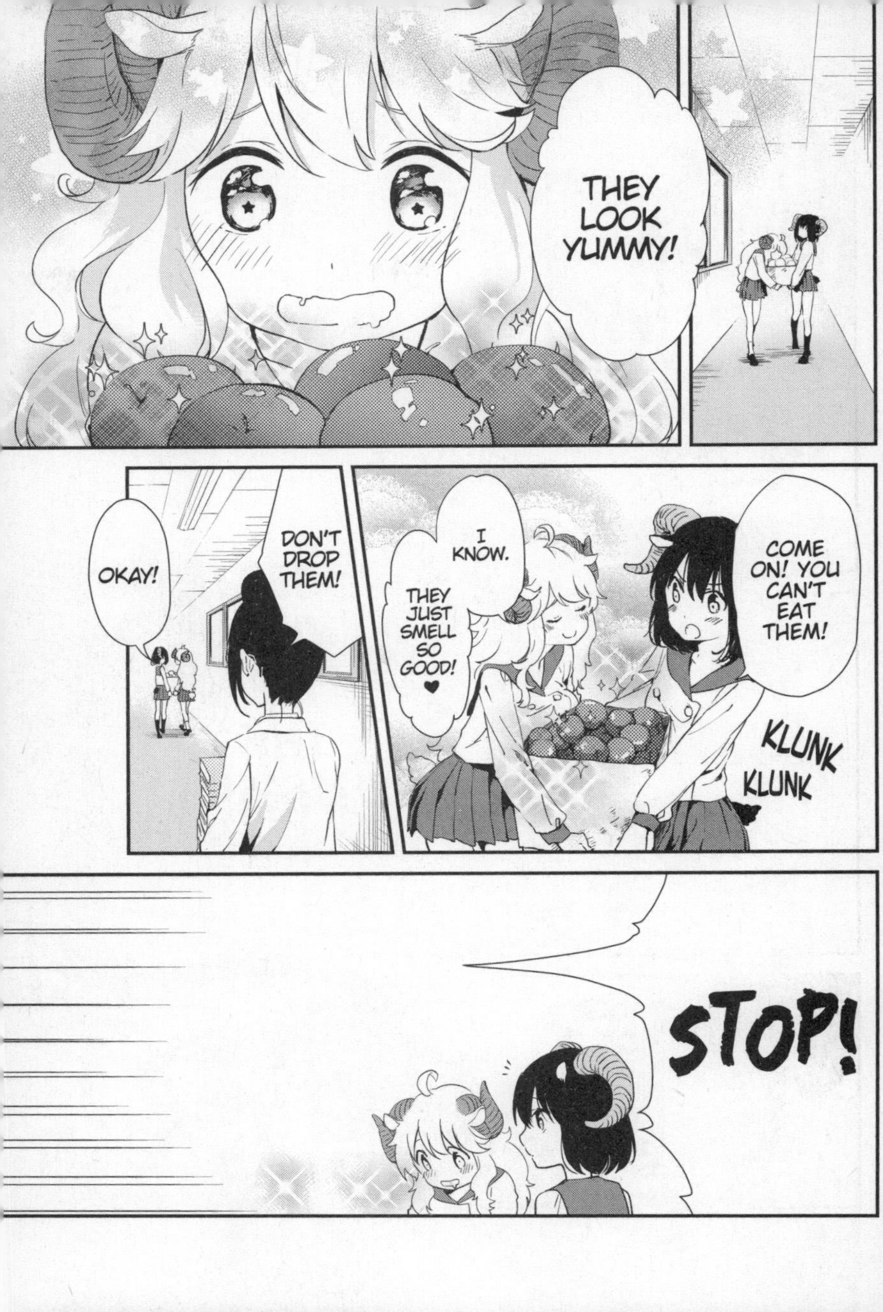
THEY LOOK YUMMY!
COME ON! YOU CAN'T EAT THEM!
I KNOW.
THEY JUST SMELL SO GOOD! ♥
KLUNK KLUNK
DON'T DROP THEM!
OKAY!
STOP!

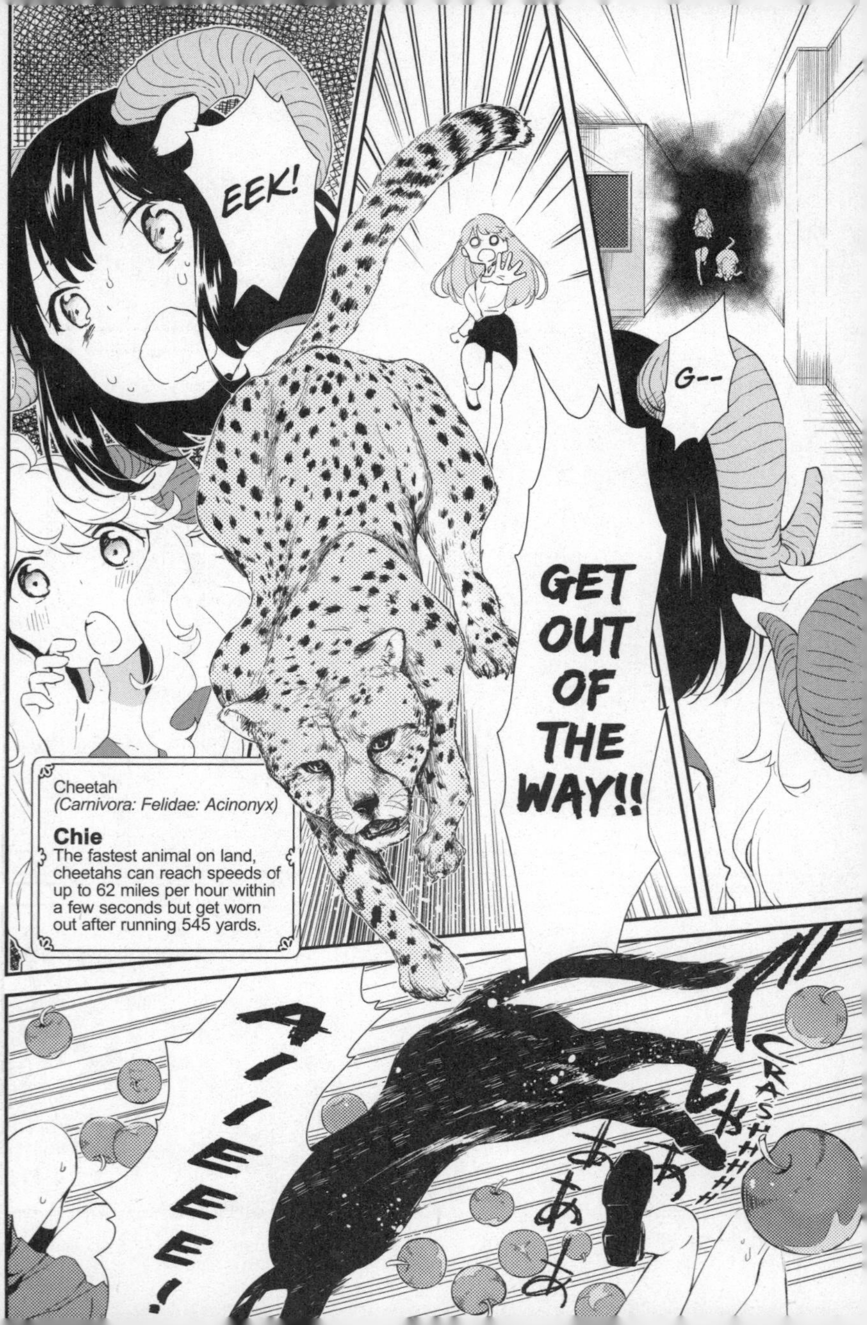
G--
GET OUT OF THE WAY!!
EEK!
Cheetah
(Carnivora: Felidae: Acinonyx)
Chie
The fastest animal on land, cheetahs can reach speeds of up to 62 miles per hour within a few seconds but get worn out after running 545 yards.
CRASHHHHH
A--EEEE!

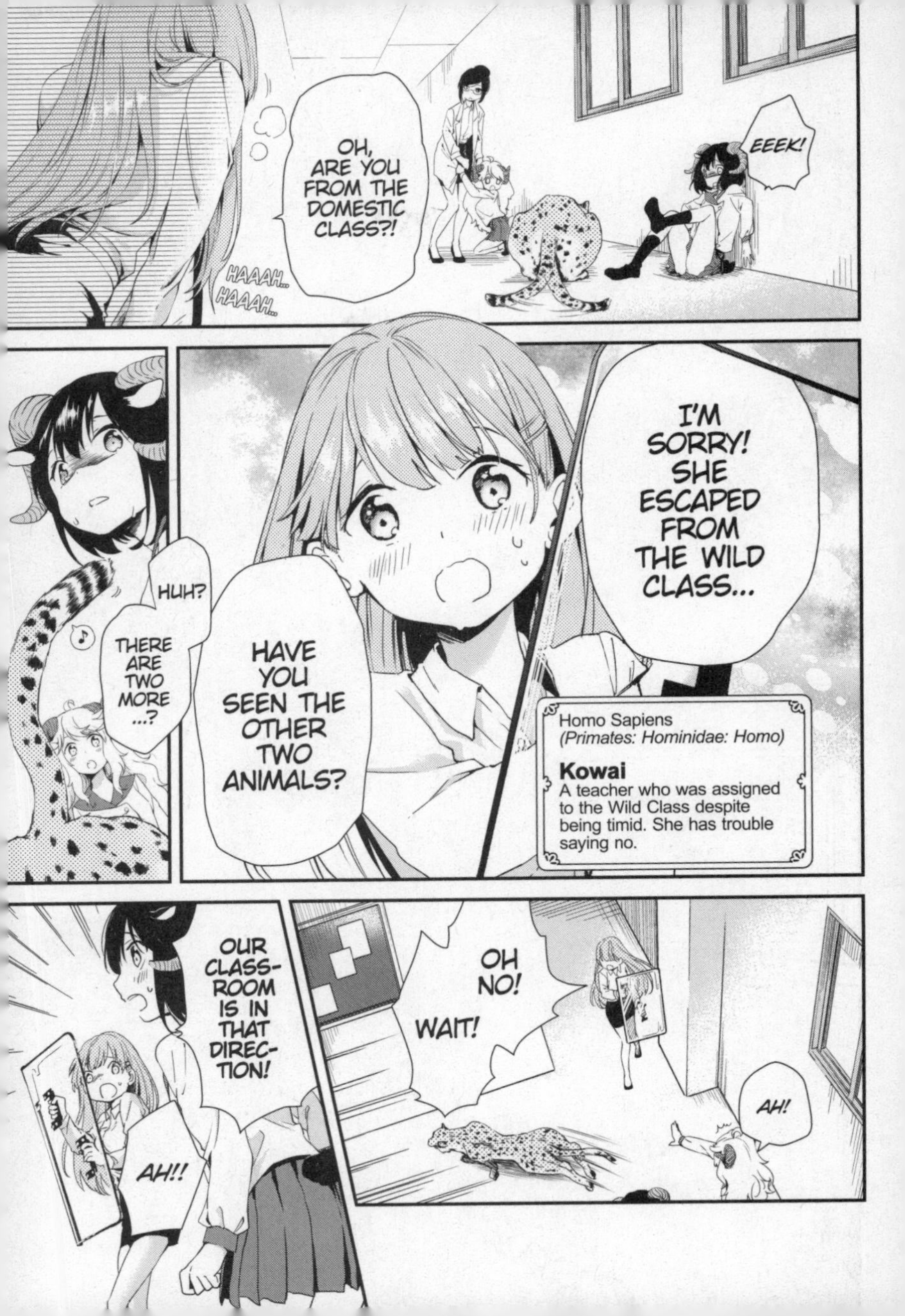
EEEK!
OH, ARE YOU FROM THE DOMESTIC CLASS?!
HAAAH... HAAAH...
I'M SORRY! SHE ESCAPED FROM THE WILD CLASS...
Homo Sapiens
(Primates: Hominidae: Homo)
Kowai
A teacher who was assigned to the Wild Class despite being timid. She has trouble saying no.
HAVE YOU SEEN THE OTHER TWO ANIMALS?
HUH?
THERE ARE TWO MORE ...?
AH!
OH NO!
WAIT!
OUR CLASSROOM IS IN THAT DIRECTION!
AH!!

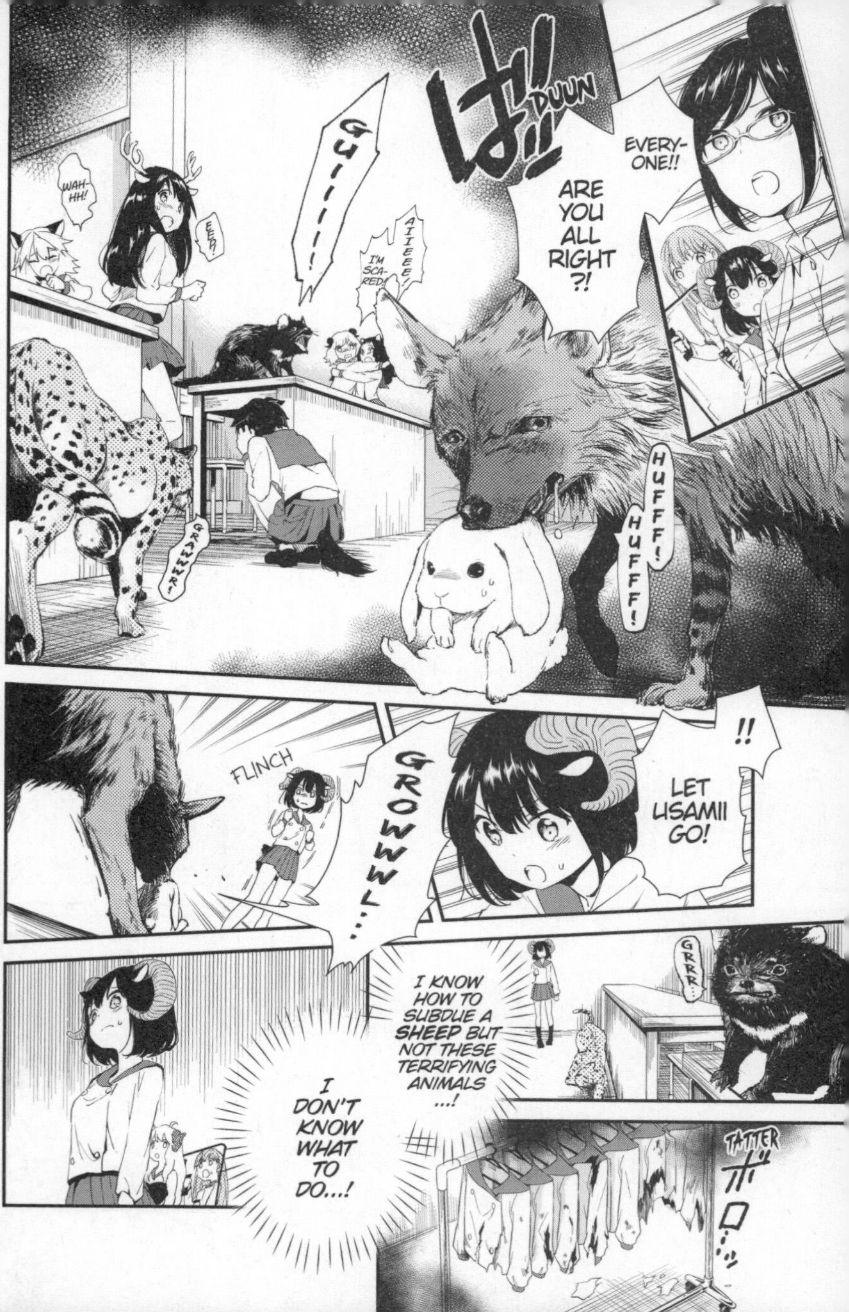
ば!! DUUN
EVERY-ONE!!
ARE YOU ALL RIGHT?!
GUIIIIII!
AIIEEEE!
I'M SCA-RED!
EEP!
WAH-HH!
HUFFF! HUFFF!
HUFFF!
GRAWWWR!
!!
LET USAMII GO!
GROWWWL...
FLINCH
GRRR...
I KNOW HOW TO SUBDUE A SHEEP BUT NOT THESE TERRIFYING ANIMALS ...!
I DON'T KNOW WHAT TO DO...!
TATTER
ボロッ

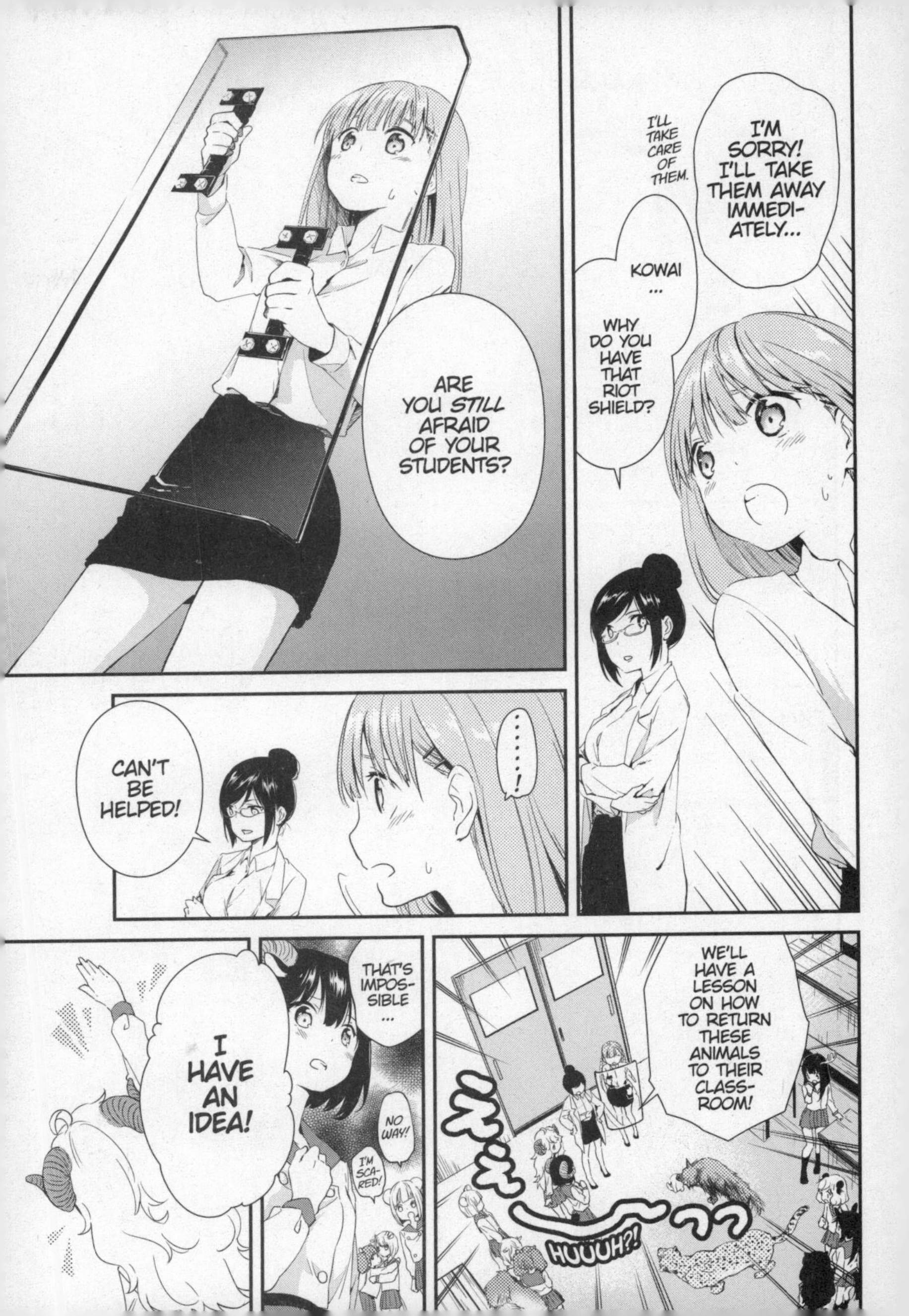
I'M SORRY! I'LL TAKE THEM AWAY IMMEDI-ATELY...
I'LL TAKE CARE OF THEM.
KOWAI ...
WHY DO YOU HAVE THAT RIOT SHIELD?
ARE YOU *STILL* AFRAID OF YOUR STUDENTS?
......!
CAN'T BE HELPED!
WE'LL HAVE A LESSON ON HOW TO RETURN THESE ANIMALS TO THEIR CLASS-ROOM!
HUUUH?!
THAT'S IMPOS-SIBLE ...
NO WAY!
I'M SCA-RED!
I HAVE AN IDEA!

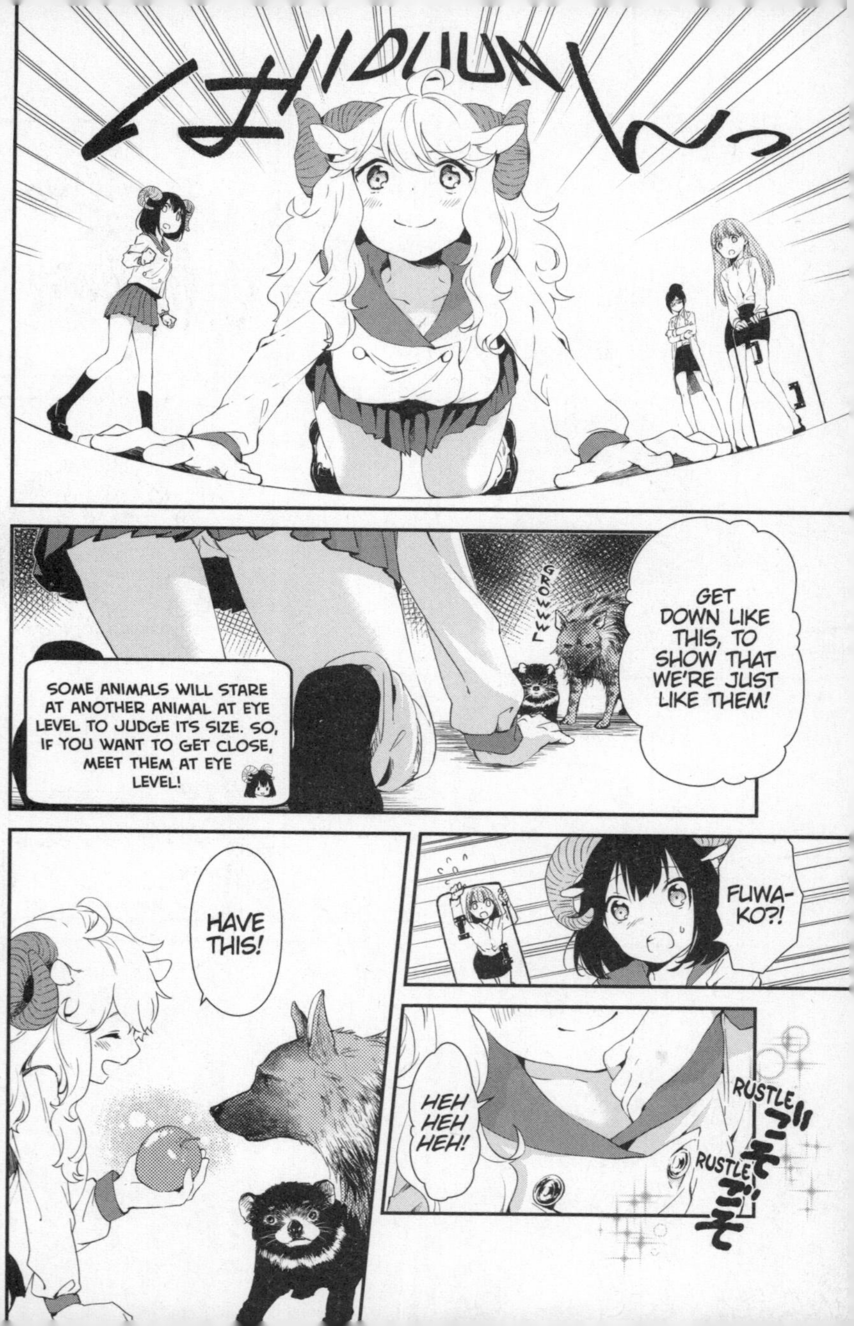
HIDUUN
GET DOWN LIKE THIS, TO SHOW THAT WE'RE JUST LIKE THEM!
GROWWWL
SOME ANIMALS WILL STARE AT ANOTHER ANIMAL AT EYE LEVEL TO JUDGE ITS SIZE. SO, IF YOU WANT TO GET CLOSE, MEET THEM AT EYE LEVEL!
FUWA-KO?!
HAVE THIS!
HEH HEH HEH!
RUSTLE
ごそ
RUSTLE
ごそ

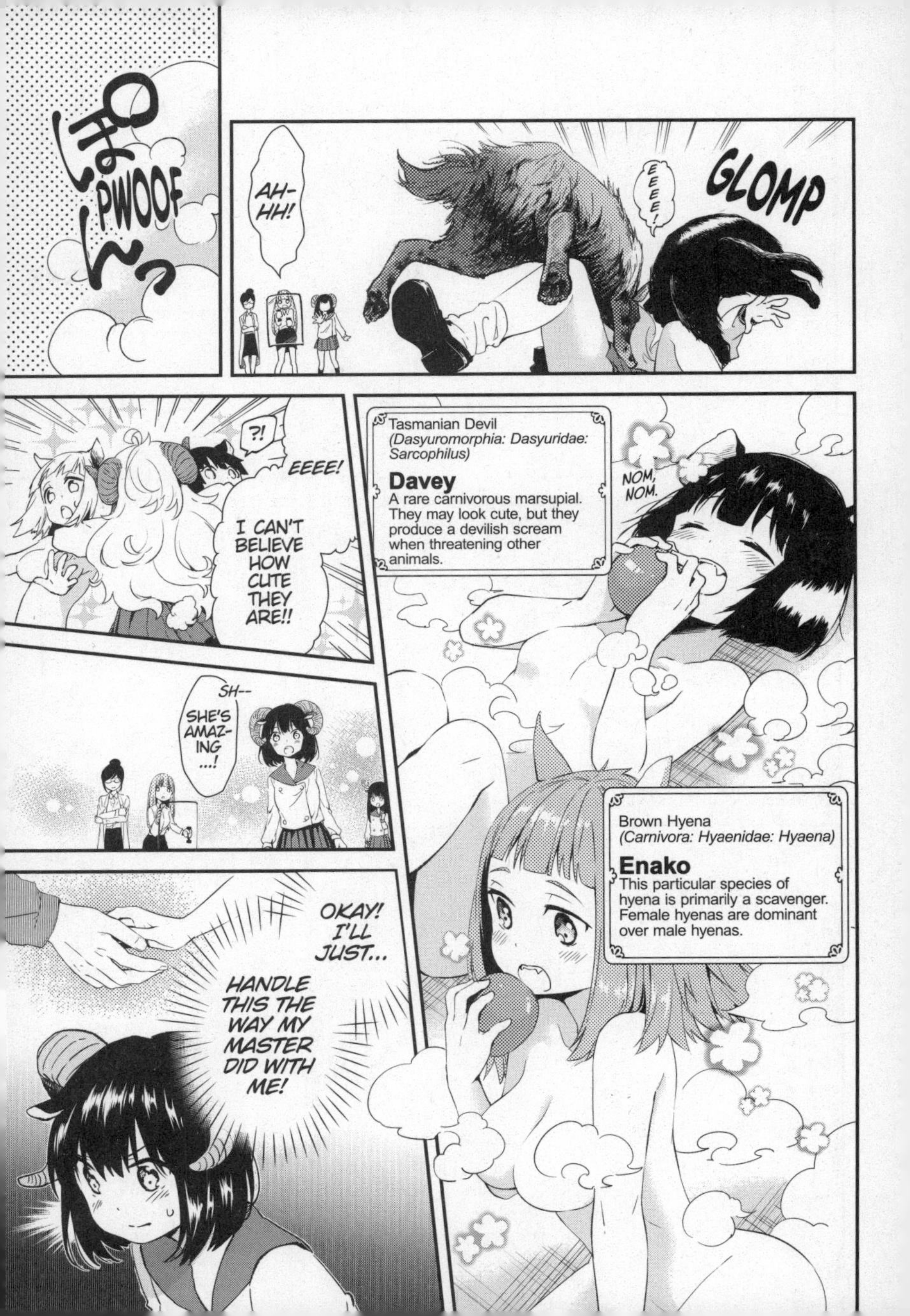

ぽんっ
PWOOF
AH-HH!
EEEE!
GLOMP
?!
EEEE!
I CAN'T BELIEVE HOW CUTE THEY ARE!!
NOM, NOM.
Tasmanian Devil
(Dasyuromorphia: Dasyuridae: Sarcophilus)
Davey
A rare carnivorous marsupial. They may look cute, but they produce a devilish scream when threatening other animals.
SH--
SHE'S AMAZING ...!
Brown Hyena
(Carnivora: Hyaenidae: Hyaena)
Enako
This particular species of hyena is primarily a scavenger. Female hyenas are dominant over male hyenas.
OKAY! I'LL JUST...
HANDLE THIS THE WAY MY MASTER DID WITH ME!

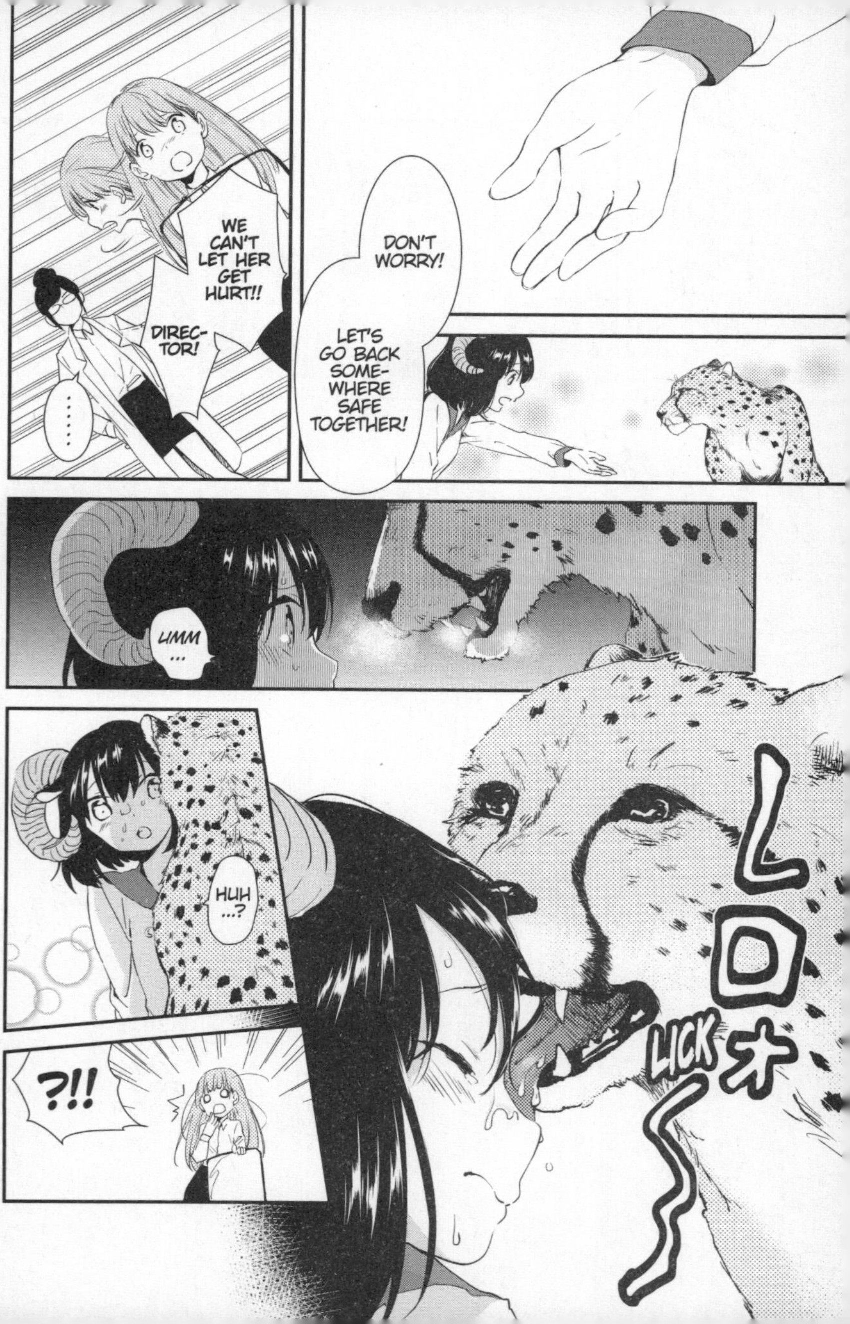
DON'T WORRY!
LET'S GO BACK SOMEWHERE SAFE TOGETHER!
WE CAN'T LET HER GET HURT!!
DIRECTOR!
......
UMM ...
HUH ...?
レロォ〜
LICK
?!!

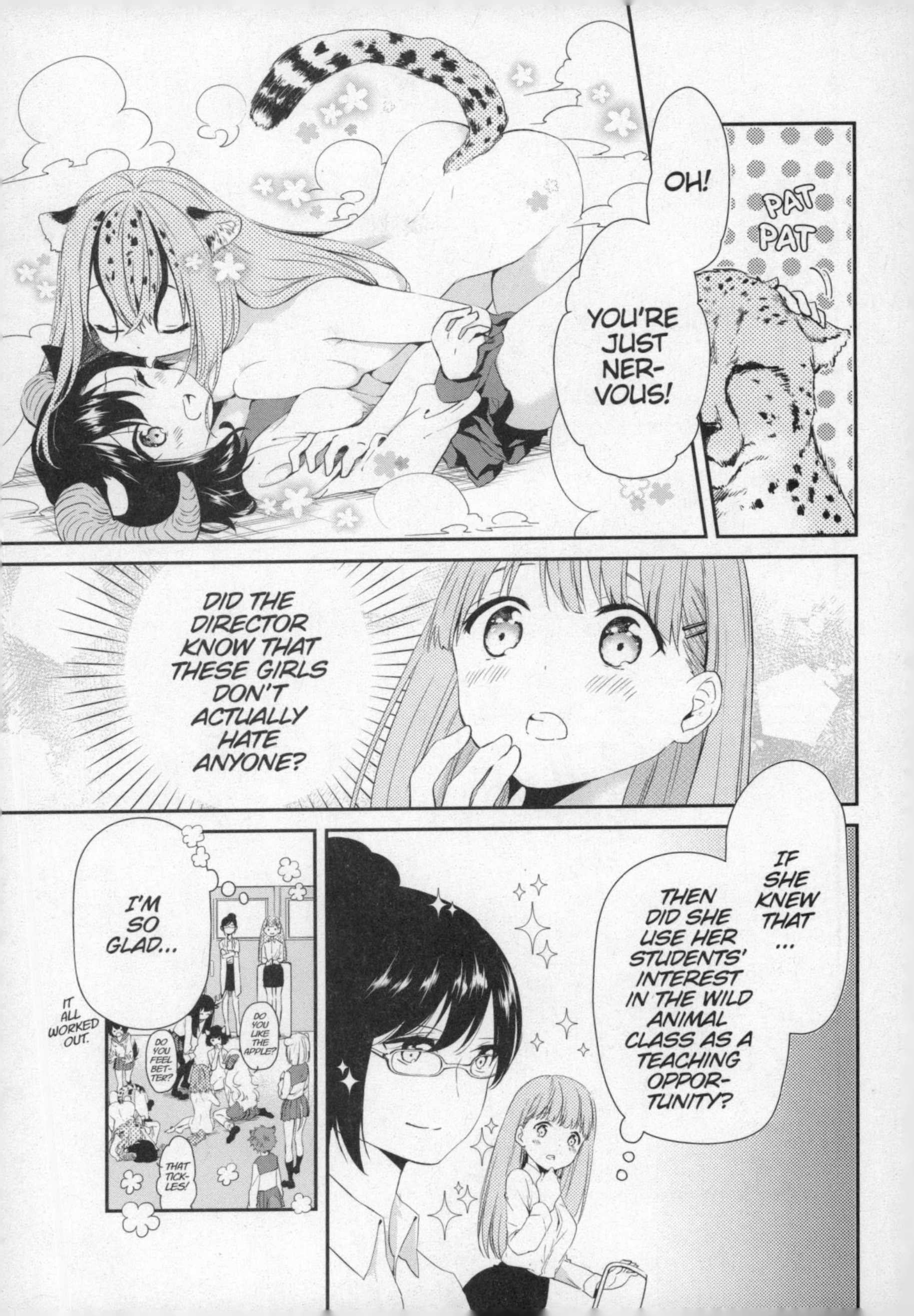
PAT PAT
OH!
YOU'RE JUST NER-VOUS!
DID THE DIRECTOR KNOW THAT THESE GIRLS DON'T ACTUALLY HATE ANYONE?
IF SHE KNEW THAT...
THEN DID SHE USE HER STUDENTS' INTEREST IN THE WILD ANIMAL CLASS AS A TEACHING OPPOR-TUNITY?
I'M SO GLAD...
IT ALL WORKED OUT.
DO YOU LIKE THE APPLE?
DO YOU FEEL BET-TER?
THAT TICK-LES!

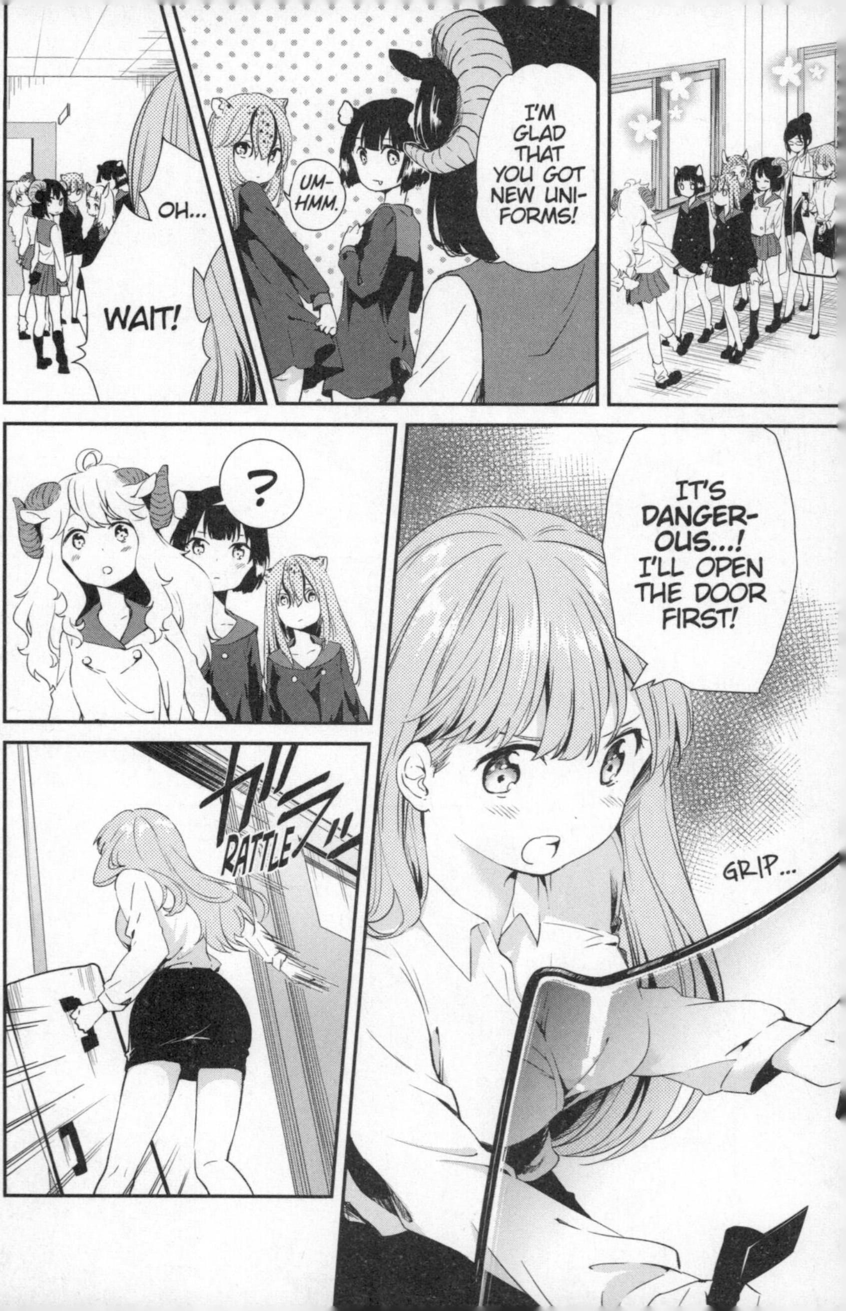
I'M GLAD THAT YOU GOT NEW UNI-FORMS!
UM-HMM.
OH...
WAIT!
IT'S DANGER-OUS...! I'LL OPEN THE DOOR FIRST!
GRIP...
?
RATTLE

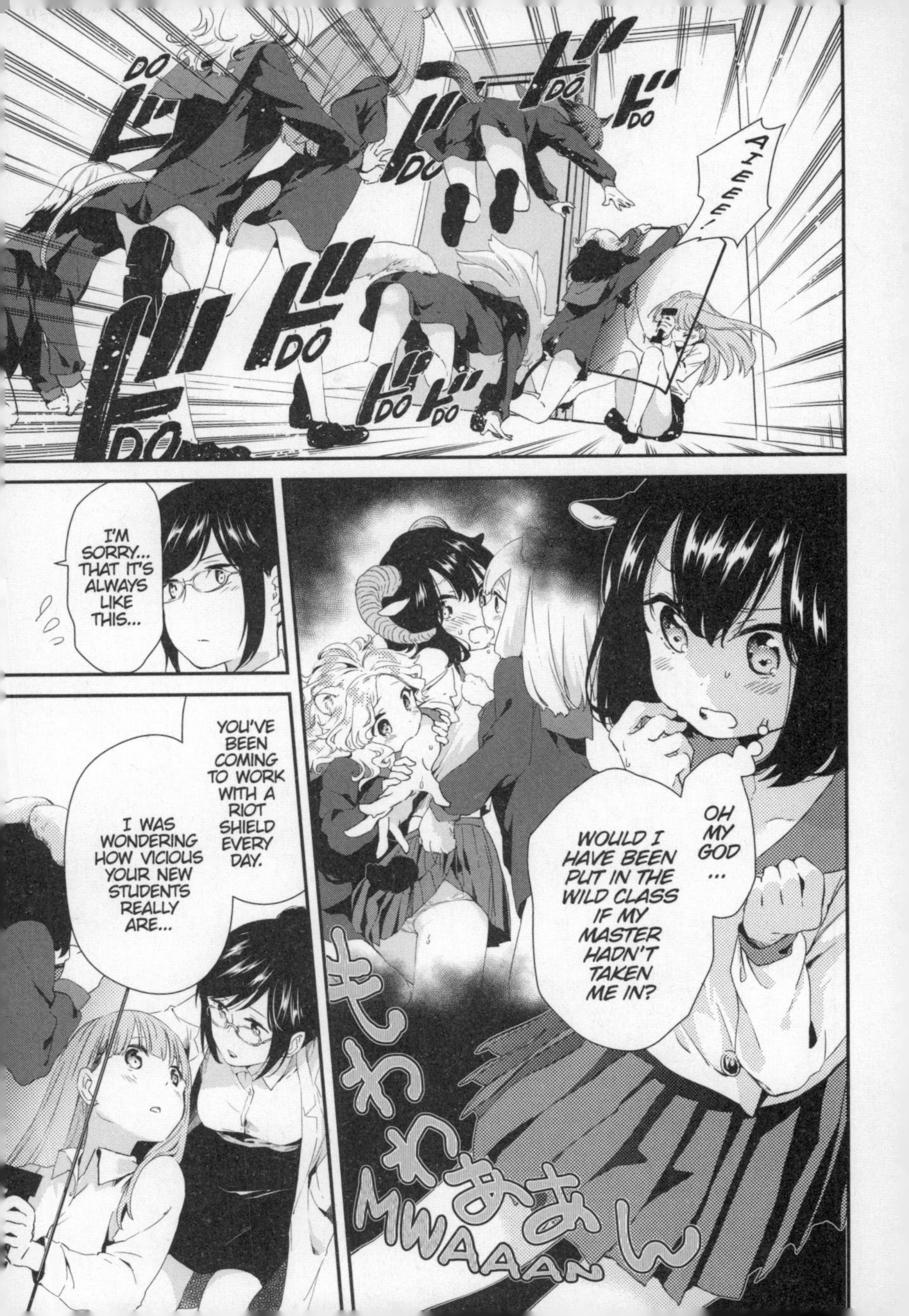
DO
DO
DO
AIEEEE!
DO
DO
DO
DO
DO
DO
I'M SORRY... THAT IT'S ALWAYS LIKE THIS...
YOU'VE BEEN COMING TO WORK WITH A RIOT SHIELD EVERY DAY.
I WAS WONDERING HOW VICIOUS YOUR NEW STUDENTS REALLY ARE...
OH MY GOD...
WOULD I HAVE BEEN PUT IN THE WILD CLASS IF MY MASTER HADN'T TAKEN ME IN?
もわわあああん
MWAAAAN

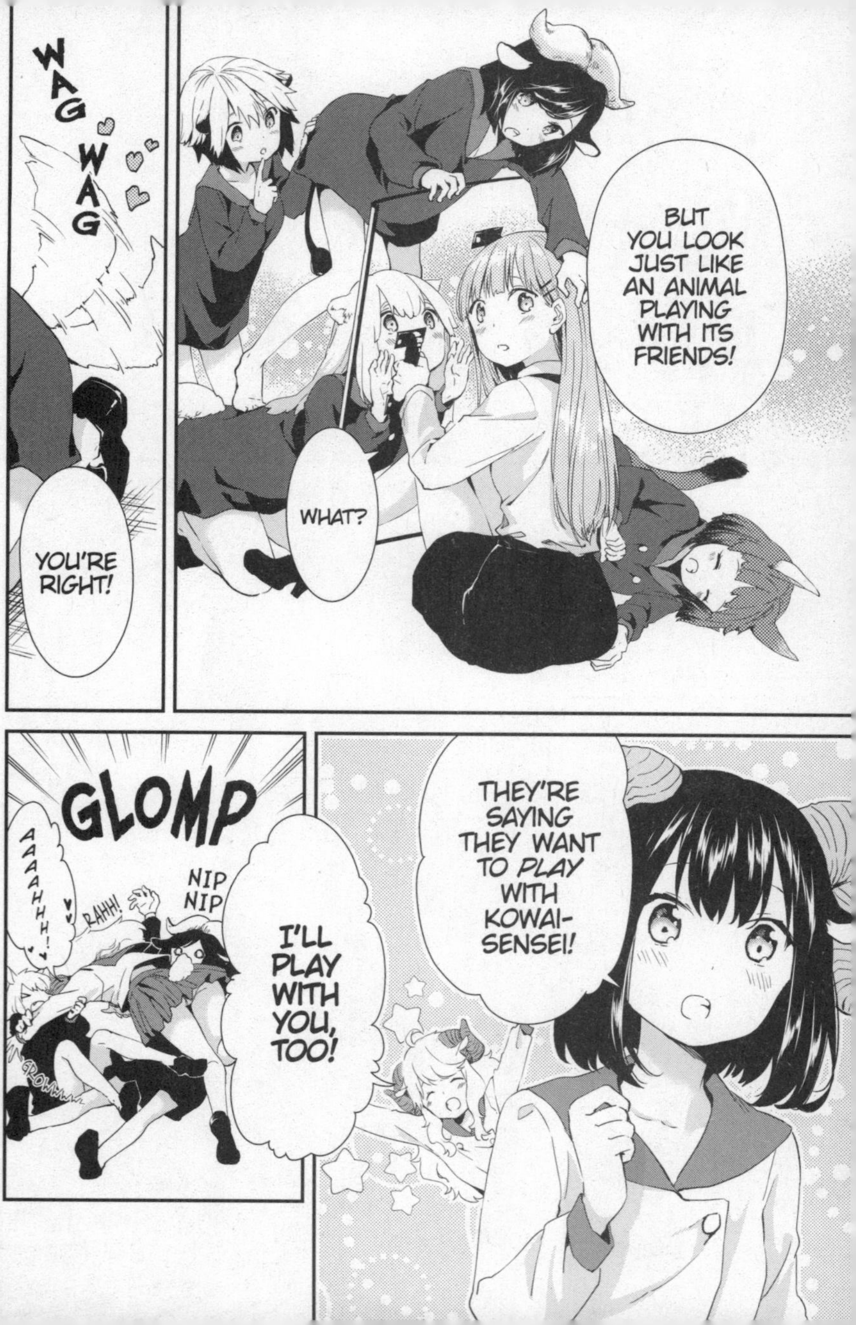
BUT YOU LOOK JUST LIKE AN ANIMAL PLAYING WITH ITS FRIENDS!
WHAT?
YOU'RE RIGHT!
WAG WAG WAG
THEY'RE SAYING THEY WANT TO *PLAY* WITH KOWAI-SENSEI!
I'LL PLAY WITH YOU, TOO!
GLOMP
NIP NIP
RAHH!
AAAAHHH!

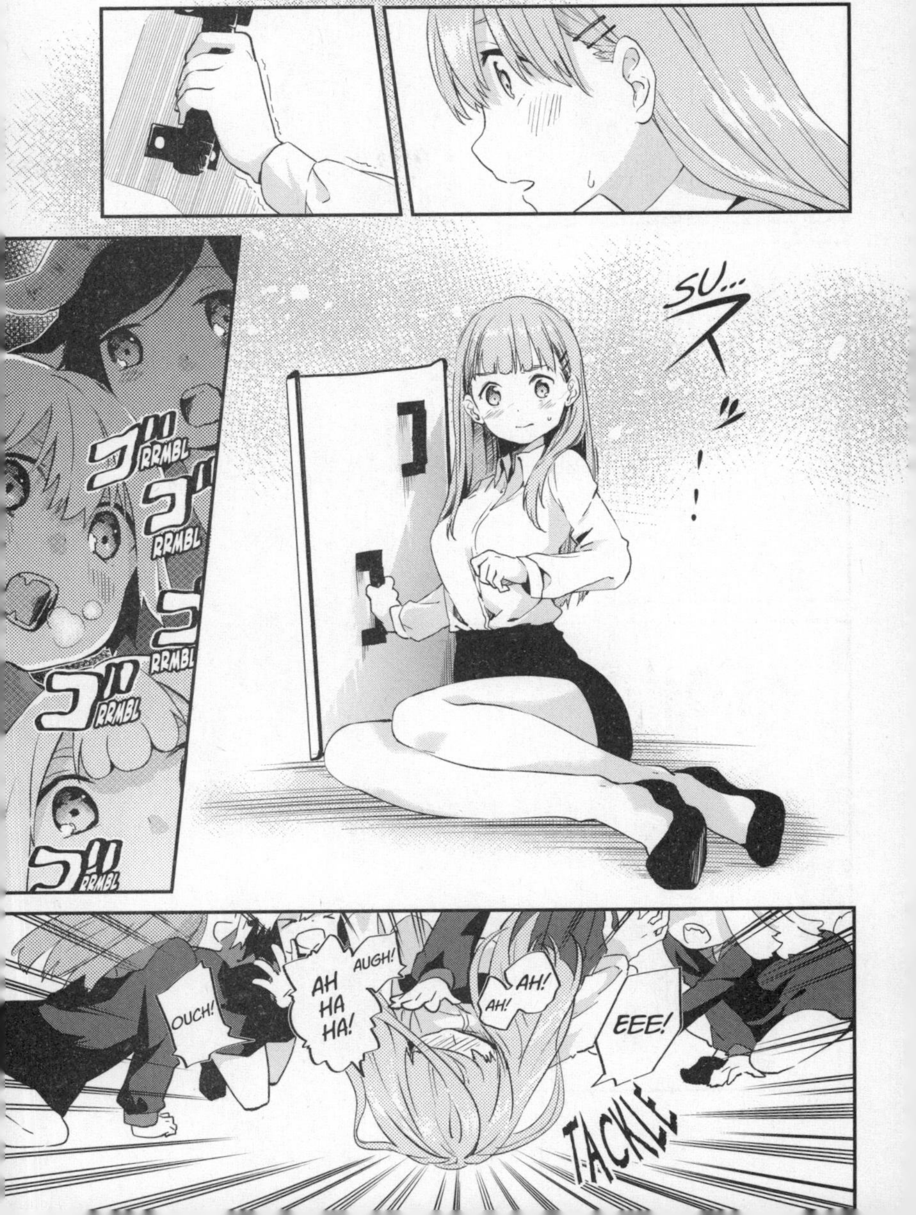

SU...
!!
RRMBL
RRMBL
RRMBL
RRMBL
RRMBL
AUGH!
AH HA HA!
OUCH!
AH!
AH!
EEE!
TACKLE

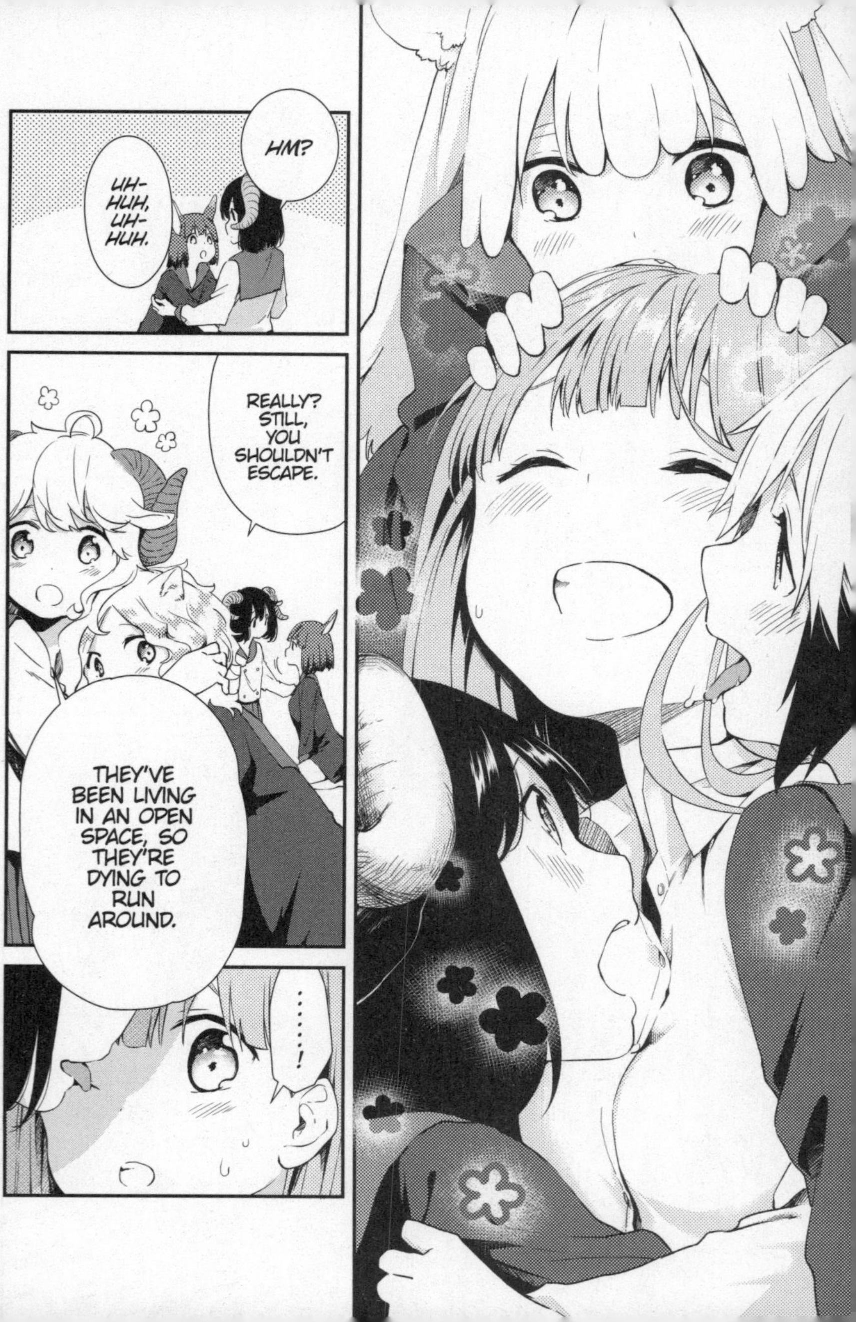
HM?
UH-HUH, UH-HUH.
REALLY? STILL, YOU SHOULDN'T ESCAPE.
THEY'VE BEEN LIVING IN AN OPEN SPACE, SO THEY'RE DYING TO RUN AROUND.
......!

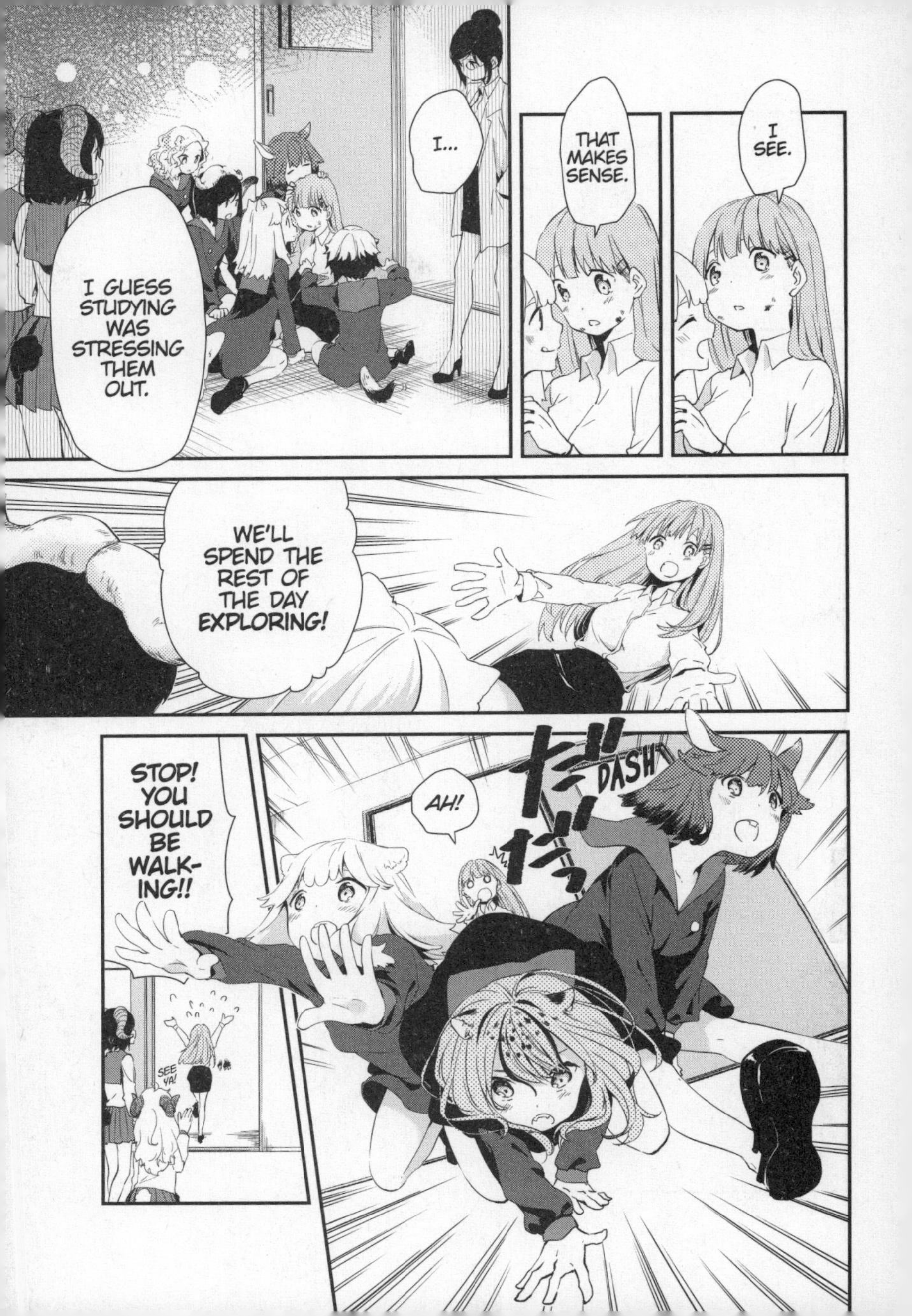
I SEE.
THAT MAKES SENSE.
I...
I GUESS STUDYING WAS STRESSING THEM OUT.
WE'LL SPEND THE REST OF THE DAY EXPLORING!
DASH
AH!
STOP! YOU SHOULD BE WALK-ING!!
SEE YA!

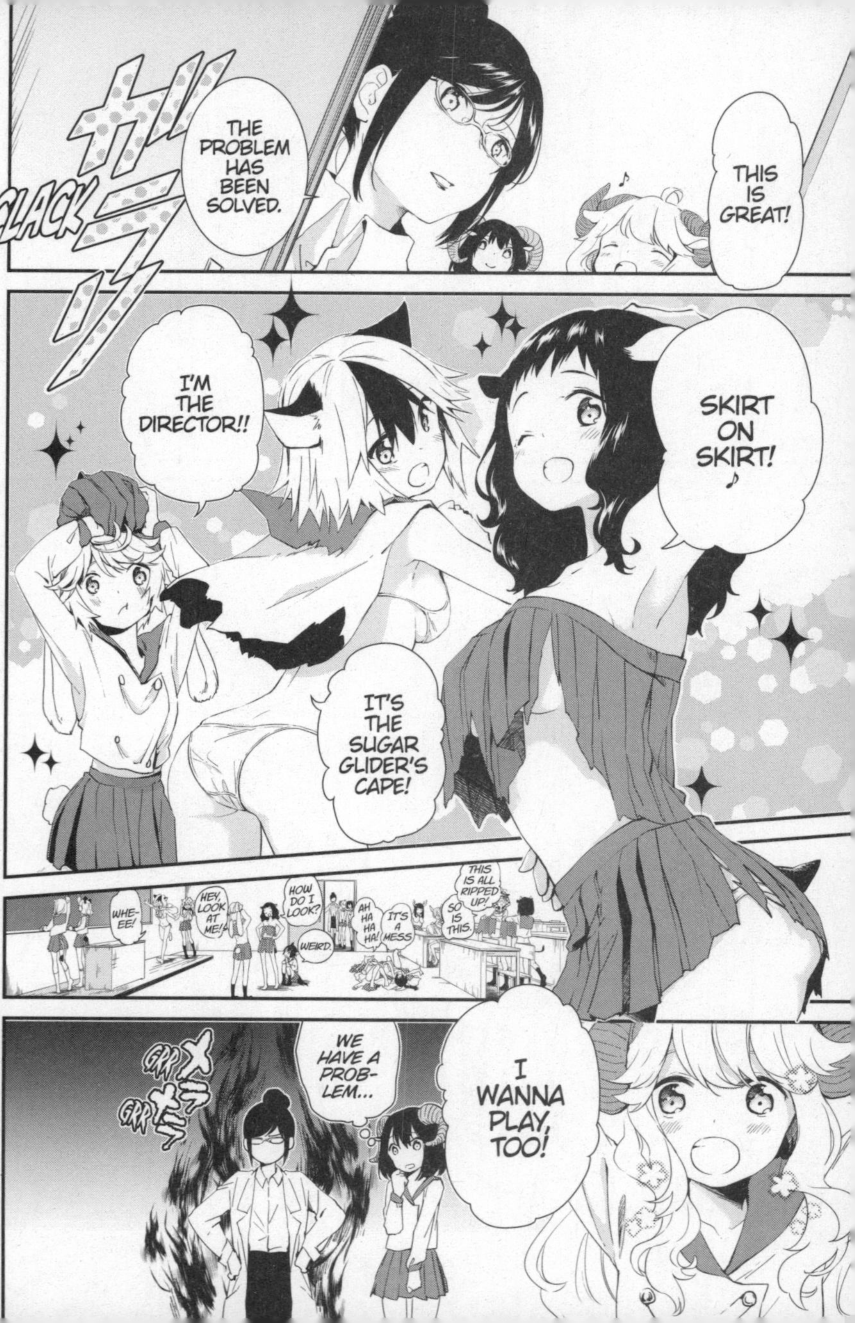
THIS IS GREAT!
THE PROBLEM HAS BEEN SOLVED.
CLACK
SKIRT ON SKIRT! ♪
I'M THE DIRECTOR!!
IT'S THE SUGAR GLIDER'S CAPE!
THIS IS ALL RIPPED UP!
SO IS THIS.
IT'S A MESS
AH HA HA HA!
HOW DO I LOOK?
WEIRD.
HEY, LOOK AT ME!
WHEE-EE!
I WANNA PLAY, TOO!
WE HAVE A PROB-LEM...
GRR
GRR

FELINE TONGUES ARE COVERED WITH TINY BARBS WHICH GIVE THEM A SCRATCHY SURFACE FOR TEARING FLESH OFF BONES, LAPPING WATER, AND GROOMING.

IT ACTU-ALLY HURTS!!
LICK LICK

DNA
DOESN'T
TELL US.

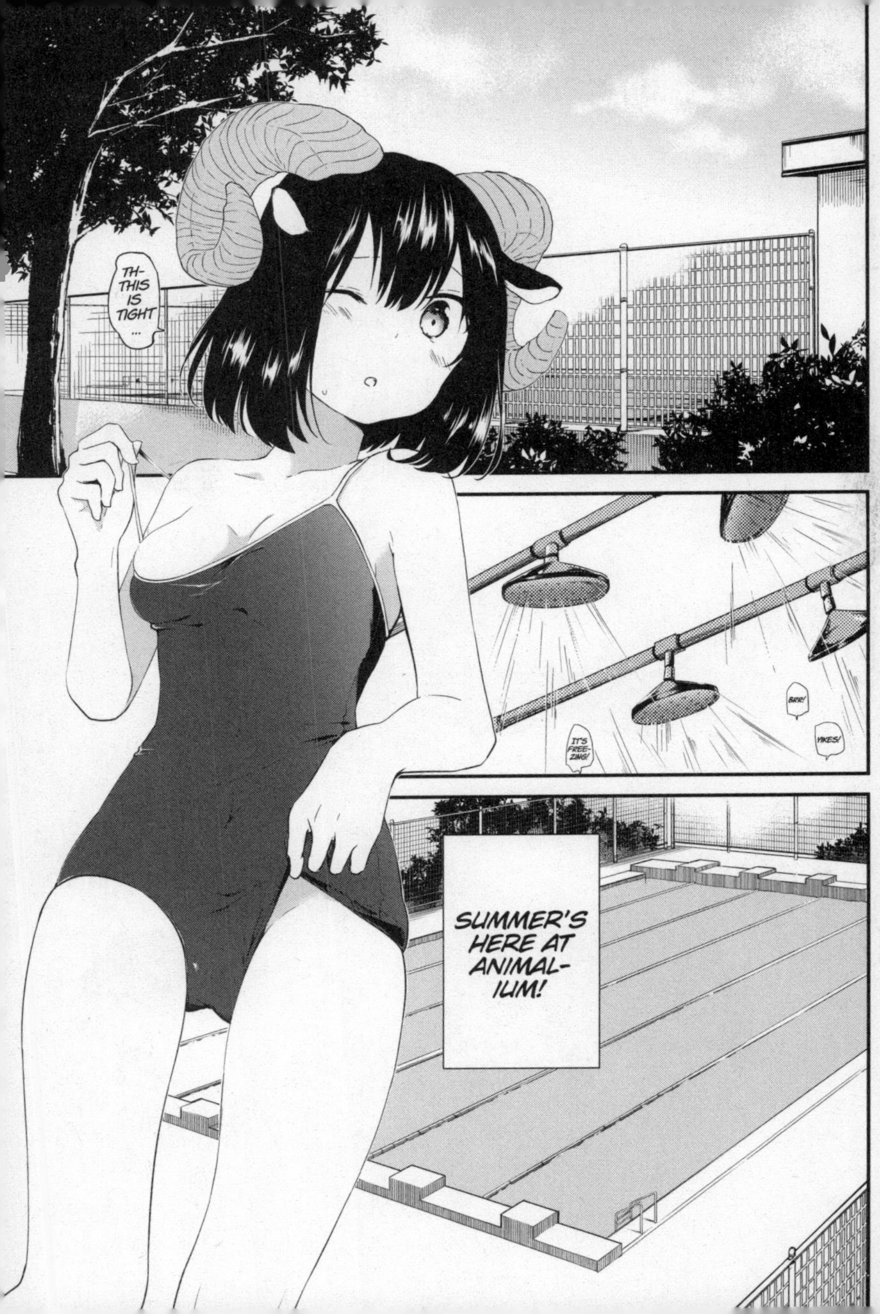
TH-THIS IS TIGHT...
BRR!
YIKES!
IT'S FREE-ZING!
SUMMER'S HERE AT ANIMAL-IUM!

Lesson 10

Girls and Water Reflections

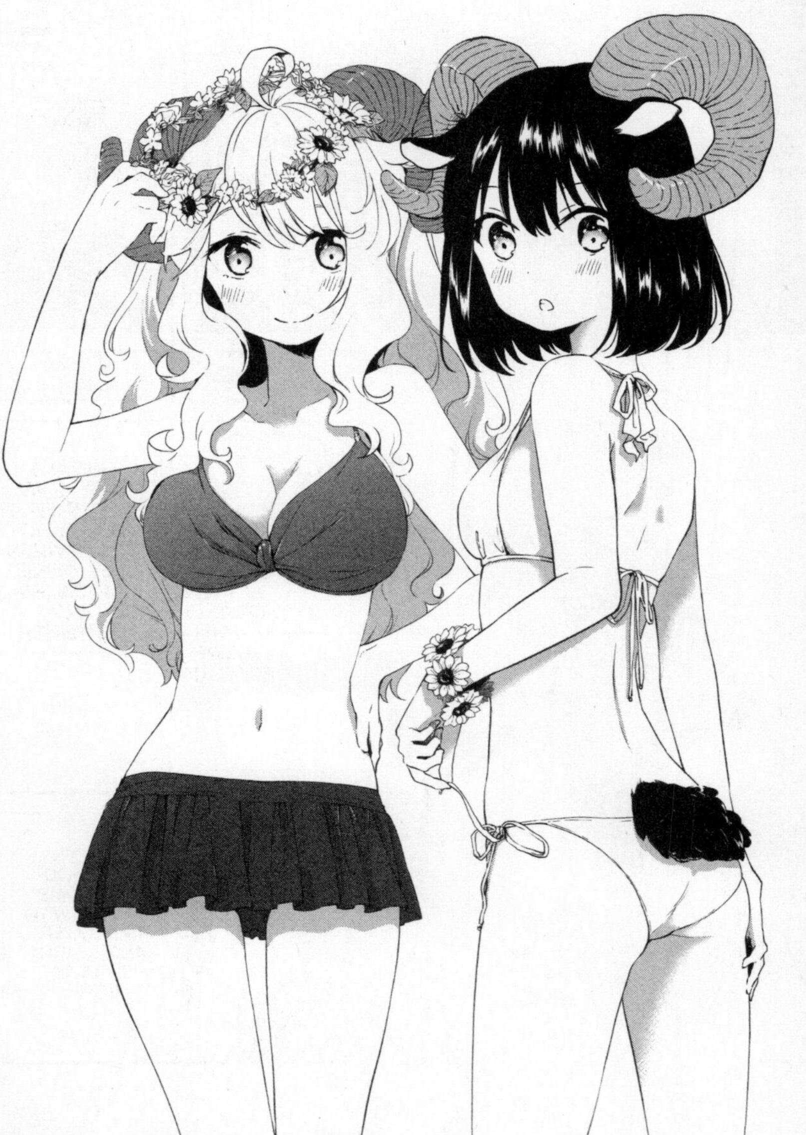

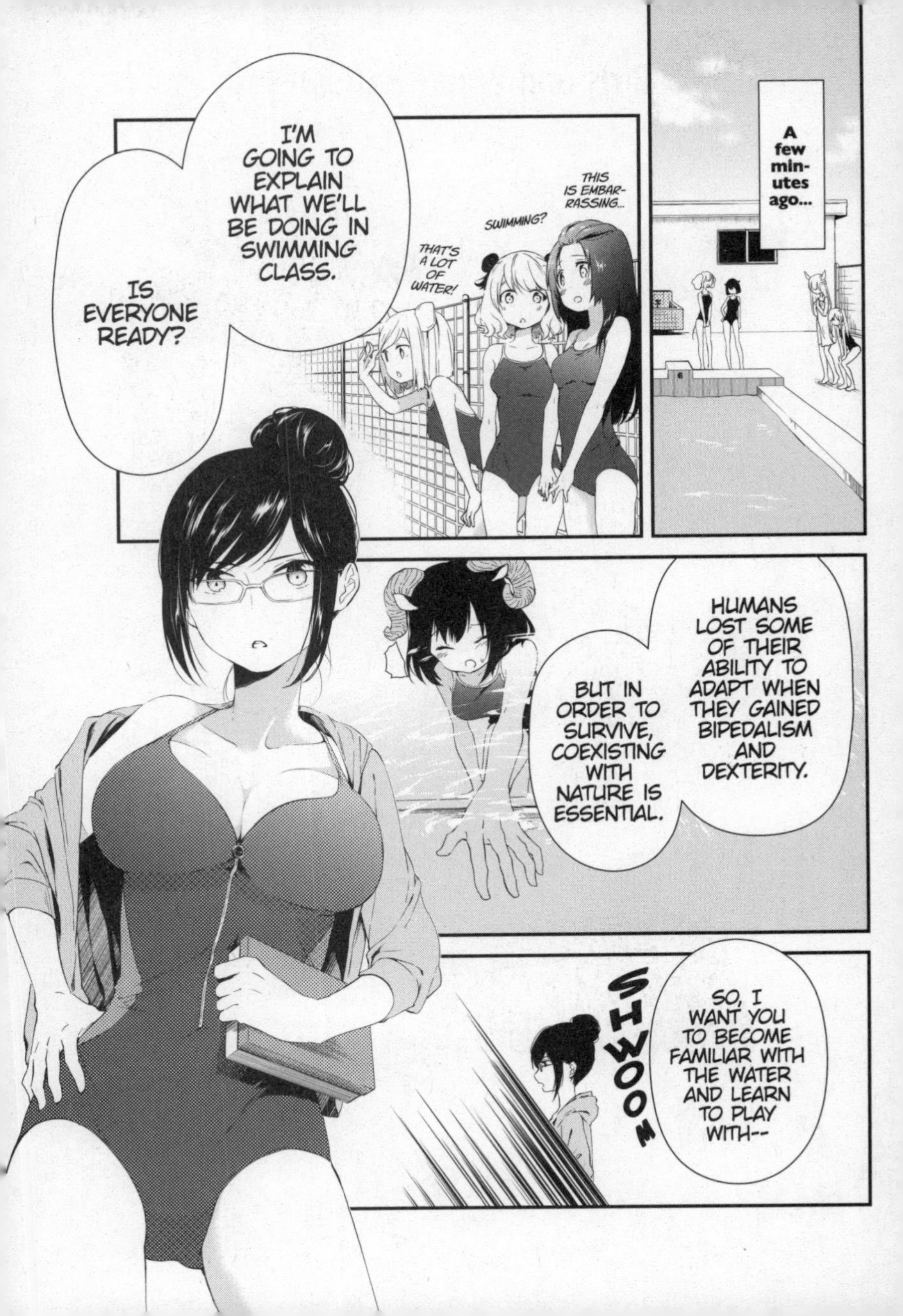
A few min-utes ago...
THIS IS EMBAR-RASSING...
SWIMMING?
THAT'S A LOT OF WATER!
I'M GOING TO EXPLAIN WHAT WE'LL BE DOING IN SWIMMING CLASS.
IS EVERYONE READY?
HUMANS LOST SOME OF THEIR ABILITY TO ADAPT WHEN THEY GAINED BIPEDALISM AND DEXTERITY.
BUT IN ORDER TO SURVIVE, COEXISTING WITH NATURE IS ESSENTIAL.
SO, I WANT YOU TO BECOME FAMILIAR WITH THE WATER AND LEARN TO PLAY WITH--
SHWOOM

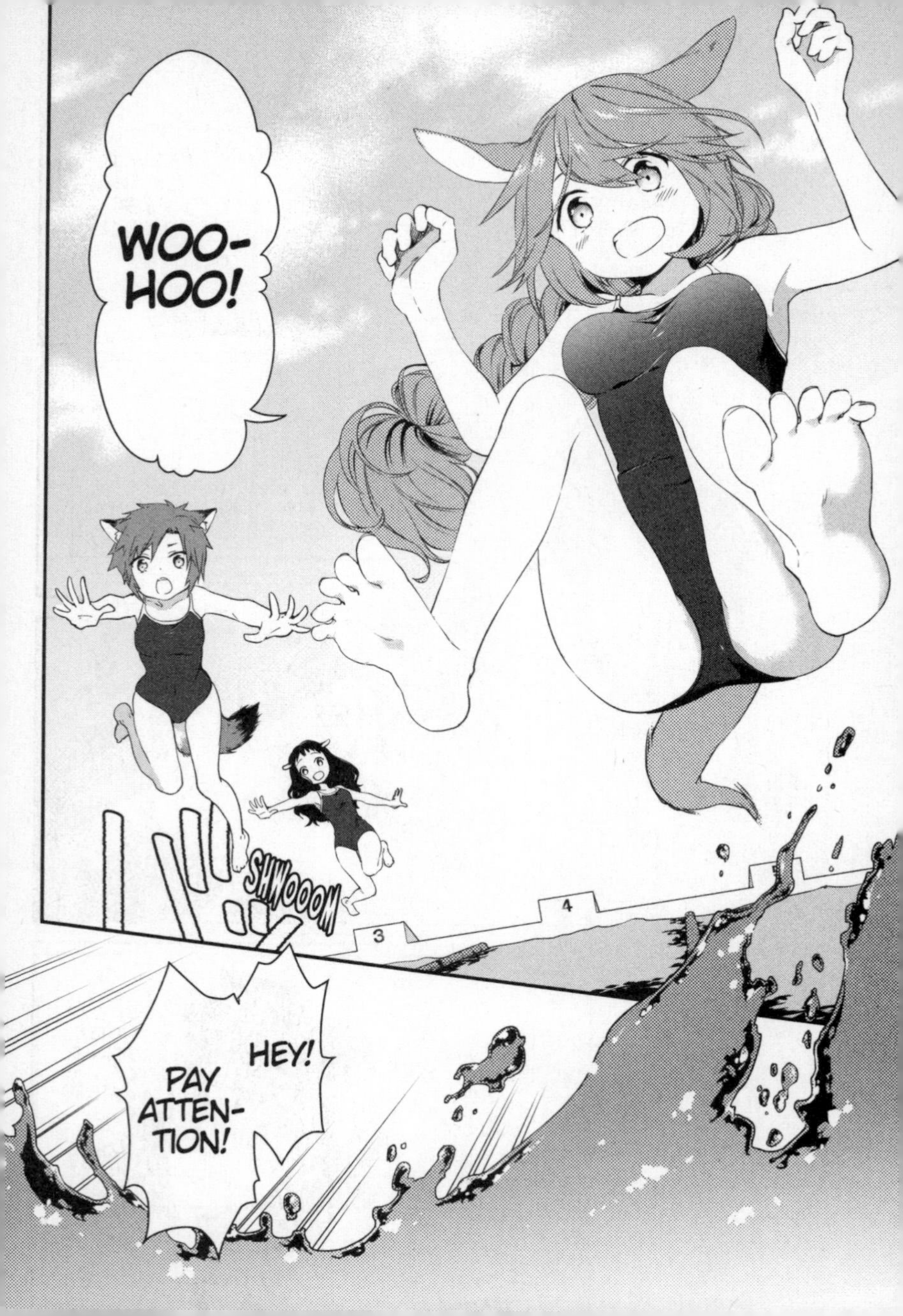
WOO-HOO!
SHWOOOM
3
4
HEY! PAY ATTEN-TION!

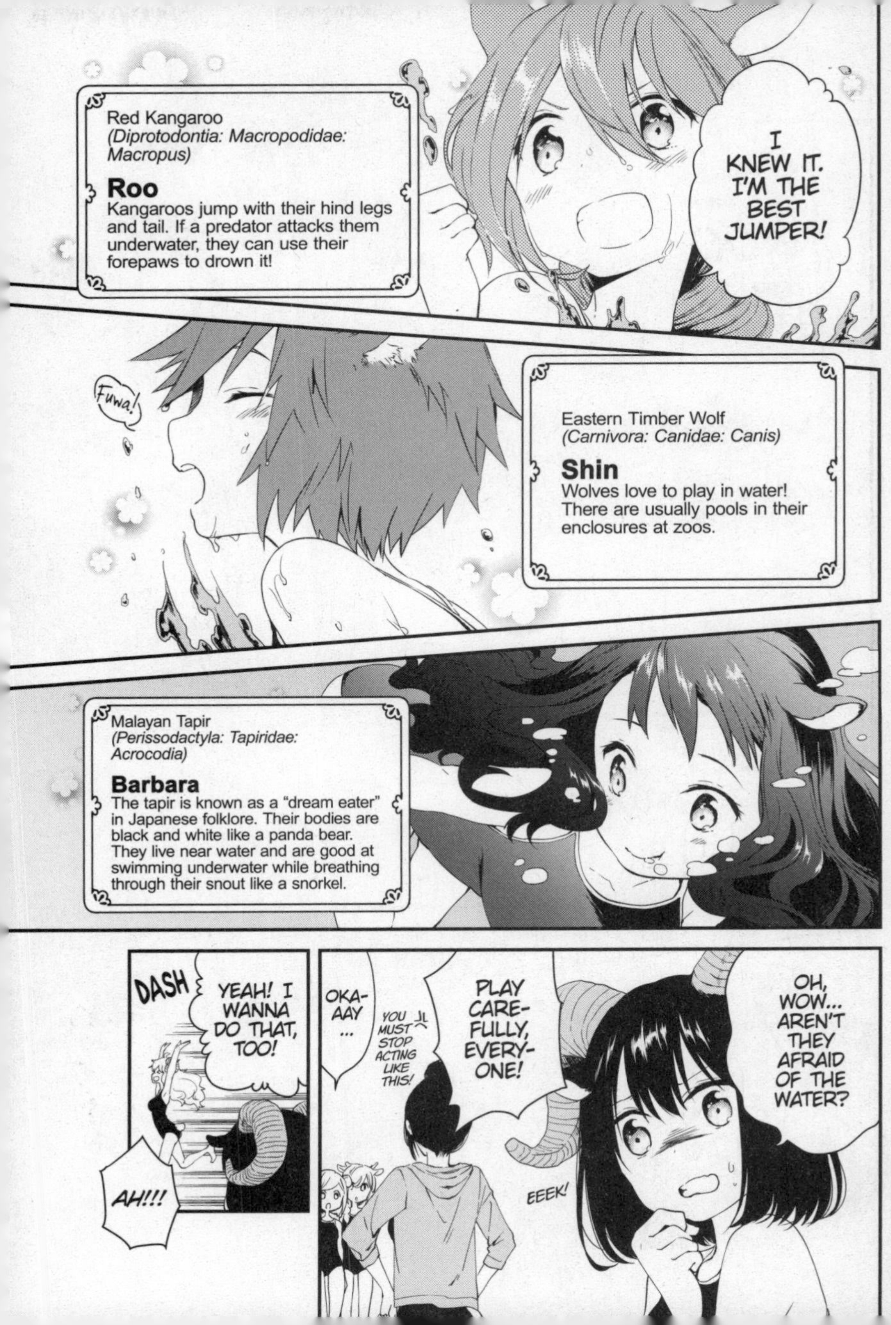
I KNEW IT. I'M THE BEST JUMPER!
Red Kangaroo
(Diprotodontia: Macropodidae: Macropus)
Roo
Kangaroos jump with their hind legs and tail. If a predator attacks them underwater, they can use their forepaws to drown it!
Eastern Timber Wolf
(Carnivora: Canidae: Canis)
Shin
Wolves love to play in water! There are usually pools in their enclosures at zoos.
Fuwa!
Malayan Tapir
(Perissodactyla: Tapiridae: Acrocodia)
Barbara
The tapir is known as a "dream eater" in Japanese folklore. Their bodies are black and white like a panda bear. They live near water and are good at swimming underwater while breathing through their snout like a snorkel.
OH, WOW... AREN'T THEY AFRAID OF THE WATER?
PLAY CARE-FULLY, EVERY-ONE!
OKA-AAY...
YOU MUST STOP ACTING LIKE THIS!
EEEK!
YEAH! I WANNA DO THAT, TOO!
DASH
AH!!!

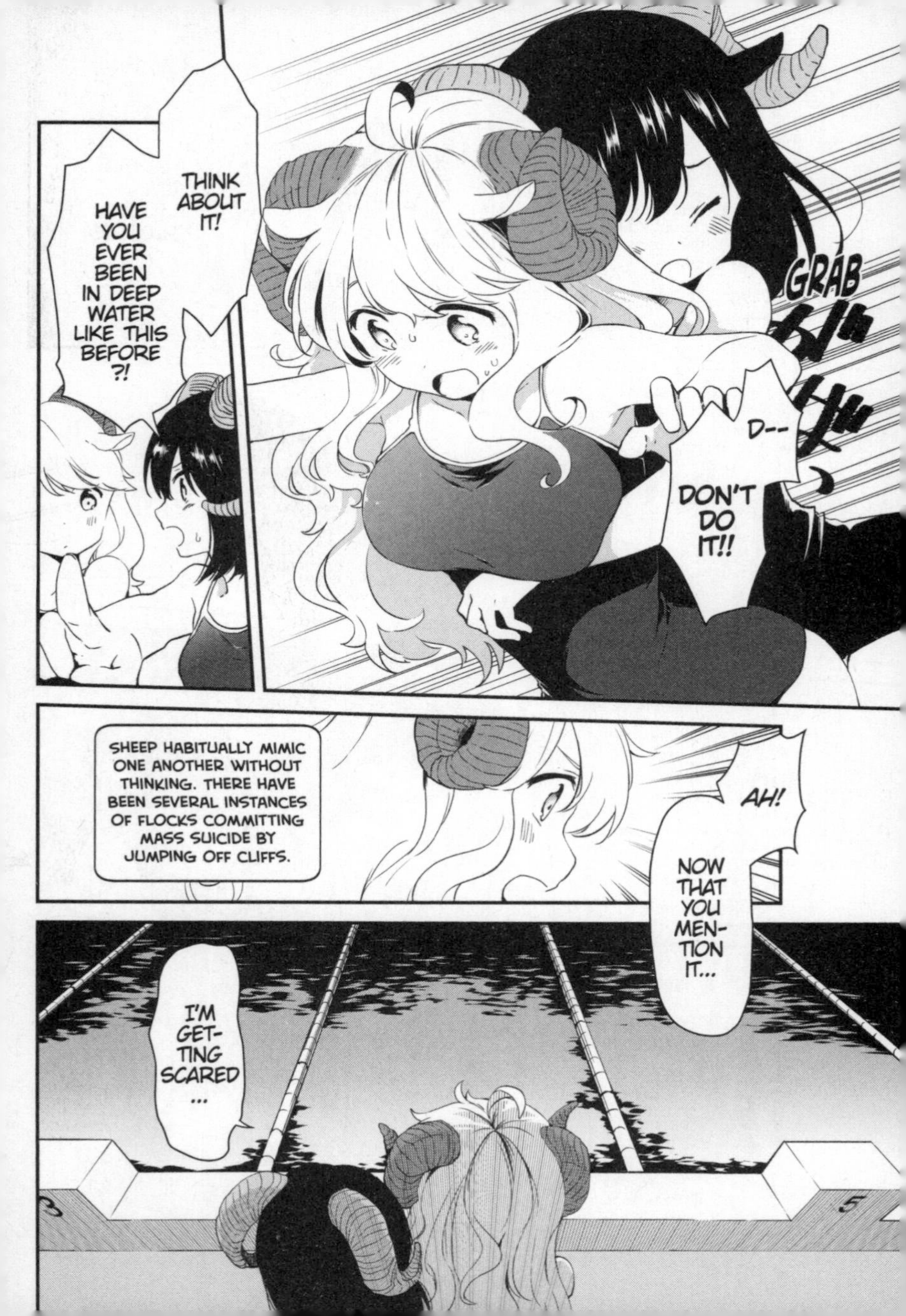
D--
DON'T DO IT!!
GRAB
THINK ABOUT IT!
HAVE YOU EVER BEEN IN DEEP WATER LIKE THIS BEFORE ?!
AH!
SHEEP HABITUALLY MIMIC ONE ANOTHER WITHOUT THINKING. THERE HAVE BEEN SEVERAL INSTANCES OF FLOCKS COMMITTING MASS SUICIDE BY JUMPING OFF CLIFFS.
NOW THAT YOU MEN-TION IT...
I'M GET-TING SCARED ...

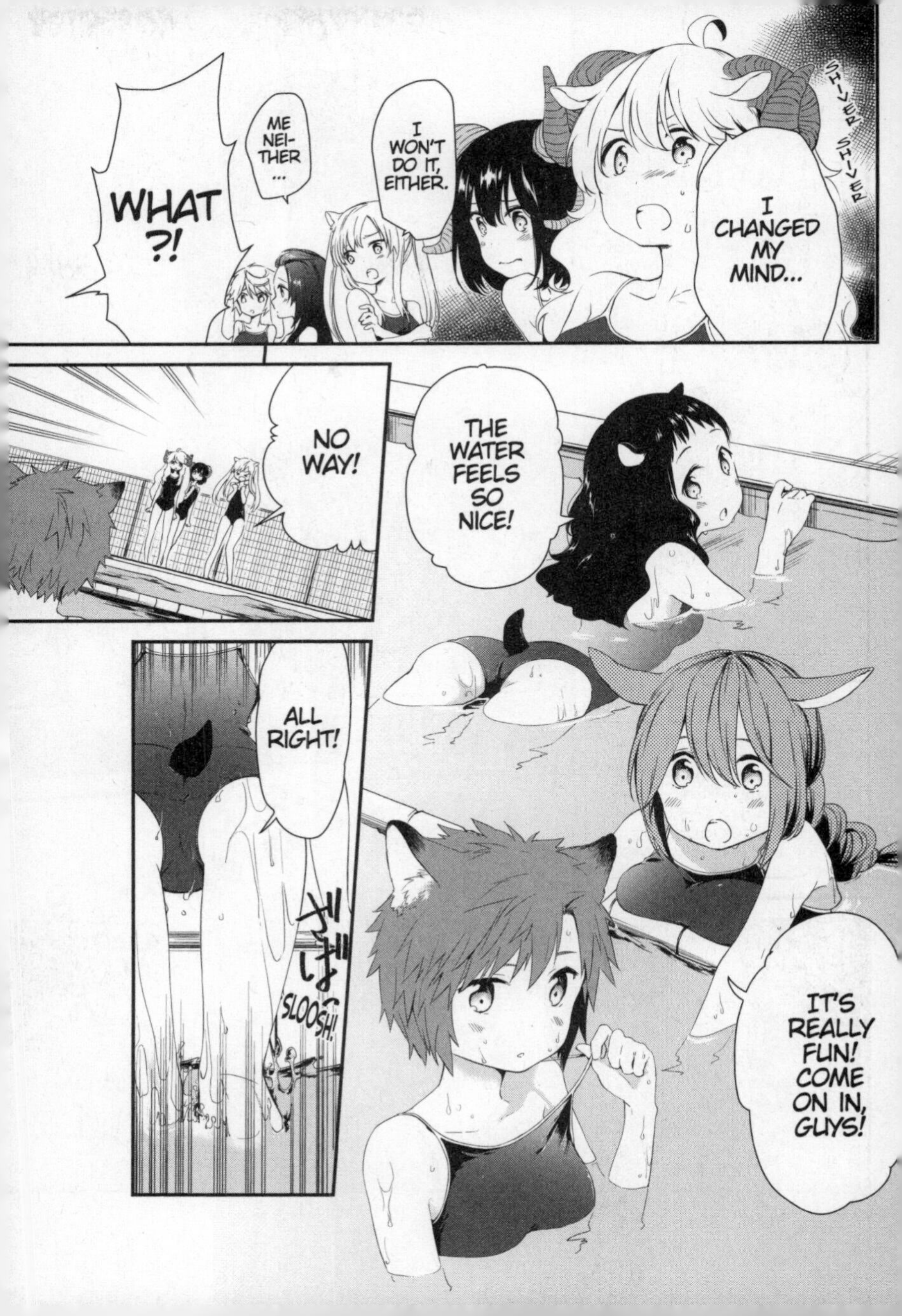
SHIVER SHIVER
I CHANGED MY MIND...
I WON'T DO IT, EITHER.
ME NEI-THER...
WHAT?!
THE WATER FEELS SO NICE!
IT'S REALLY FUN! COME ON IN, GUYS!
NO WAY!
ALL RIGHT!
SLOOSH!

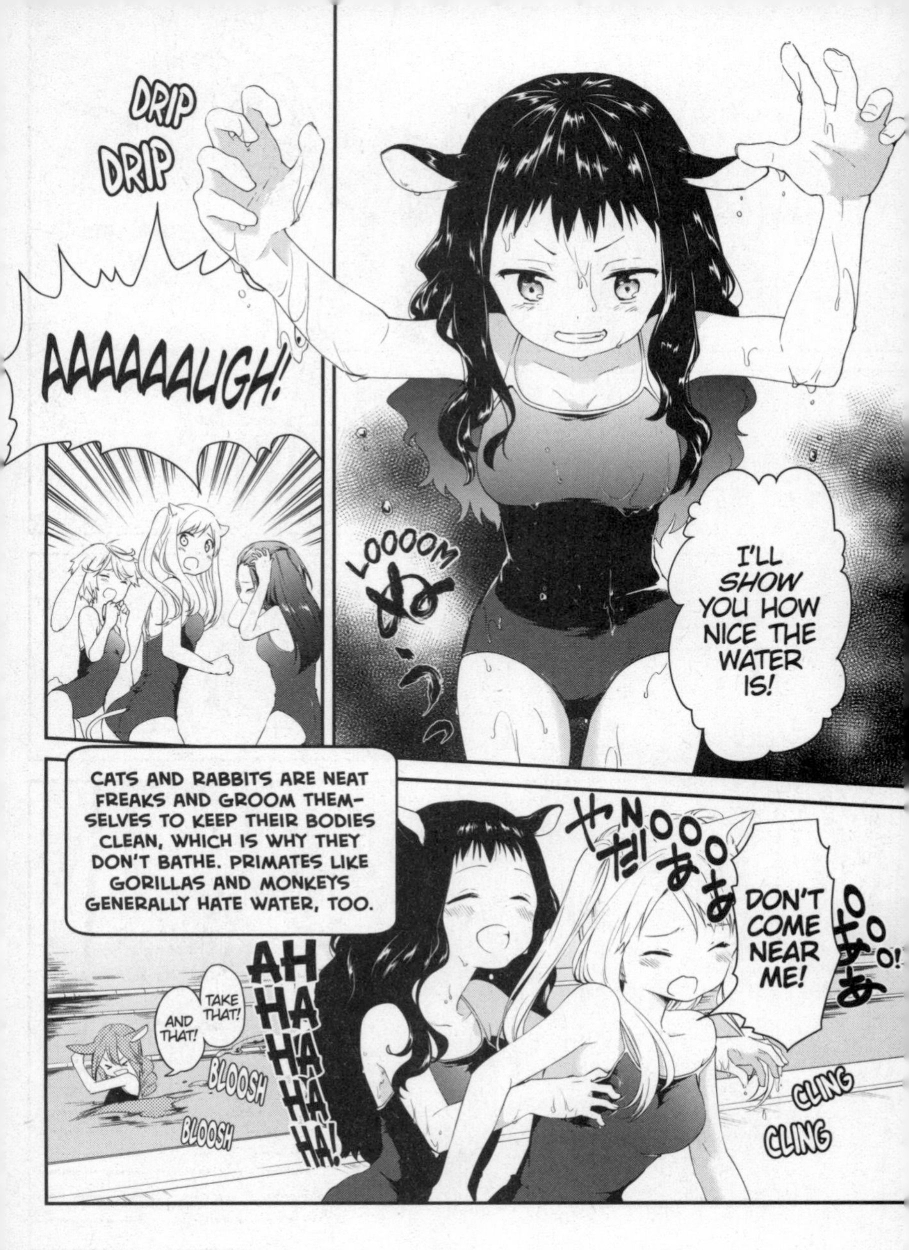

LOOOOM
I'LL SHOW YOU HOW NICE THE WATER IS!
DRIP
DRIP
AAAAAAUGH!
NOOOO
DON'T COME NEAR ME!
AH HA HA HA HA HA!
CATS AND RABBITS ARE NEAT FREAKS AND GROOM THEMSELVES TO KEEP THEIR BODIES CLEAN, WHICH IS WHY THEY DON'T BATHE. PRIMATES LIKE GORILLAS AND MONKEYS GENERALLY HATE WATER, TOO.
CLING
CLING
TAKE THAT!
AND THAT!
BLOOSH
BLOOSH

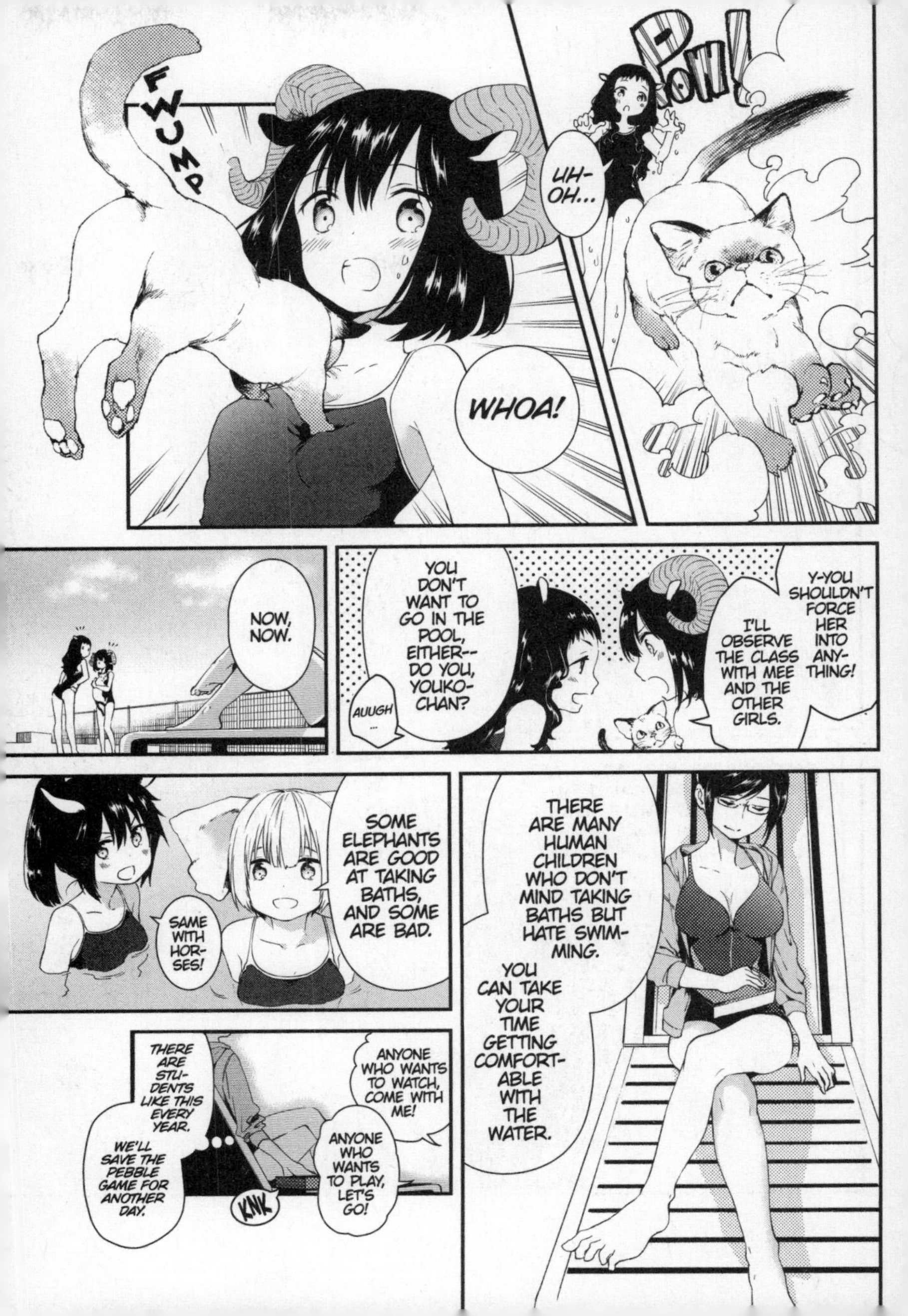
POW!
UH-OH...
FWUMP
WHOA!
Y-YOU SHOULDN'T FORCE HER INTO ANYTHING!
I'LL OBSERVE THE CLASS WITH MEE AND THE OTHER GIRLS.
YOU DON'T WANT TO GO IN THE POOL, EITHER-- DO YOU, YOUKO-CHAN?
AUUGH ...
NOW, NOW.
THERE ARE MANY HUMAN CHILDREN WHO DON'T MIND TAKING BATHS BUT HATE SWIMMING.
YOU CAN TAKE YOUR TIME GETTING COMFORTABLE WITH THE WATER.
SOME ELEPHANTS ARE GOOD AT TAKING BATHS, AND SOME ARE BAD.
SAME WITH HORSES!
ANYONE WHO WANTS TO WATCH, COME WITH ME!
ANYONE WHO WANTS TO PLAY, LET'S GO!
KNK
...
THERE ARE STUDENTS LIKE THIS EVERY YEAR.
WE'LL SAVE THE PEBBLE GAME FOR ANOTHER DAY.

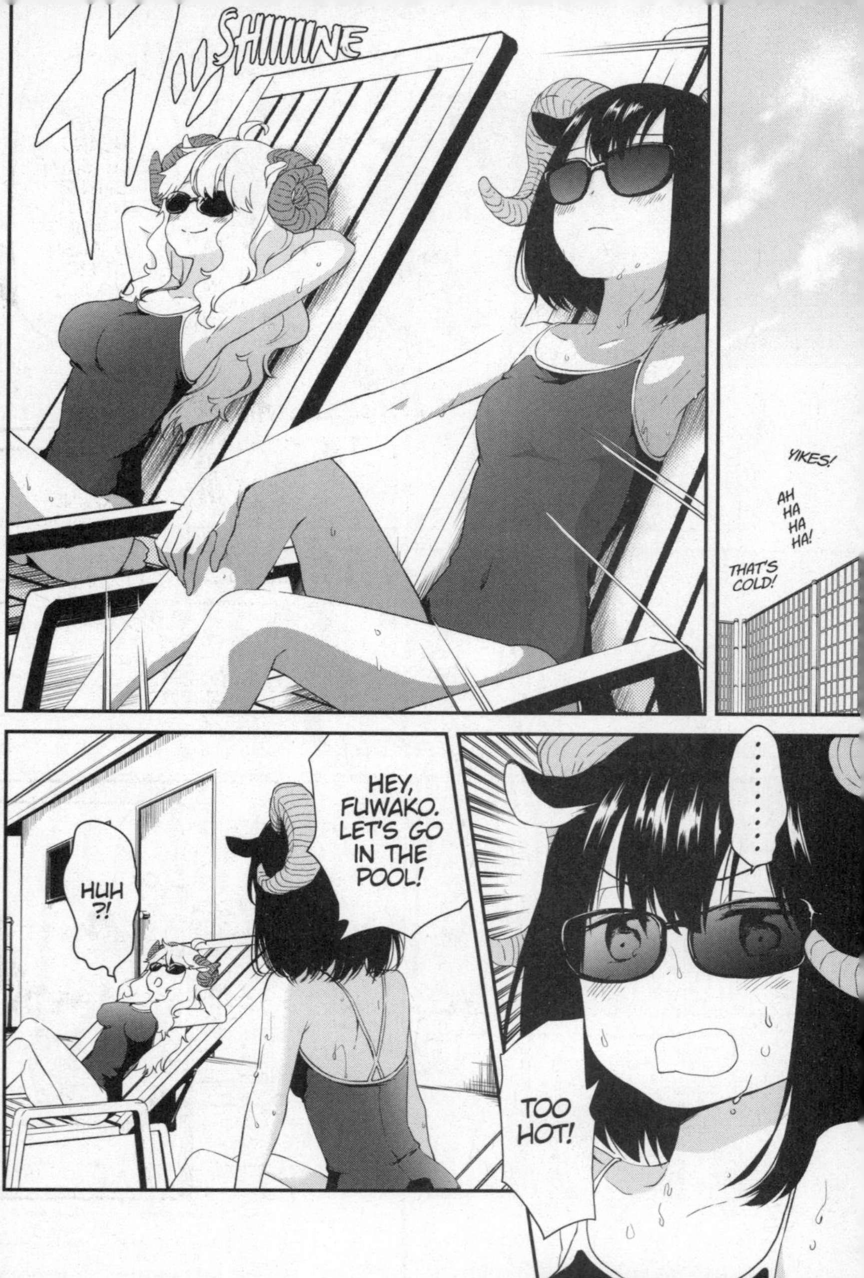

SHIIIIINE
YIKES!
AH HA HA HA!
THAT'S COLD!
......
TOO HOT!
HEY, FUWAKO. LET'S GO IN THE POOL!
HUH ?!

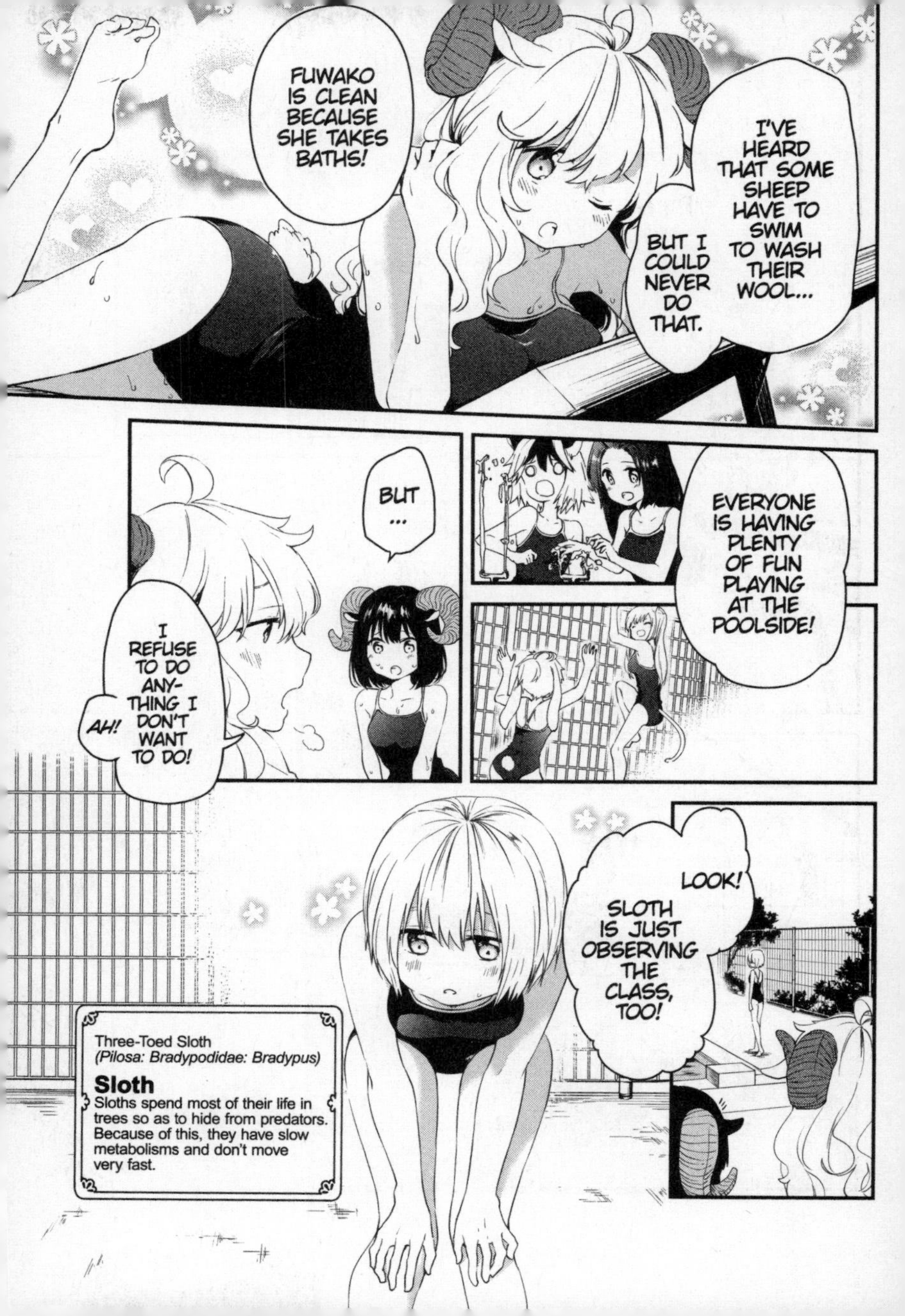
I'VE HEARD THAT SOME SHEEP HAVE TO SWIM TO WASH THEIR WOOL...
BUT I COULD NEVER DO THAT.
FUWAKO IS CLEAN BECAUSE SHE TAKES BATHS!
EVERYONE IS HAVING PLENTY OF FUN PLAYING AT THE POOLSIDE!
BUT ...
I REFUSE TO DO ANY-THING I DON'T WANT TO DO!
AH!
LOOK!
SLOTH IS JUST OBSERVING THE CLASS, TOO!

Three-Toed Sloth
(Pilosa: Bradypodidae: Bradypus)

Sloth

Sloths spend most of their life in trees so as to hide from predators. Because of this, they have slow metabolisms and don't move very fast.

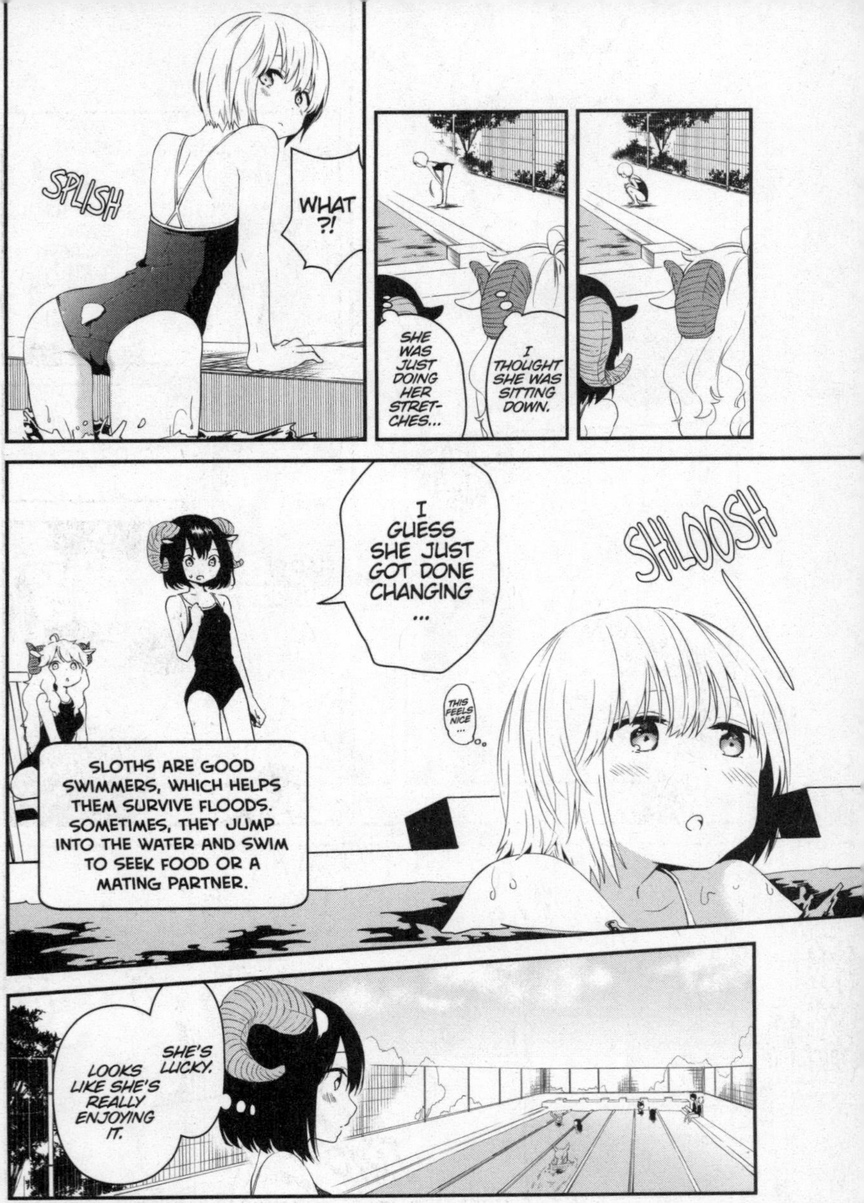
I THOUGHT SHE WAS SITTING DOWN.
SHE WAS JUST DOING HER STRETCHES...
WHAT?!
SPLISH
SHLOOSH
THIS FEELS NICE...
I GUESS SHE JUST GOT DONE CHANGING...
SLOTHS ARE GOOD SWIMMERS, WHICH HELPS THEM SURVIVE FLOODS. SOMETIMES, THEY JUMP INTO THE WATER AND SWIM TO SEEK FOOD OR A MATING PARTNER.
SHE'S LUCKY.
LOOKS LIKE SHE'S REALLY ENJOYING IT.

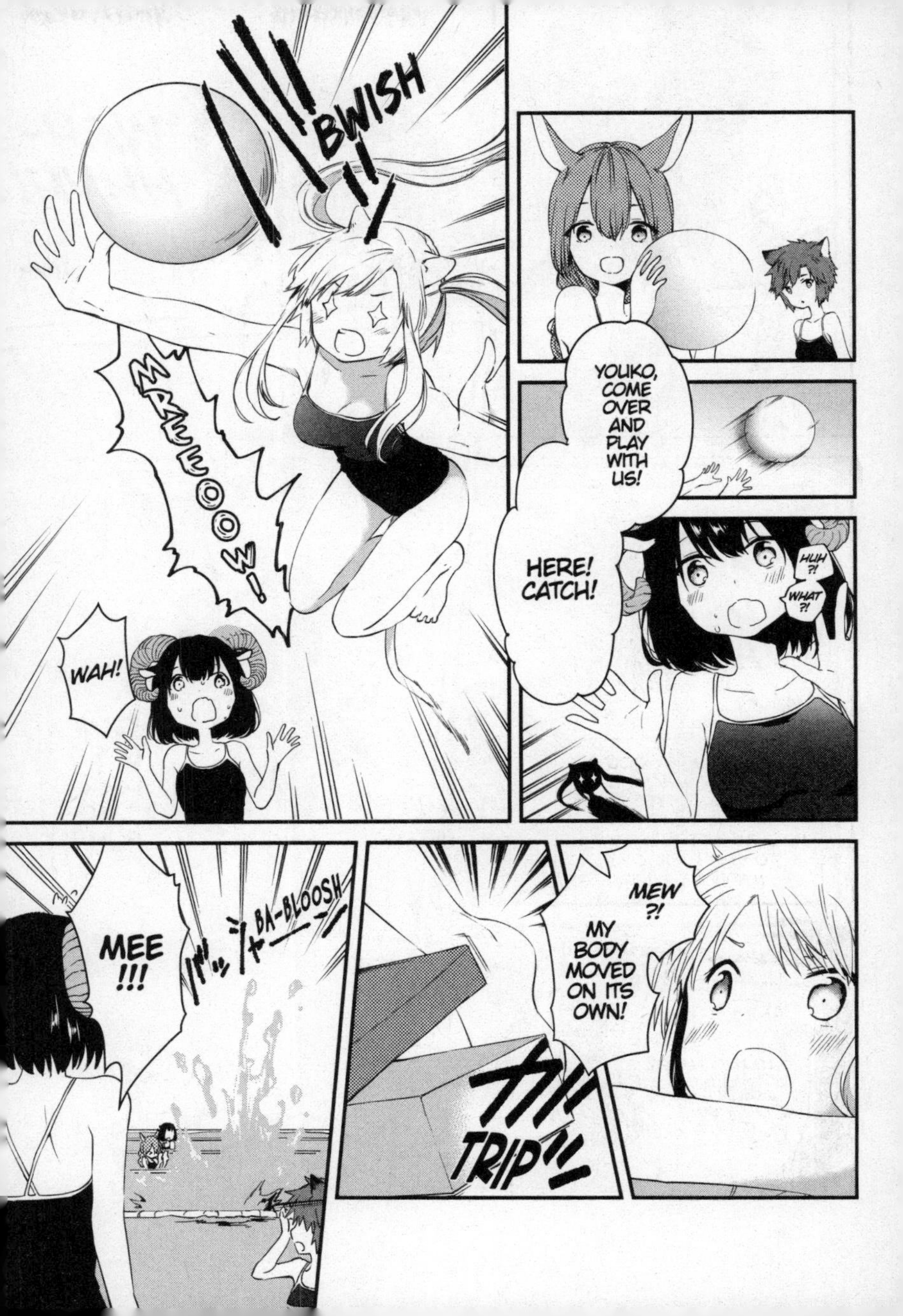
YOUKO, COME OVER AND PLAY WITH US!
HERE! CATCH!
HUH?!
WHAT?!
BWISH
MREEOOOW!
WAH!
MEW?!
MY BODY MOVED ON ITS OWN!
TRIP
BA-BLOOSH
MEE!!!

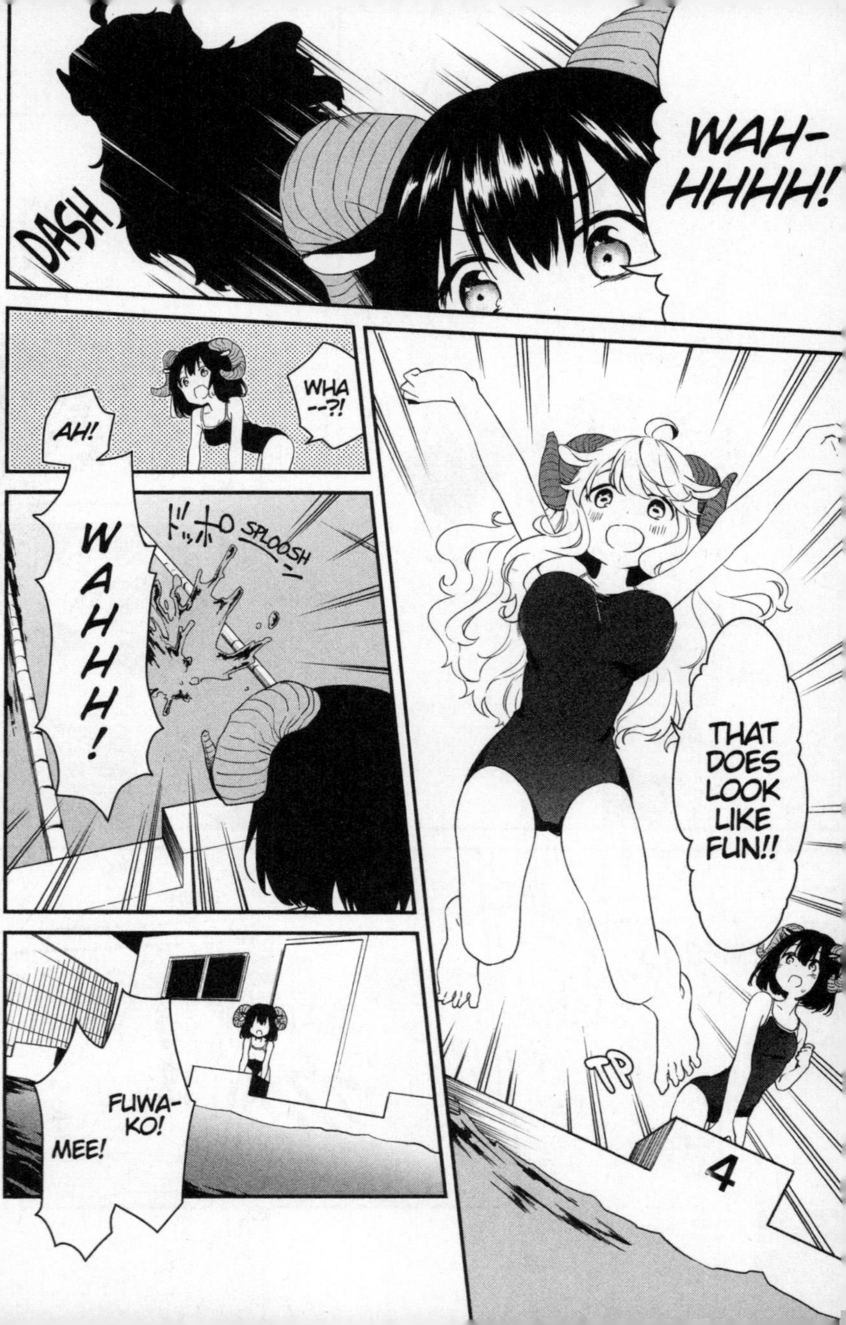
WAH-HHHH!
DASH
WHA--?!
AH!
THAT DOES LOOK LIKE FUN!!
TP
4
ドッボーン SPLOOSH
WAHHHH!
FUWA-KO!
MEE!

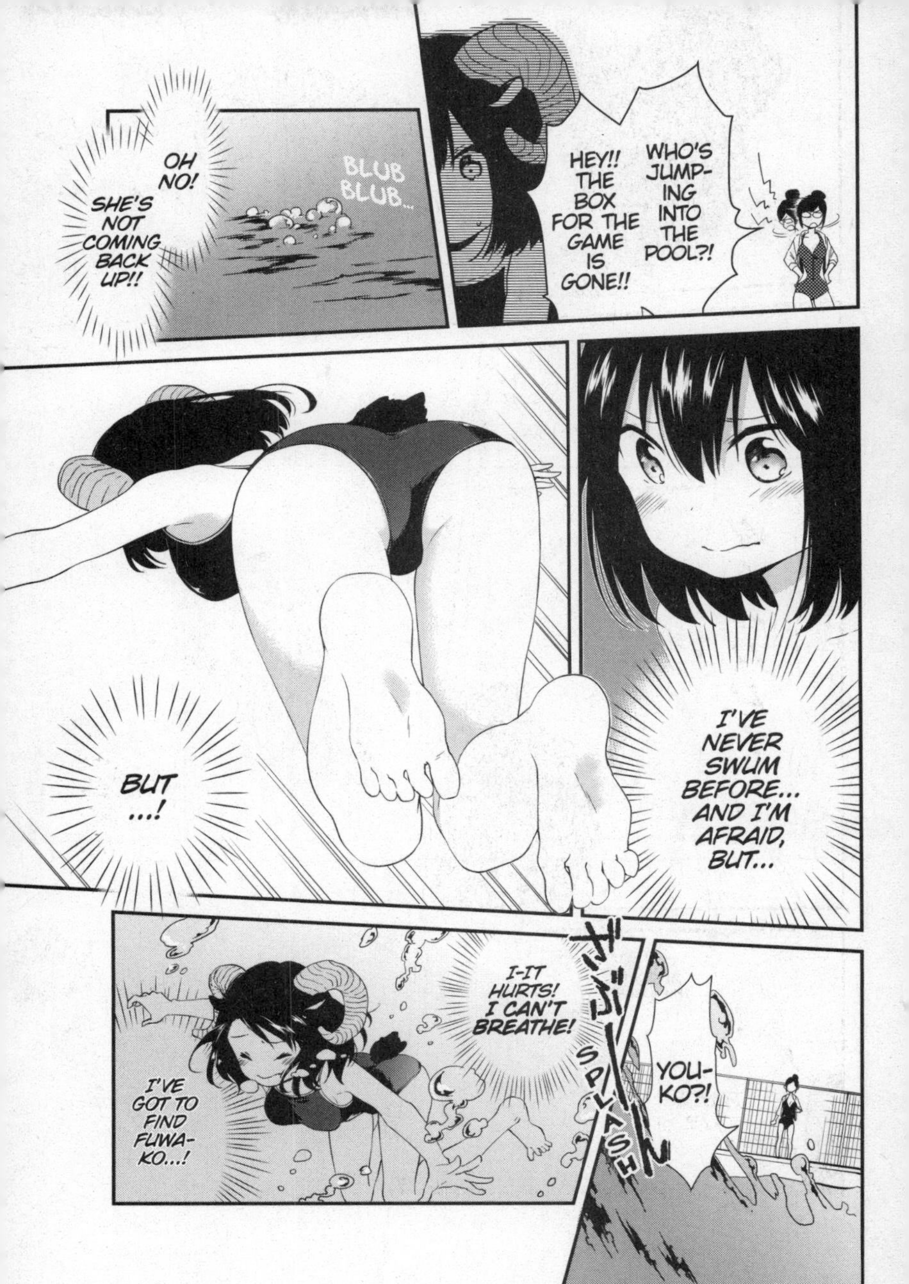
WHO'S JUMPING INTO THE POOL?!
HEY!! THE BOX FOR THE GAME IS GONE!!
BLUB BLUB...
OH NO! SHE'S NOT COMING BACK UP!!
I'VE NEVER SWUM BEFORE... AND I'M AFRAID, BUT...
BUT ...!
YOU-KO?!
SPLASH
I-IT HURTS! I CAN'T BREATHE!
I'VE GOT TO FIND FUWA-KO...!

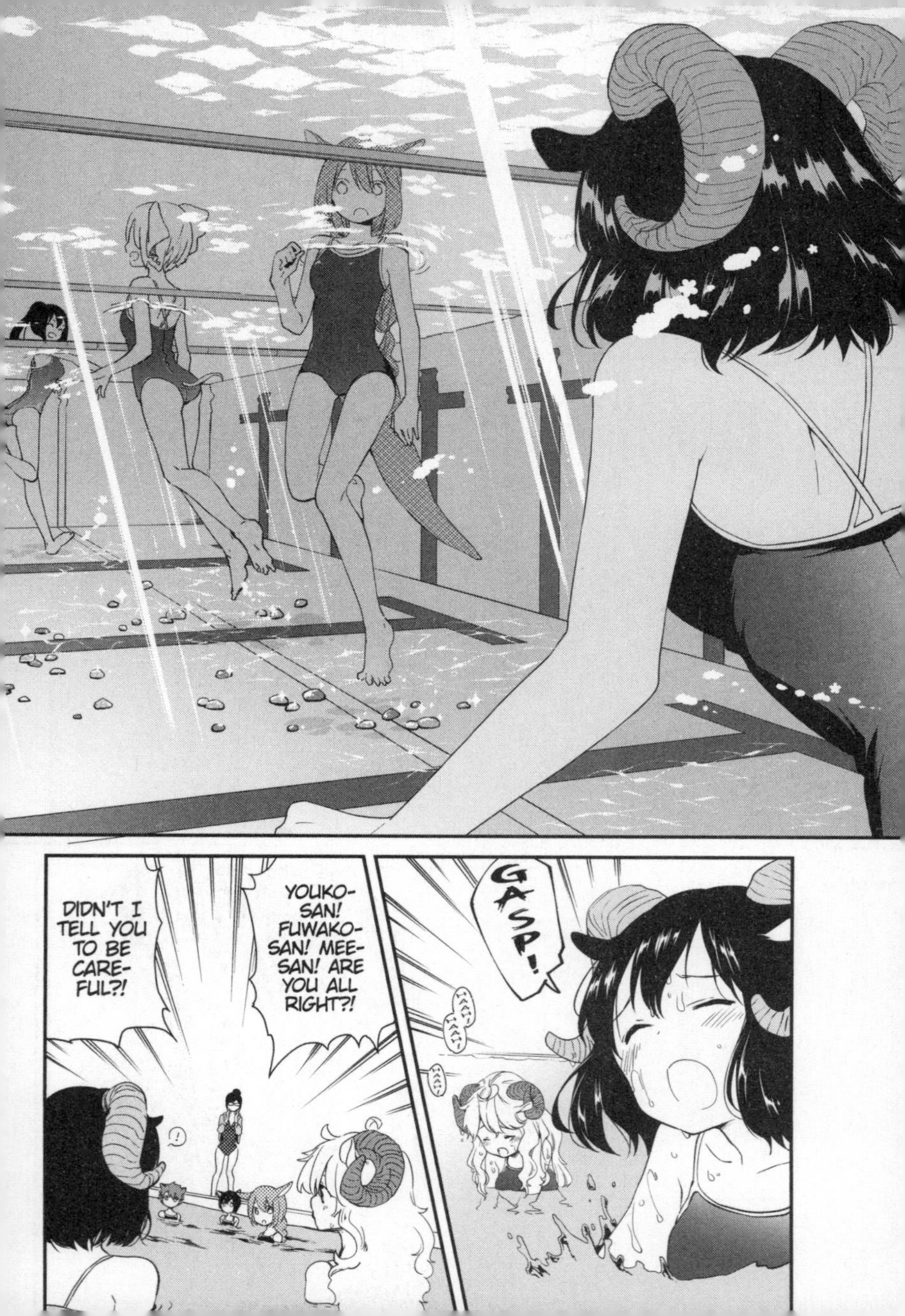
GASP!
YOUKO-SAN! FUWAKO-SAN! MEE-SAN! ARE YOU ALL RIGHT?!
DIDN'T I TELL YOU TO BE CAREFUL?!
!

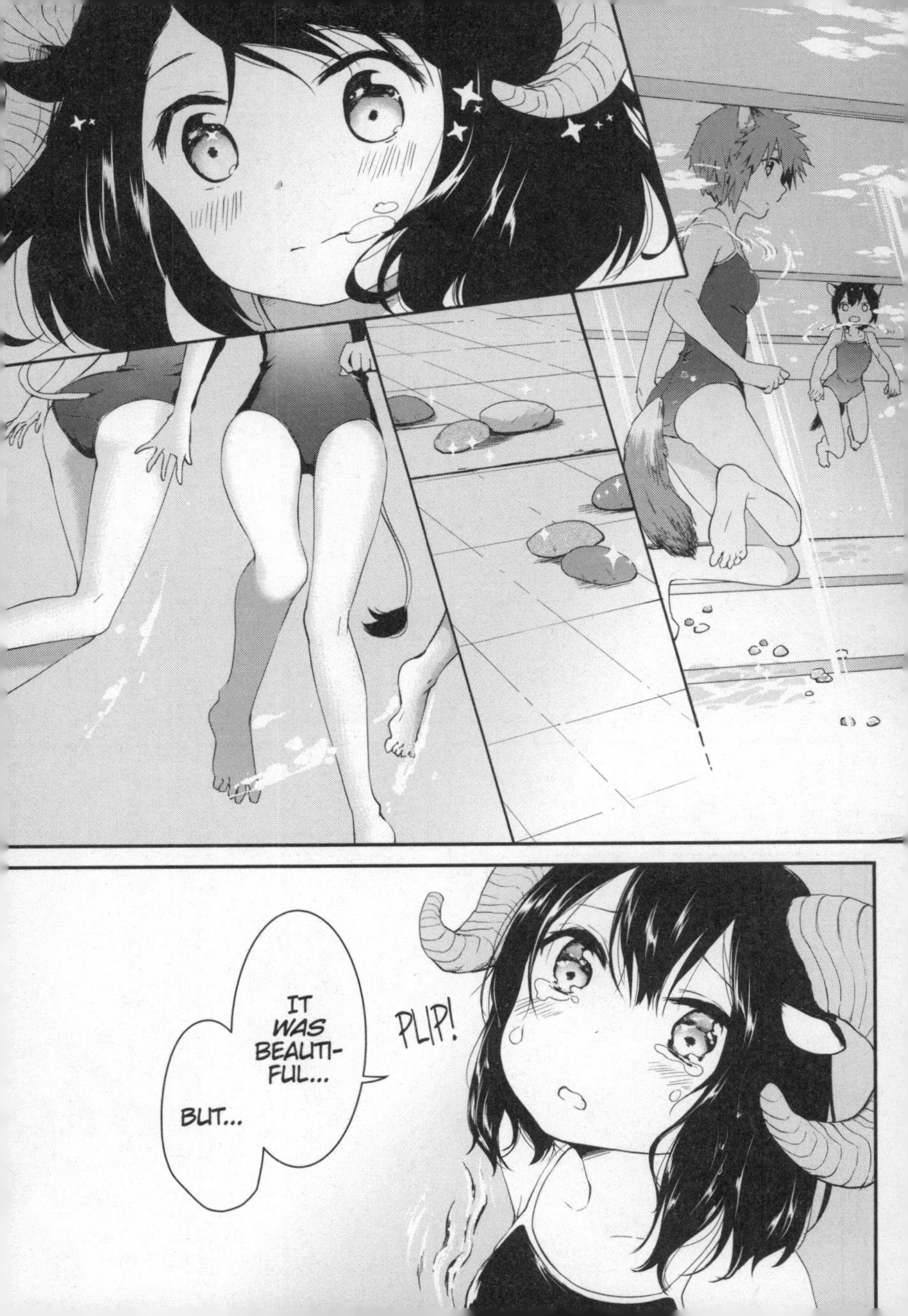
IT WAS BEAUTIFUL...
BUT...
PLIP!

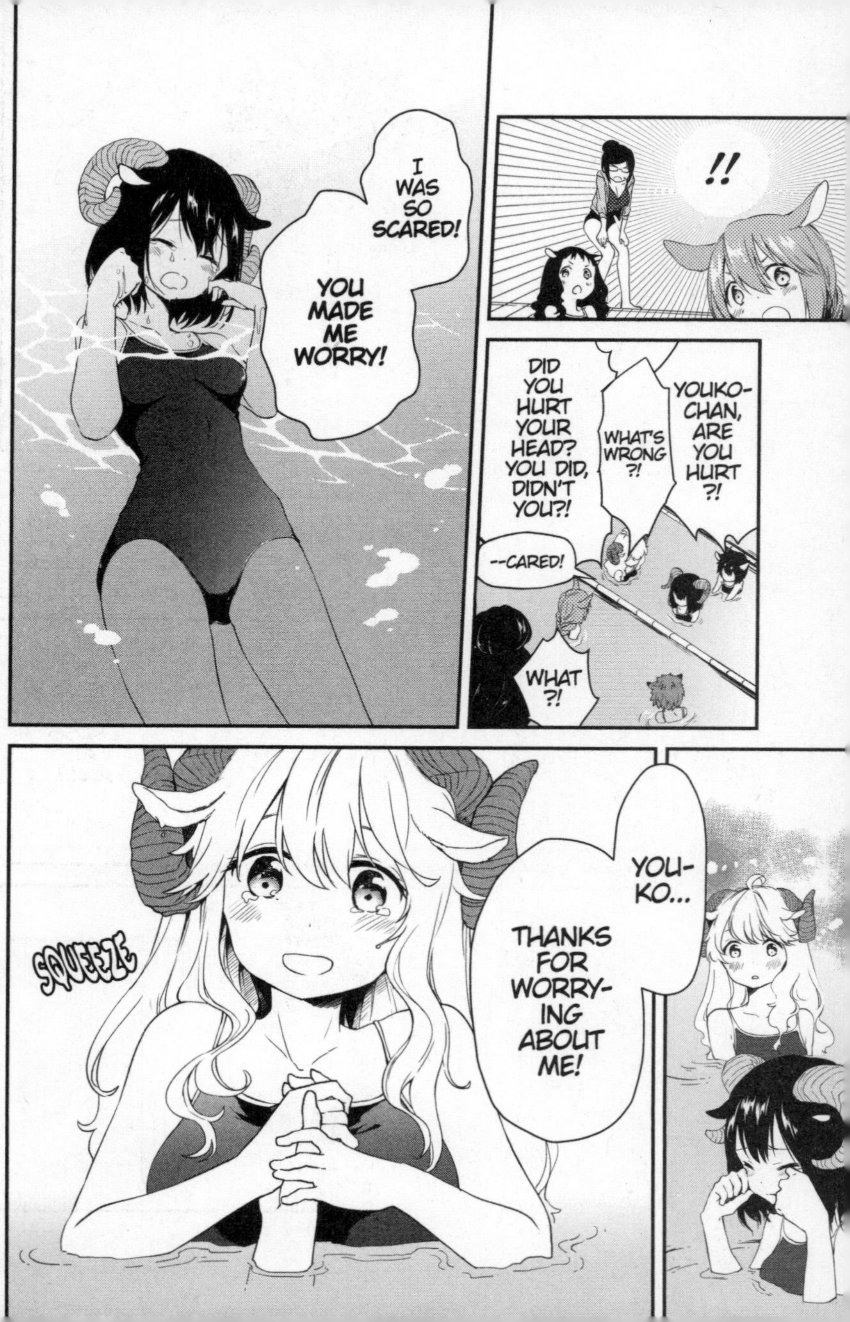
!!
YOUKO-CHAN, ARE YOU HURT?!
WHAT'S WRONG?!
DID YOU HURT YOUR HEAD? YOU DID, DIDN'T YOU?!
--CARED!
WHAT?!
I WAS SO SCARED!
YOU MADE ME WORRY!
YOU-KO...
THANKS FOR WORRY-ING ABOUT ME!
SQUEEZE

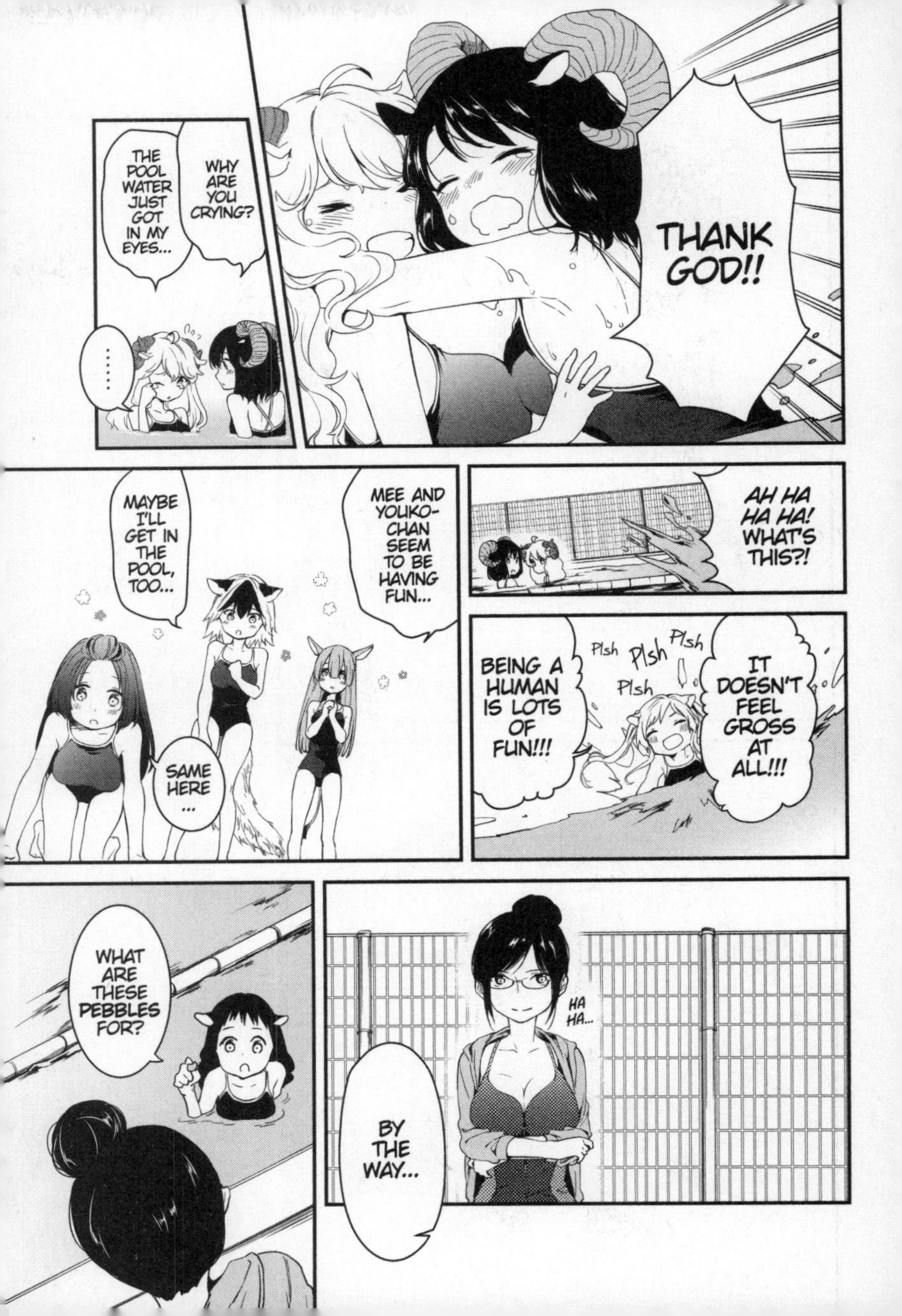
THANK GOD!!
WHY ARE YOU CRYING?
THE POOL WATER JUST GOT IN MY EYES...
......
AH HA HA HA! WHAT'S THIS?!
MEE AND YOUKO-CHAN SEEM TO BE HAVING FUN...
MAYBE I'LL GET IN THE POOL, TOO...
SAME HERE ...
Plsh Plsh Plsh Plsh
IT DOESN'T FEEL GROSS AT ALL!!!
BEING A HUMAN IS LOTS OF FUN!!!
HA HA...
BY THE WAY...
WHAT ARE THESE PEBBLES FOR?

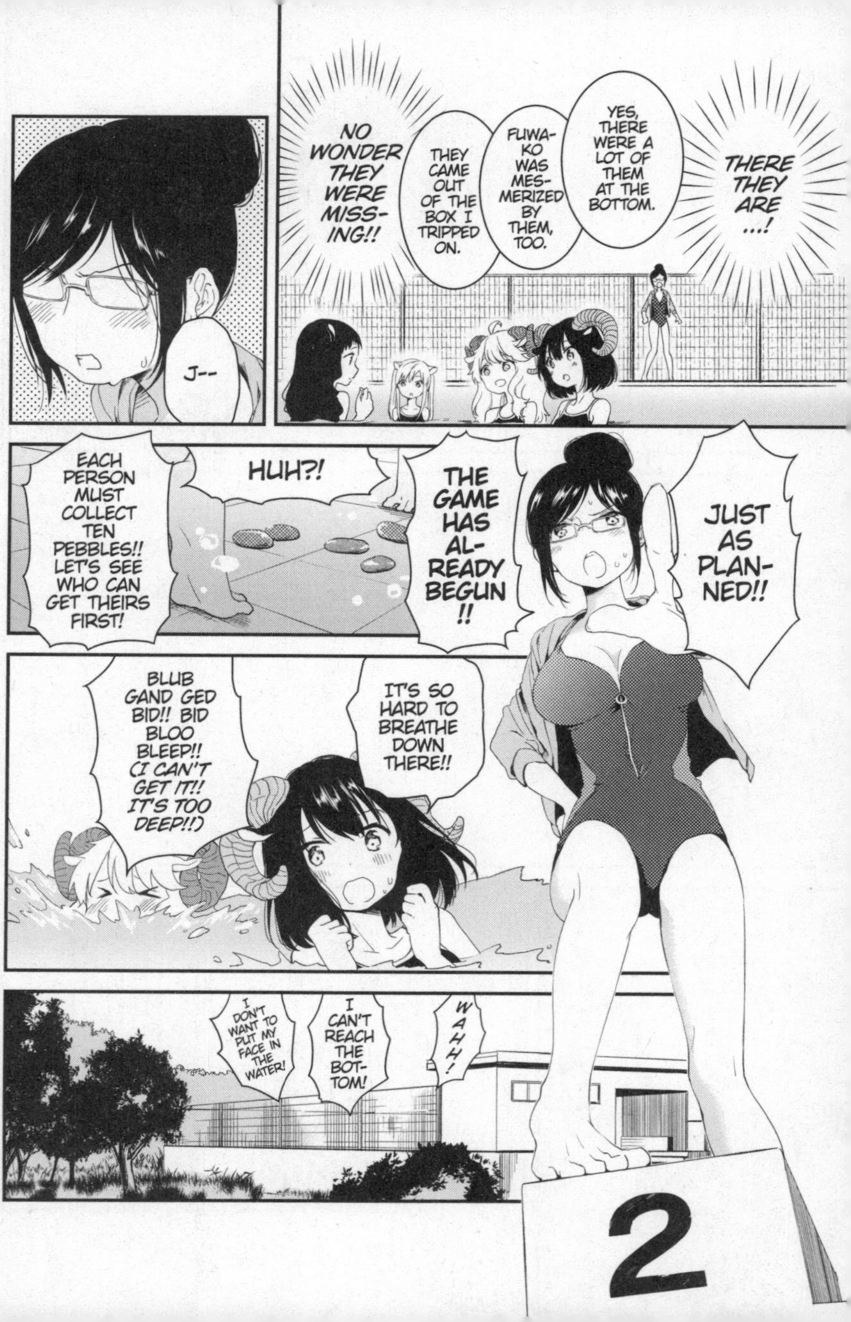
THERE THEY ARE ...!
YES, THERE WERE A LOT OF THEM AT THE BOTTOM.
FUWA-KO WAS MES-MERIZED BY THEM, TOO.
THEY CAME OUT OF THE BOX I TRIPPED ON.
NO WONDER THEY WERE MISS-ING!!
J--
JUST AS PLAN-NED!!
THE GAME HAS AL-READY BEGUN!!
HUH?!
EACH PERSON MUST COLLECT TEN PEBBLES!! LET'S SEE WHO CAN GET THEIRS FIRST!
IT'S SO HARD TO BREATHE DOWN THERE!!
BLUB GAND GED BID!! BID BLOO BLEEP!! (I CAN'T GET IT!! IT'S TOO DEEP!!)
WAHH!
I CAN'T REACH THE BOT-TOM!
I DON'T WANT TO PUT MY FACE IN THE WATER!
2

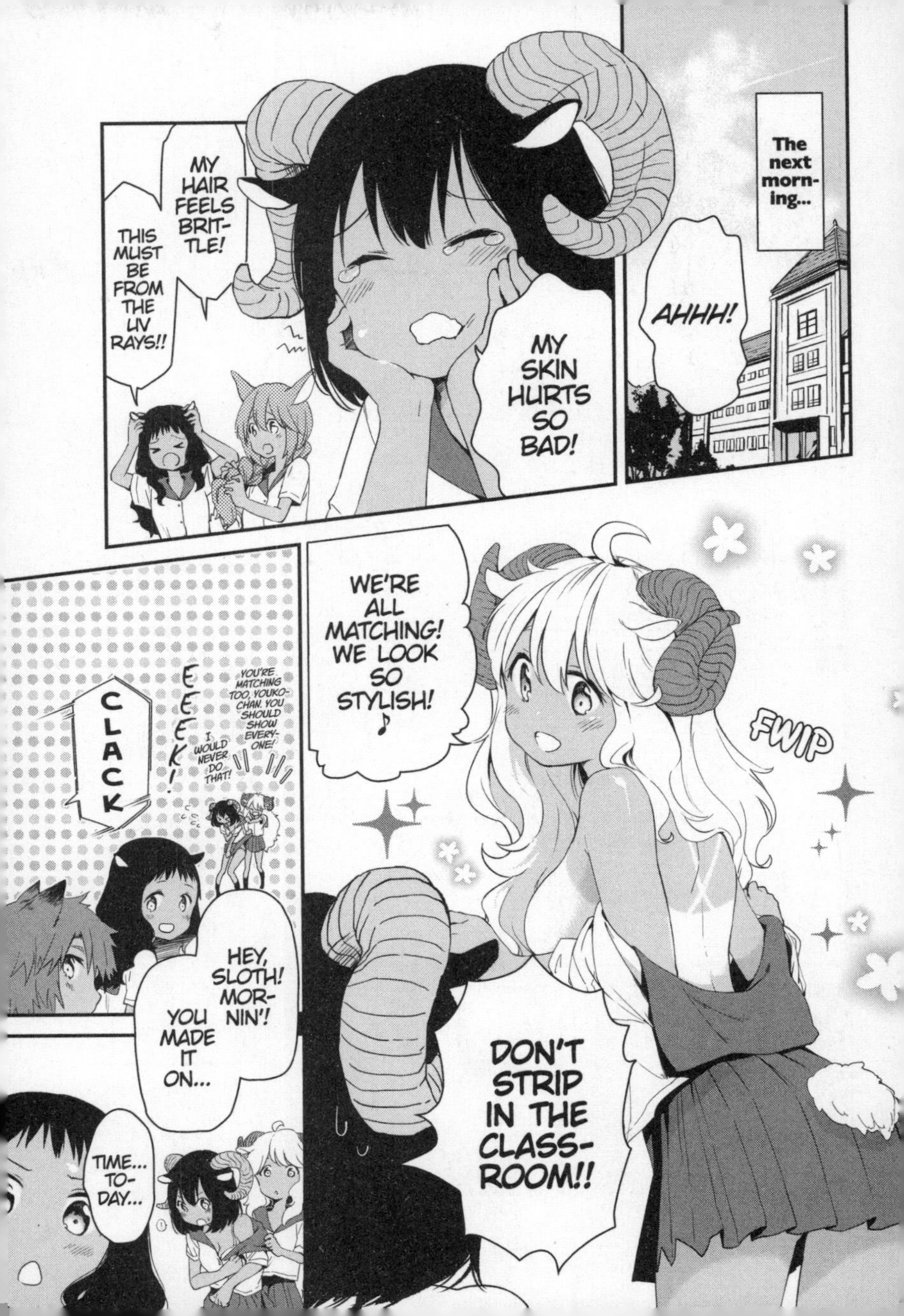

The next morning...
AHHH!
MY SKIN HURTS SO BAD!
MY HAIR FEELS BRITTLE!
THIS MUST BE FROM THE UV RAYS!!
FWIP
WE'RE ALL MATCHING! WE LOOK SO STYLISH! ♪
DON'T STRIP IN THE CLASSROOM!!
CLACK
EEEEK!
YOU'RE MATCHING TOO, YOUKO-CHAN. YOU SHOULD SHOW EVERYONE!
I WOULD NEVER DO THAT!
HEY, SLOTH! MORNIN'!
YOU MADE IT ON...
TIME... TODAY...

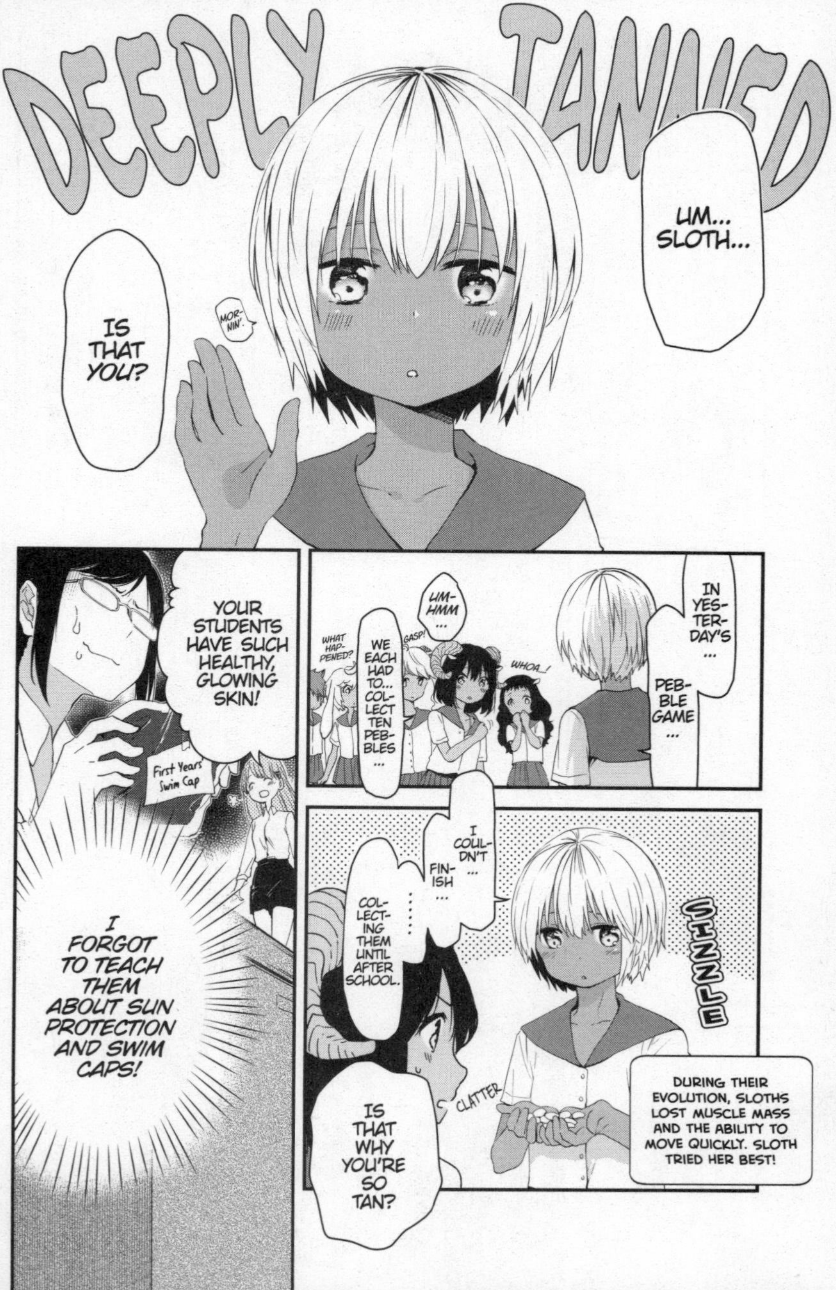
DEEPLY TANNED
UM... SLOTH...
MOR-NIN'.
IS THAT YOU?
IN YES-TER-DAY'S ... PEB-BLE GAME ...
UM-HMM ...
WE EACH HAD TO... COL-LECT TEN PEB-BLES ...
GASP!
WHAT HAP-PENED?
WHOA...!
YOUR STUDENTS HAVE SUCH HEALTHY, GLOWING SKIN!
First Years Swim Cap
I FORGOT TO TEACH THEM ABOUT SUN PROTECTION AND SWIM CAPS!
I COUL-DN'T ...
FIN-ISH ...
COL-LECT-ING THEM UNTIL AFTER SCHOOL.
SIZZLE
CLATTER
IS THAT WHY YOU'RE SO TAN?
DURING THEIR EVOLUTION, SLOTHS LOST MUSCLE MASS AND THE ABILITY TO MOVE QUICKLY. SLOTH TRIED HER BEST!

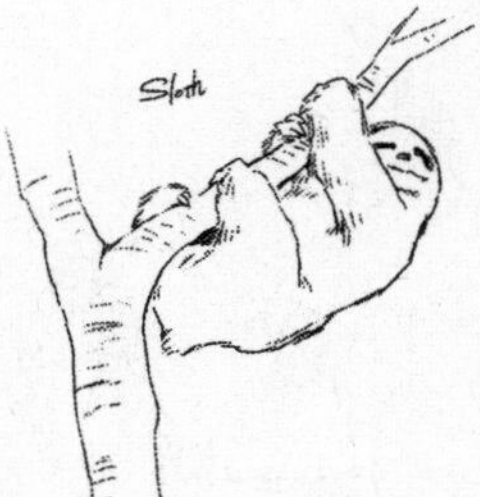
Sloth

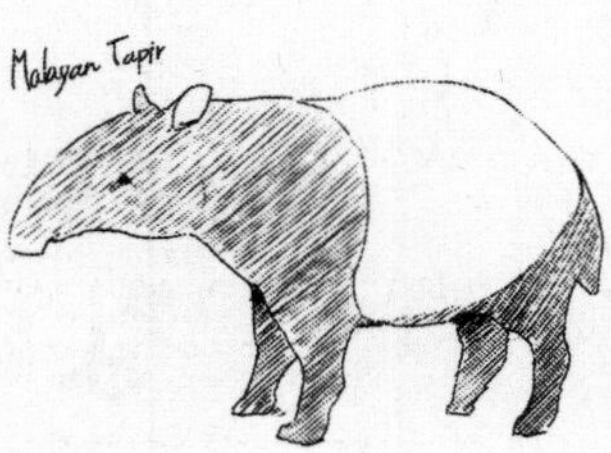
Malayan Tapir

DNAは教えてくれない

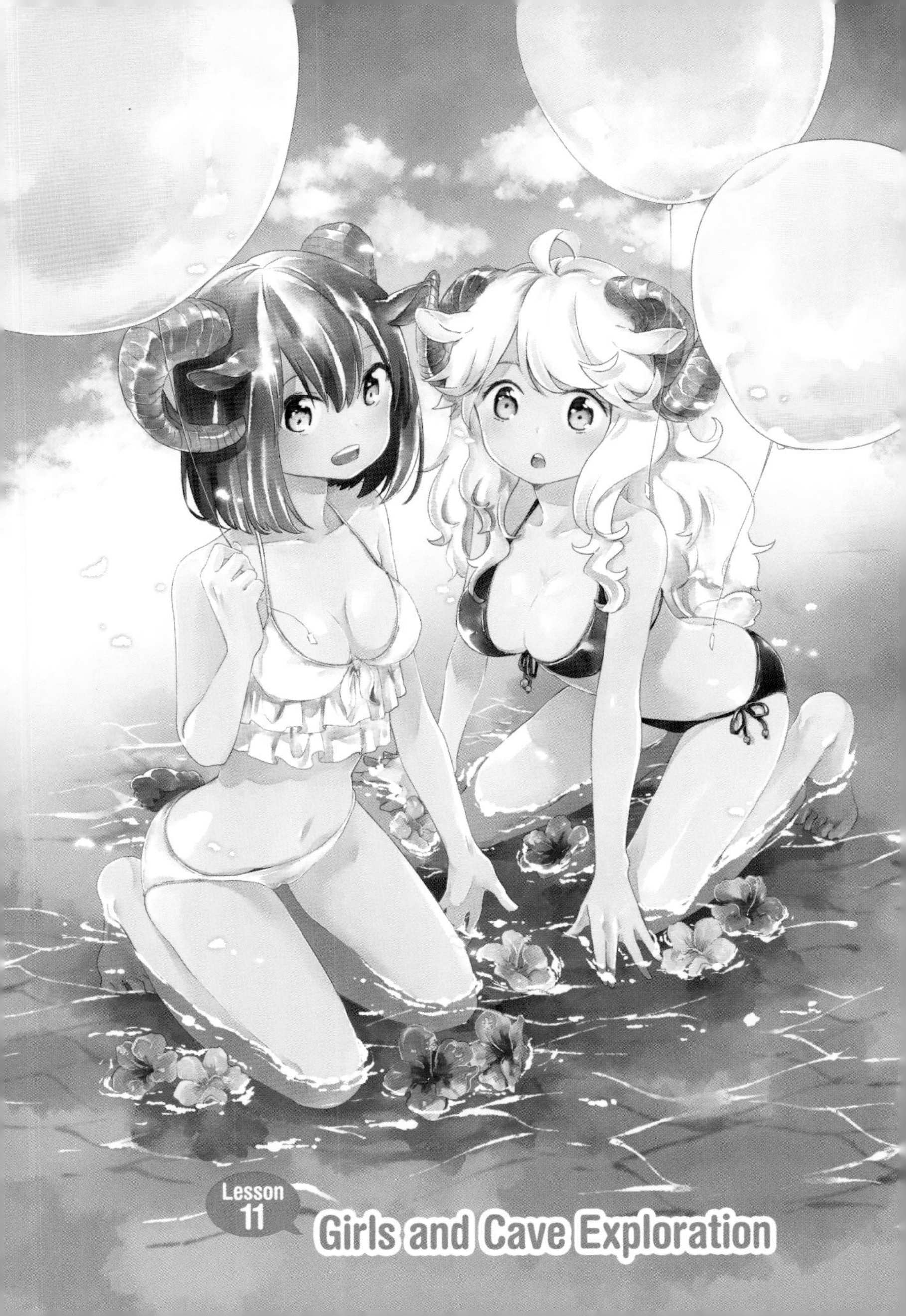
Lesson 11
Girls and Cave Exploration

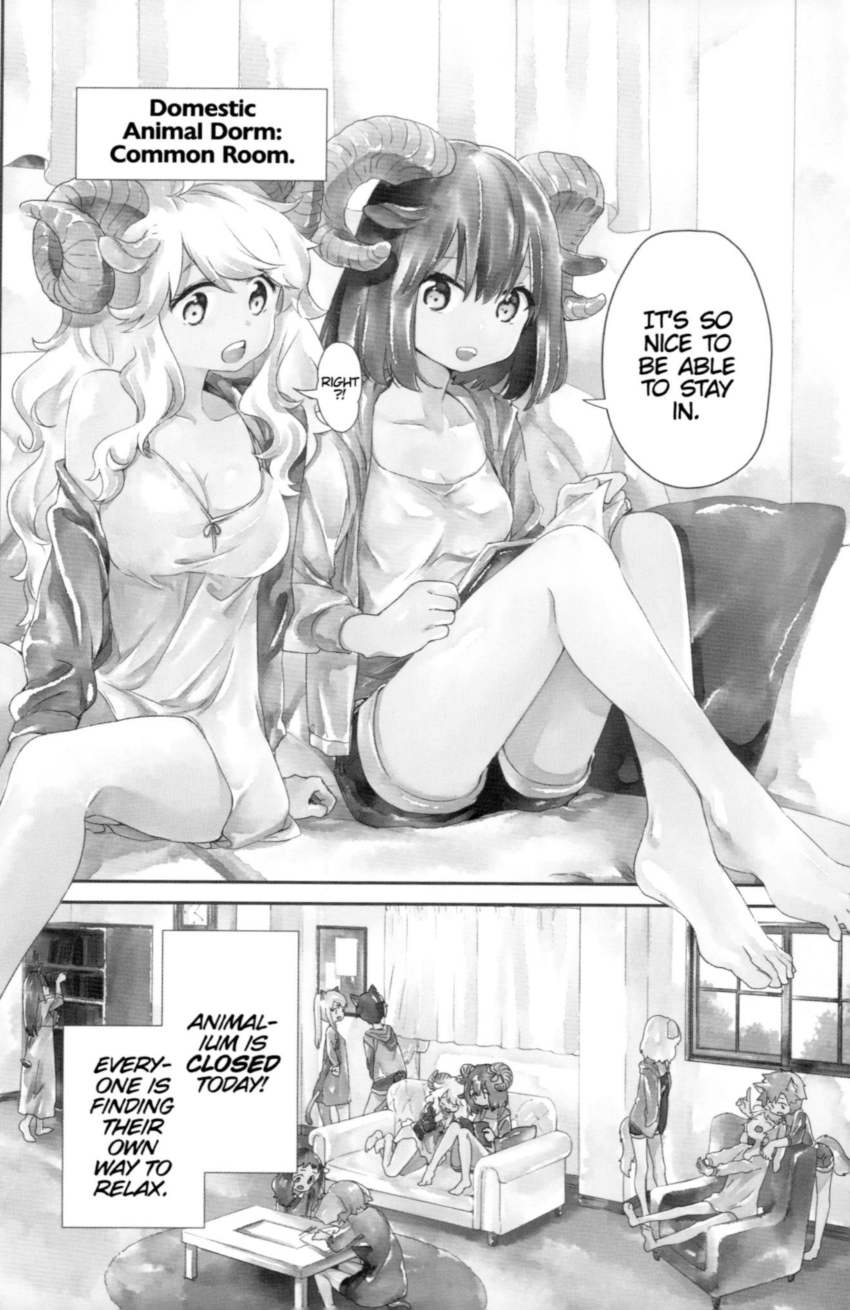
Domestic Animal Dorm: Common Room.
IT'S SO NICE TO BE ABLE TO STAY IN.
RIGHT ?!
ANIMAL-IUM IS CLOSED TODAY!
EVERY-ONE IS FINDING THEIR OWN WAY TO RELAX.

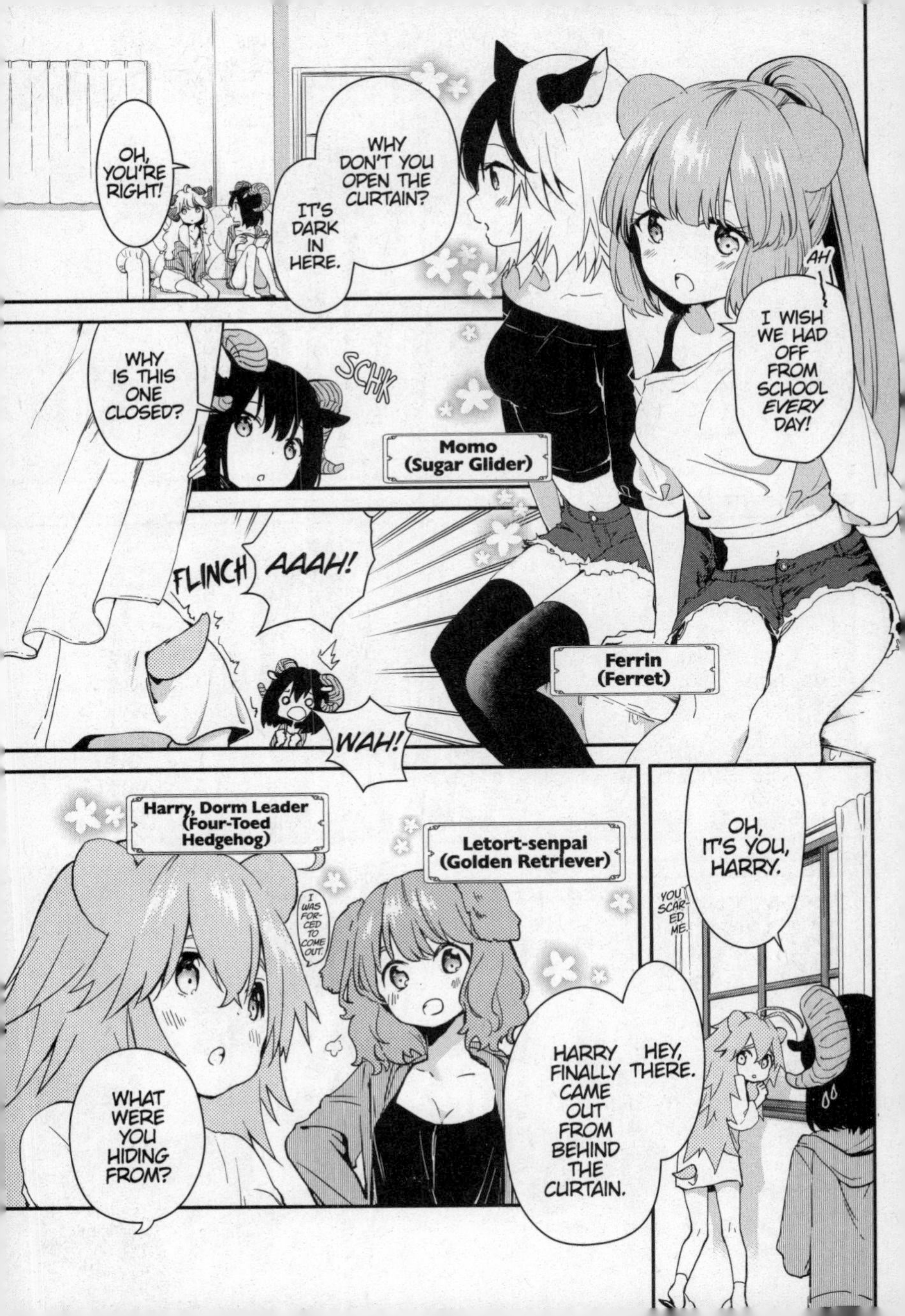
AH~
I WISH WE HAD OFF FROM SCHOOL *EVERY* DAY!
WHY DON'T YOU OPEN THE CURTAIN?
IT'S DARK IN HERE.
OH, YOU'RE RIGHT!
Momo (Sugar Glider)
Ferrin (Ferret)
SCHK
WHY IS THIS ONE CLOSED?
AAAH!
FLINCH
WAH!
OH, IT'S YOU, HARRY.
YOU SCARED ME.
HEY, THERE.
HARRY FINALLY CAME OUT FROM BEHIND THE CURTAIN.
Letort-senpai (Golden Retriever)
Harry, Dorm Leader (Four-Toed Hedgehog)
I WAS FORCED TO COME OUT.
WHAT WERE YOU HIDING FROM?

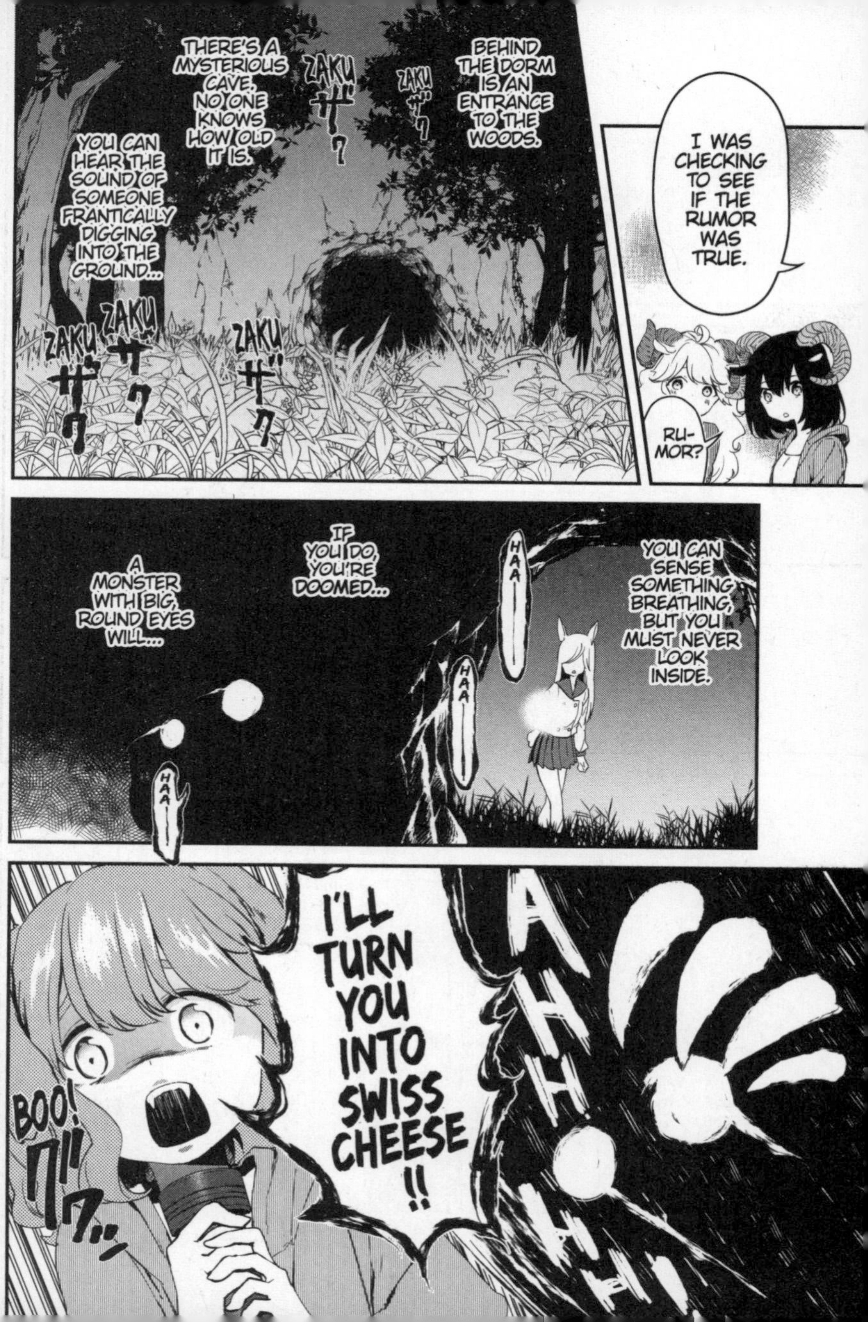
I WAS CHECKING TO SEE IF THE RUMOR WAS TRUE.
RU-MOR?
BEHIND THE DORM IS AN ENTRANCE TO THE WOODS.
ZAKU
ZAKU
THERE'S A MYSTERIOUS CAVE. NO ONE KNOWS HOW OLD IT IS.
YOU CAN HEAR THE SOUND OF SOMEONE FRANTICALLY DIGGING INTO THE GROUND...
ZAKU
ZAKU
ZAKU
YOU CAN SENSE SOMETHING BREATHING, BUT YOU MUST NEVER LOOK INSIDE.
HAA
HAA
IF YOU DO, YOU'RE DOOMED...
A MONSTER WITH BIG, ROUND EYES WILL...
HAA
AHHHHH
I'LL TURN YOU INTO SWISS CHEESE!!
BOO!

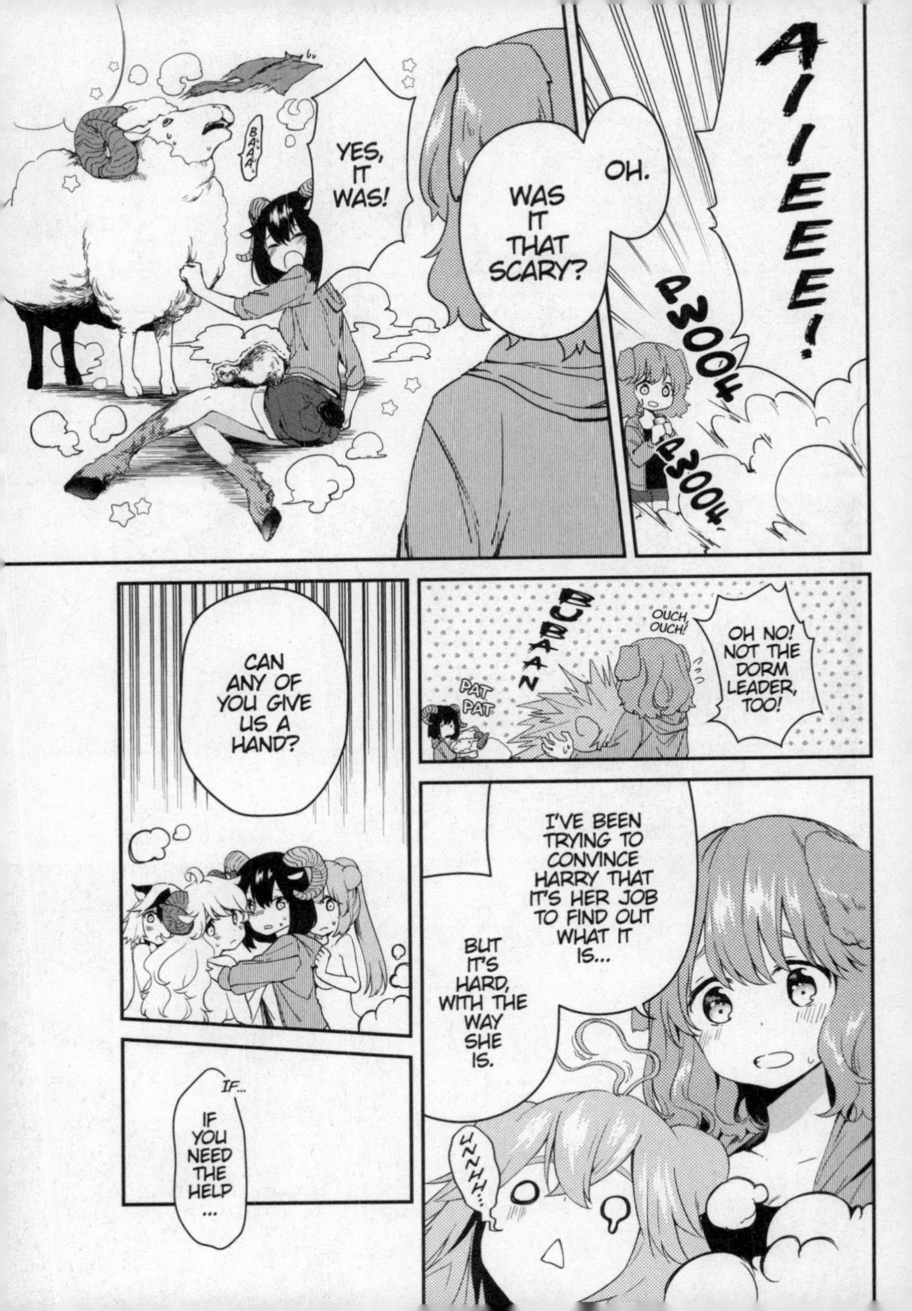
AIIEEE!
PWOOH
PWOOH
OH. WAS IT THAT SCARY?
BAAA
YES, IT WAS!
BUBAAN
OUCH, OUCH!
OH NO! NOT THE DORM LEADER, TOO!
PAT PAT
CAN ANY OF YOU GIVE US A HAND?
I'VE BEEN TRYING TO CONVINCE HARRY THAT IT'S HER JOB TO FIND OUT WHAT IT IS...
BUT IT'S HARD, WITH THE WAY SHE IS.
UNNH...
IF... IF YOU NEED THE HELP...

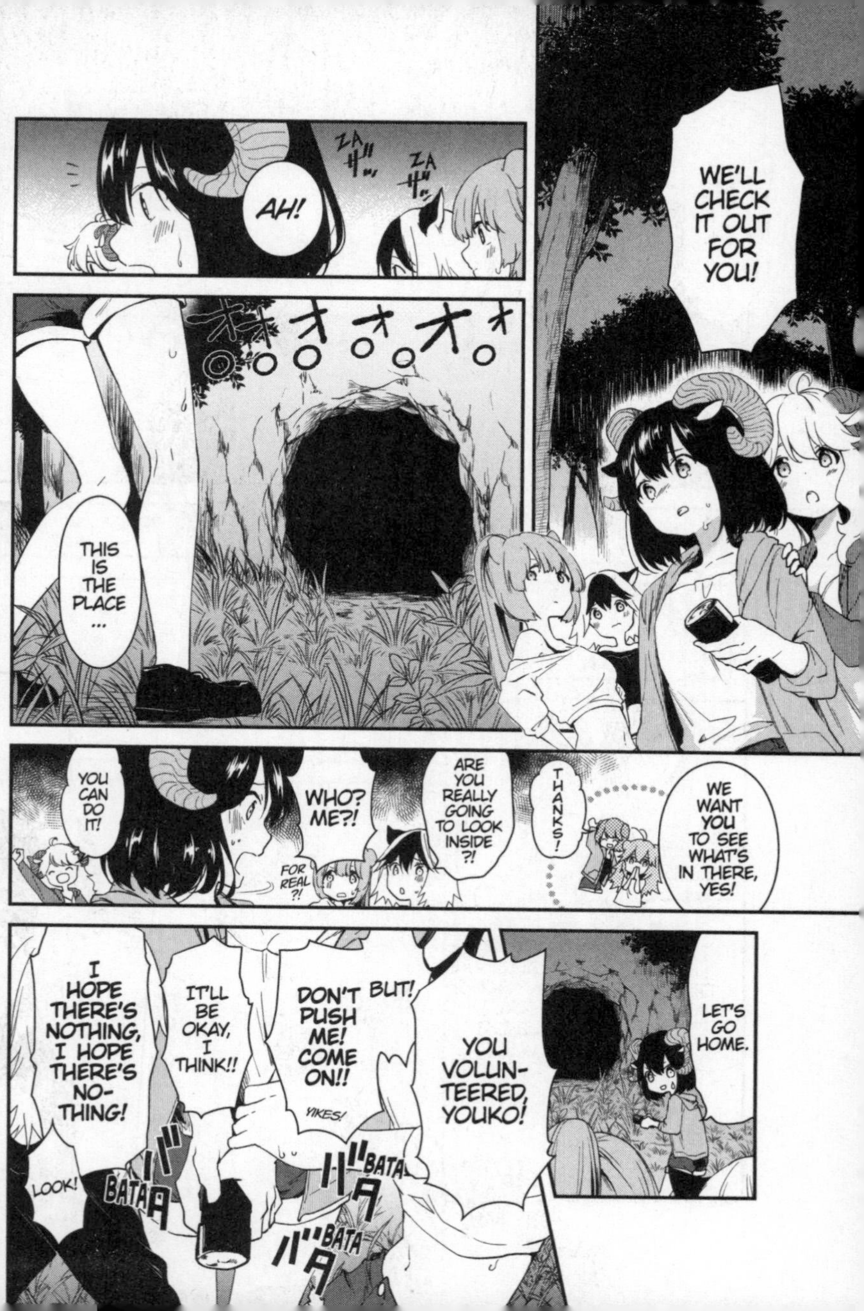
WE'LL CHECK IT OUT FOR YOU!
ZA
ZA
AH!
THIS IS THE PLACE...
WE WANT YOU TO SEE WHAT'S IN THERE, YES!
THANKS!
ARE YOU REALLY GOING TO LOOK INSIDE?!
FOR REAL?!
WHO? ME?!
YOU CAN DO IT!
LET'S GO HOME.
YOU VOLUNTEERED, YOUKO!
BUT!
DON'T PUSH ME! COME ON!!
YIKES!
IT'LL BE OKAY, I THINK!!
I HOPE THERE'S NOTHING, I HOPE THERE'S NO-THING!
BATA
BATA
BATA
LOOK!

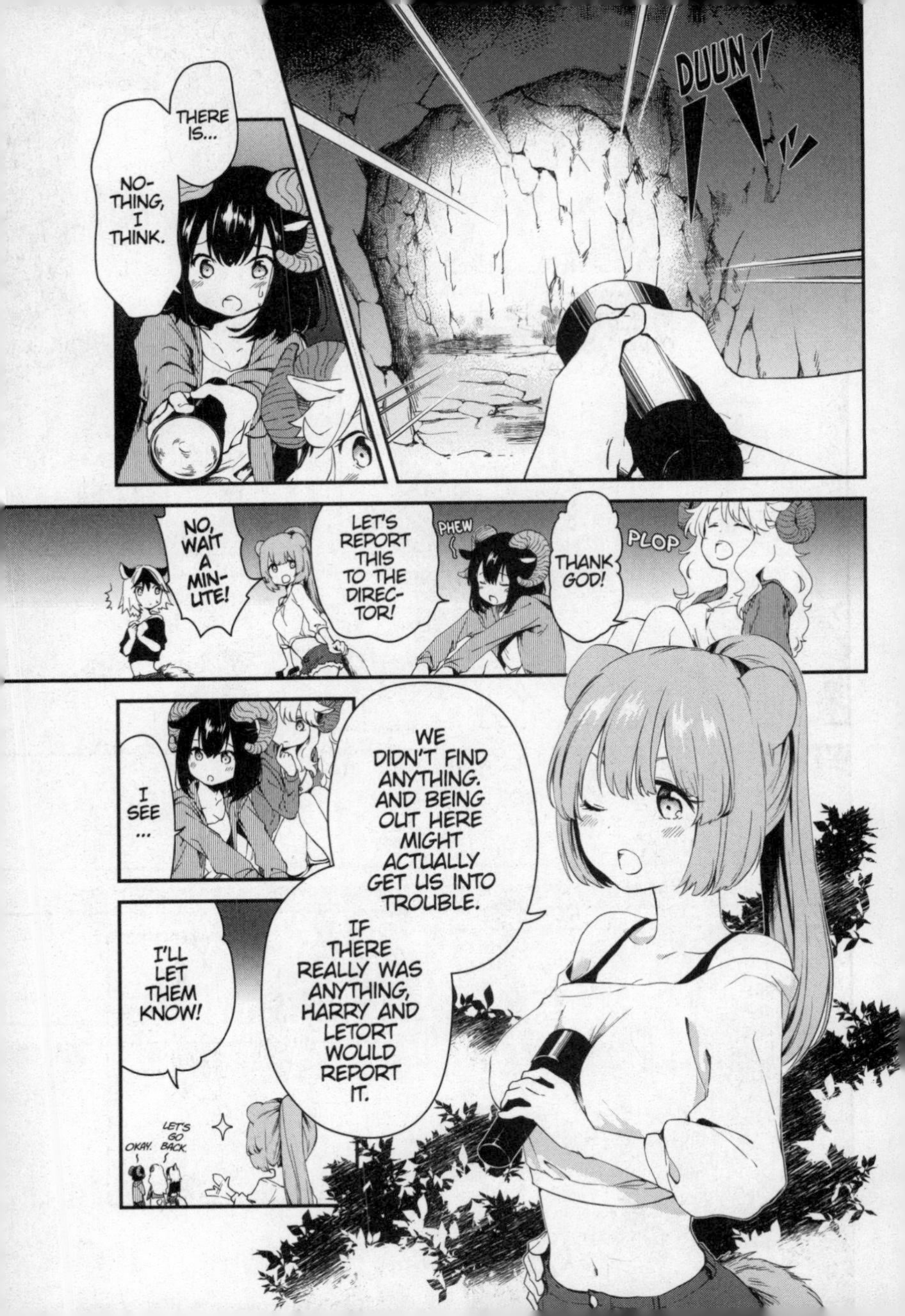
DUUN
THERE IS...
NOTHING, I THINK.
THANK GOD!
PLOP
PHEW
LET'S REPORT THIS TO THE DIRECTOR!
NO, WAIT A MINUTE!
WE DIDN'T FIND ANYTHING. AND BEING OUT HERE MIGHT ACTUALLY GET US INTO TROUBLE.
IF THERE REALLY WAS ANYTHING, HARRY AND LETORT WOULD REPORT IT.
I SEE...
I'LL LET THEM KNOW!
LET'S GO BACK.
OKAY.

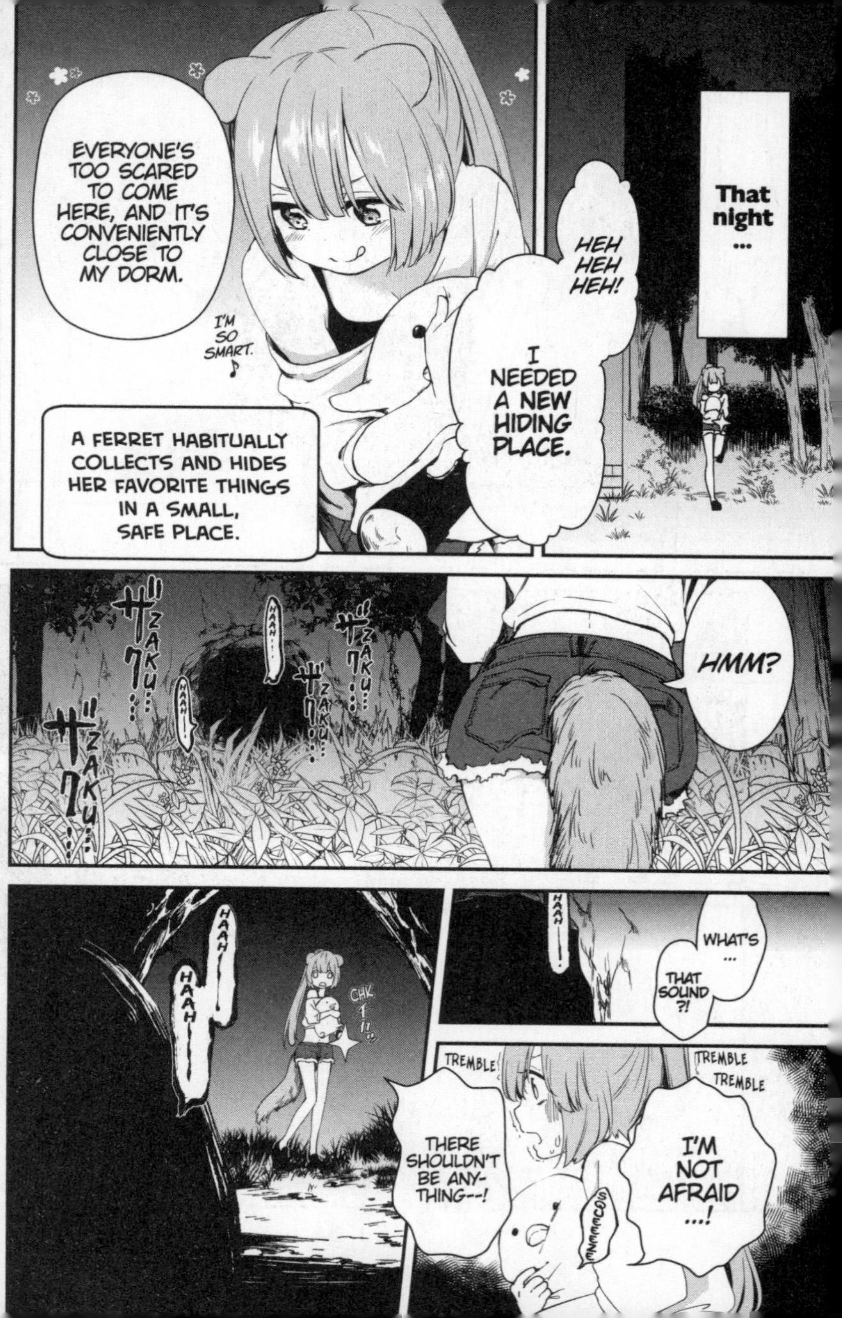

That night ...
HEH HEH HEH!
I NEEDED A NEW HIDING PLACE.
EVERYONE'S TOO SCARED TO COME HERE, AND IT'S CONVENIENTLY CLOSE TO MY DORM.
I'M SO SMART. ♪
A FERRET HABITUALLY COLLECTS AND HIDES HER FAVORITE THINGS IN A SMALL, SAFE PLACE.
HMM?
ZAKU...
ZAKU...
HAAH...
ZAKU...
HAAH...
ZAKU...
WHAT'S ... THAT SOUND ?!
HAAH
HAAH
HAAH
CHK
TREMBLE
TREMBLE
TREMBLE
I'M NOT AFRAID ...!
THERE SHOULDN'T BE ANY-THING--!

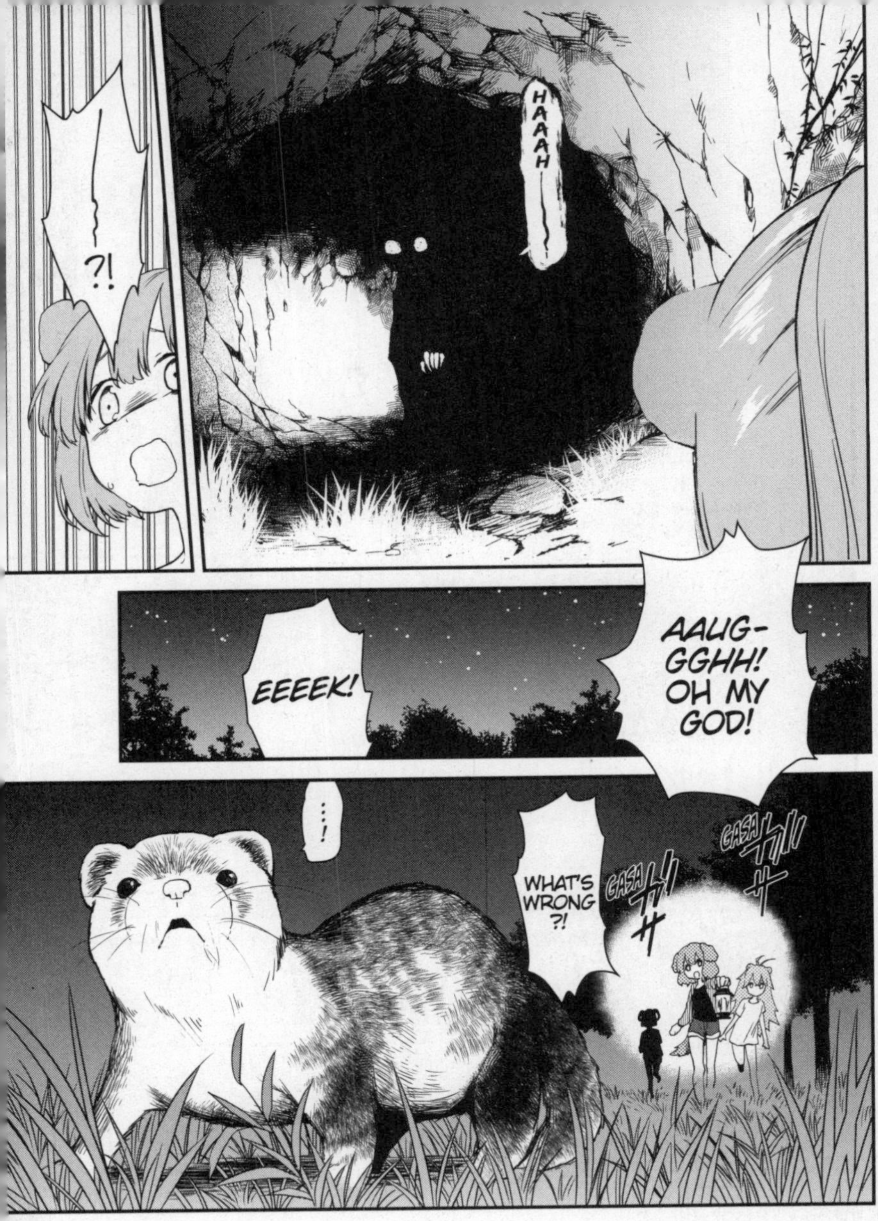
HAAAAH
—?!
AAUG-GGHH! OH MY GOD!
EEEEK!
WHAT'S WRONG?!
…!
GASA
GASA

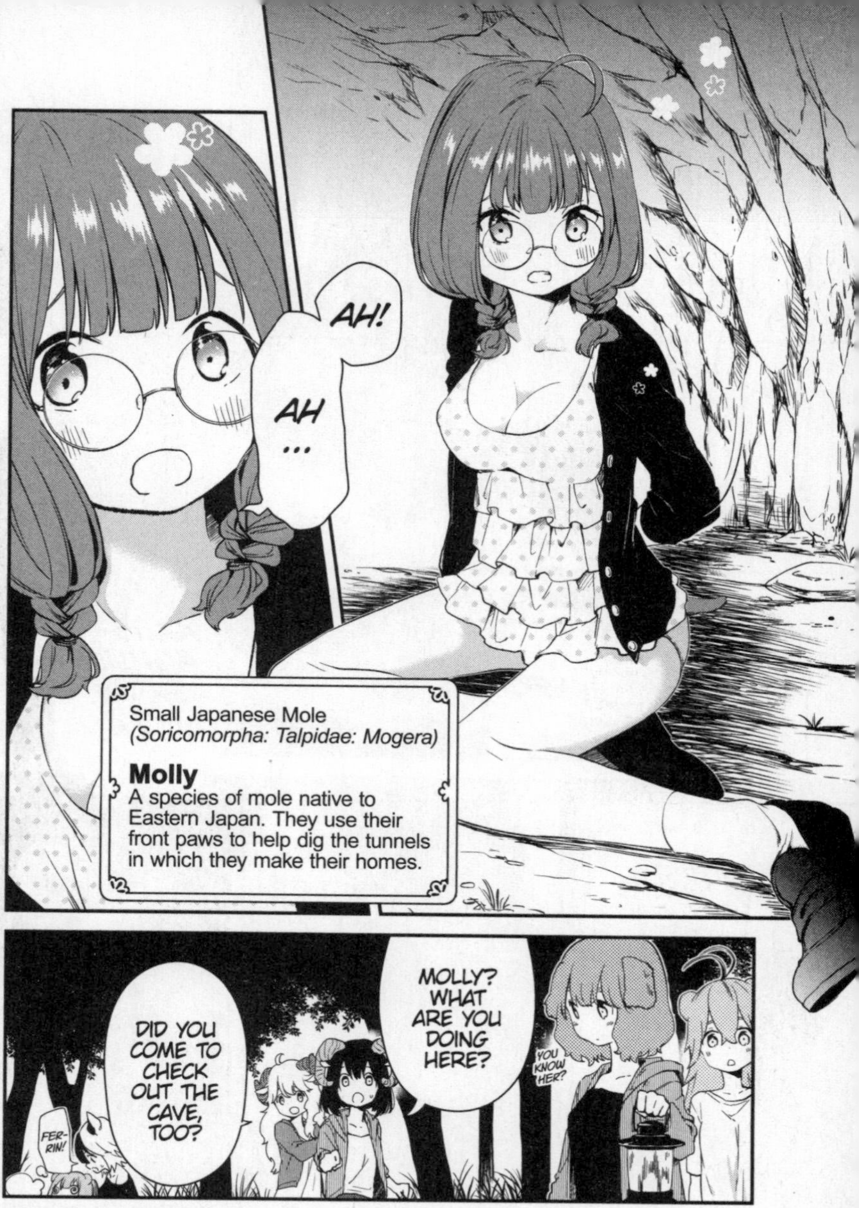
AH!
AH ...
Small Japanese Mole
(Soricomorpha: Talpidae: Mogera)
Molly
A species of mole native to Eastern Japan. They use their front paws to help dig the tunnels in which they make their homes.
MOLLY? WHAT ARE YOU DOING HERE?
YOU KNOW HER?
DID YOU COME TO CHECK OUT THE CAVE, TOO?
FER-RIN!

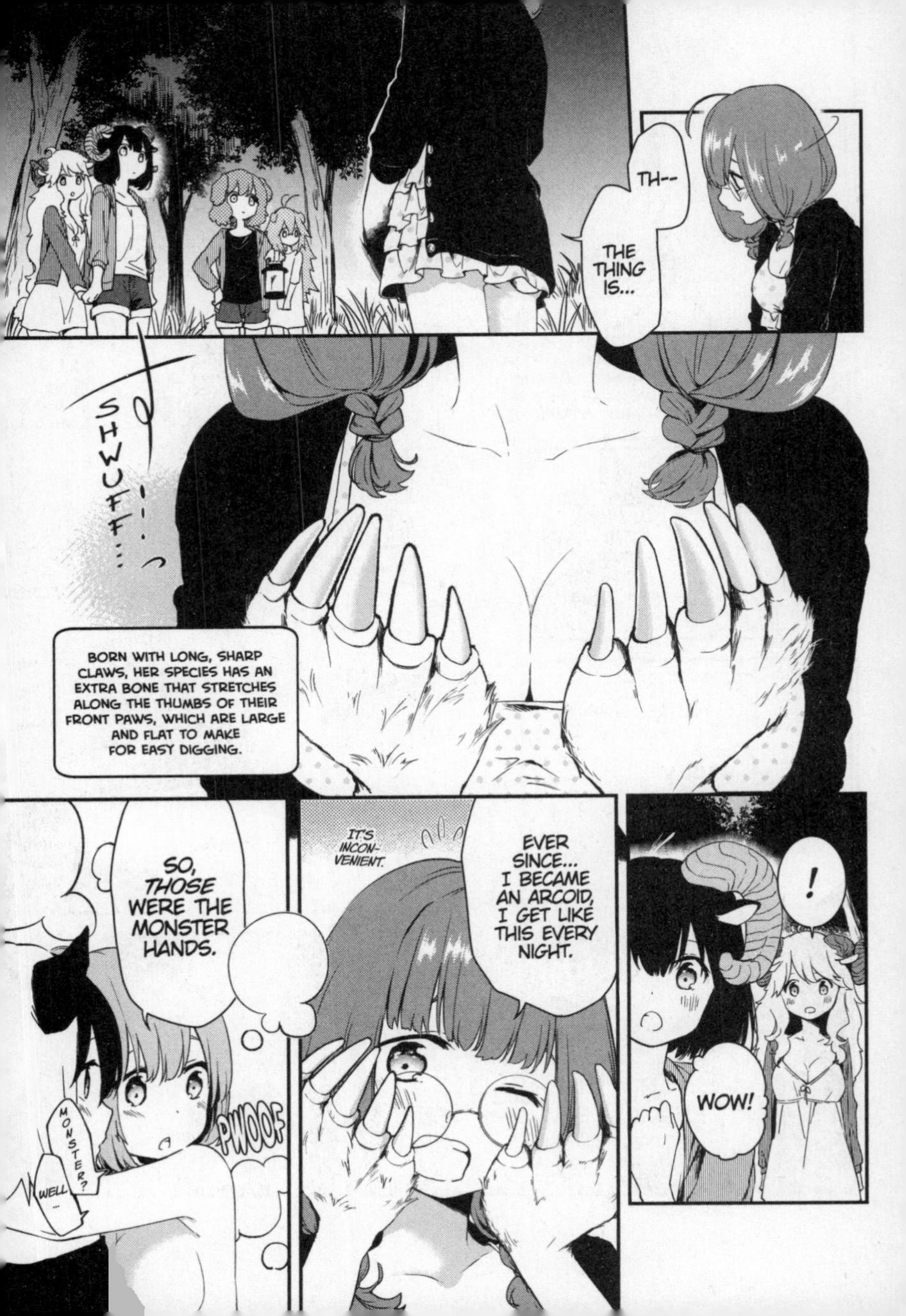
TH--
THE THING IS...
SHWUFF...
BORN WITH LONG, SHARP CLAWS, HER SPECIES HAS AN EXTRA BONE THAT STRETCHES ALONG THE THUMBS OF THEIR FRONT PAWS, WHICH ARE LARGE AND FLAT TO MAKE FOR EASY DIGGING.
!
WOW!
EVER SINCE... I BECAME AN ARCOID, I GET LIKE THIS EVERY NIGHT.
IT'S INCONVENIENT.
SO, *THOSE* WERE THE MONSTER HANDS.
PWOOF
MONSTER?
WELL...

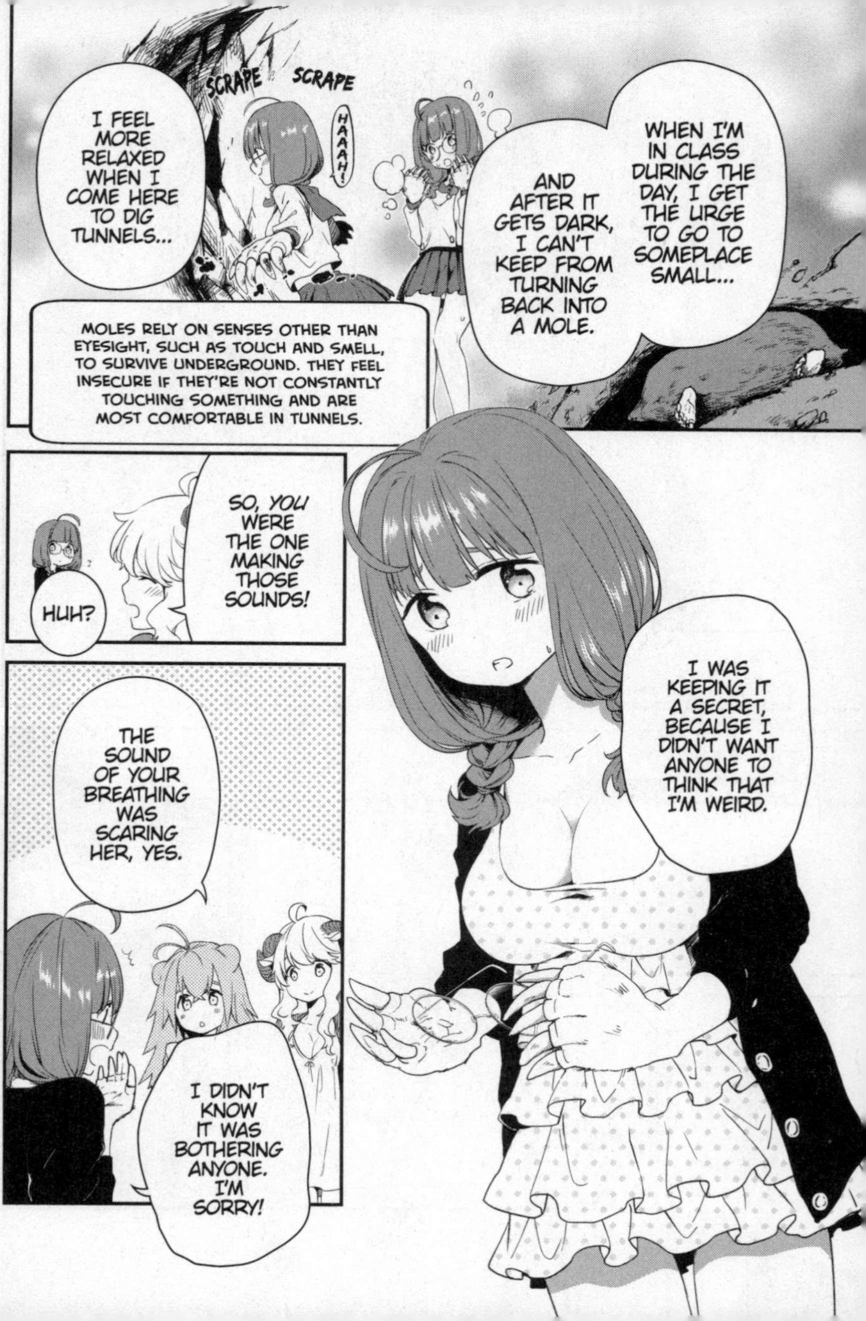
WHEN I'M IN CLASS DURING THE DAY, I GET THE URGE TO GO TO SOMEPLACE SMALL...
AND AFTER IT GETS DARK, I CAN'T KEEP FROM TURNING BACK INTO A MOLE.
SCRAPE SCRAPE
HAAAH!
I FEEL MORE RELAXED WHEN I COME HERE TO DIG TUNNELS...
MOLES RELY ON SENSES OTHER THAN EYESIGHT, SUCH AS TOUCH AND SMELL, TO SURVIVE UNDERGROUND. THEY FEEL INSECURE IF THEY'RE NOT CONSTANTLY TOUCHING SOMETHING AND ARE MOST COMFORTABLE IN TUNNELS.
I WAS KEEPING IT A SECRET, BECAUSE I DIDN'T WANT ANYONE TO THINK THAT I'M WEIRD.
SO, YOU WERE THE ONE MAKING THOSE SOUNDS!
HUH?
THE SOUND OF YOUR BREATHING WAS SCARING HER, YES.
I DIDN'T KNOW IT WAS BOTHERING ANYONE. I'M SORRY!

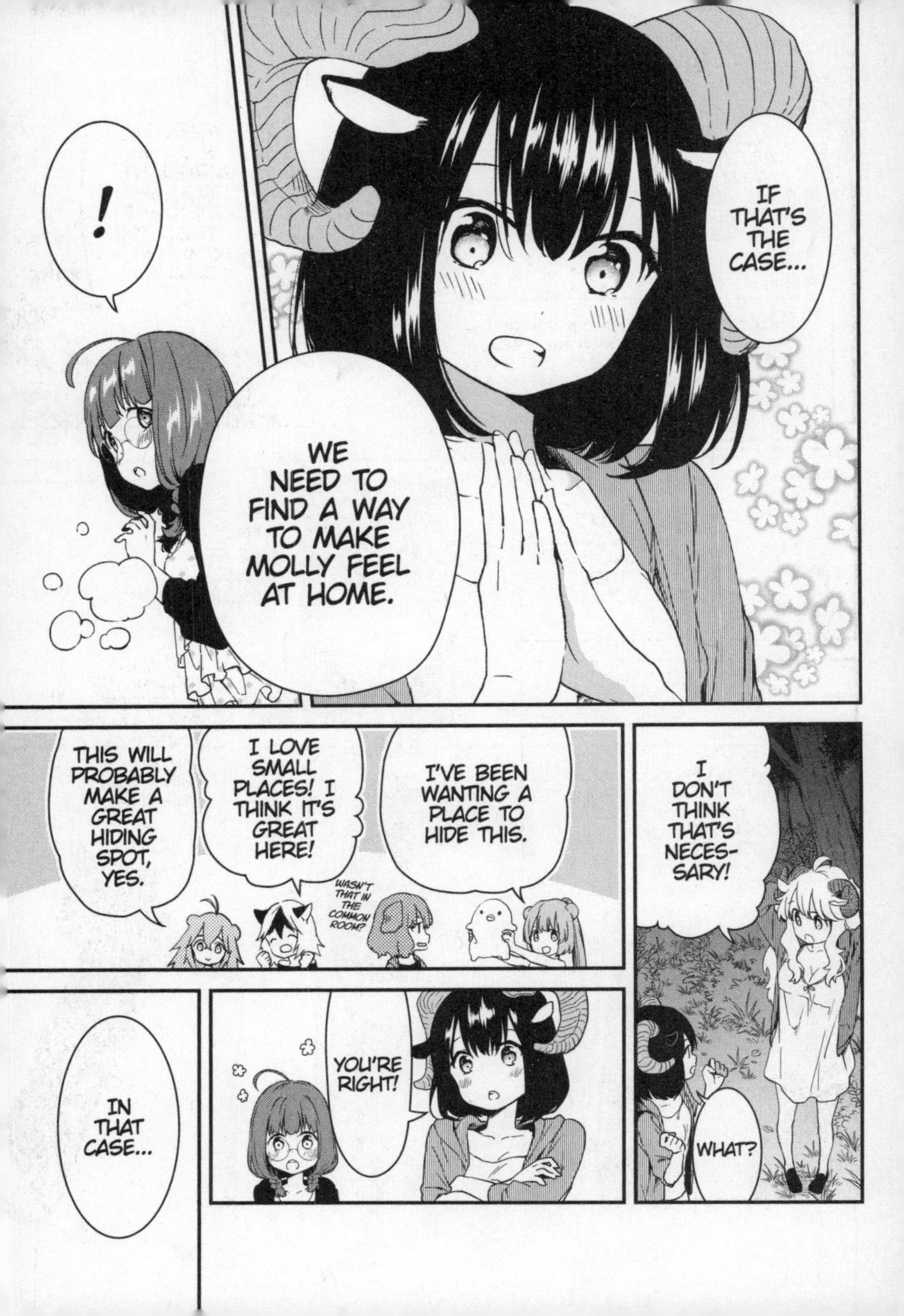
IF THAT'S THE CASE...
WE NEED TO FIND A WAY TO MAKE MOLLY FEEL AT HOME.
!
I'VE BEEN WANTING A PLACE TO HIDE THIS.
WASN'T THAT IN THE COMMON ROOM?
I LOVE SMALL PLACES! I THINK IT'S GREAT HERE!
THIS WILL PROBABLY MAKE A GREAT HIDING SPOT, YES.
I DON'T THINK THAT'S NECES-SARY!
WHAT?
YOU'RE RIGHT!
IN THAT CASE...

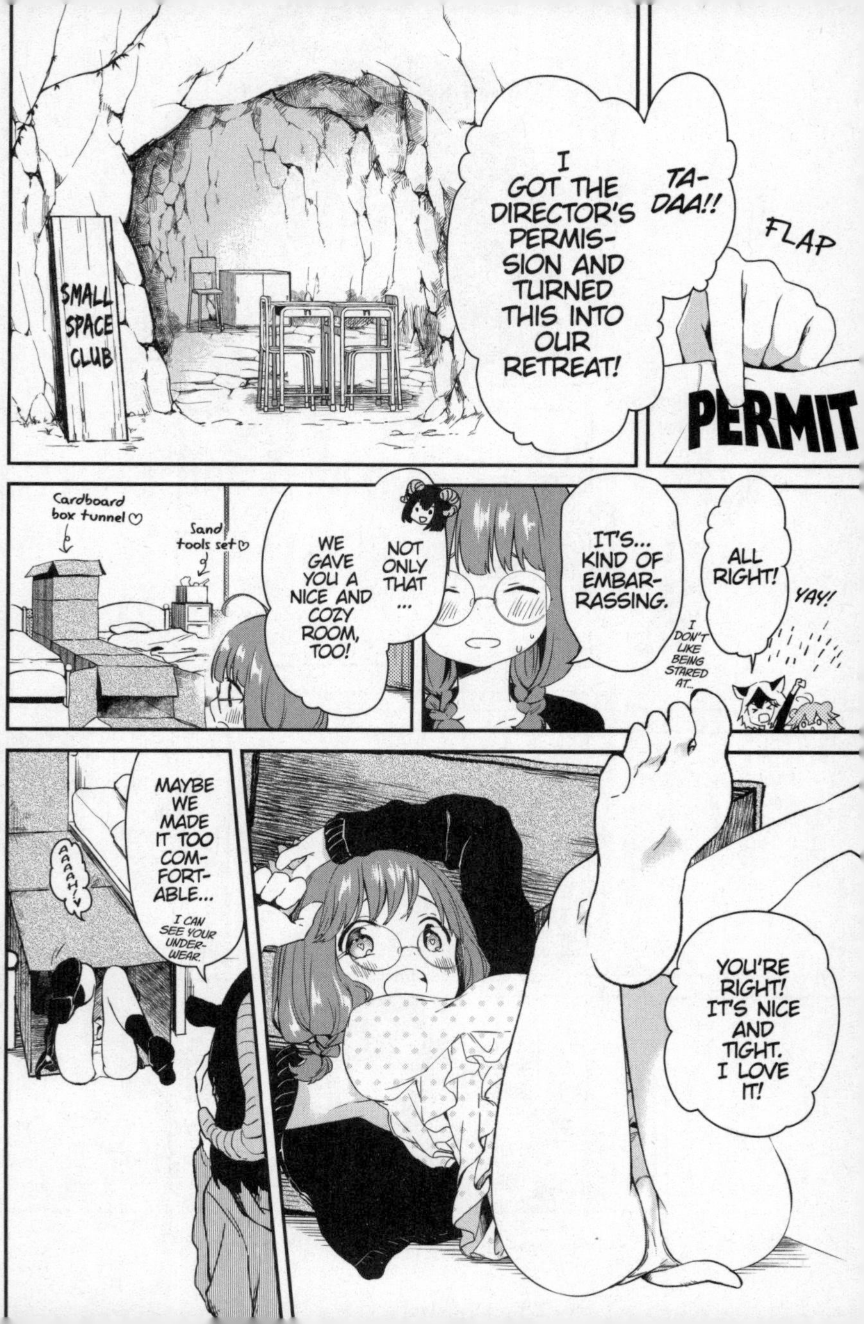
TA-DAA!!
I GOT THE DIRECTOR'S PERMISSION AND TURNED THIS INTO OUR RETREAT!
FLAP
PERMIT
SMALL SPACE CLUB
ALL RIGHT!
YAY!
I DON'T LIKE BEING STARED AT...
IT'S... KIND OF EMBARRASSING.
NOT ONLY THAT...
WE GAVE YOU A NICE AND COZY ROOM, TOO!
Sand tools set♡
Cardboard box tunnel♡
YOU'RE RIGHT! IT'S NICE AND TIGHT. I LOVE IT!
MAYBE WE MADE IT TOO COMFORTABLE...
I CAN SEE YOUR UNDERWEAR.
AAAAH!♥

Overwhelming Instinct

Okay! Let's get this weeding done!
Moku
Pwop
Moku
Pwop
Skritch
Skritch
I don't think you need to dig that deep.
Oh? Molly?
I thought I could dig a tunnel to the cave from here.
We'll get into even more trouble ...

DNA
DOESN'T
TELL US.

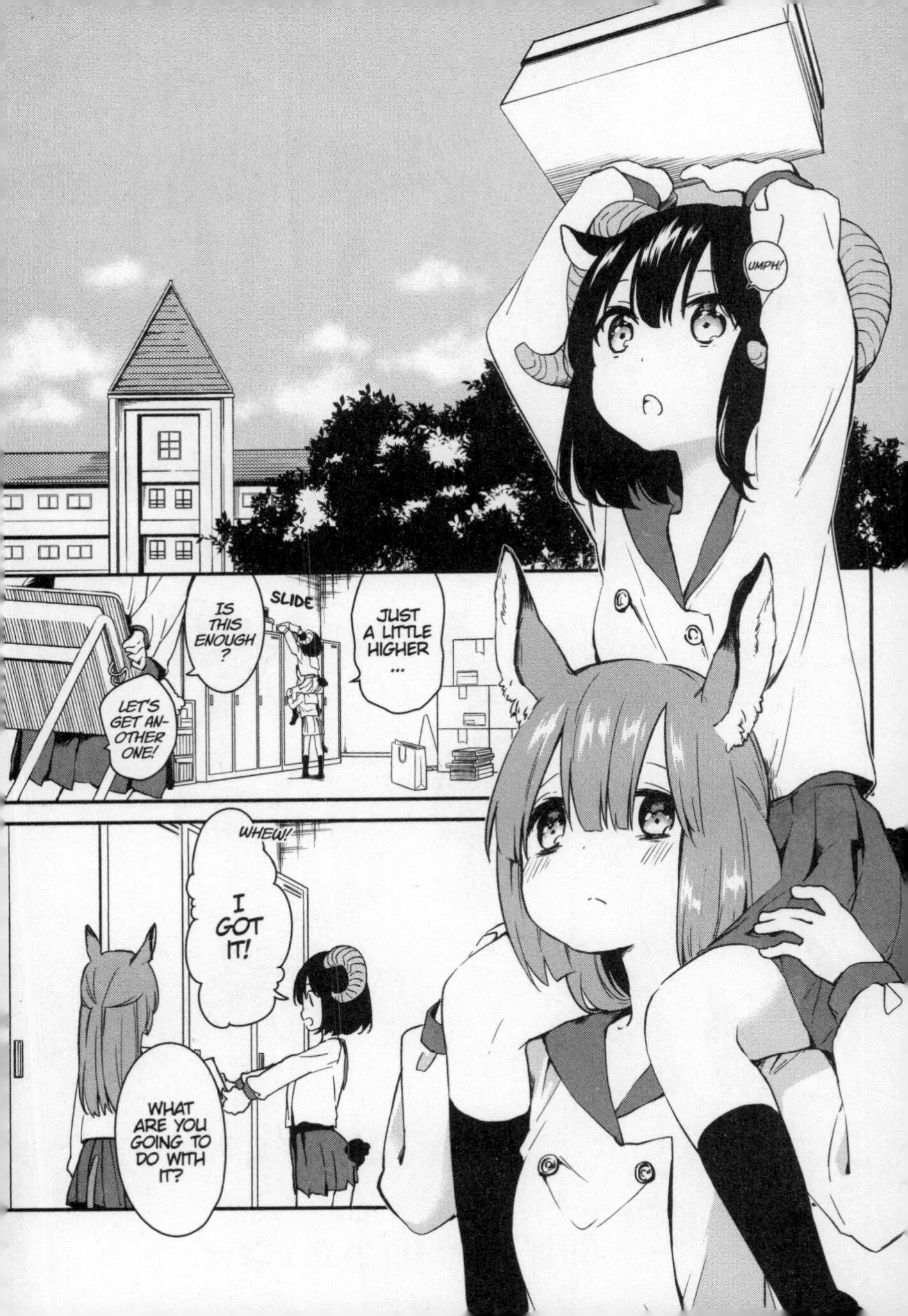
UMPH!
JUST A LITTLE HIGHER ...
SLIDE
IS THIS ENOUGH?
LET'S GET AN-OTHER ONE!
WHEW!
I GOT IT!
WHAT ARE YOU GOING TO DO WITH IT?

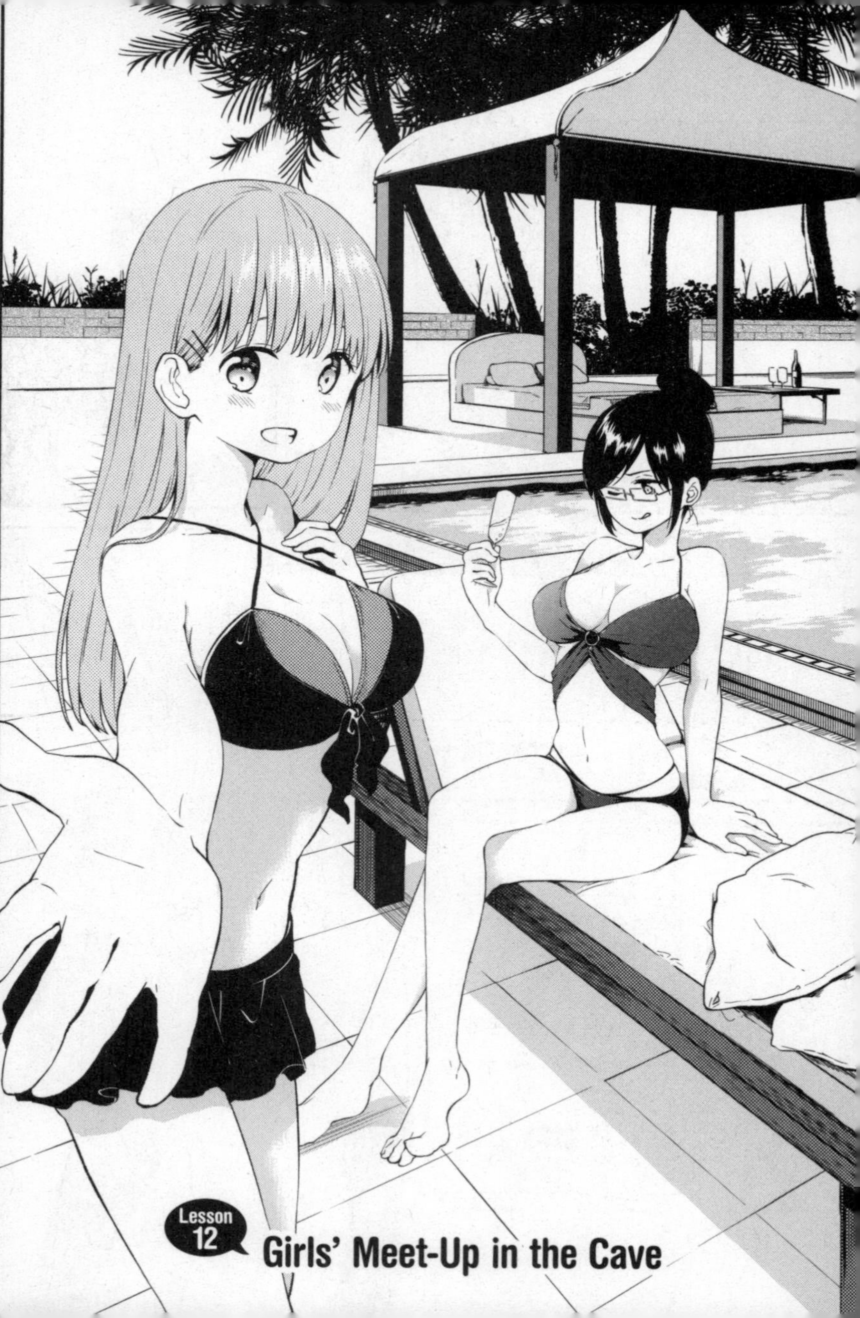
Lesson 12
Girls' Meet-Up in the Cave

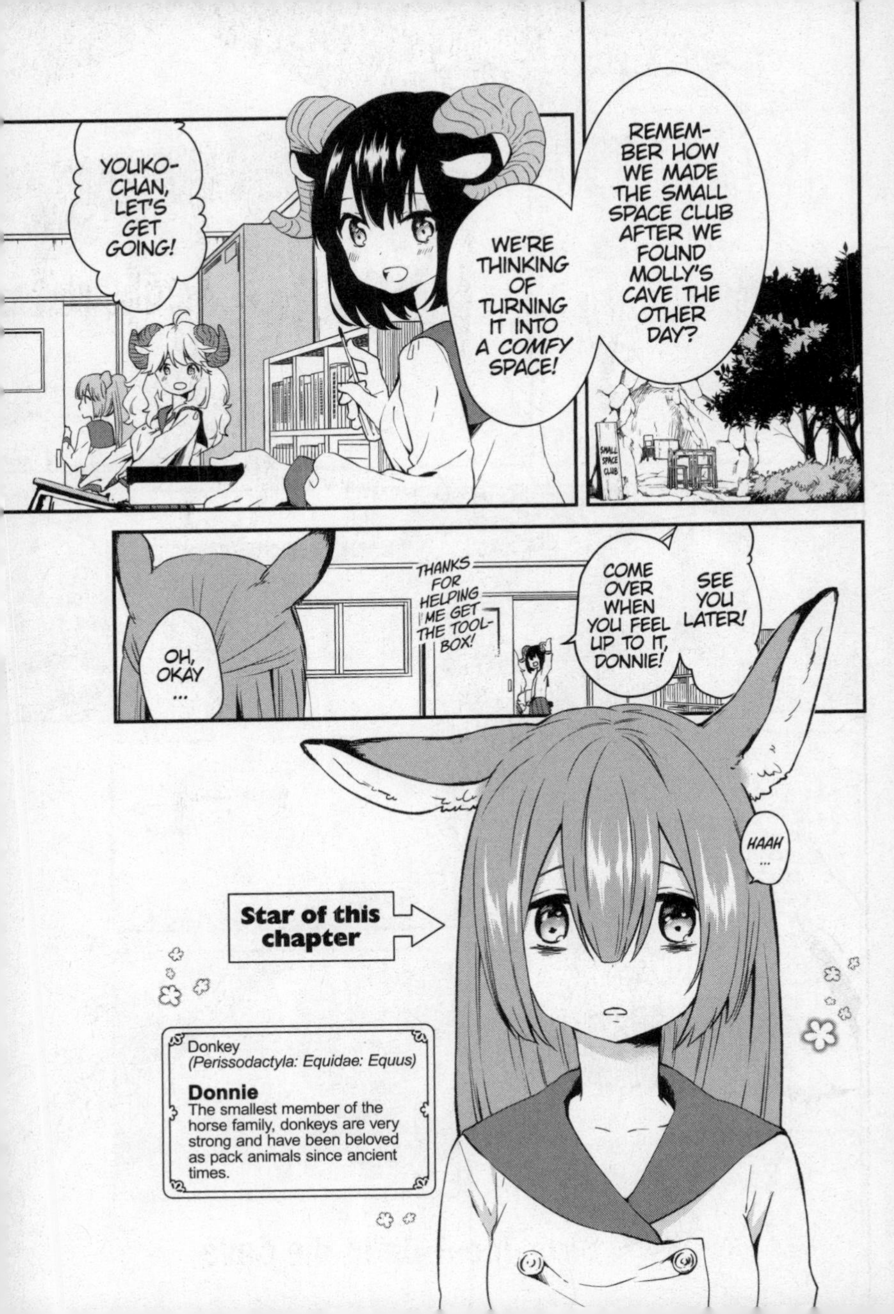
REMEMBER HOW WE MADE THE SMALL SPACE CLUB AFTER WE FOUND MOLLY'S CAVE THE OTHER DAY?
SMALL SPACE CLUB
WE'RE THINKING OF TURNING IT INTO A *COMFY* SPACE!
YOUKO-CHAN, LET'S GET GOING!
SEE YOU LATER!
COME OVER WHEN YOU FEEL UP TO IT, DONNIE!
THANKS FOR HELPING ME GET THE TOOLBOX!
OH, OKAY ...
HAAH ...
Star of this chapter
Donkey
(Perissodactyla: Equidae: Equus)
Donnie
The smallest member of the horse family, donkeys are very strong and have been beloved as pack animals since ancient times.

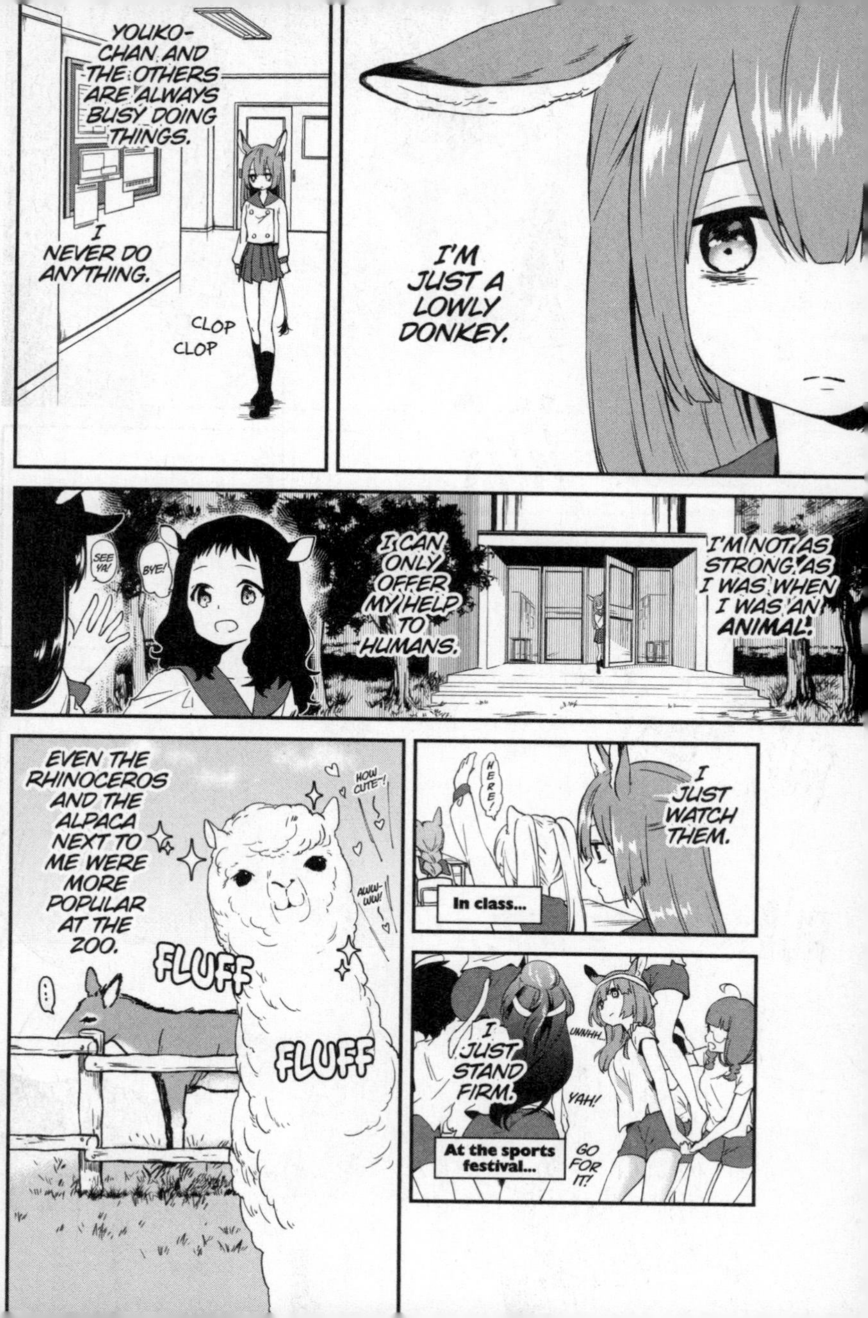
I'M JUST A LOWLY DONKEY.
YOUKO-CHAN AND THE OTHERS ARE ALWAYS BUSY DOING THINGS.
I NEVER DO ANYTHING.
CLOP
CLOP
I'M NOT AS STRONG AS I WAS WHEN I WAS AN ANIMAL.
I CAN ONLY OFFER MY HELP TO HUMANS.
BYE!
SEE YA!
HERE!
I JUST WATCH THEM.
In class...
I JUST STAND FIRM.
UNNHH...
YAH!
GO FOR IT!
At the sports festival...
EVEN THE RHINOCEROS AND THE ALPACA NEXT TO ME WERE MORE POPULAR AT THE ZOO.
HOW CUTE!
AWW-WW!
FLUFF
FLUFF
...

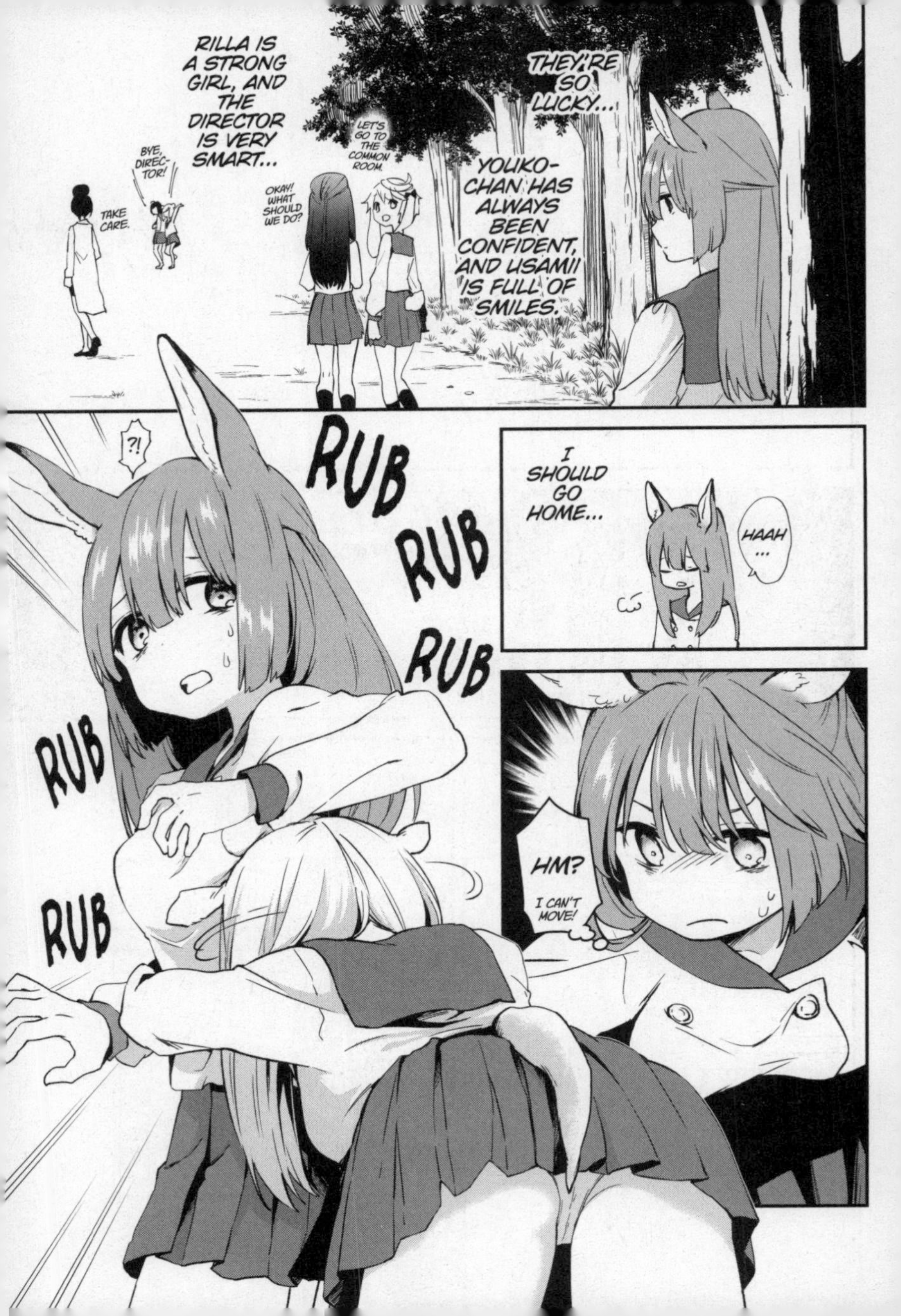
THEY'RE SO LUCKY...
YOUKO-CHAN HAS ALWAYS BEEN CONFIDENT, AND USAMII IS FULL OF SMILES.
LET'S GO TO THE COMMON ROOM.
OKAY! WHAT SHOULD WE DO?
RILLA IS A STRONG GIRL, AND THE DIRECTOR IS VERY SMART...
BYE, DIRECTOR!
TAKE CARE.
I SHOULD GO HOME...
HAAH...
HM?
I CAN'T MOVE!
?!
RUB
RUB
RUB
RUB
RUB

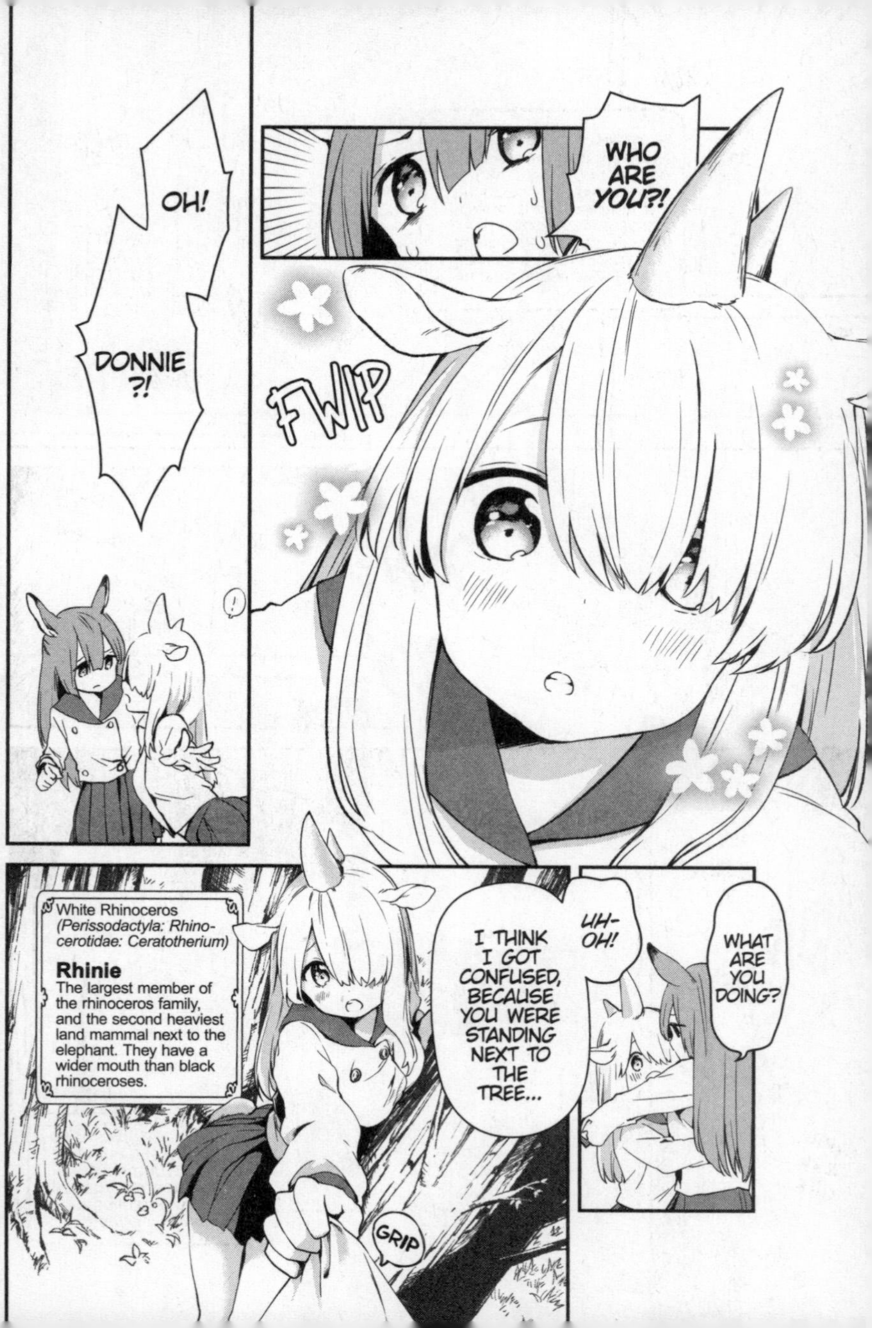
WHO ARE YOU?!
FWIP
!
OH!
DONNIE ?!
WHAT ARE YOU DOING?
UH-OH!
I THINK I GOT CONFUSED, BECAUSE YOU WERE STANDING NEXT TO THE TREE...
GRIP
White Rhinoceros
(Perissodactyla: Rhinocerotidae: Ceratotherium)
Rhinie
The largest member of the rhinoceros family, and the second heaviest land mammal next to the elephant. They have a wider mouth than black rhinoceroses.

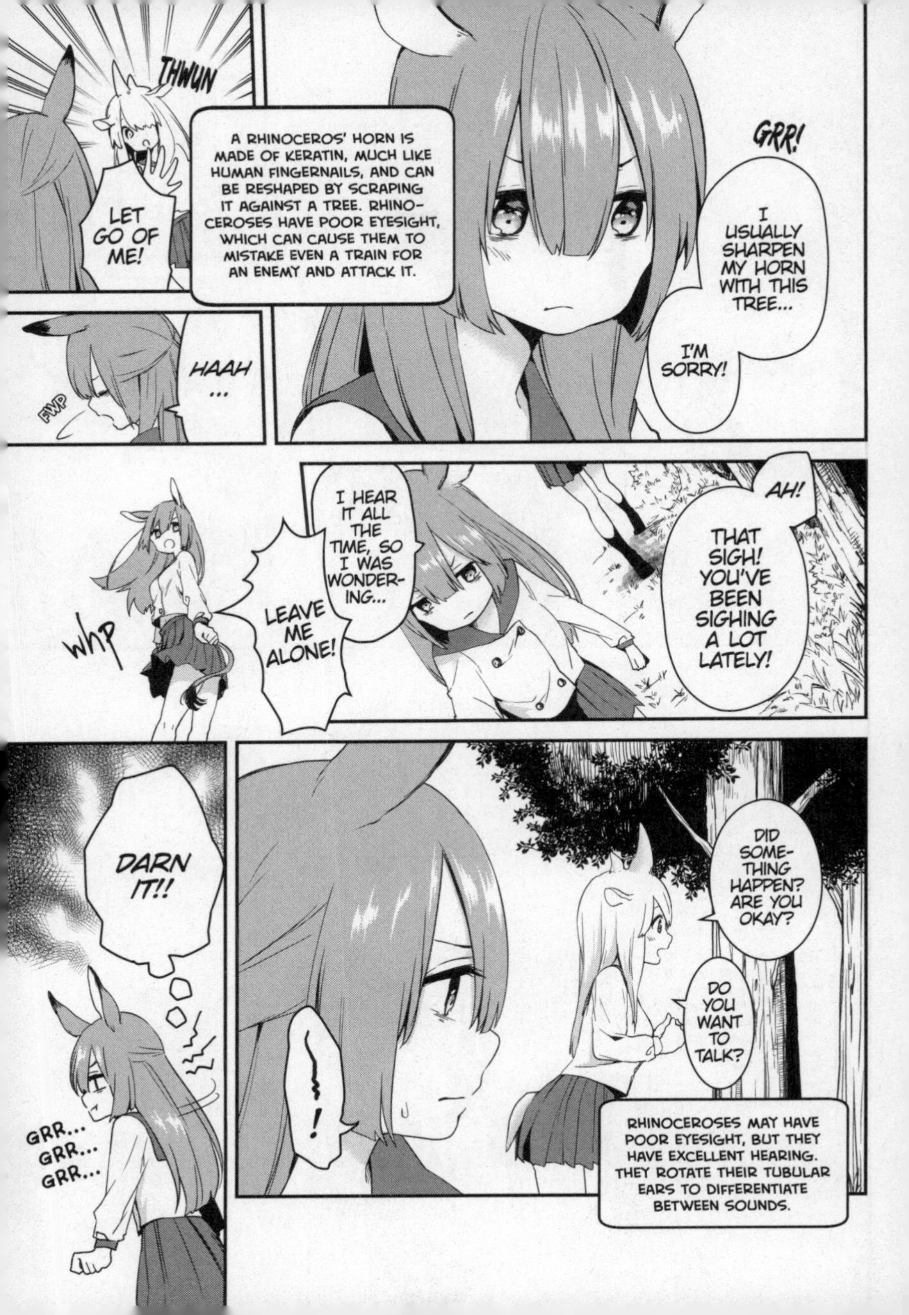

GRR!
I USUALLY SHARPEN MY HORN WITH THIS TREE...
I'M SORRY!
THWUN
LET GO OF ME!
A RHINOCEROS' HORN IS MADE OF KERATIN, MUCH LIKE HUMAN FINGERNAILS, AND CAN BE RESHAPED BY SCRAPING IT AGAINST A TREE. RHINOCEROSES HAVE POOR EYESIGHT, WHICH CAN CAUSE THEM TO MISTAKE EVEN A TRAIN FOR AN ENEMY AND ATTACK IT.
HAAH ...
FWP
AH!
THAT SIGH! YOU'VE BEEN SIGHING A LOT LATELY!
I HEAR IT ALL THE TIME, SO I WAS WONDERING...
LEAVE ME ALONE!
whp
DID SOMETHING HAPPEN? ARE YOU OKAY?
DO YOU WANT TO TALK?
RHINOCEROSES MAY HAVE POOR EYESIGHT, BUT THEY HAVE EXCELLENT HEARING. THEY ROTATE THEIR TUBULAR EARS TO DIFFERENTIATE BETWEEN SOUNDS.
DARN IT!!
GRR... GRR... GRR...

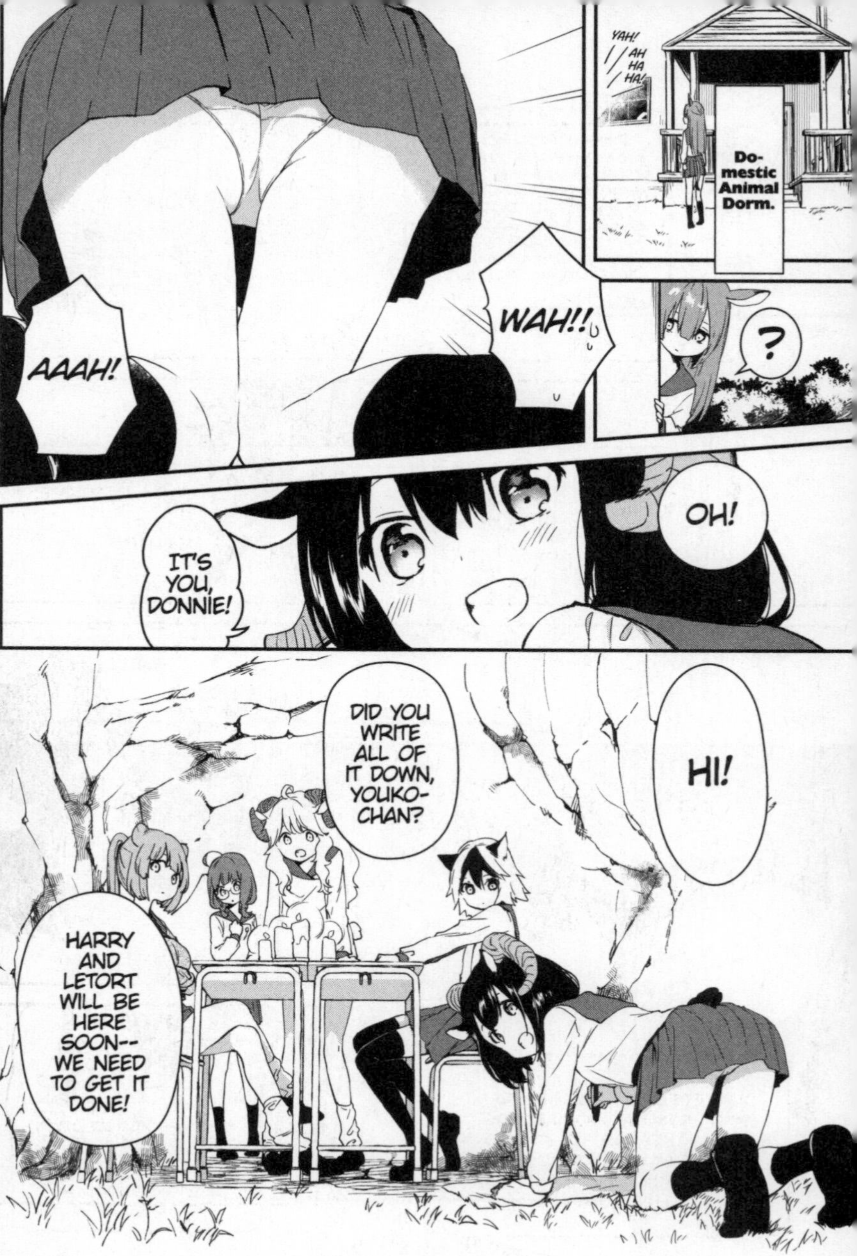
YAH!
AH HA HA!
Do-mestic Animal Dorm.
?
WAH!!
AAAH!
OH!
IT'S YOU, DONNIE!
HI!
DID YOU WRITE ALL OF IT DOWN, YOUKO-CHAN?
HARRY AND LETORT WILL BE HERE SOON--WE NEED TO GET IT DONE!

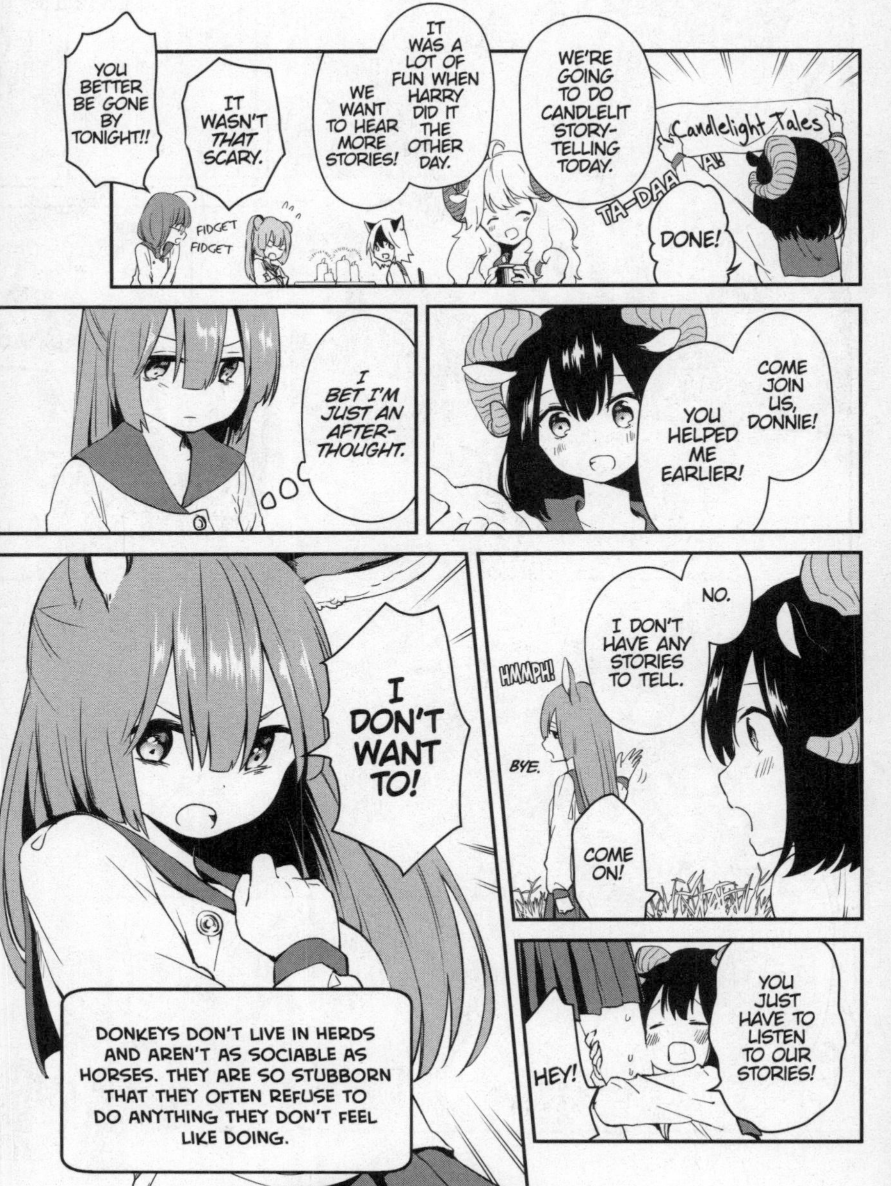

DONE!
TA-DAAAA!
Candlelight Tales
WE'RE GOING TO DO CANDLELIT STORY-TELLING TODAY.
IT WAS A LOT OF FUN WHEN HARRY DID IT THE OTHER DAY.
WE WANT TO HEAR MORE STORIES!
FIDGET FIDGET
IT WASN'T THAT SCARY.
YOU BETTER BE GONE BY TONIGHT!!
COME JOIN US, DONNIE!
YOU HELPED ME EARLIER!
I BET I'M JUST AN AFTER-THOUGHT.
NO.
I DON'T HAVE ANY STORIES TO TELL.
HMMPH!
BYE.
COME ON!
YOU JUST HAVE TO LISTEN TO OUR STORIES!
HEY!
I DON'T WANT TO!
DONKEYS DON'T LIVE IN HERDS AND AREN'T AS SOCIABLE AS HORSES. THEY ARE SO STUBBORN THAT THEY OFTEN REFUSE TO DO ANYTHING THEY DON'T FEEL LIKE DOING.

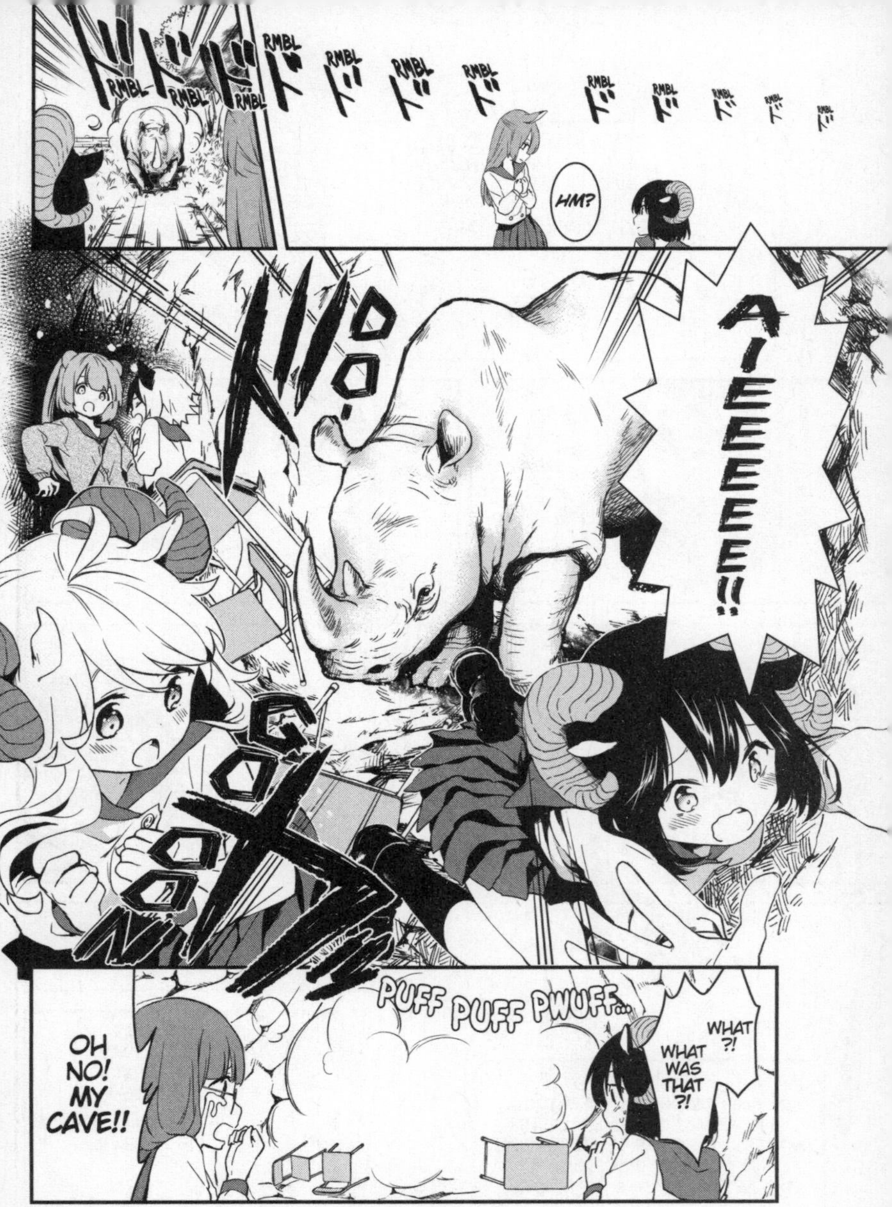

RMBL RMBL RMBL RMBL RMBL RMBL RMBL RMBL RMBL RMBL RMBL
ドドドドドドドドドド
HM?
AIEEEEEE!!
DOO
GOOOON
WHAT?!
WHAT WAS THAT?!
PUFF PUFF PWUFF...
OH NO! MY CAVE!!

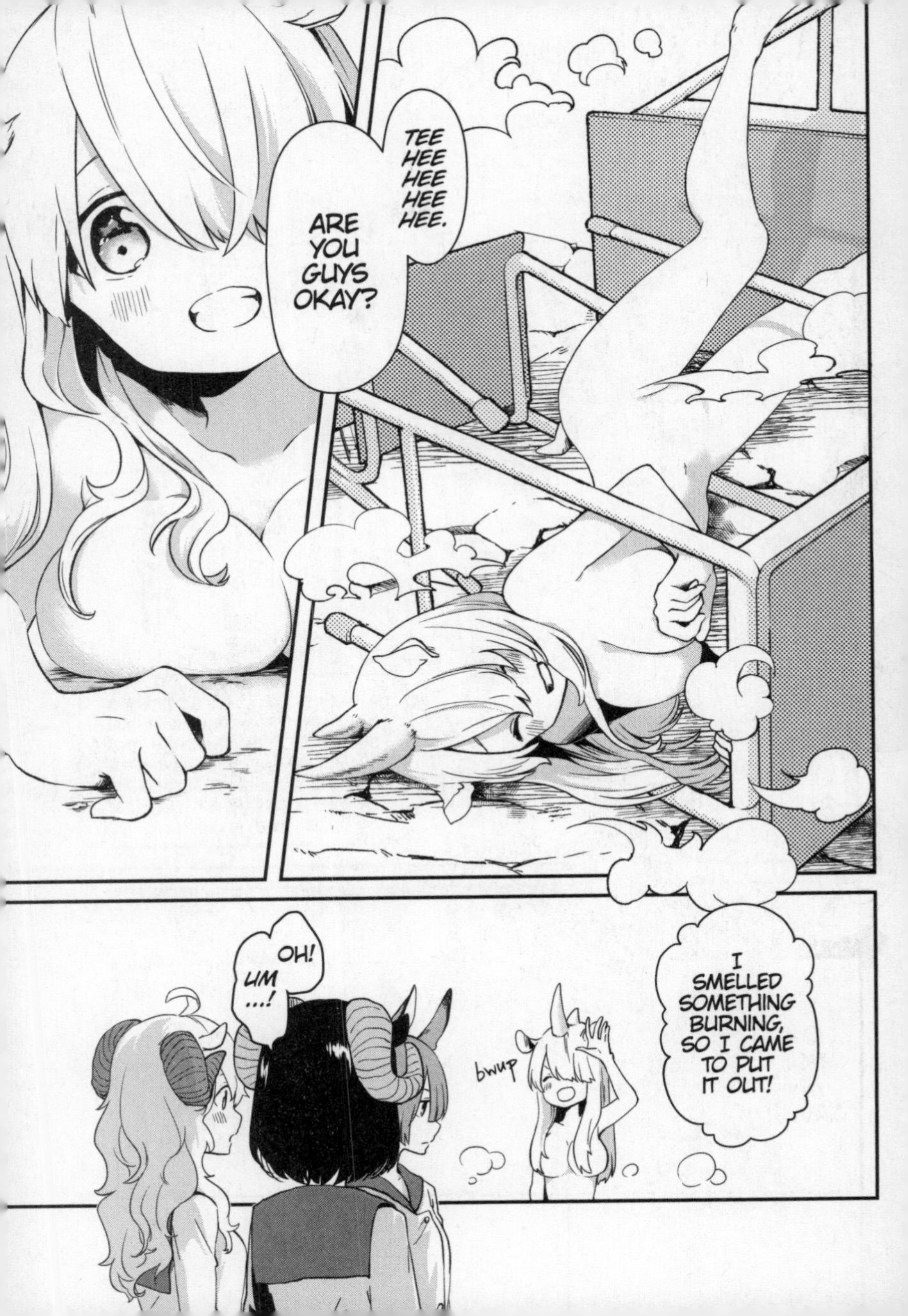
TEE HEE HEE HEE HEE.
ARE YOU GUYS OKAY?
I SMELLED SOMETHING BURNING, SO I CAME TO PUT IT OUT!
bwup
OH! UM ...!

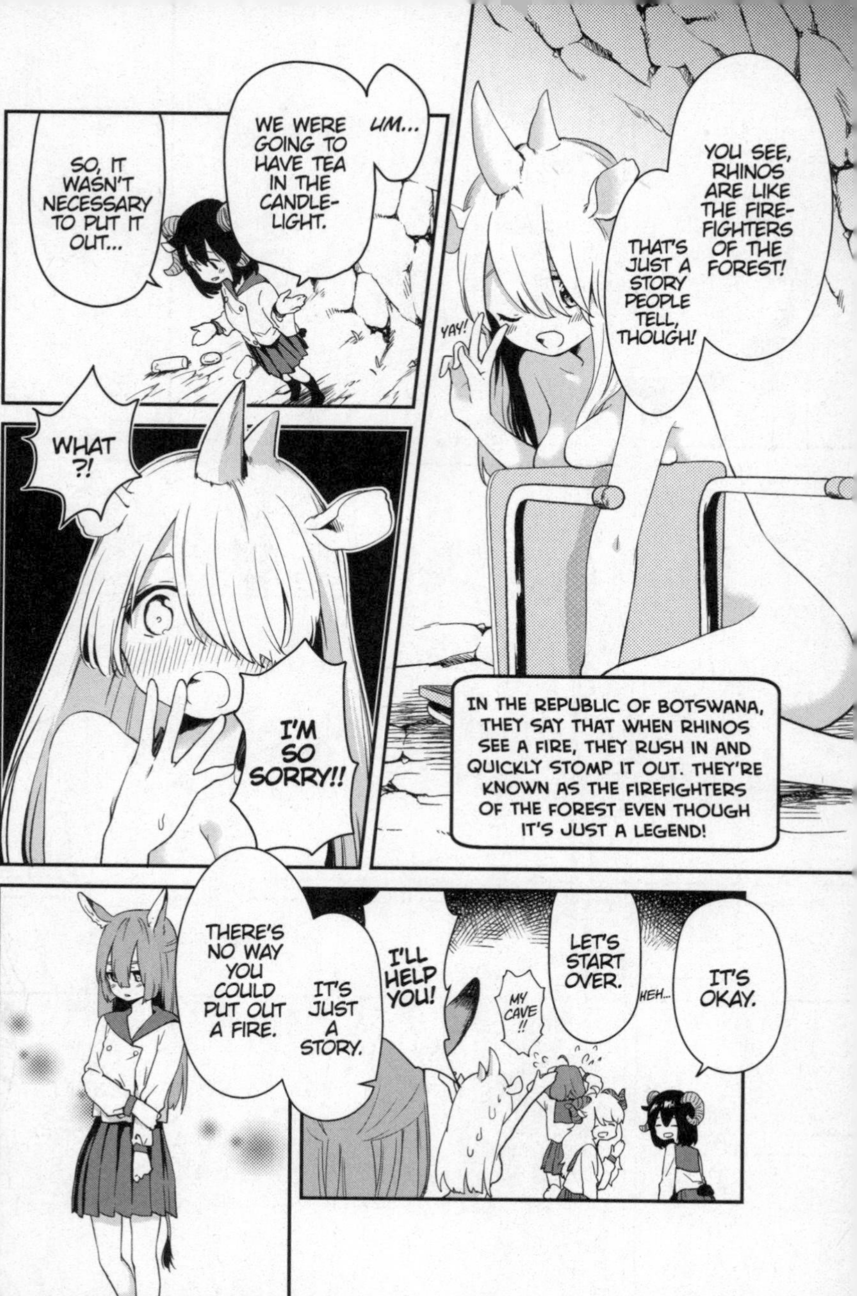
YOU SEE, RHINOS ARE LIKE THE FIRE-FIGHTERS OF THE FOREST!
THAT'S JUST A STORY PEOPLE TELL, THOUGH!
YAY!
IN THE REPUBLIC OF BOTSWANA, THEY SAY THAT WHEN RHINOS SEE A FIRE, THEY RUSH IN AND QUICKLY STOMP IT OUT. THEY'RE KNOWN AS THE FIREFIGHTERS OF THE FOREST EVEN THOUGH IT'S JUST A LEGEND!
UM...
WE WERE GOING TO HAVE TEA IN THE CANDLE-LIGHT.
SO, IT WASN'T NECESSARY TO PUT IT OUT...
WHAT?!
I'M SO SORRY!!
IT'S OKAY.
HEH...
LET'S START OVER.
MY CAVE!!
I'LL HELP YOU!
IT'S JUST A STORY.
THERE'S NO WAY YOU COULD PUT OUT A FIRE.

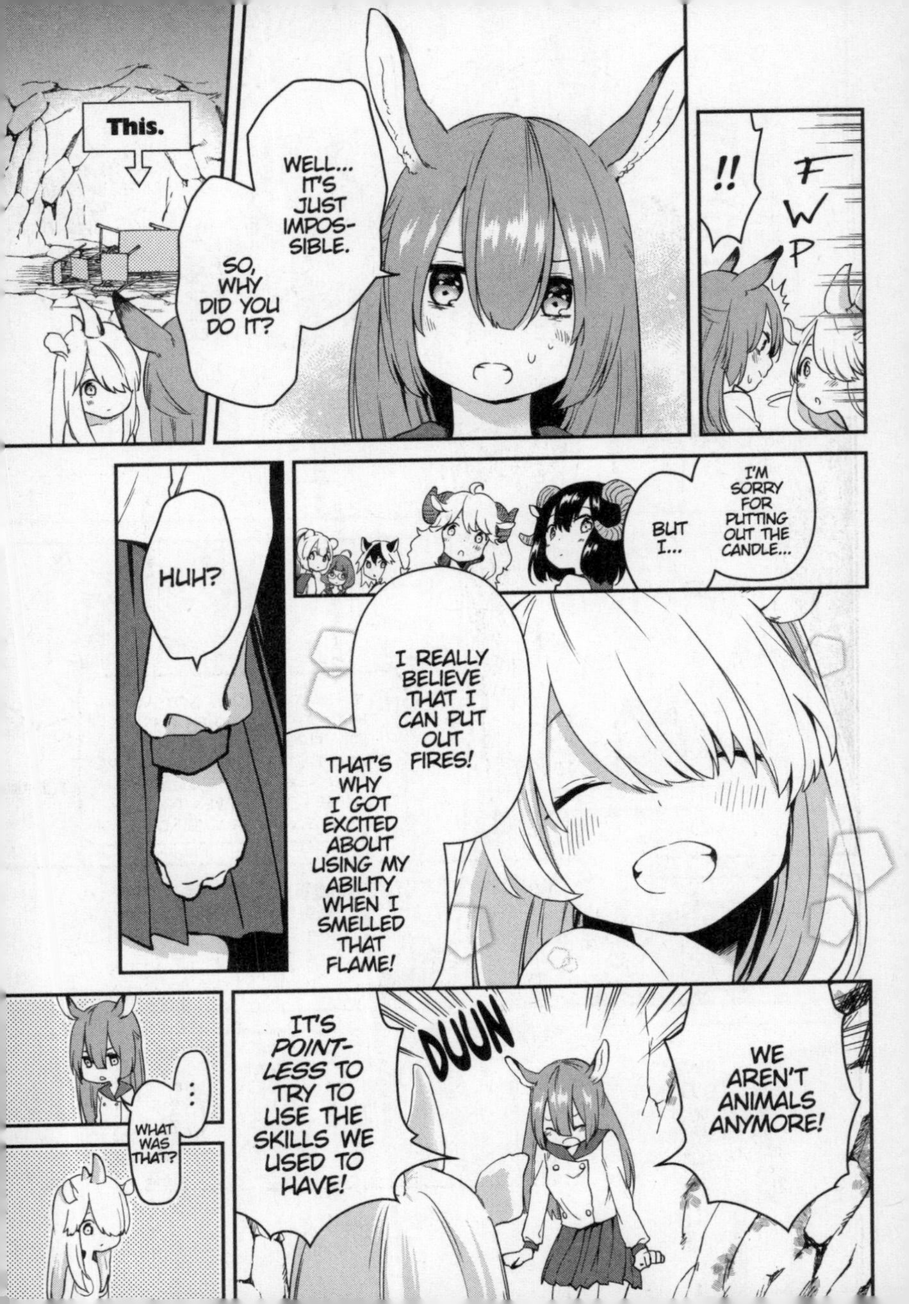

This.
WELL... IT'S JUST IMPOSSIBLE.
SO, WHY DID YOU DO IT?
!!
FWP
HUH?
I'M SORRY FOR PUTTING OUT THE CANDLE...
BUT I...
I REALLY BELIEVE THAT I CAN PUT OUT FIRES!
THAT'S WHY I GOT EXCITED ABOUT USING MY ABILITY WHEN I SMELLED THAT FLAME!
IT'S POINTLESS TO TRY TO USE THE SKILLS WE USED TO HAVE!
DUUN
WE AREN'T ANIMALS ANYMORE!
...
WHAT WAS THAT?

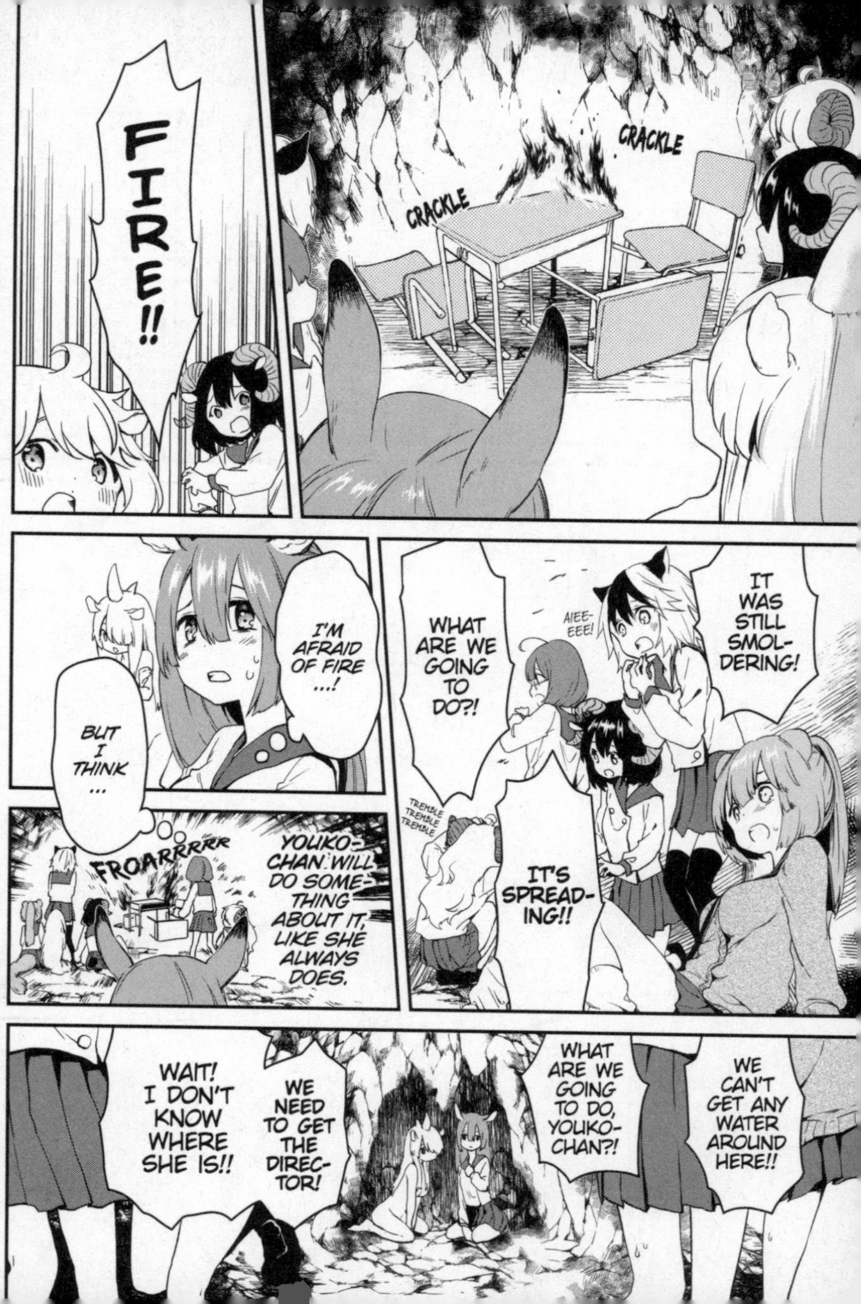
CRACKLE
CRACKLE
FIRE!!
IT WAS STILL SMOLDERING!
AIEE-EEE!
WHAT ARE WE GOING TO DO?!
TREMBLE TREMBLE TREMBLE
IT'S SPREADING!!
I'M AFRAID OF FIRE ...!
BUT I THINK ...
FROARRRRR
YOUKO-CHAN WILL DO SOMETHING ABOUT IT, LIKE SHE ALWAYS DOES.
WE CAN'T GET ANY WATER AROUND HERE!!
WHAT ARE WE GOING TO DO, YOUKO-CHAN?!
WE NEED TO GET THE DIRECTOR!
WAIT! I DON'T KNOW WHERE SHE IS!!

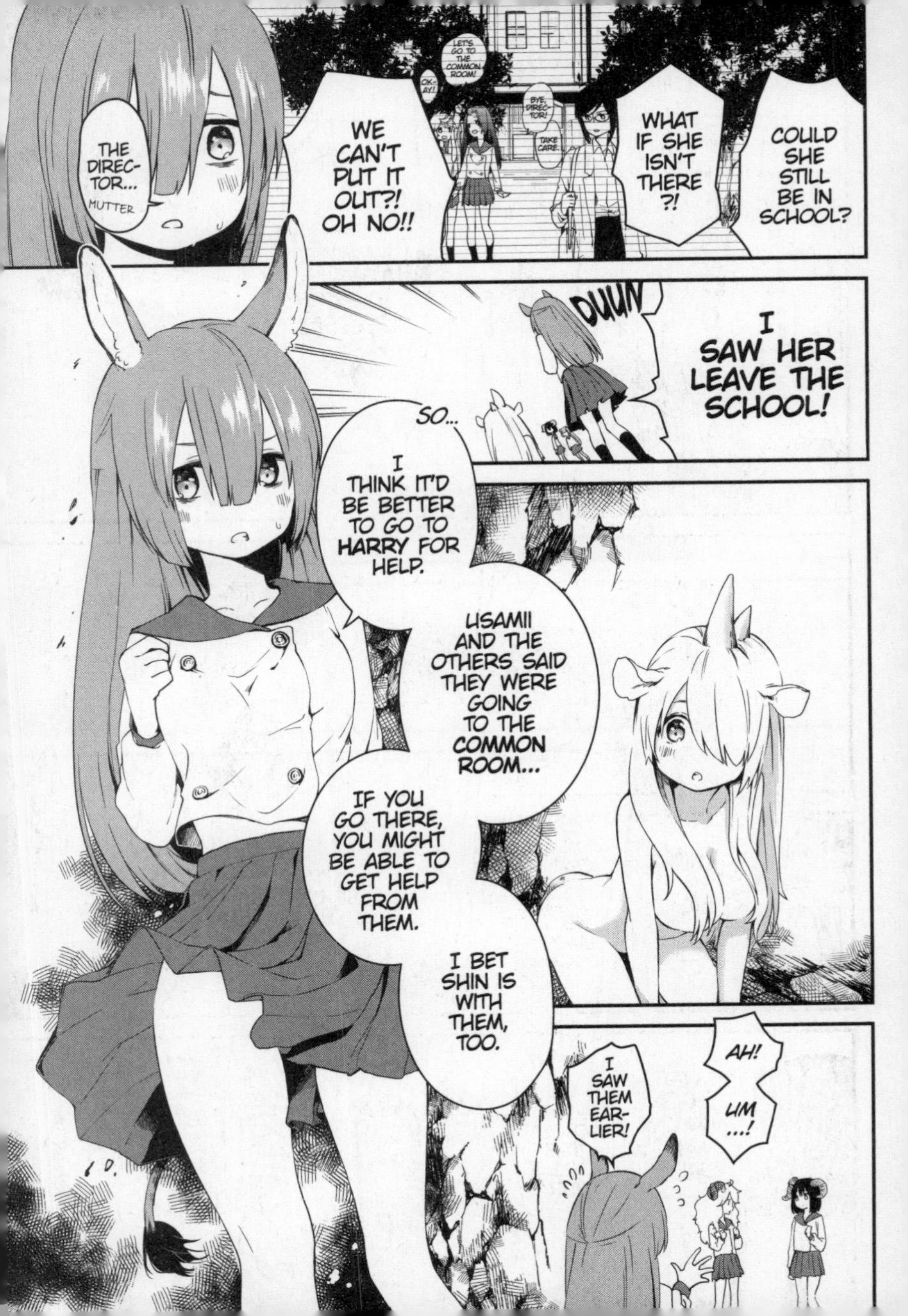
COULD SHE STILL BE IN SCHOOL?
WHAT IF SHE ISN'T THERE?!
LET'S GO TO THE COMMON ROOM!
OK-AY!
BYE, DIRECTOR!
TAKE CARE.
WE CAN'T PUT IT OUT?! OH NO!!
THE DIRECTOR... MUTTER
I SAW HER LEAVE THE SCHOOL!
DUUN
SO...
I THINK IT'D BE BETTER TO GO TO HARRY FOR HELP.
USAMII AND THE OTHERS SAID THEY WERE GOING TO THE COMMON ROOM...
IF YOU GO THERE, YOU MIGHT BE ABLE TO GET HELP FROM THEM.
I BET SHIN IS WITH THEM, TOO.
AH!
UM...!
I SAW THEM EAR-LIER!

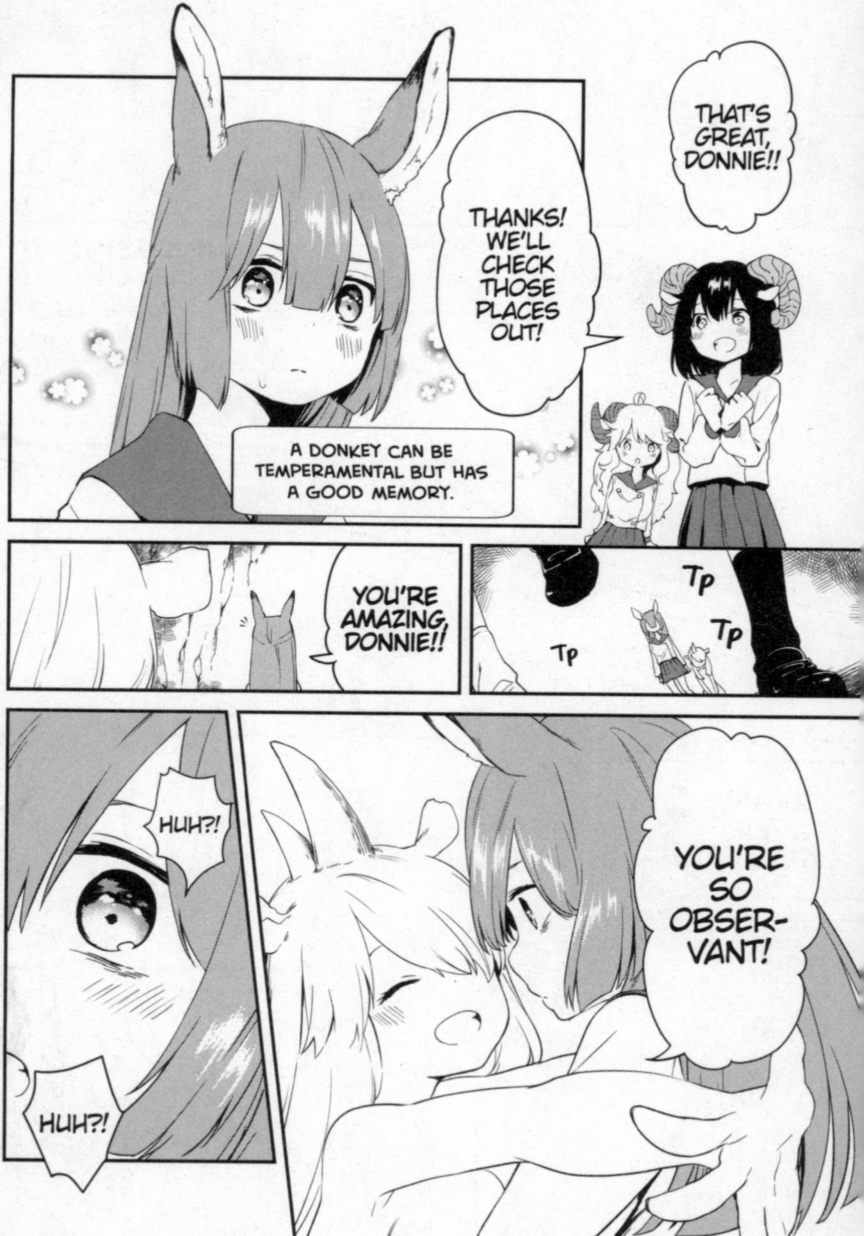
THAT'S GREAT, DONNIE!!
THANKS! WE'LL CHECK THOSE PLACES OUT!
A DONKEY CAN BE TEMPERAMENTAL BUT HAS A GOOD MEMORY.
Tp
Tp
Tp
YOU'RE AMAZING, DONNIE!!
YOU'RE SO OBSER-VANT!
HUH?!
HUH?!

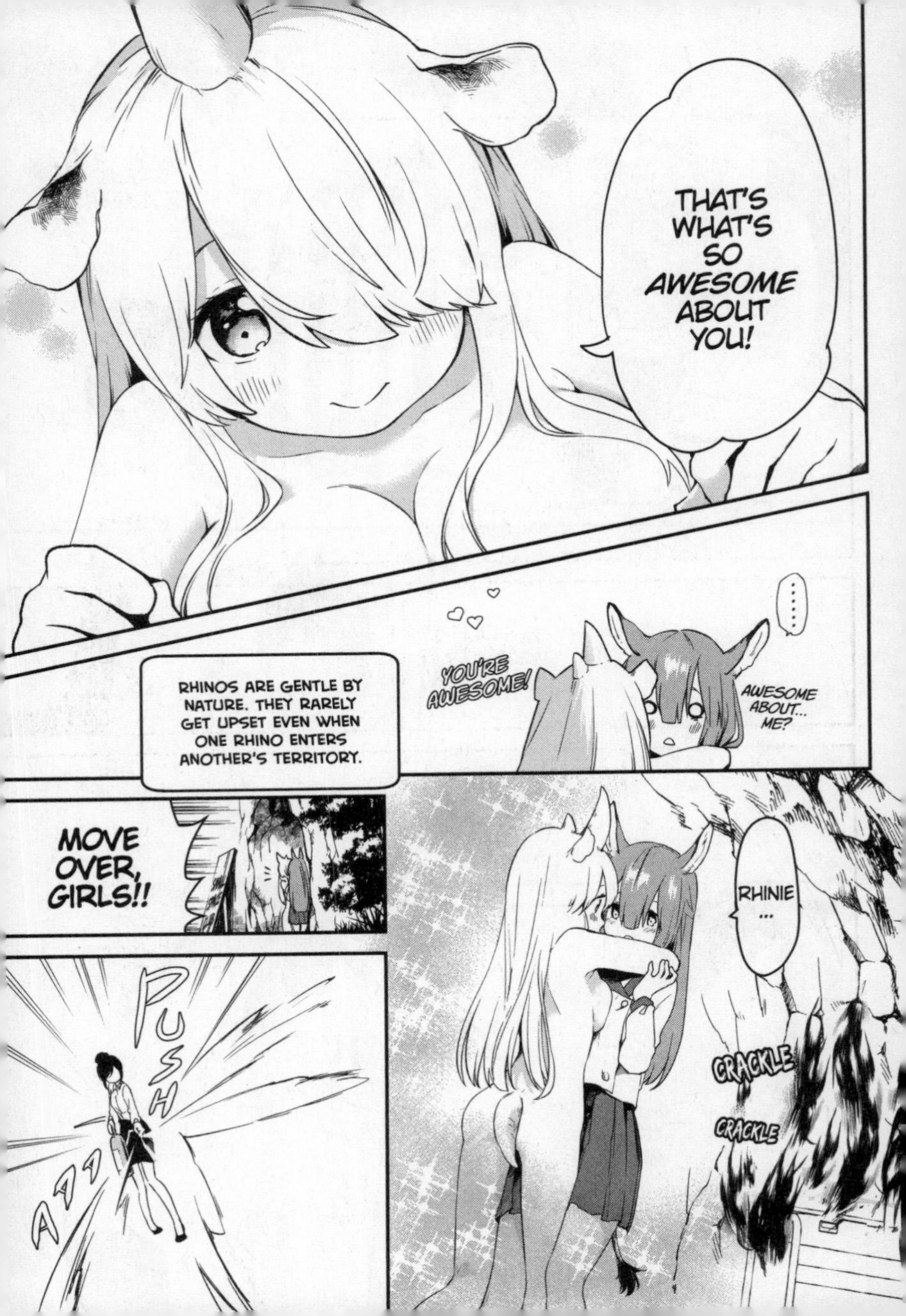
THAT'S WHAT'S SO AWESOME ABOUT YOU!
......
YOU'RE AWESOME!
AWESOME ABOUT... ME?
RHINOS ARE GENTLE BY NATURE. THEY RARELY GET UPSET EVEN WHEN ONE RHINO ENTERS ANOTHER'S TERRITORY.
RHINIE ...
MOVE OVER, GIRLS!!
CRACKLE
CRACKLE
PUSH
AAAA

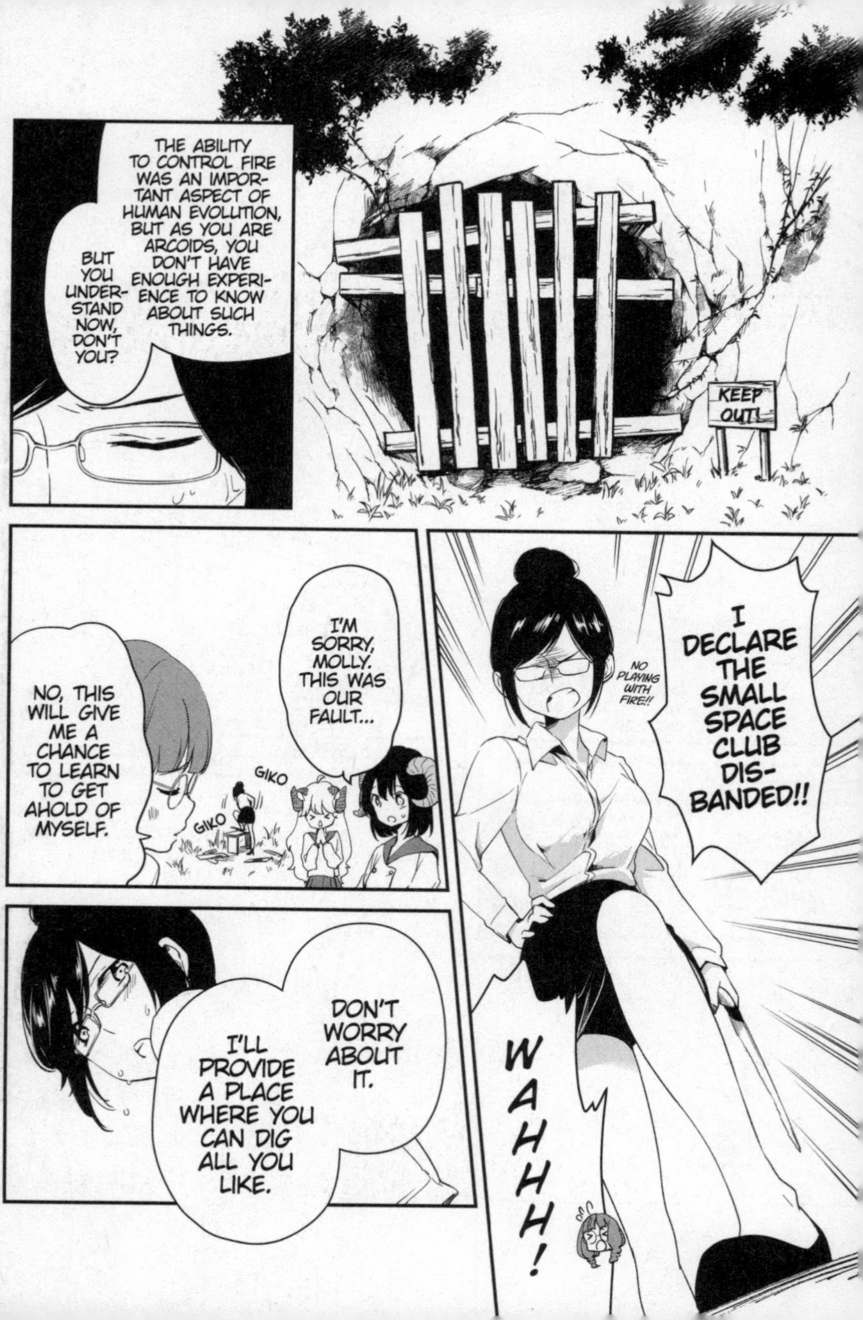
KEEP OUT!
THE ABILITY TO CONTROL FIRE WAS AN IMPORTANT ASPECT OF HUMAN EVOLUTION, BUT AS YOU ARE ARCOIDS, YOU DON'T HAVE ENOUGH EXPERIENCE TO KNOW ABOUT SUCH THINGS.
BUT YOU UNDERSTAND NOW, DON'T YOU?
I DECLARE THE SMALL SPACE CLUB DISBANDED!!
NO PLAYING WITH FIRE!!
WAHHH!
I'M SORRY, MOLLY. THIS WAS OUR FAULT...
GIKO
GIKO
NO, THIS WILL GIVE ME A CHANCE TO LEARN TO GET AHOLD OF MYSELF.
DON'T WORRY ABOUT IT.
I'LL PROVIDE A PLACE WHERE YOU CAN DIG ALL YOU LIKE.

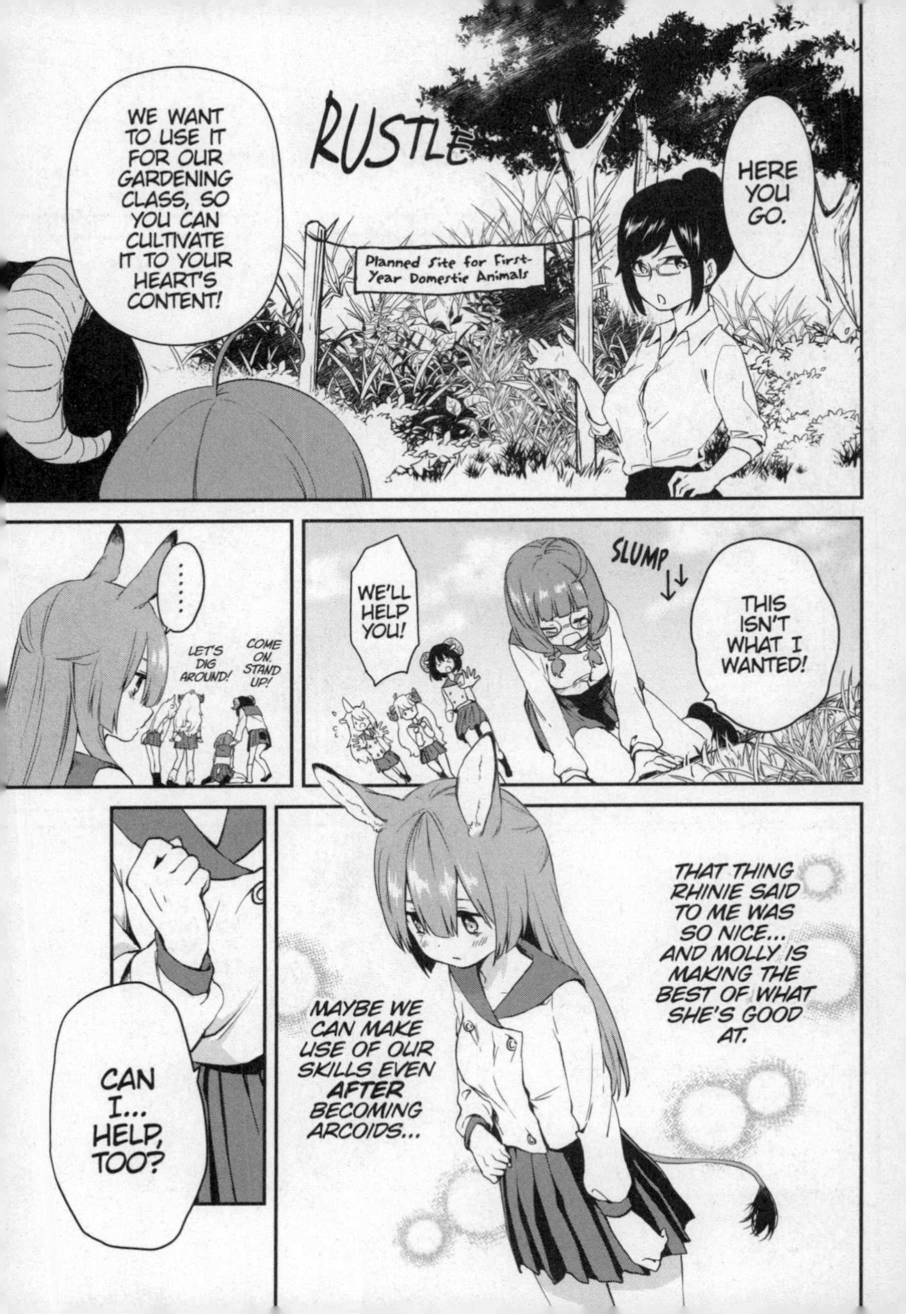
RUSTLE
HERE YOU GO.
WE WANT TO USE IT FOR OUR GARDENING CLASS, SO YOU CAN CULTIVATE IT TO YOUR HEART'S CONTENT!
Planned Site for First-Year Domestic Animals
SLUMP
THIS ISN'T WHAT I WANTED!
WE'LL HELP YOU!
......
COME ON. STAND UP!
LET'S DIG AROUND!
THAT THING RHINIE SAID TO ME WAS SO NICE... AND MOLLY IS MAKING THE BEST OF WHAT SHE'S GOOD AT.
MAYBE WE CAN MAKE USE OF OUR SKILLS EVEN AFTER BECOMING ARCOIDS...
CAN I... HELP, TOO?

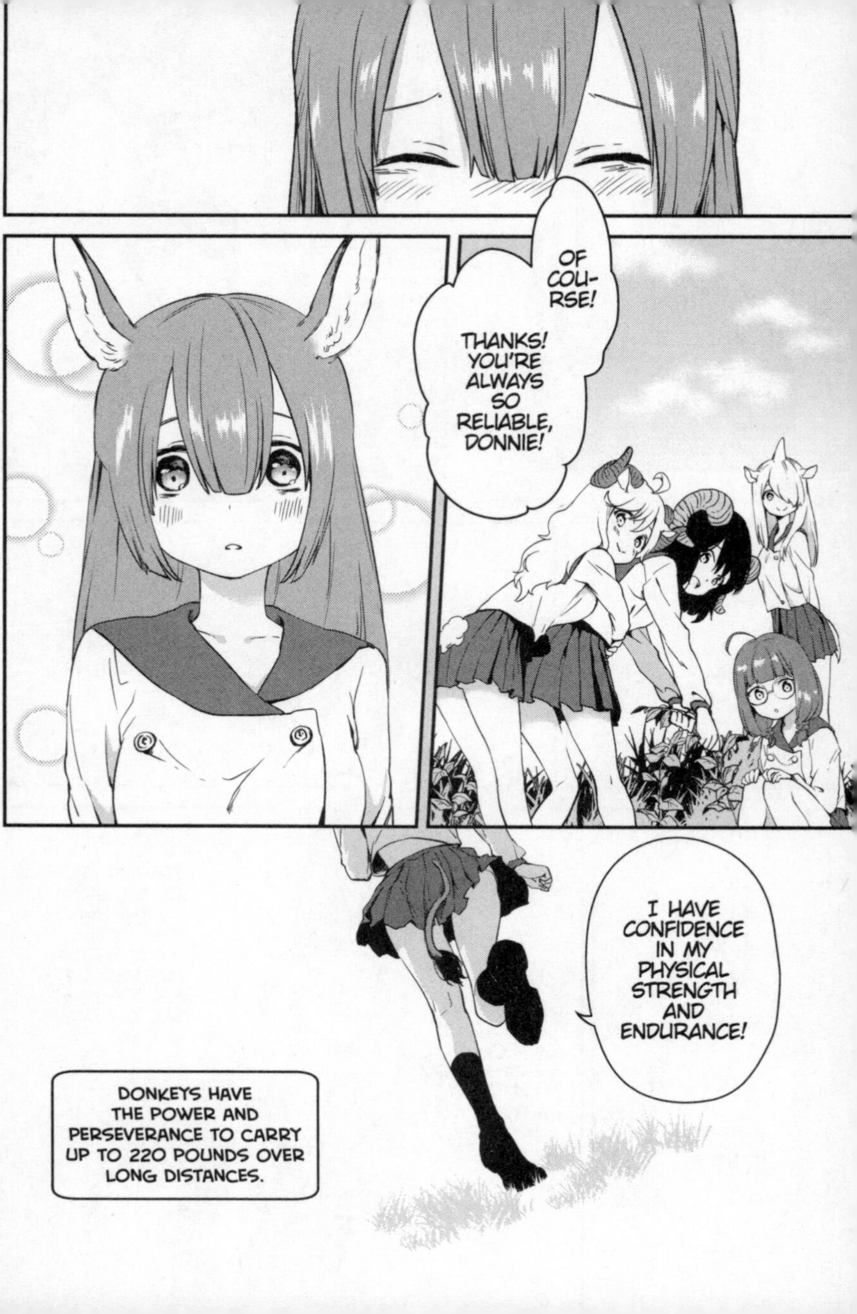
OF COURSE!
THANKS! YOU'RE ALWAYS SO RELIABLE, DONNIE!
I HAVE CONFIDENCE IN MY PHYSICAL STRENGTH AND ENDURANCE!
DONKEYS HAVE THE POWER AND PERSEVERANCE TO CARRY UP TO 220 POUNDS OVER LONG DISTANCES.

Donkey

White Rhinoceros

DNAは教えてくれない

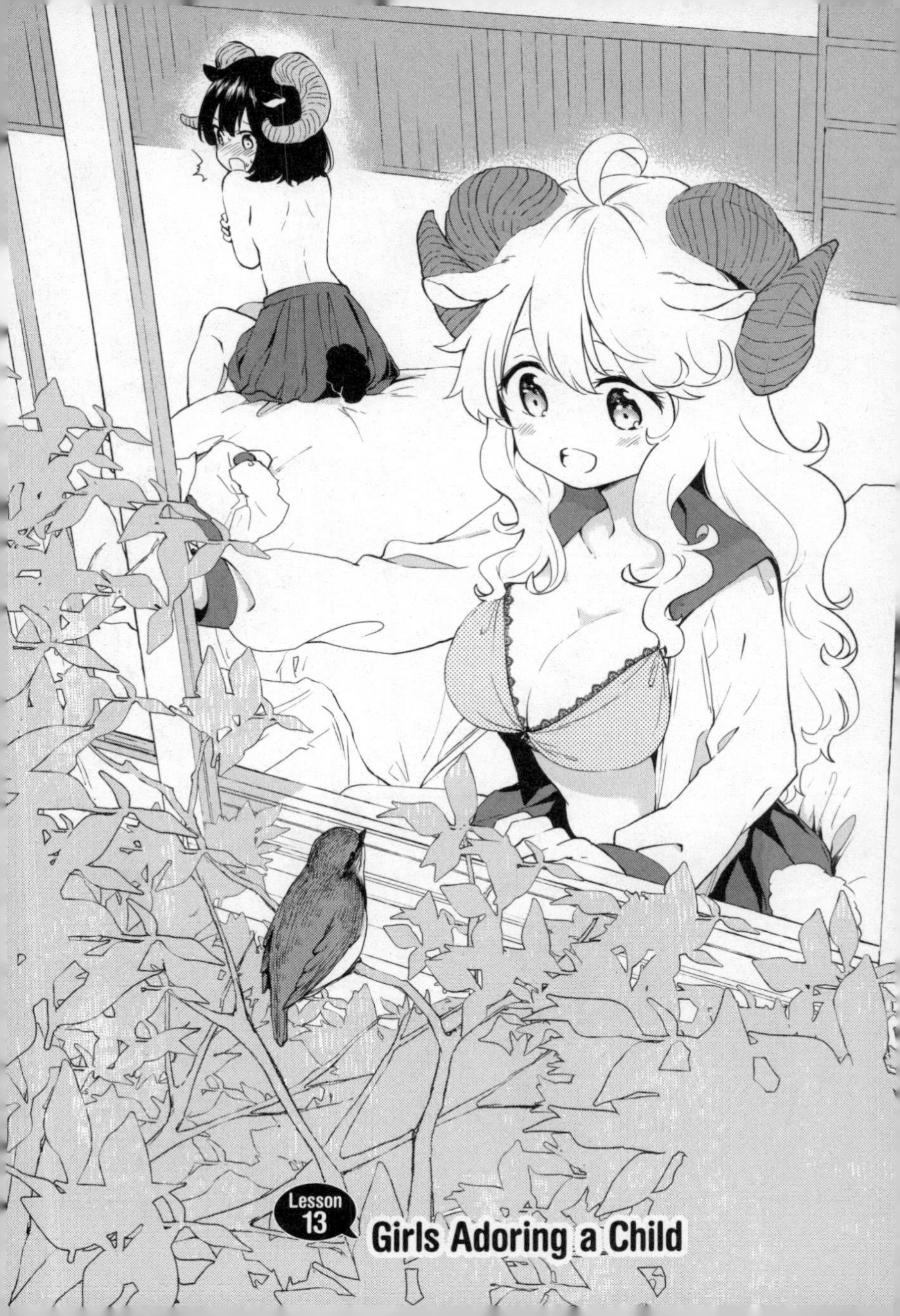
Lesson
13
Girls Adoring a Child

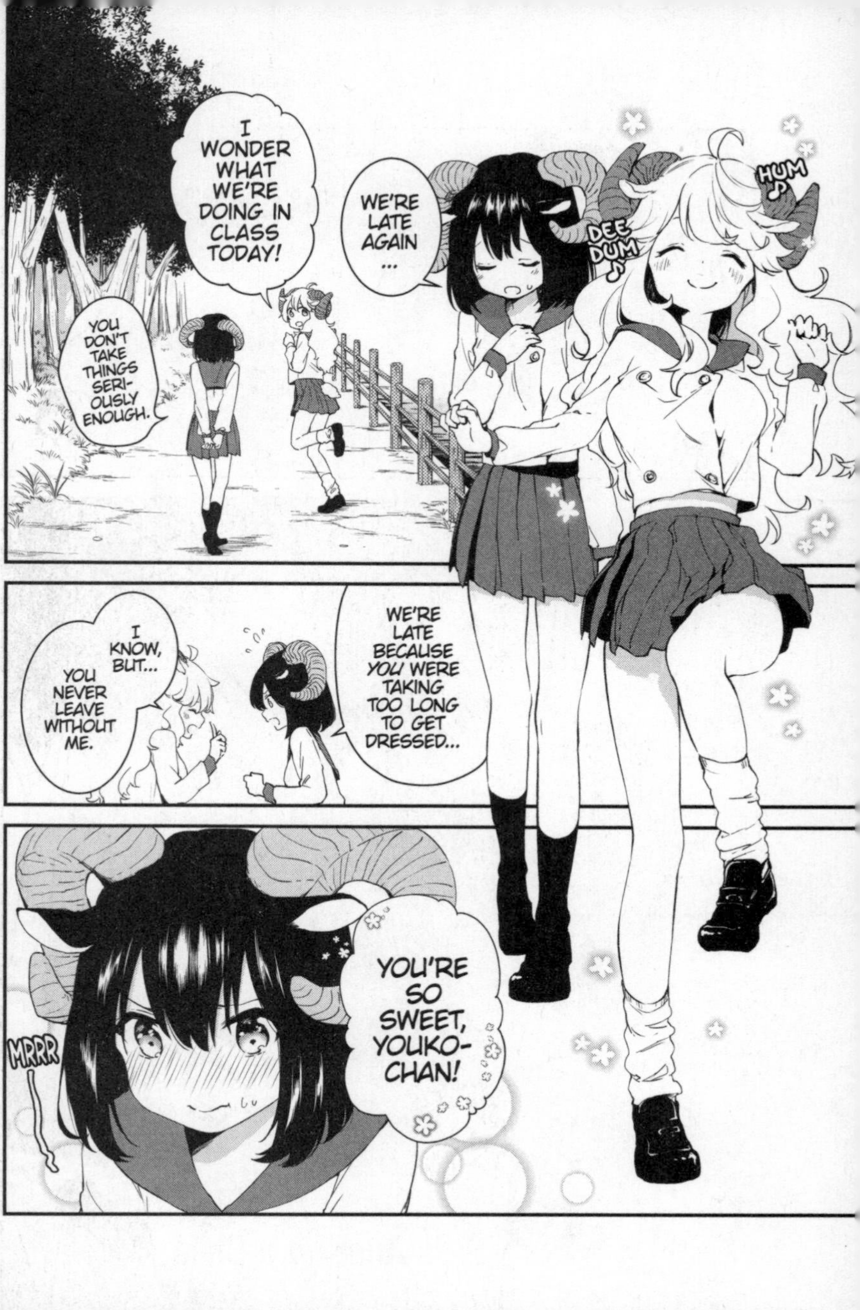
HUM ♪
DEE DUM ♪
WE'RE LATE AGAIN ...
I WONDER WHAT WE'RE DOING IN CLASS TODAY!
YOU DON'T TAKE THINGS SERI-OUSLY ENOUGH.
WE'RE LATE BECAUSE *YOU* WERE TAKING TOO LONG TO GET DRESSED...
I KNOW, BUT...
YOU NEVER LEAVE WITHOUT ME.
YOU'RE SO SWEET, YOUKO-CHAN!
MRRR

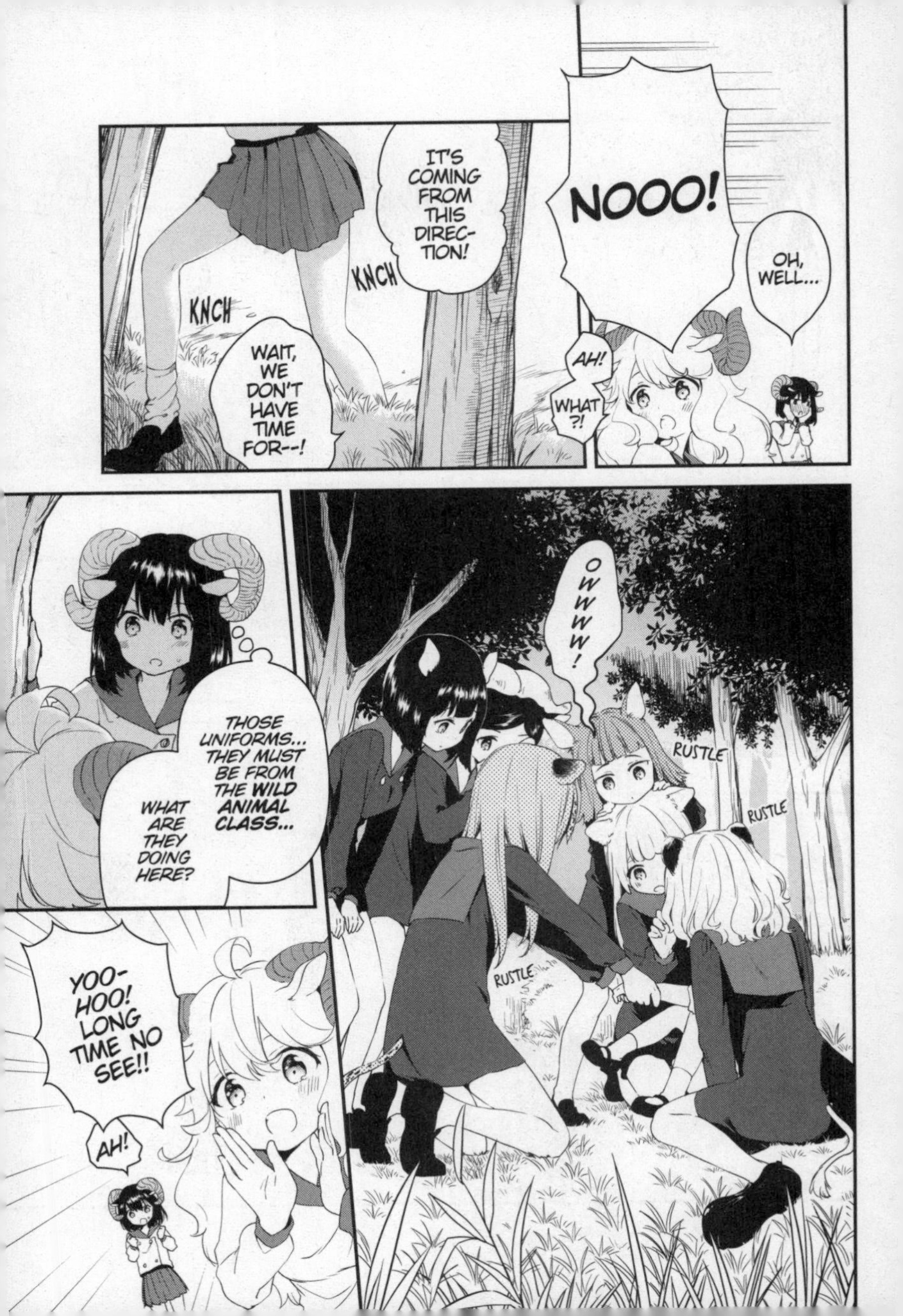
NOOO!
OH, WELL...
AH!
WHAT?!
IT'S COMING FROM THIS DIRECTION!
KNCH
KNCH
WAIT, WE DON'T HAVE TIME FOR--!
OWWWWW!
RUSTLE
RUSTLE
RUSTLE
THOSE UNIFORMS... THEY MUST BE FROM THE WILD ANIMAL CLASS...
WHAT ARE THEY DOING HERE?
YOO-HOO! LONG TIME NO SEE!!
AH!

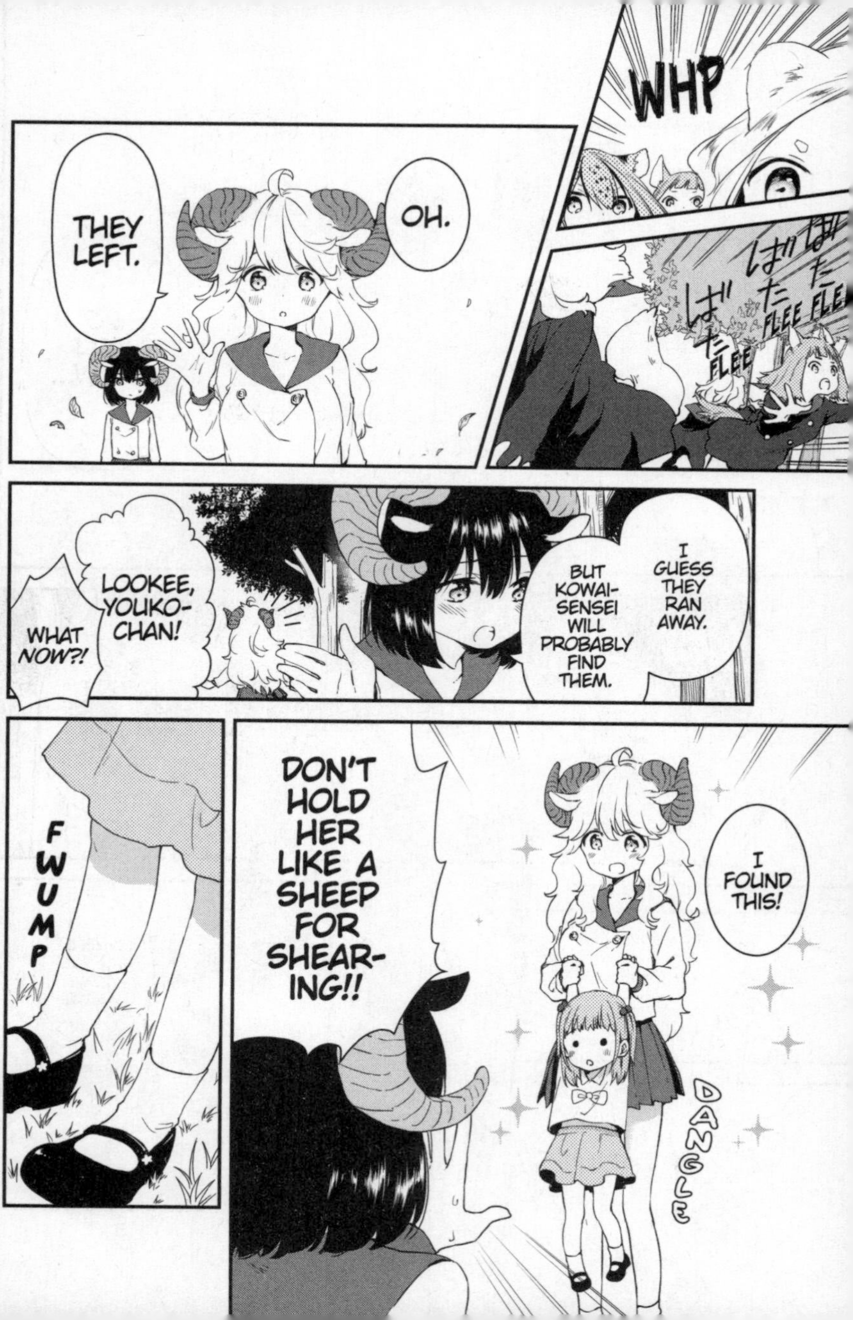
WHP
ばたばた
FLEE FLEE FLEE
OH.
THEY LEFT.
I GUESS THEY RAN AWAY.
BUT KOWAI-SENSEI WILL PROBABLY FIND THEM.
LOOKEE, YOUKO-CHAN!
WHAT NOW?!
I FOUND THIS!
DANGLE
DON'T HOLD HER LIKE A SHEEP FOR SHEAR-ING!!
FWUMP

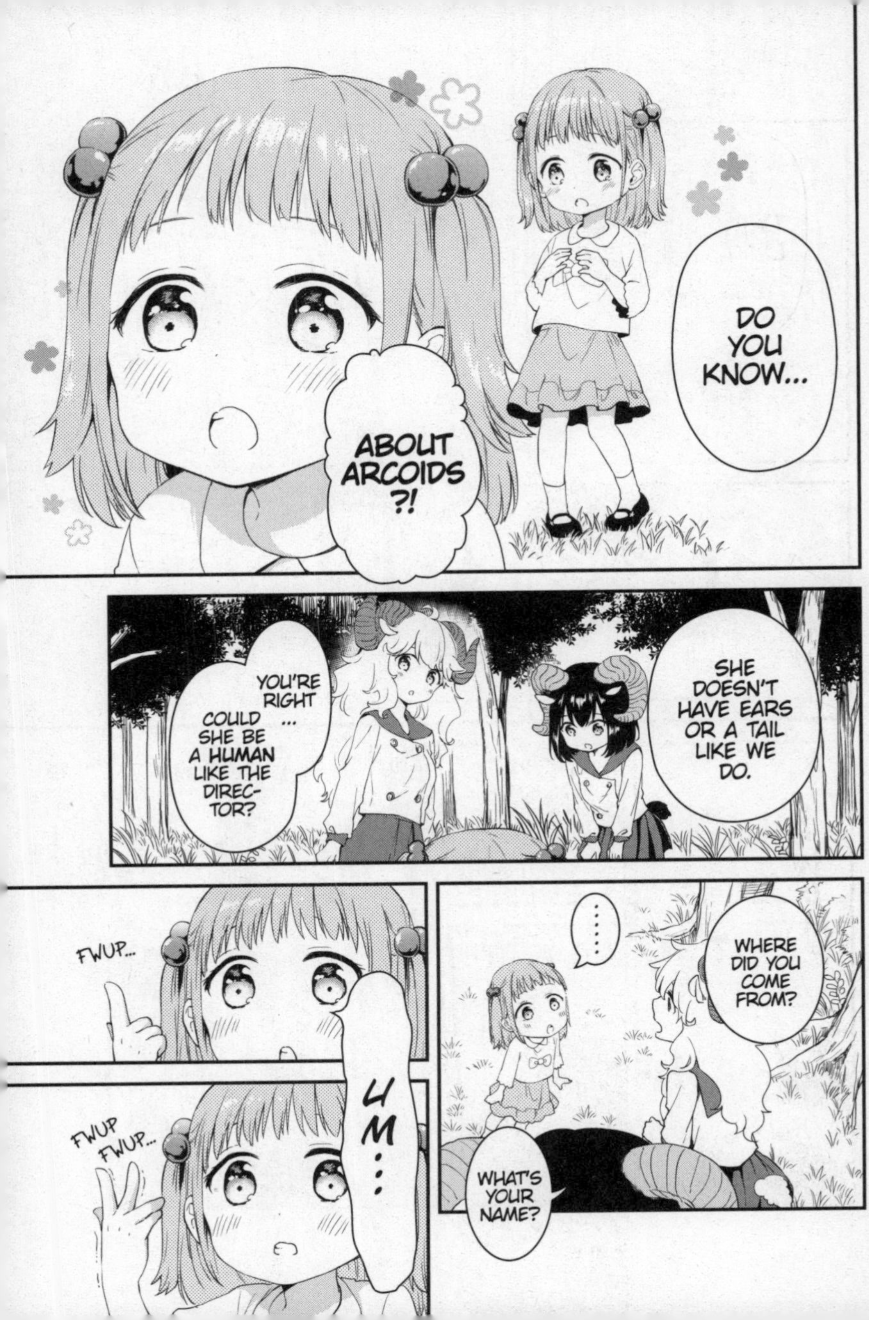
DO YOU KNOW...
ABOUT ARCOIDS ?!
SHE DOESN'T HAVE EARS OR A TAIL LIKE WE DO.
YOU'RE RIGHT ...
COULD SHE BE A HUMAN LIKE THE DIREC-TOR?
WHERE DID YOU COME FROM?
......
WHAT'S YOUR NAME?
FWUP...
UM...
FWUP FWUP...

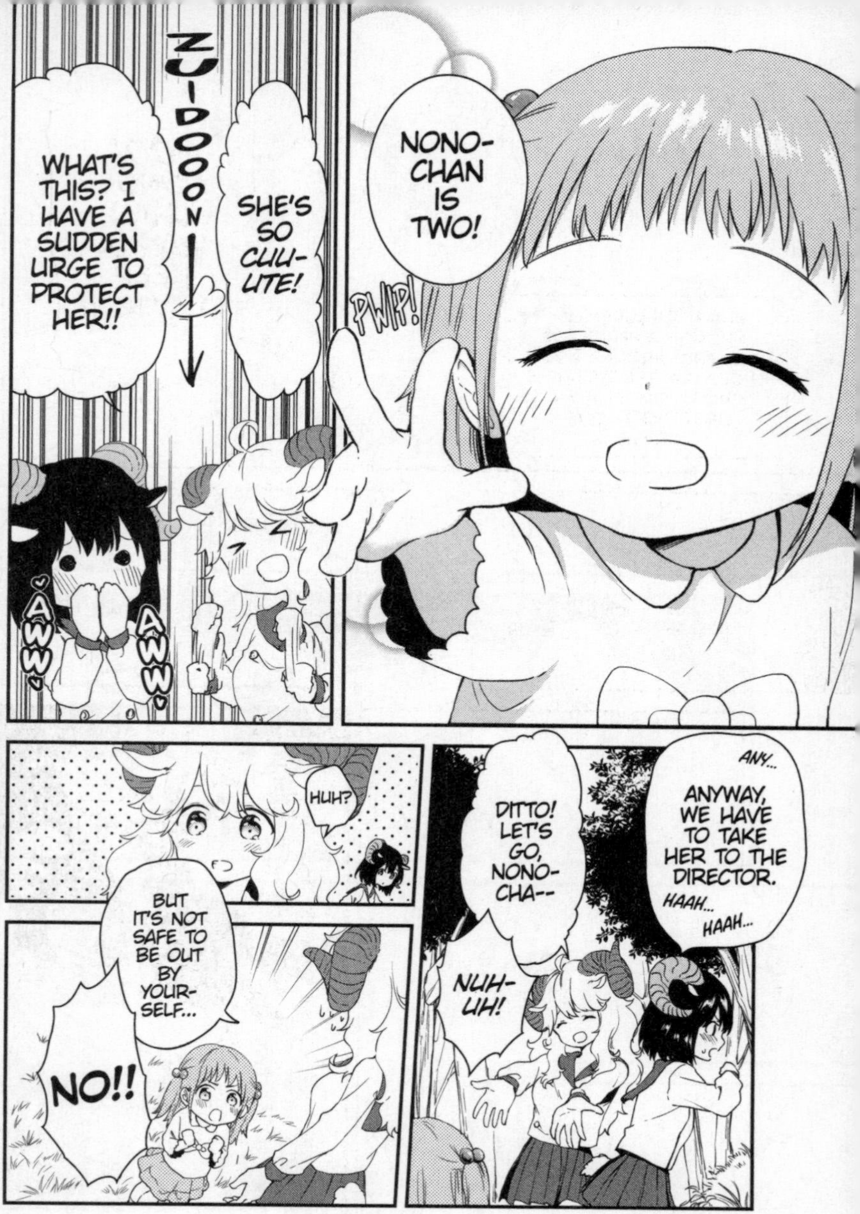

NONO-CHAN IS TWO!
PWIP!
SHE'S SO CUUU-UTE!
WHAT'S THIS? I HAVE A SUDDEN URGE TO PROTECT HER!!
ZUIDOOOON
AWW
AWW
ANY... ANYWAY, WE HAVE TO TAKE HER TO THE DIRECTOR.
HAAH... HAAH...
DITTO! LET'S GO, NONO-CHA--
NUH-UH!
HUH?
BUT IT'S NOT SAFE TO BE OUT BY YOURSELF...
NO!!

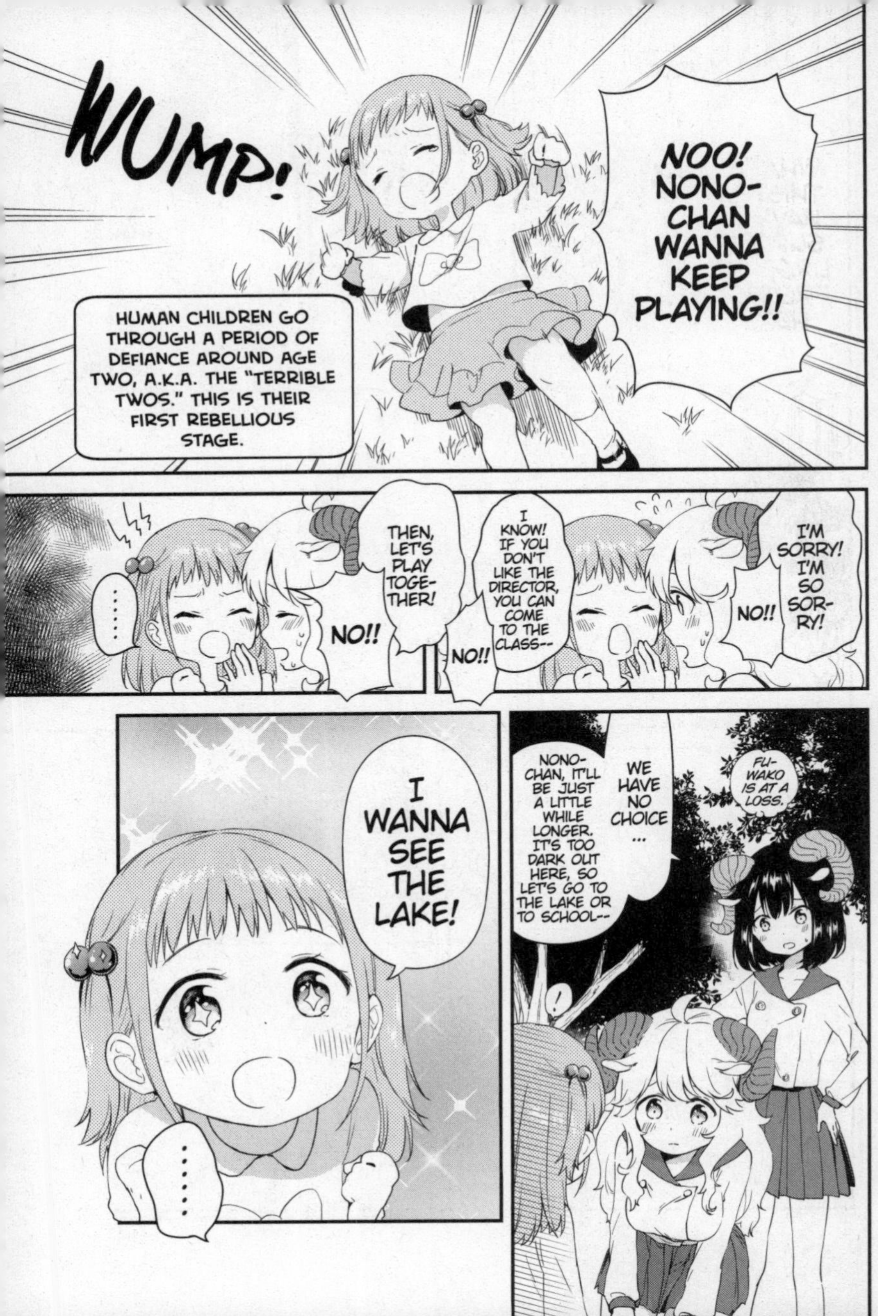
WUMP!
NOO! NONO-CHAN WANNA KEEP PLAYING!!
HUMAN CHILDREN GO THROUGH A PERIOD OF DEFIANCE AROUND AGE TWO, A.K.A. THE "TERRIBLE TWOS." THIS IS THEIR FIRST REBELLIOUS STAGE.
I'M SORRY! I'M SO SOR-RY!
NO!!
I KNOW! IF YOU DON'T LIKE THE DIRECTOR, YOU CAN COME TO THE CLASS--
NO!!
THEN, LET'S PLAY TOGE-THER!
NO!!
......
FU-WAKO IS AT A LOSS.
WE HAVE NO CHOICE ...
NONO-CHAN, IT'LL BE JUST A LITTLE WHILE LONGER. IT'S TOO DARK OUT HERE, SO LET'S GO TO THE LAKE OR TO SCHOOL--
!
I WANNA SEE THE LAKE!
......

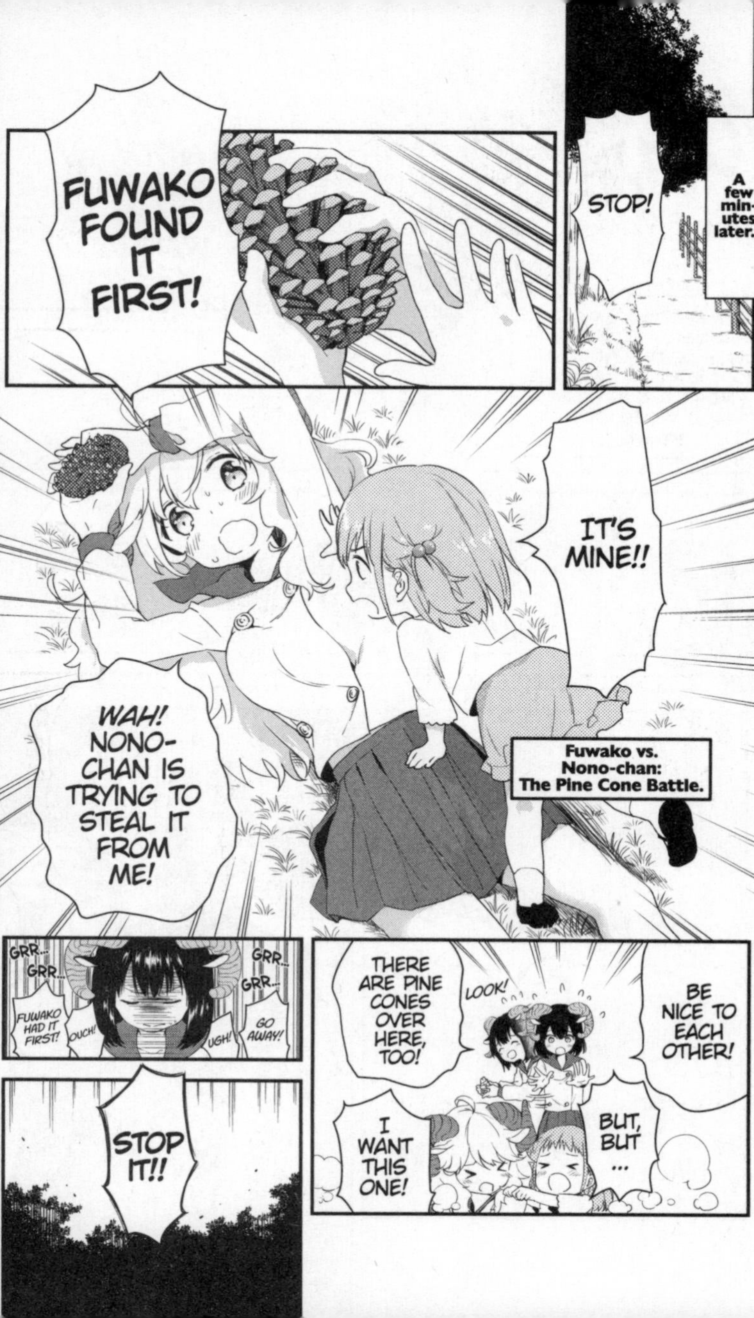

A few min-utes later...
STOP!
FUWAKO FOUND IT FIRST!
IT'S MINE!!
WAH! NONO-CHAN IS TRYING TO STEAL IT FROM ME!
Fuwako vs. Nono-chan: The Pine Cone Battle.
BE NICE TO EACH OTHER!
THERE ARE PINE CONES OVER HERE, TOO!
LOOK!
BUT, BUT ...
I WANT THIS ONE!
GRR... GRR...
GRR... GRR...
FUWAKO HAD IT FIRST!
OUCH!
UGH!
GO AWAY!
STOP IT!!

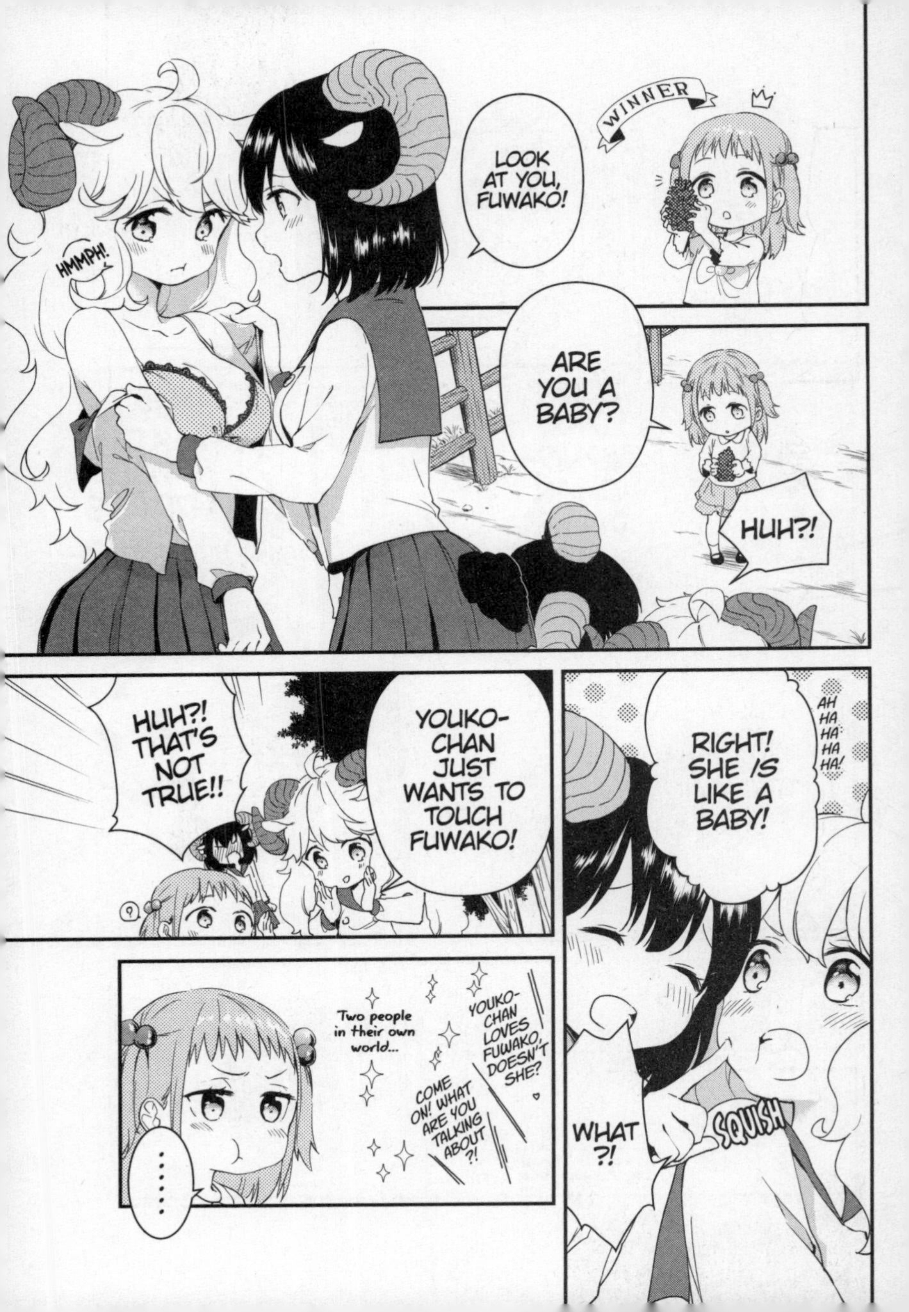
WINNER
LOOK AT YOU, FUWAKO!
HMMPH!
ARE YOU A BABY?
HUH?!
RIGHT! SHE IS LIKE A BABY!
AH HA HA HA HA!
YOUKO-CHAN JUST WANTS TO TOUCH FUWAKO!
HUH?! THAT'S NOT TRUE!!
?
SQUISH
WHAT?!
YOUKO-CHAN LOVES FUWAKO, DOESN'T SHE?
COME ON! WHAT ARE YOU TALKING ABOUT?!
Two people in their own world...
......

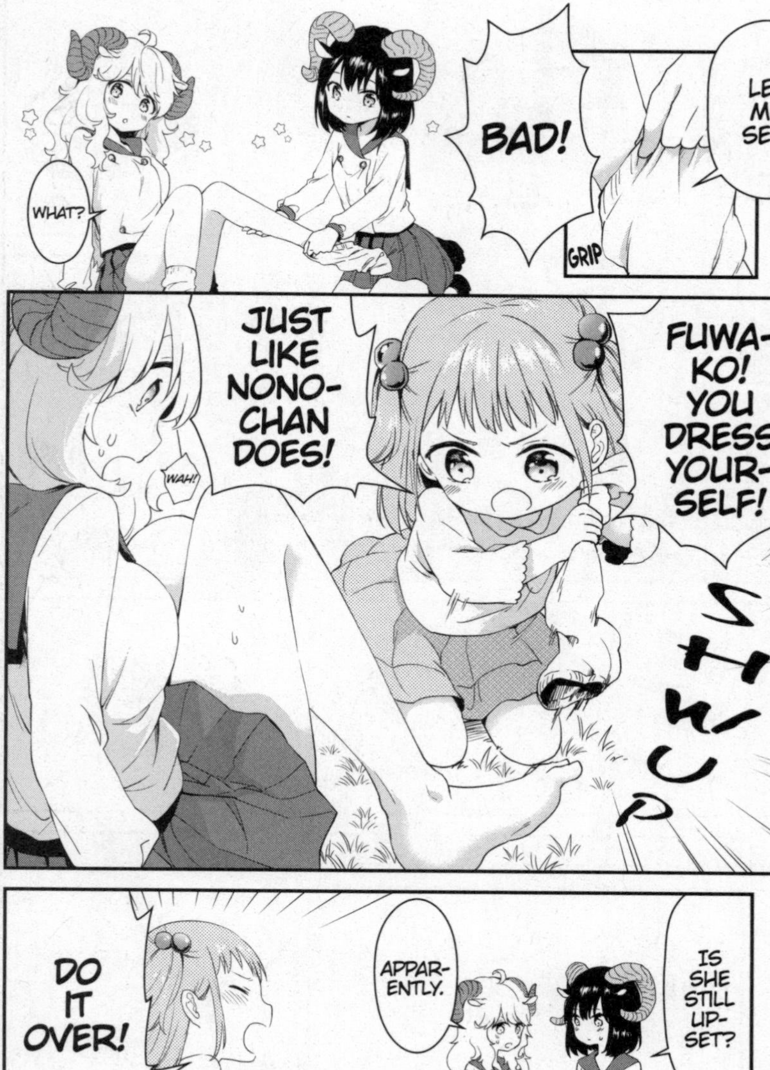

LET ME SEE.
GRIP
BAD!
WHAT?
FUWA-KO! YOU DRESS YOUR-SELF!
JUST LIKE NONO-CHAN DOES!
WAH!
SHWUP
IS SHE STILL UP-SET?
APPAR-ENTLY.
DO IT OVER!
A two-year old who begs for attention.

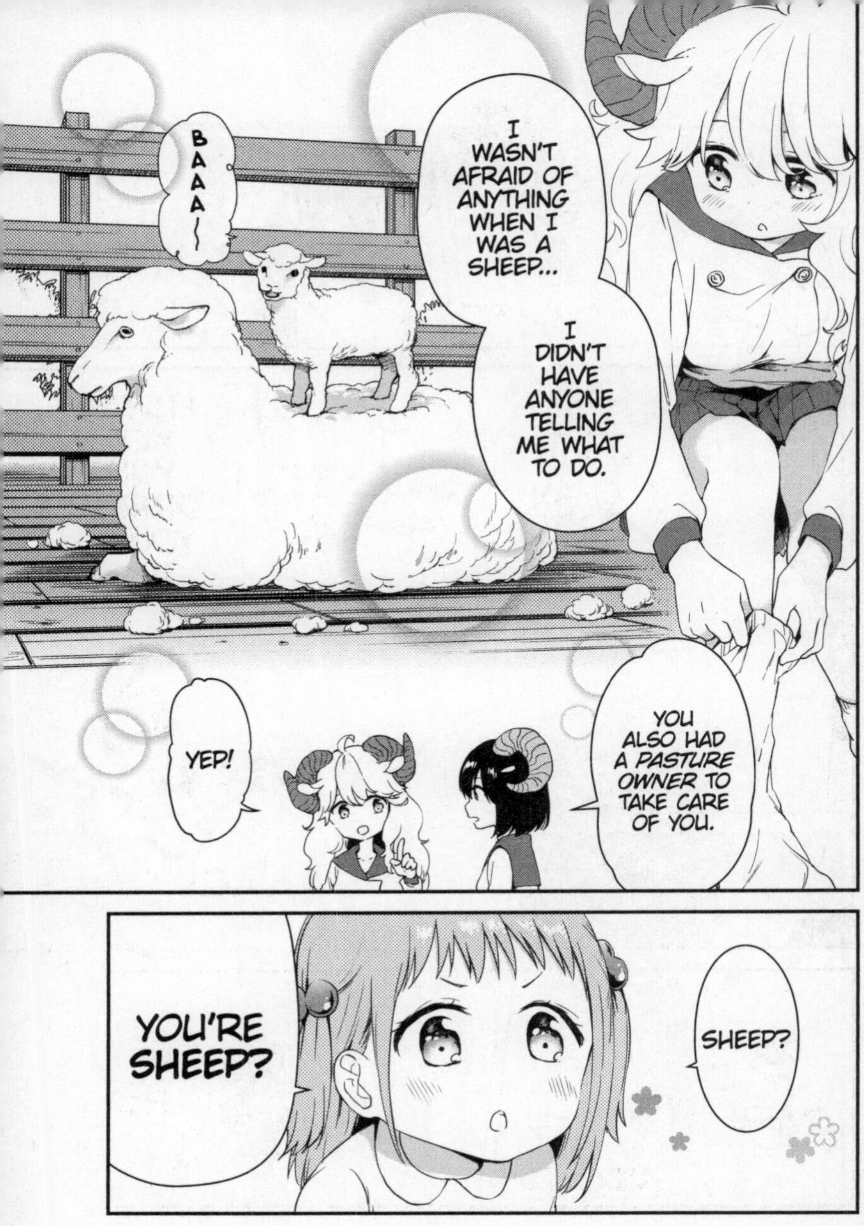
I WASN'T AFRAID OF ANYTHING WHEN I WAS A SHEEP...
I DIDN'T HAVE ANYONE TELLING ME WHAT TO DO.
BAAA~
YOU ALSO HAD A *PASTURE OWNER* TO TAKE CARE OF YOU.
YEP!
SHEEP?
YOU'RE SHEEP?

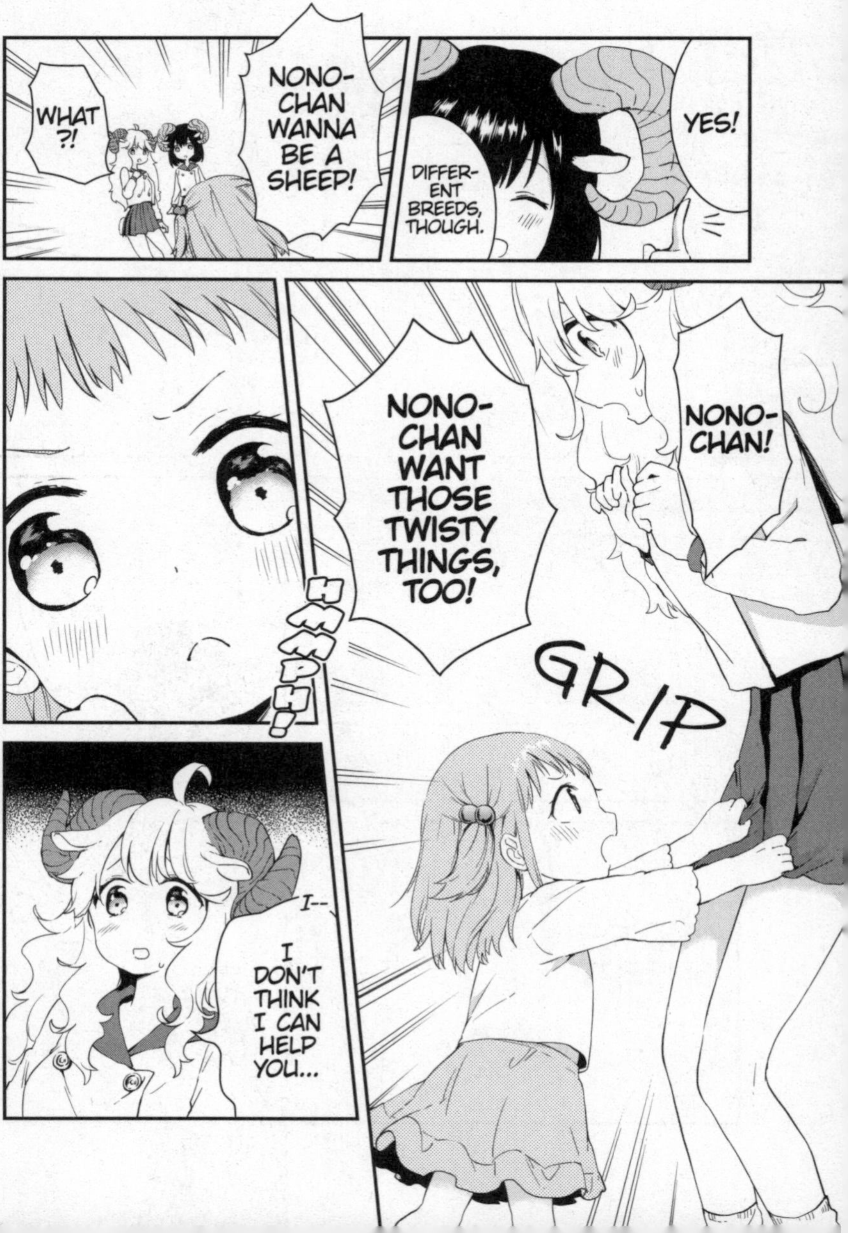
YES!
DIFFER-ENT BREEDS, THOUGH.
NONO-CHAN WANNA BE A SHEEP!
WHAT?!
NONO-CHAN!
NONO-CHAN WANT THOSE TWISTY THINGS, TOO!
GRIP
HMMPH!
I--
I DON'T THINK I CAN HELP YOU...

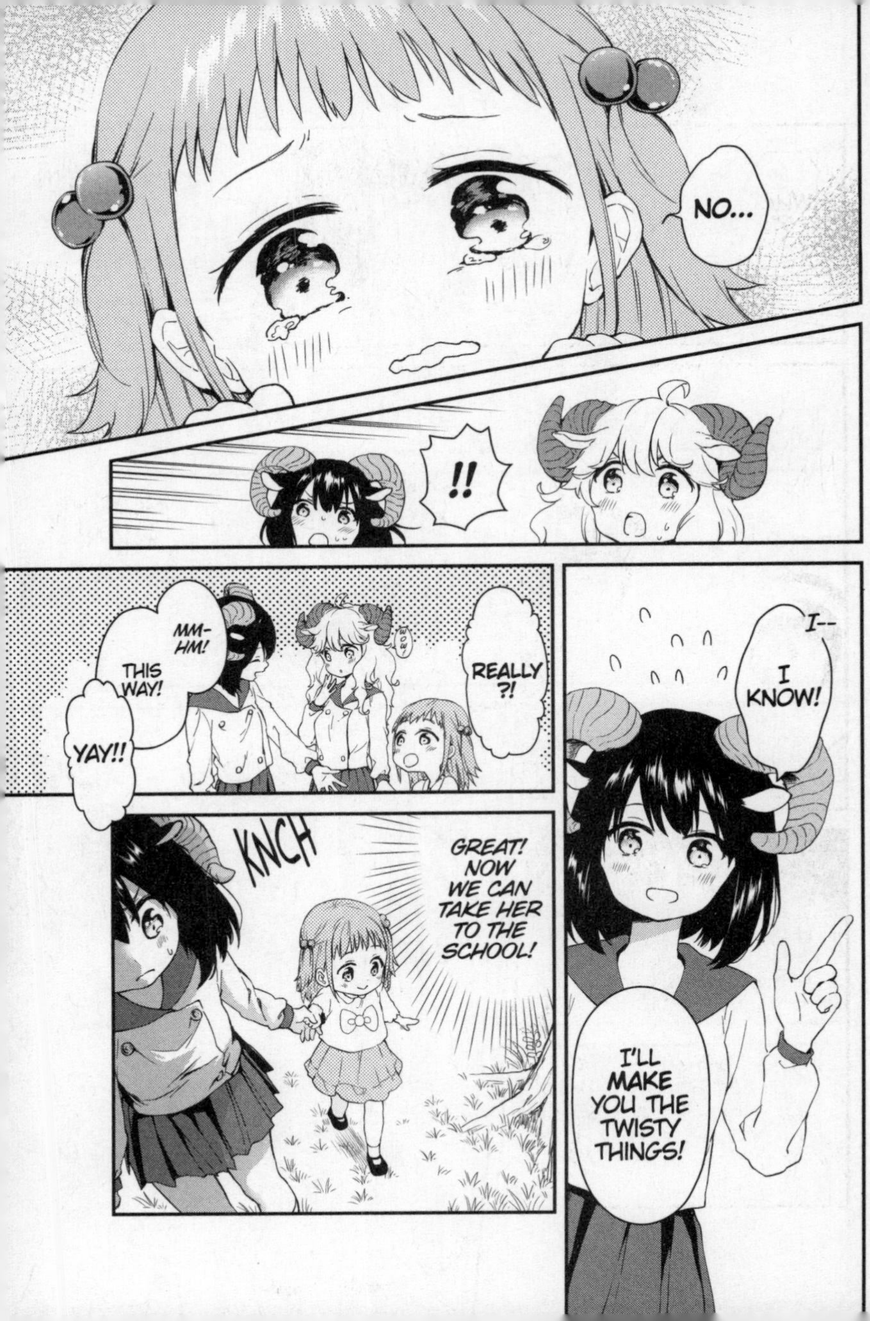
NO...
!!
I--
I KNOW!
I'LL MAKE YOU THE TWISTY THINGS!
REALLY?!
MM-HM! THIS WAY!
YAY!!
KNCH
GREAT! NOW WE CAN TAKE HER TO THE SCHOOL!

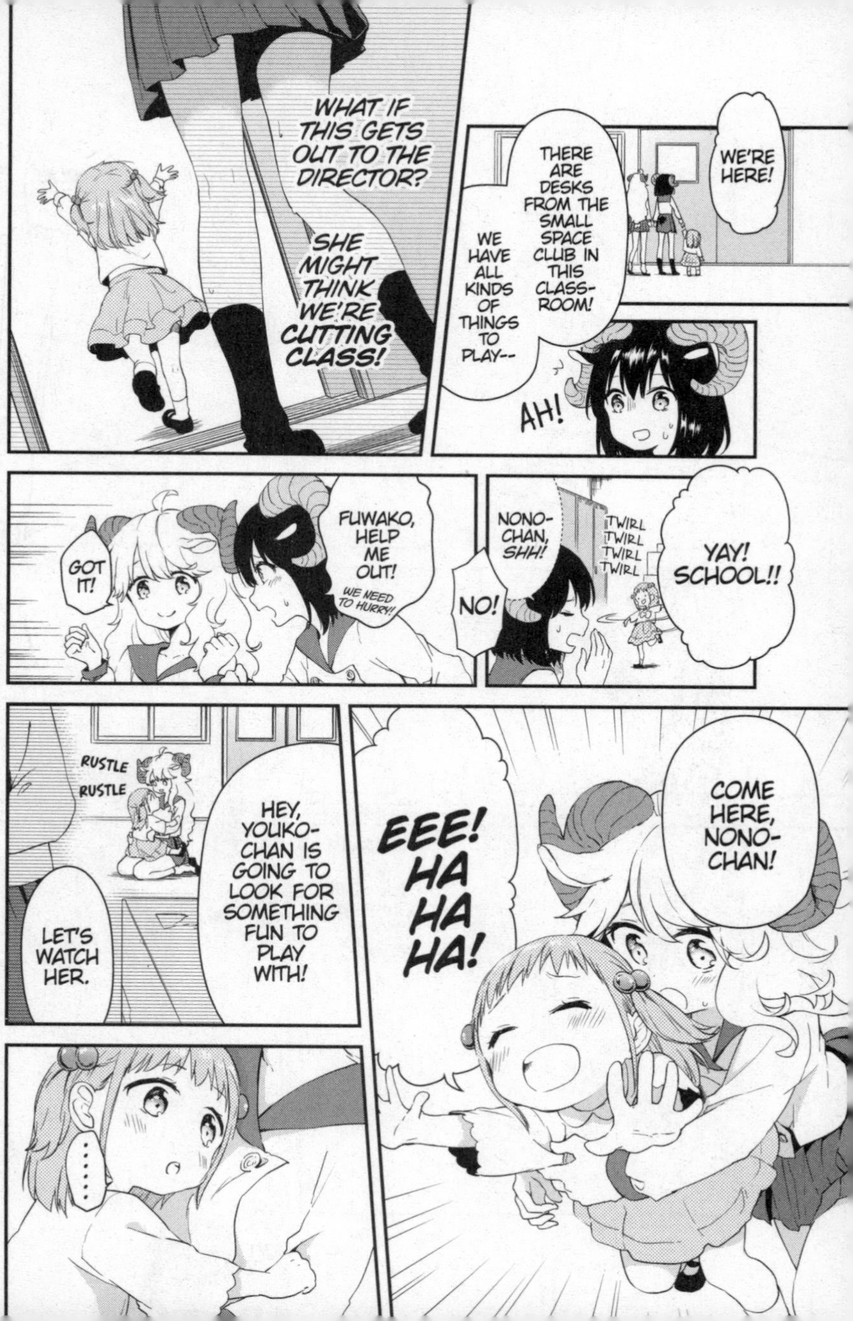

WE'RE HERE!
THERE ARE DESKS FROM THE SMALL SPACE CLUB IN THIS CLASSROOM!
WE HAVE ALL KINDS OF THINGS TO PLAY--
AH!
WHAT IF THIS GETS OUT TO THE DIRECTOR?
SHE MIGHT THINK WE'RE CUTTING CLASS!
YAY! SCHOOL!!
TWIRL TWIRL TWIRL TWIRL
NONO-CHAN, SHH!
NO!
FUWAKO, HELP ME OUT!
WE NEED TO HURRY!!
GOT IT!
COME HERE, NONO-CHAN!
EEE! HA HA HA HA!
RUSTLE
RUSTLE
HEY, YOUKO-CHAN IS GOING TO LOOK FOR SOMETHING FUN TO PLAY WITH!
LET'S WATCH HER.
......

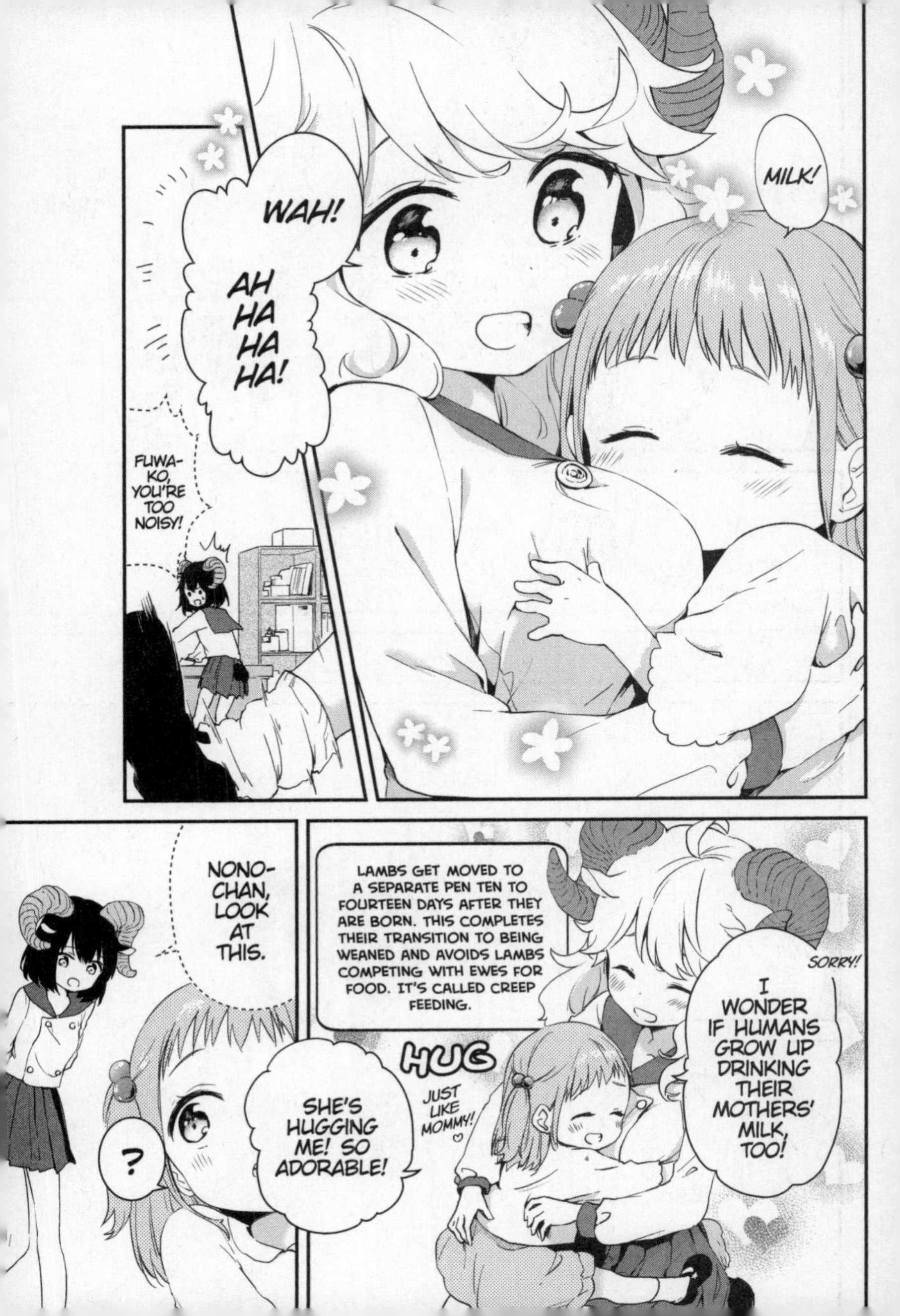
MILK!
WAH!
AH HA HA HA!
FUWA-KO, YOU'RE TOO NOISY!
LAMBS GET MOVED TO A SEPARATE PEN TEN TO FOURTEEN DAYS AFTER THEY ARE BORN. THIS COMPLETES THEIR TRANSITION TO BEING WEANED AND AVOIDS LAMBS COMPETING WITH EWES FOR FOOD. IT'S CALLED CREEP FEEDING.
SORRY!
I WONDER IF HUMANS GROW UP DRINKING THEIR MOTHERS' MILK, TOO!
HUG
JUST LIKE MOMMY!
SHE'S HUGGING ME! SO ADORABLE!
NONO-CHAN, LOOK AT THIS.
?

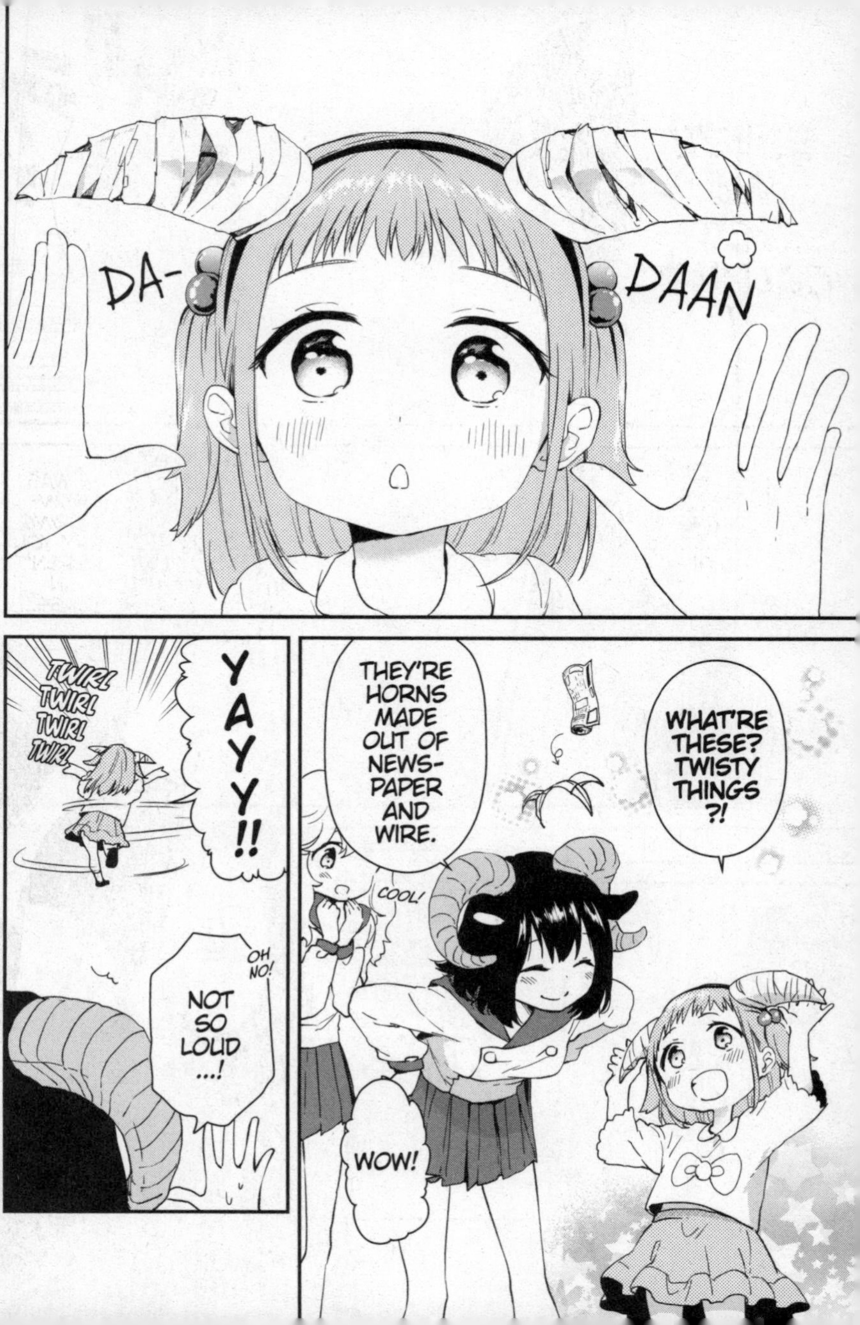

DA-
DAAN
WHAT'RE THESE? TWISTY THINGS?!
THEY'RE HORNS MADE OUT OF NEWS-PAPER AND WIRE.
COOL!
WOW!
YAYY!!
TWIRL TWIRL TWIRL TWIRL
OH NO!
NOT SO LOUD ...!

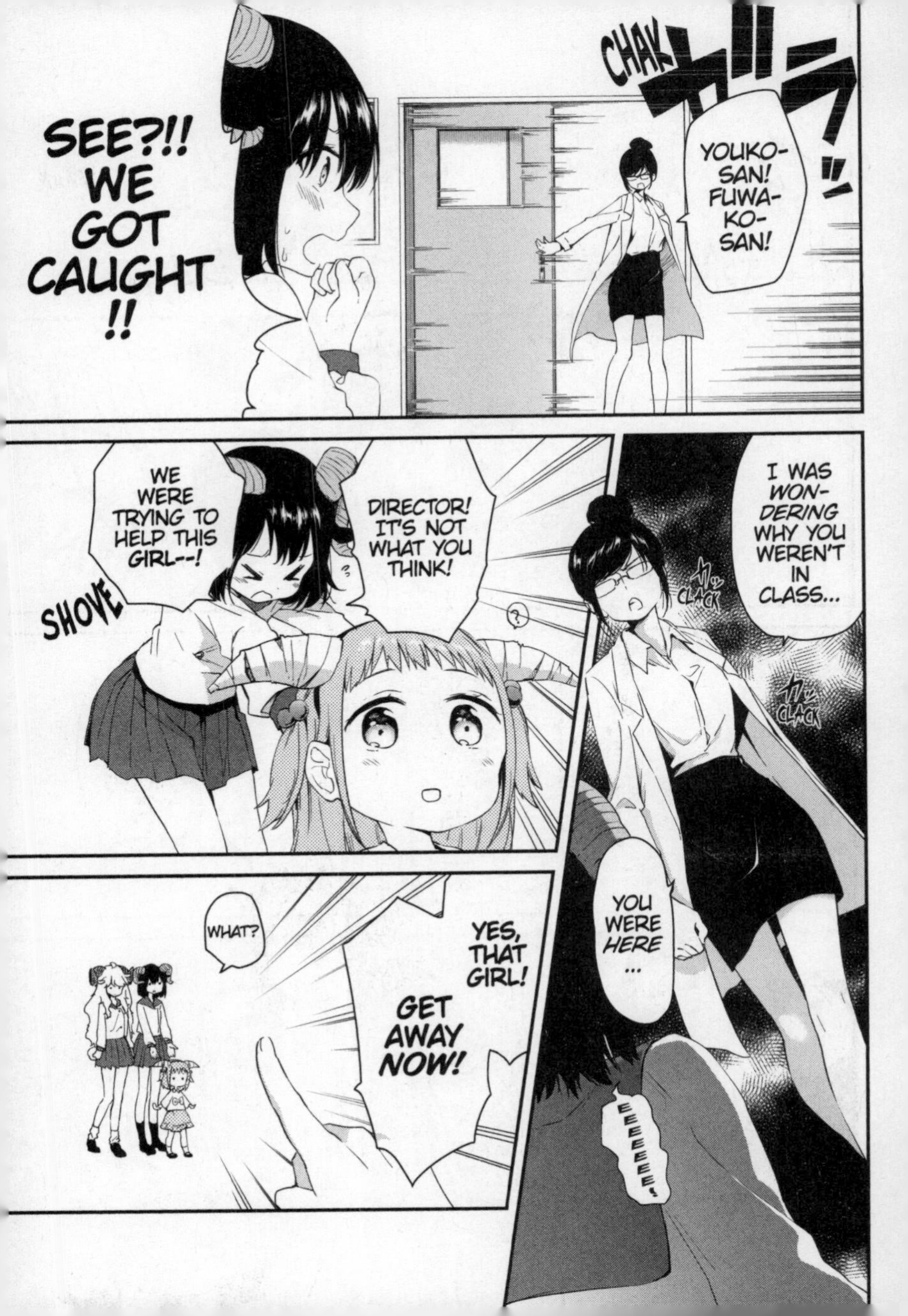
CHAK
YOUKO-SAN! FUWAKO-SAN!
SEE?!! WE GOT CAUGHT!!
I WAS WONDERING WHY YOU WEREN'T IN CLASS...
CLACK
CLACK
YOU WERE HERE...
EEEEEEE!
DIRECTOR! IT'S NOT WHAT YOU THINK!
WE WERE TRYING TO HELP THIS GIRL--!
SHOVE
?
YES, THAT GIRL!
GET AWAY NOW!
WHAT?

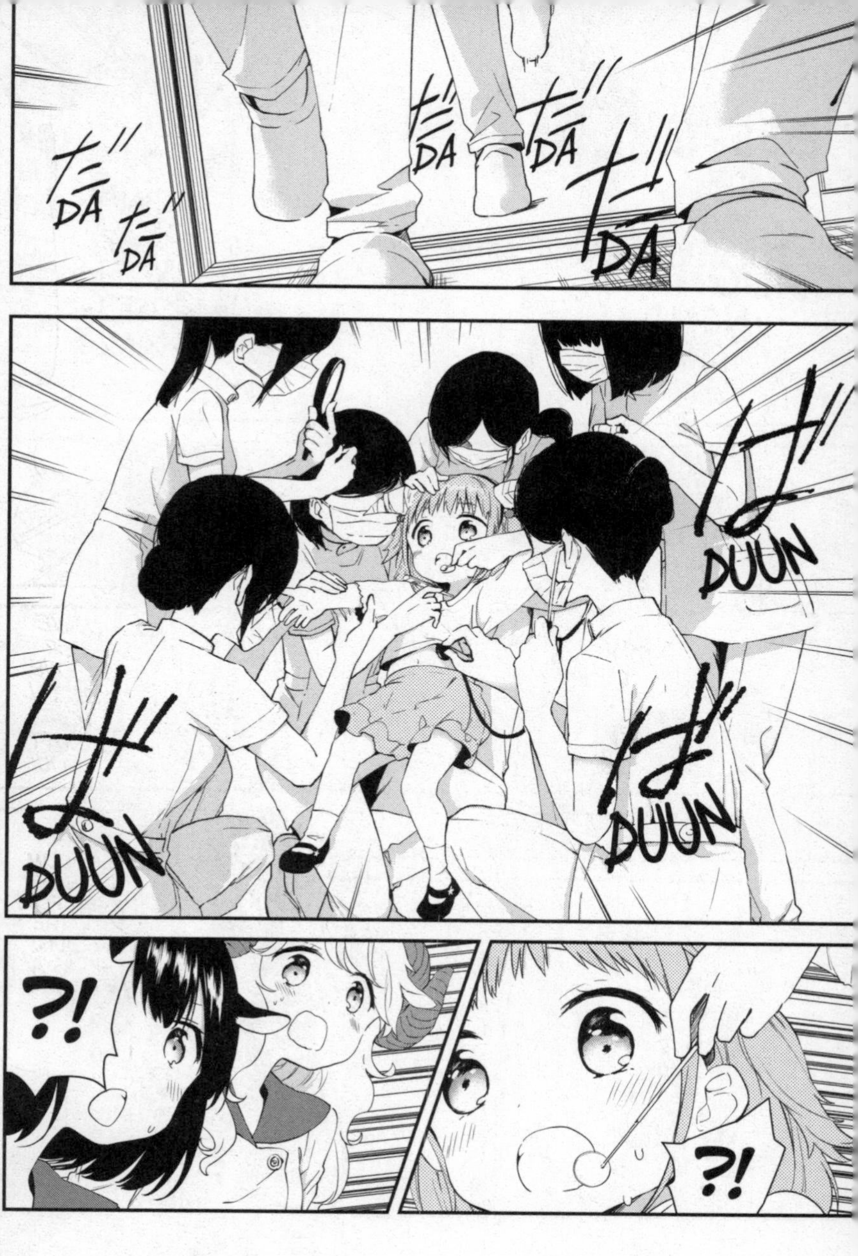
だ DA
だ DA
だ DA
だ DA
だ DA
ば DUUN
ば DUUN
ば DUUN
?!
?!

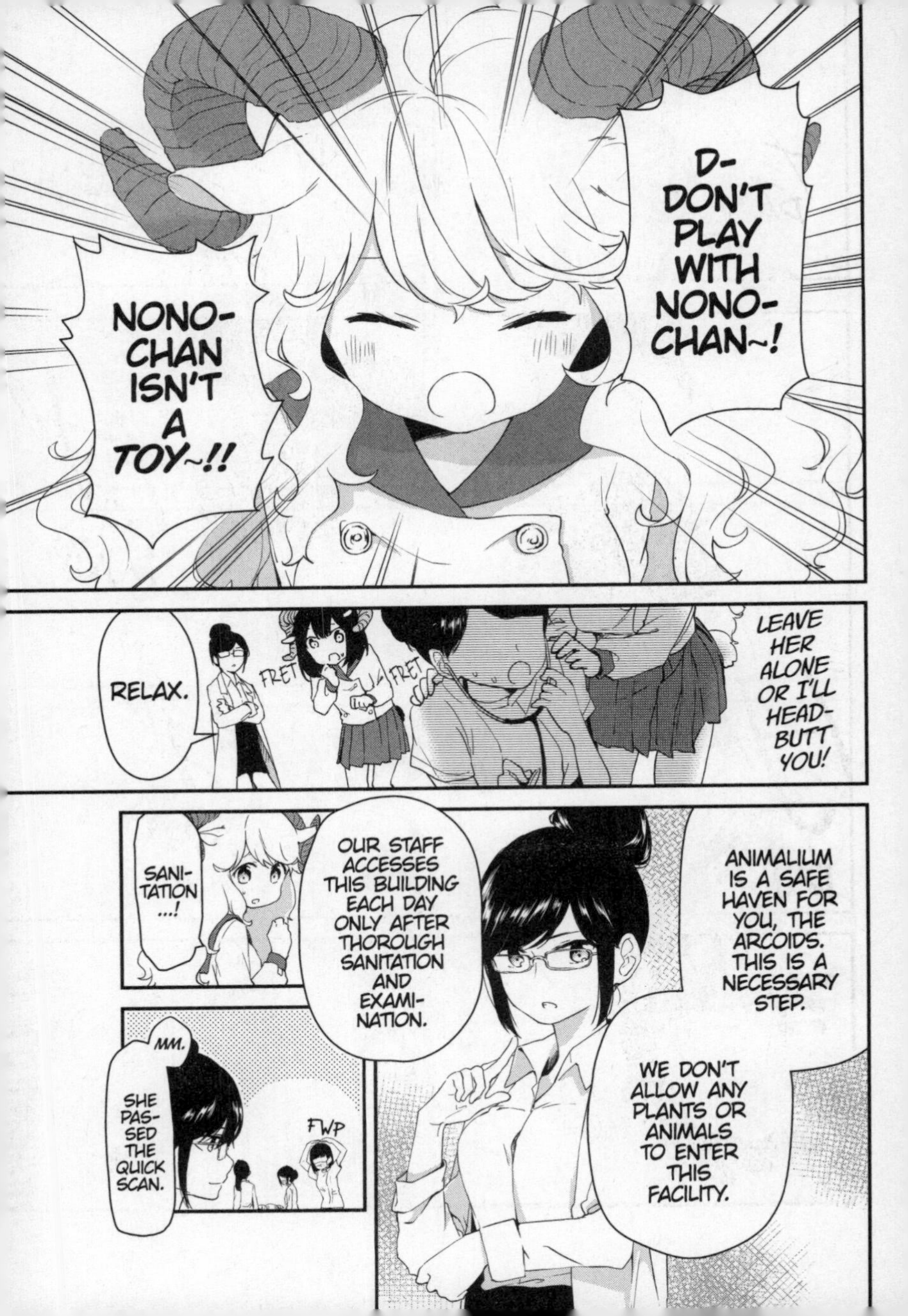
D-DON'T PLAY WITH NONO-CHAN~!
NONO-CHAN ISN'T A TOY~!!
LEAVE HER ALONE OR I'LL HEAD-BUTT YOU!
FRET
FRET
RELAX.
ANIMALIUM IS A SAFE HAVEN FOR YOU, THE ARCOIDS. THIS IS A NECESSARY STEP.
OUR STAFF ACCESSES THIS BUILDING EACH DAY ONLY AFTER THOROUGH SANITATION AND EXAMINATION.
SANITATION...!
WE DON'T ALLOW ANY PLANTS OR ANIMALS TO ENTER THIS FACILITY.
FWP
MM.
SHE PASSED THE QUICK SCAN.

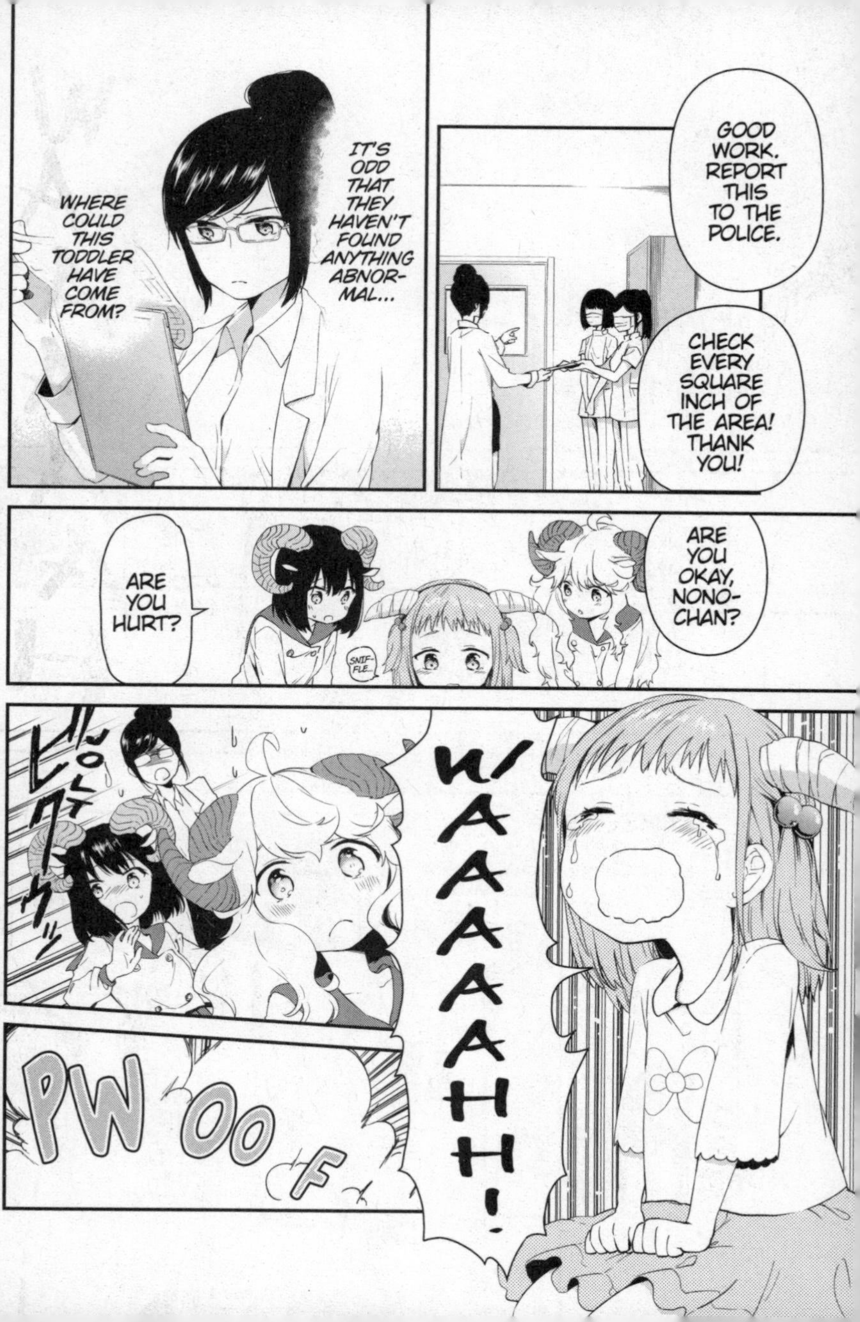
GOOD WORK. REPORT THIS TO THE POLICE.
CHECK EVERY SQUARE INCH OF THE AREA! THANK YOU!
IT'S ODD THAT THEY HAVEN'T FOUND ANYTHING ABNOR-MAL...
WHERE COULD THIS TODDLER HAVE COME FROM?
ARE YOU OKAY, NONO-CHAN?
SNIFF-FLE...
ARE YOU HURT?
WAAAAAAH!
JOLT
PWOOF

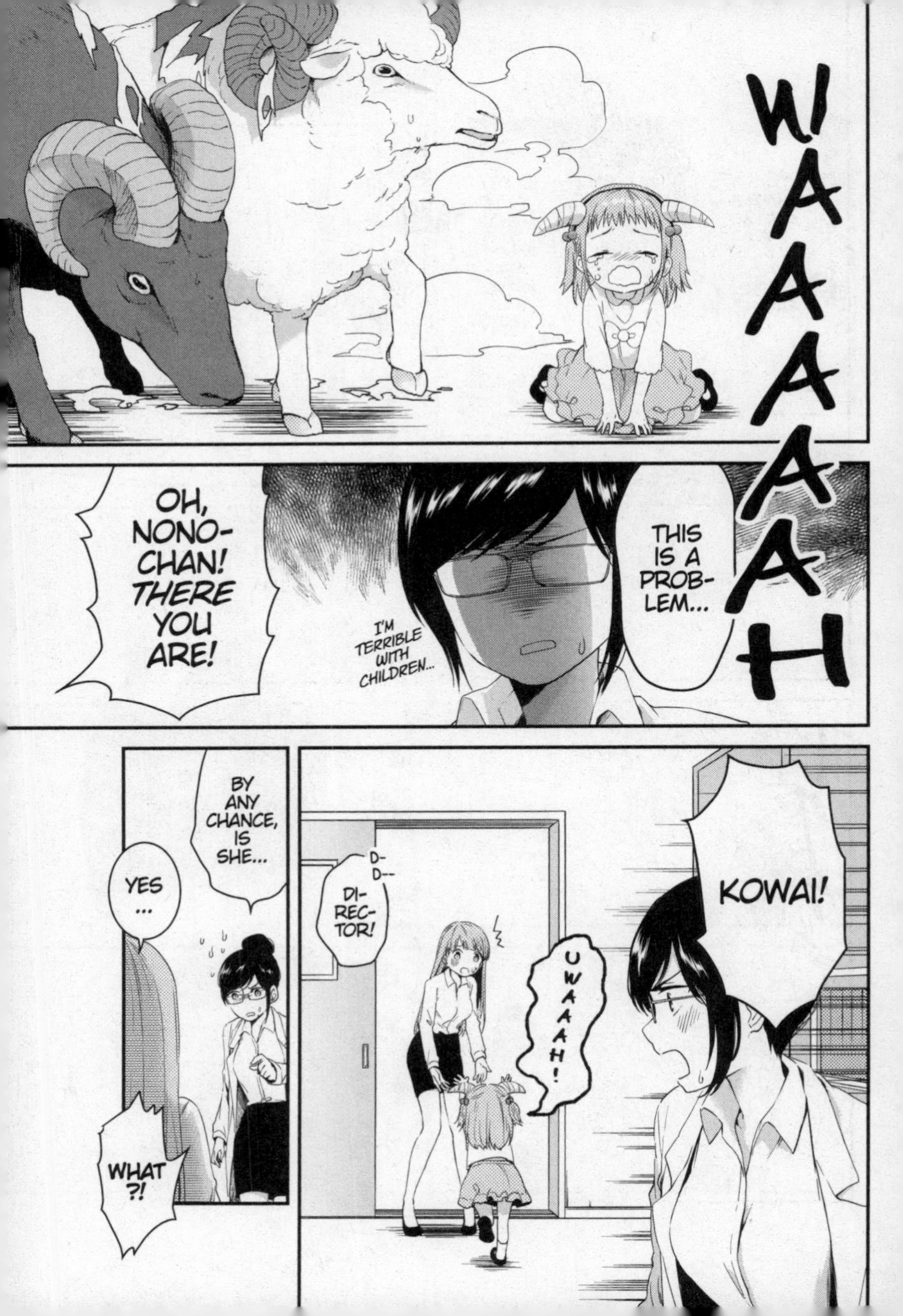

WAAAAAAH
THIS IS A PROBLEM...
I'M TERRIBLE WITH CHILDREN...
OH, NONO-CHAN! THERE YOU ARE!
KOWAI!
UWAAAAH!
D-D-- DIRECTOR!
BY ANY CHANCE, IS SHE...
YES ...
WHAT ?!

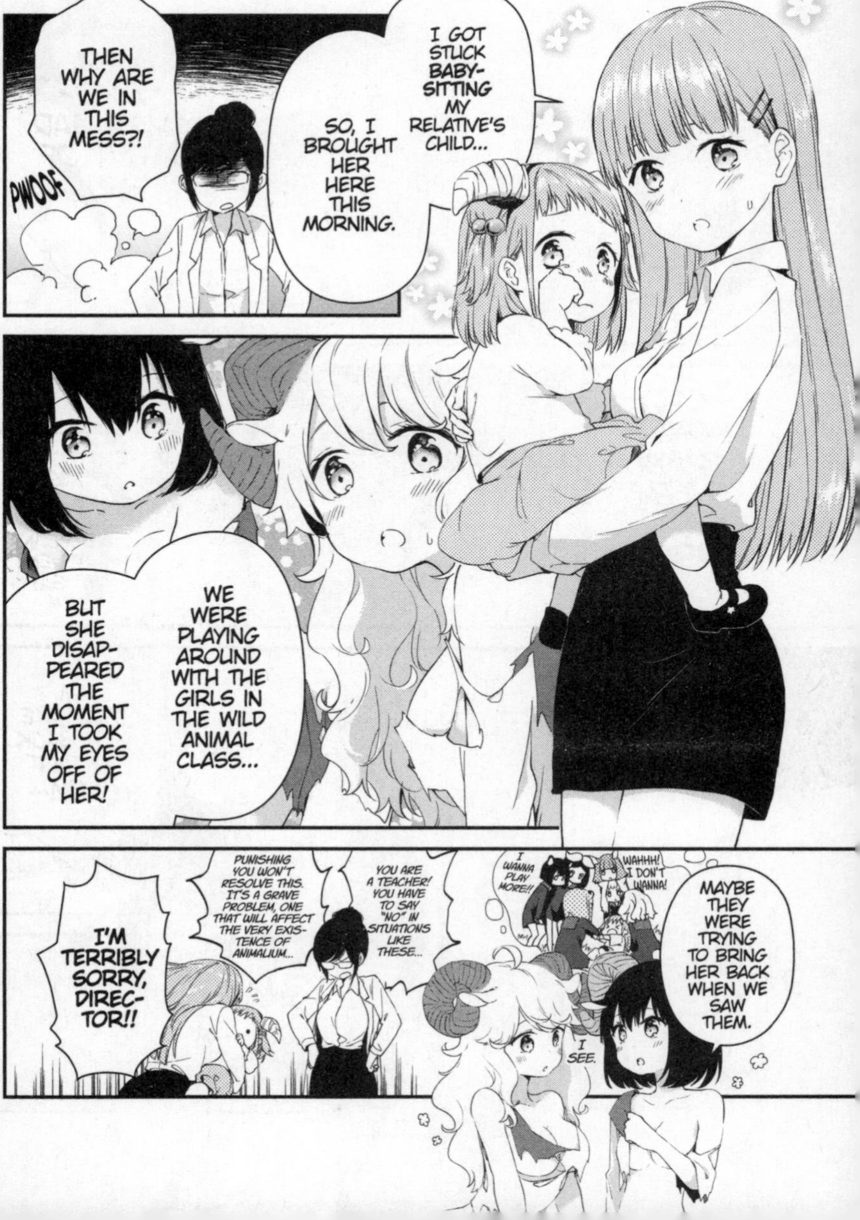
I GOT STUCK BABY-SITTING MY RELATIVE'S CHILD...
SO, I BROUGHT HER HERE THIS MORNING.
THEN WHY ARE WE IN THIS MESS?!
PWOOF
WE WERE PLAYING AROUND WITH THE GIRLS IN THE WILD ANIMAL CLASS...
BUT SHE DISAPPEARED THE MOMENT I TOOK MY EYES OFF OF HER!
MAYBE THEY WERE TRYING TO BRING HER BACK WHEN WE SAW THEM.
I SEE.
WAHHH! I DON'T WANNA!
I WANNA PLAY MORE!!
YOU ARE A TEACHER! YOU HAVE TO SAY "NO" IN SITUATIONS LIKE THESE...
PUNISHING YOU WON'T RESOLVE THIS. IT'S A GRAVE PROBLEM, ONE THAT WILL AFFECT THE VERY EXISTENCE OF ANIMALIUM...
I'M TERRIBLY SORRY, DIRECTOR!!

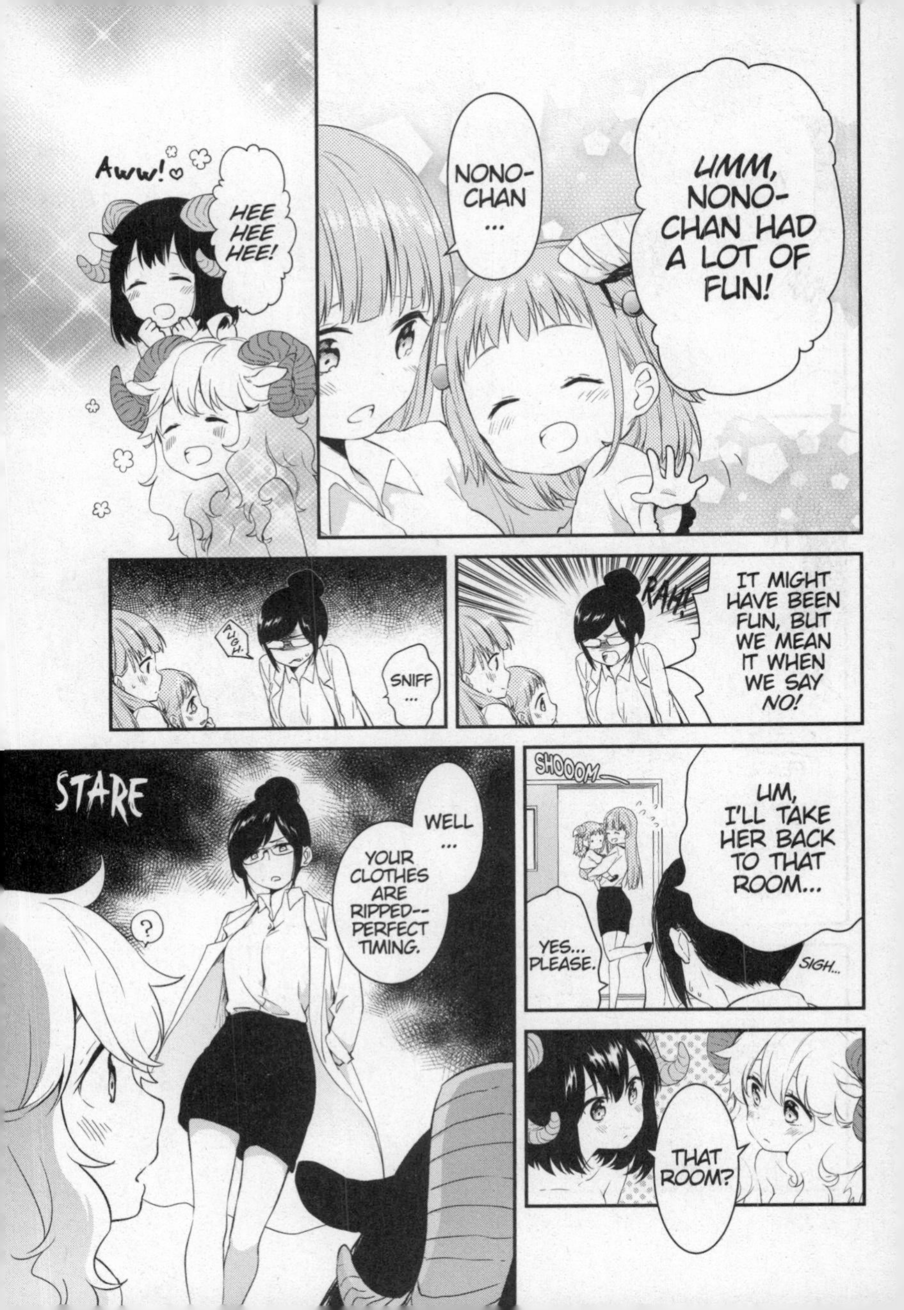
UMM, NONO-CHAN HAD A LOT OF FUN!
NONO-CHAN ...
HEE HEE HEE!
Aww!
RAH!
IT MIGHT HAVE BEEN FUN, BUT WE MEAN IT WHEN WE SAY NO!
AUGH.
SNIFF ...
SHOOOM
UM, I'LL TAKE HER BACK TO THAT ROOM...
YES... PLEASE.
SIGH...
THAT ROOM?
STARE
WELL ...
YOUR CLOTHES ARE RIPPED-- PERFECT TIMING.
?

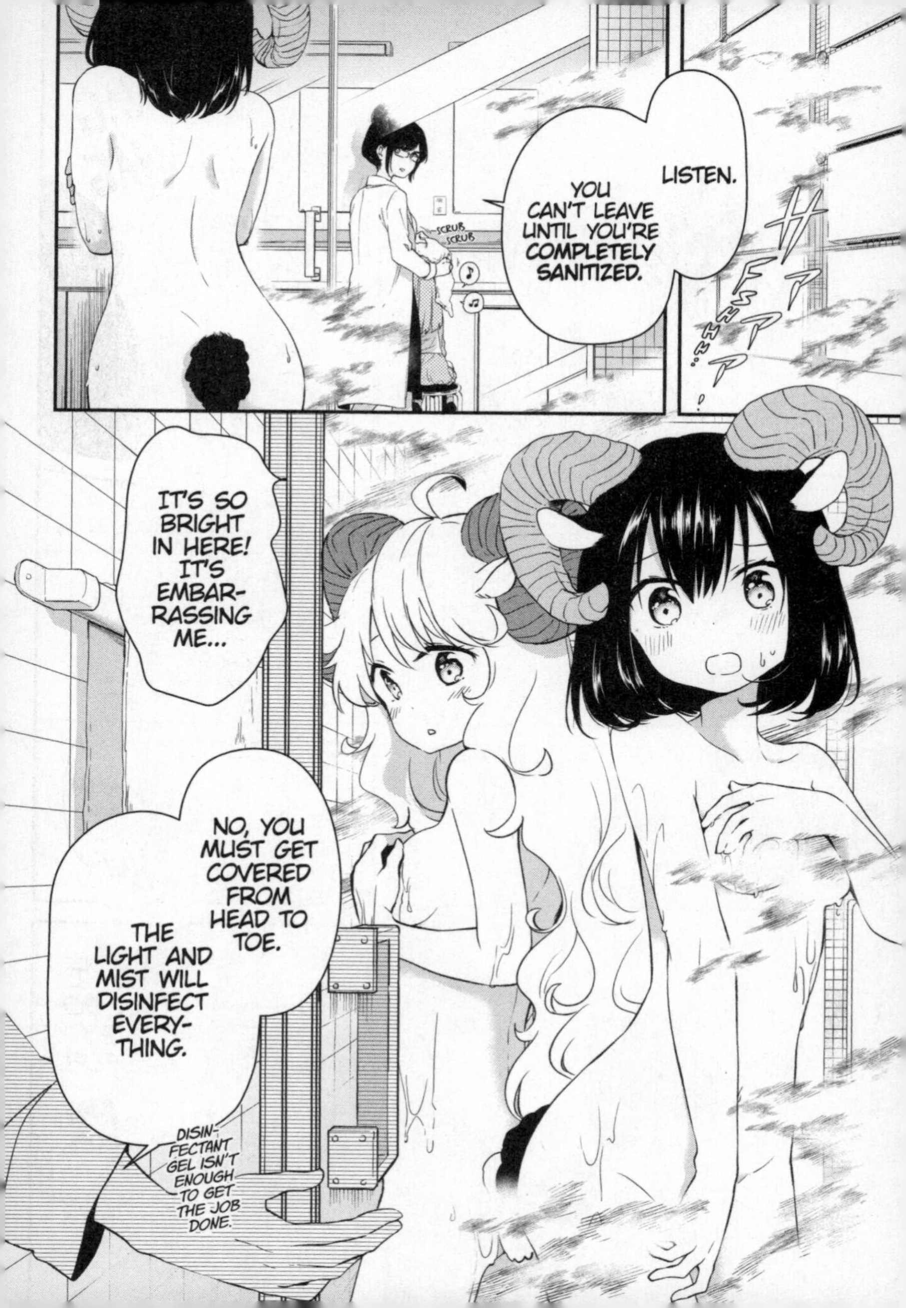
LISTEN.
YOU CAN'T LEAVE UNTIL YOU'RE COMPLETELY SANITIZED.
FSHHH...
SCRUB SCRUB
IT'S SO BRIGHT IN HERE! IT'S EMBARRASSING ME...
NO, YOU MUST GET COVERED FROM HEAD TO TOE.
THE LIGHT AND MIST WILL DISINFECT EVERYTHING.
DISINFECTANT GEL ISN'T ENOUGH TO GET THE JOB DONE.

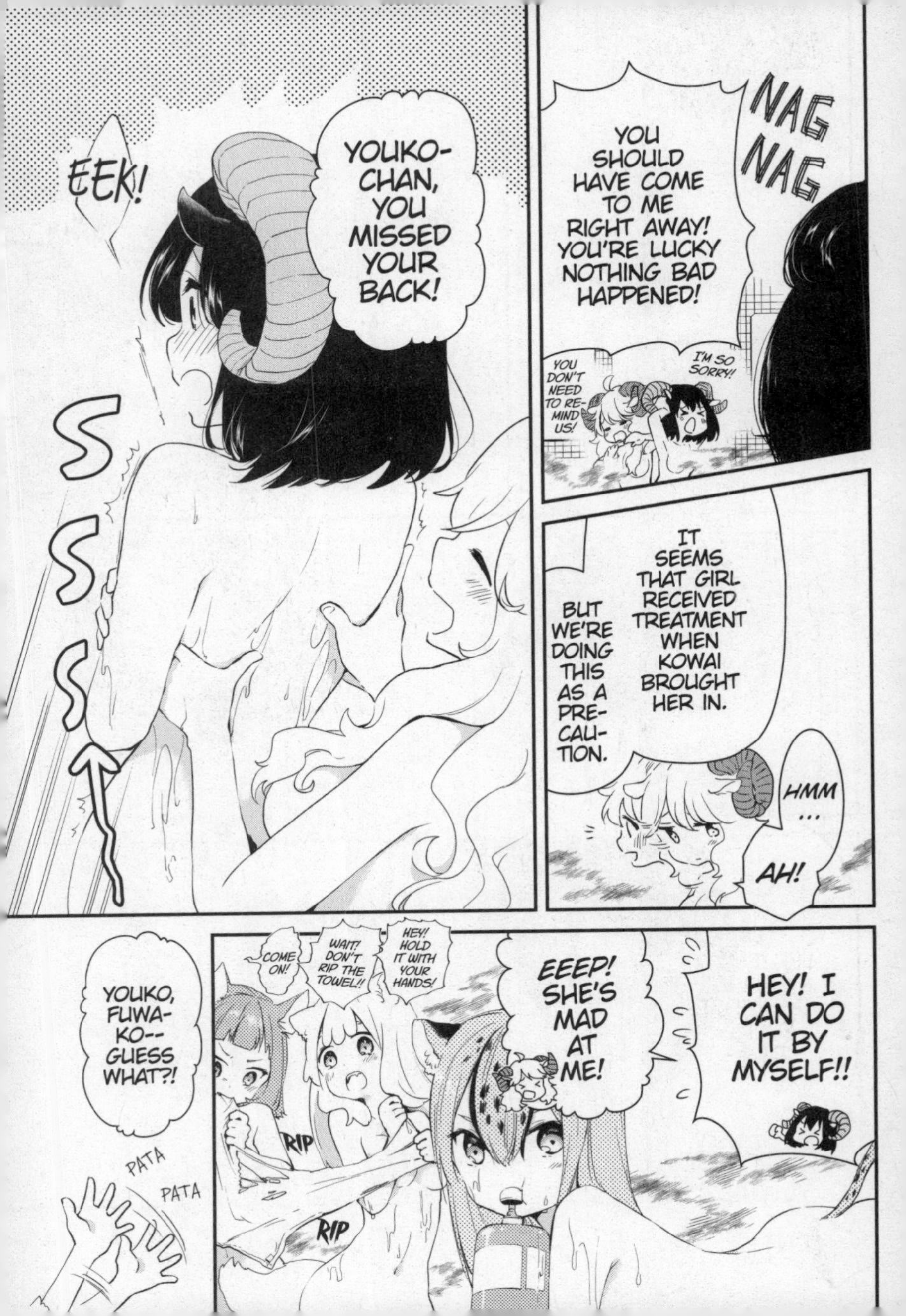
NAG NAG
YOU SHOULD HAVE COME TO ME RIGHT AWAY! YOU'RE LUCKY NOTHING BAD HAPPENED!
I'M SO SORRY!!
YOU DON'T NEED TO RE-MIND US!
IT SEEMS THAT GIRL RECEIVED TREATMENT WHEN KOWAI BROUGHT HER IN.
BUT WE'RE DOING THIS AS A PRE-CAU-TION.
HMM...
AH!
YOUKO-CHAN, YOU MISSED YOUR BACK!
EEK!
SSS
HEY! I CAN DO IT BY MYSELF!!
EEEP! SHE'S MAD AT ME!
HEY! HOLD IT WITH YOUR HANDS!
WAIT! DON'T RIP THE TOWEL!!
COME ON!
RIP
RIP
YOUKO, FUWA-KO-- GUESS WHAT?!
PATA
PATA

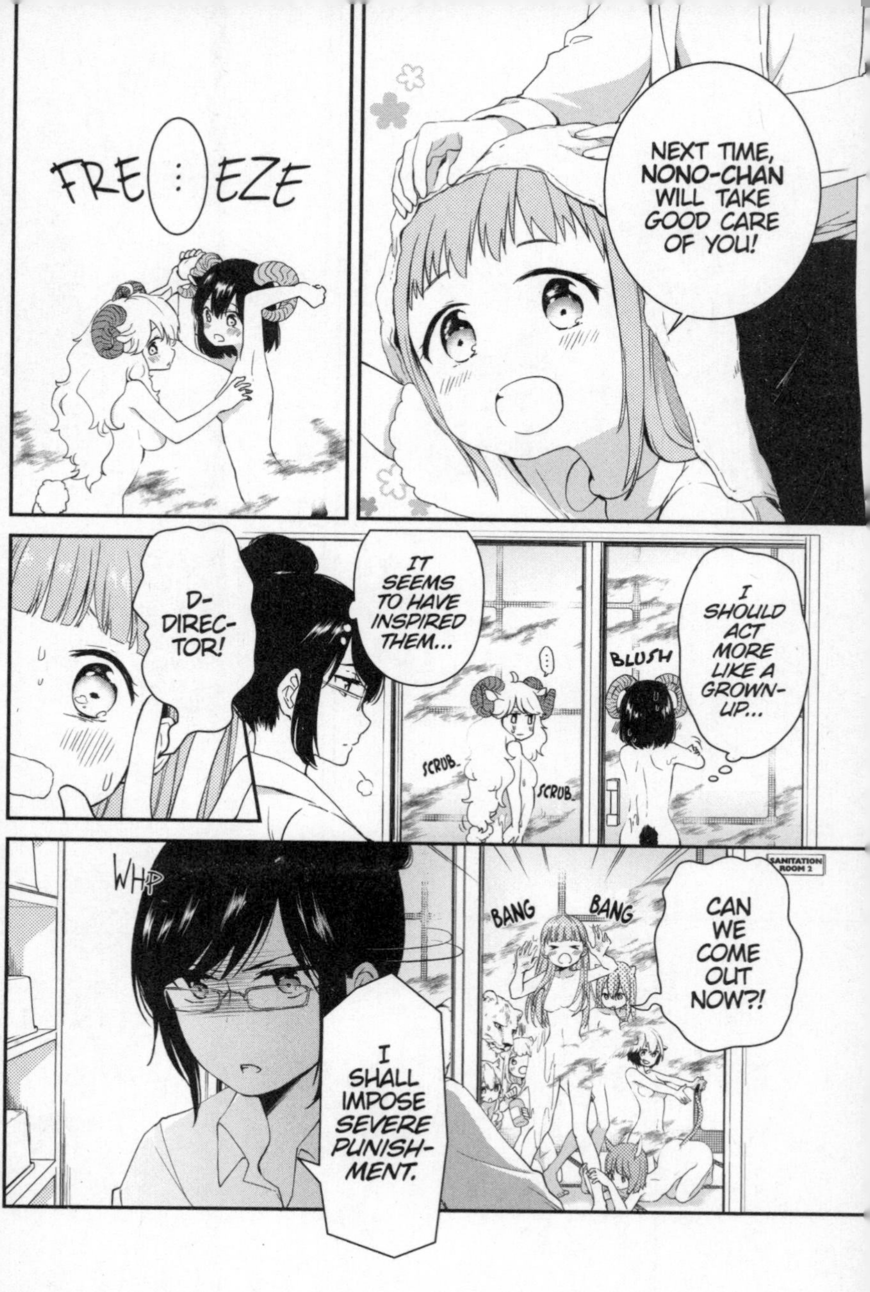
NEXT TIME, NONO-CHAN WILL TAKE GOOD CARE OF YOU!
FRE EZE
…
I SHOULD ACT MORE LIKE A GROWN-UP...
BLUSH
…
SCRUB
SCRUB
IT SEEMS TO HAVE INSPIRED THEM...
D-DIRECTOR!
SANITATION ROOM 2
BANG
BANG
CAN WE COME OUT NOW?!
WHIP
I SHALL IMPOSE SEVERE PUNISHMENT.

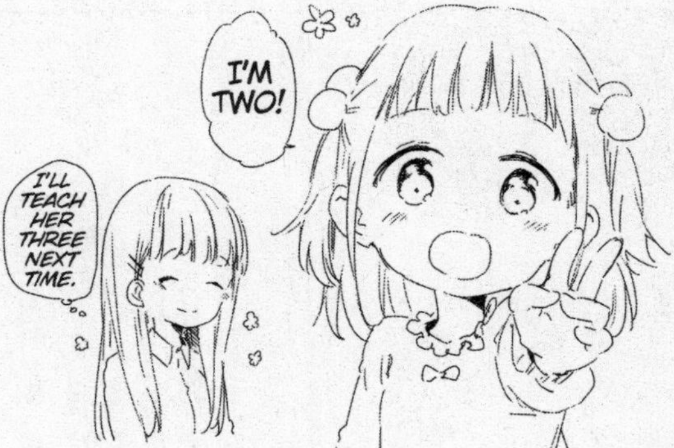
I'M TWO!
I'LL TEACH HER THREE NEXT TIME.

DNA
DOESN'T
TELL US.

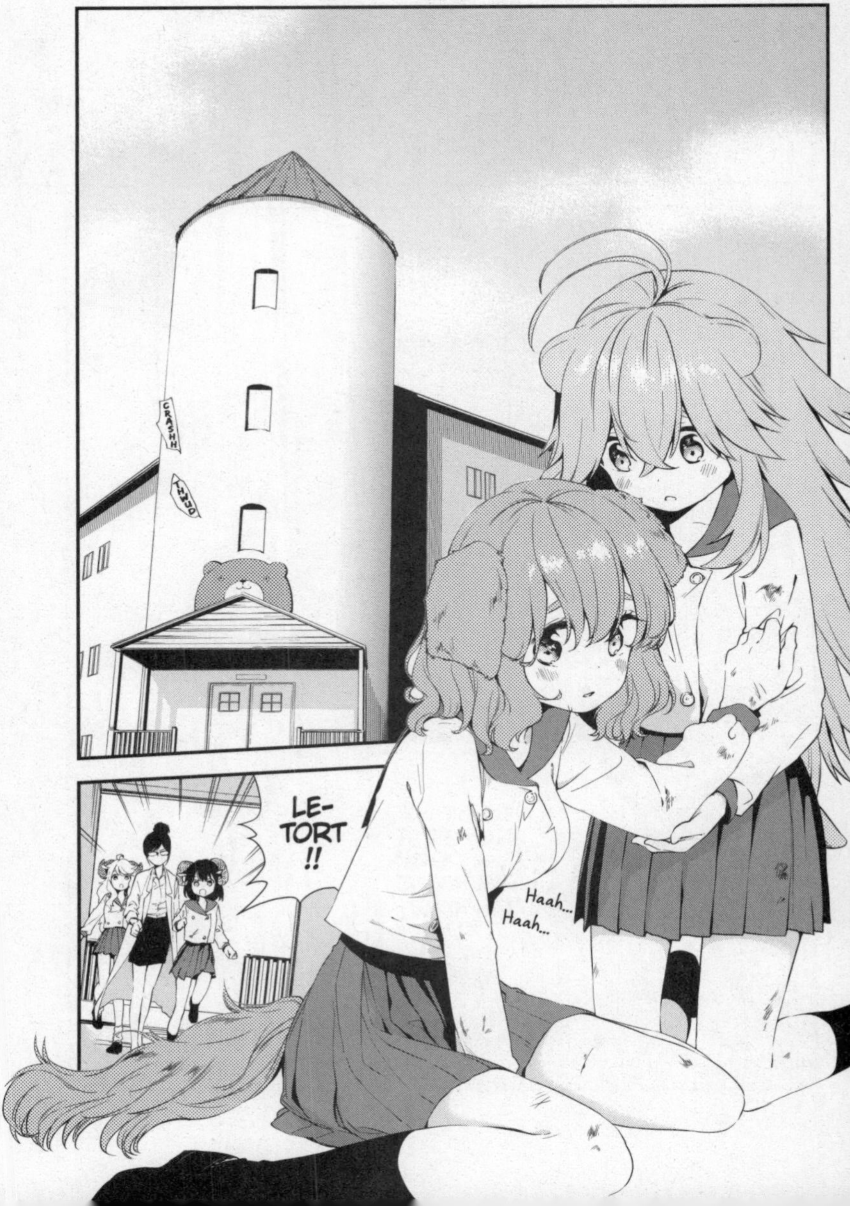
CRASHH
THWUD
LE-TORT!!
Haah...
Haah...

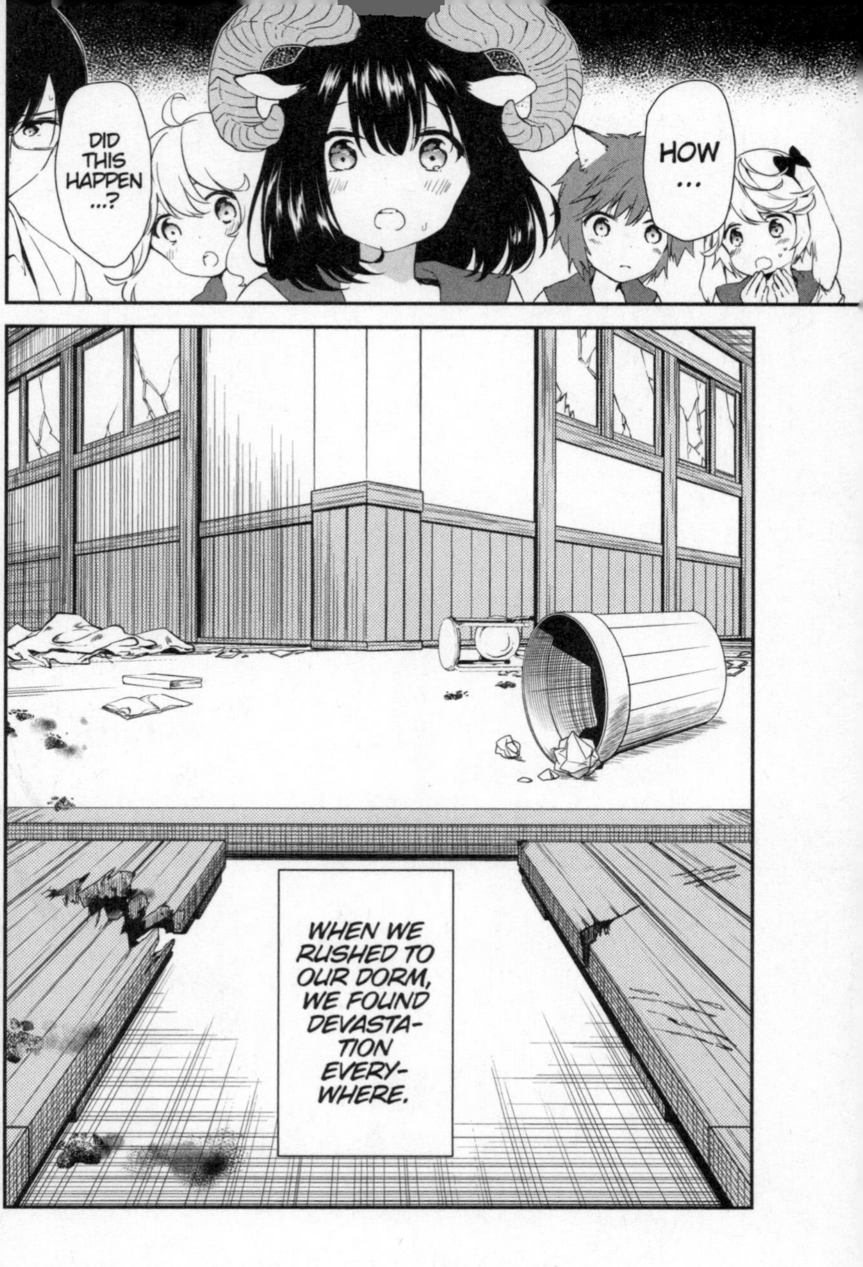
HOW ...
DID THIS HAPPEN ...?
WHEN WE RUSHED TO OUR DORM, WE FOUND DEVASTATION EVERYWHERE.

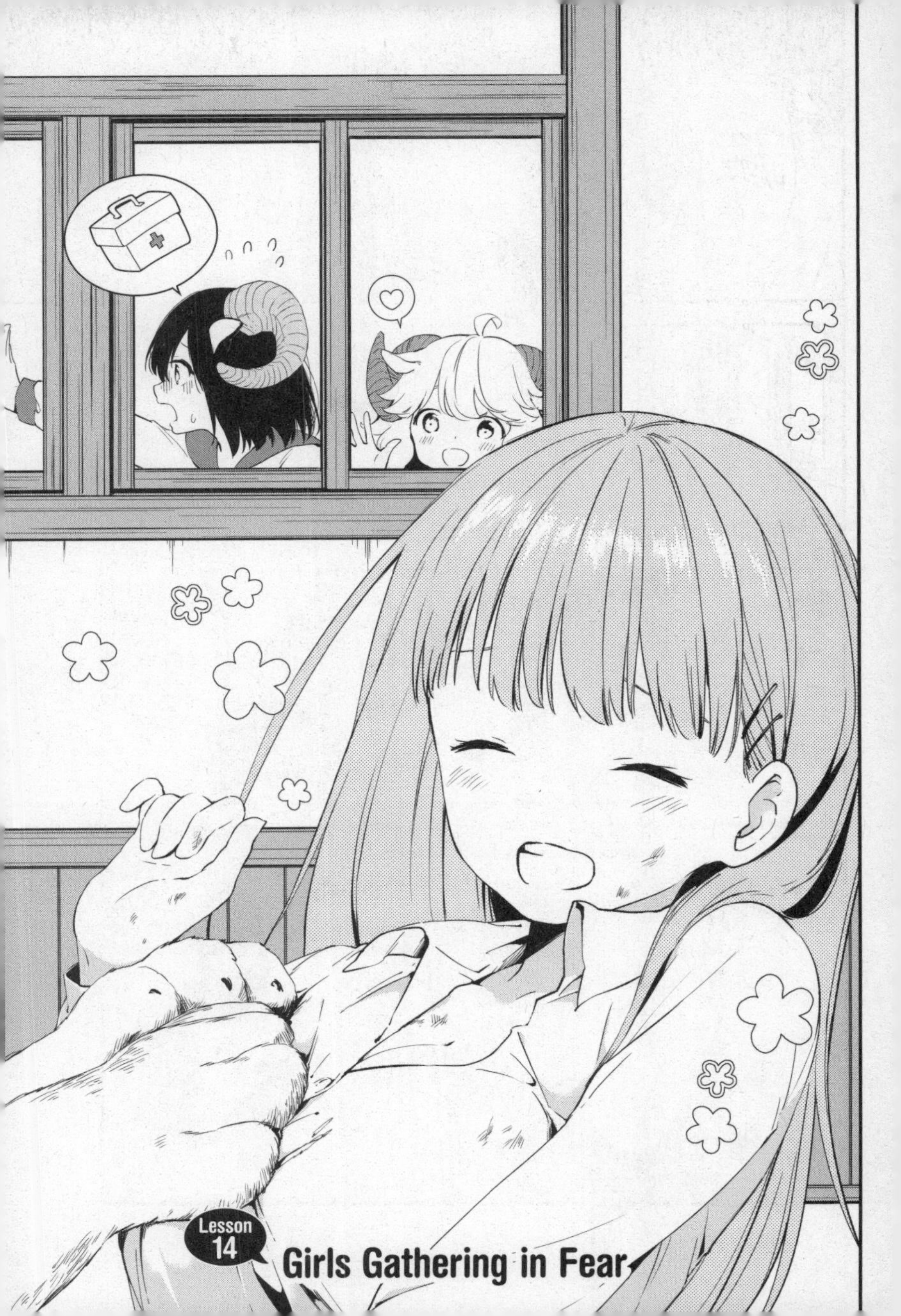
Lesson 14
Girls Gathering in Fear

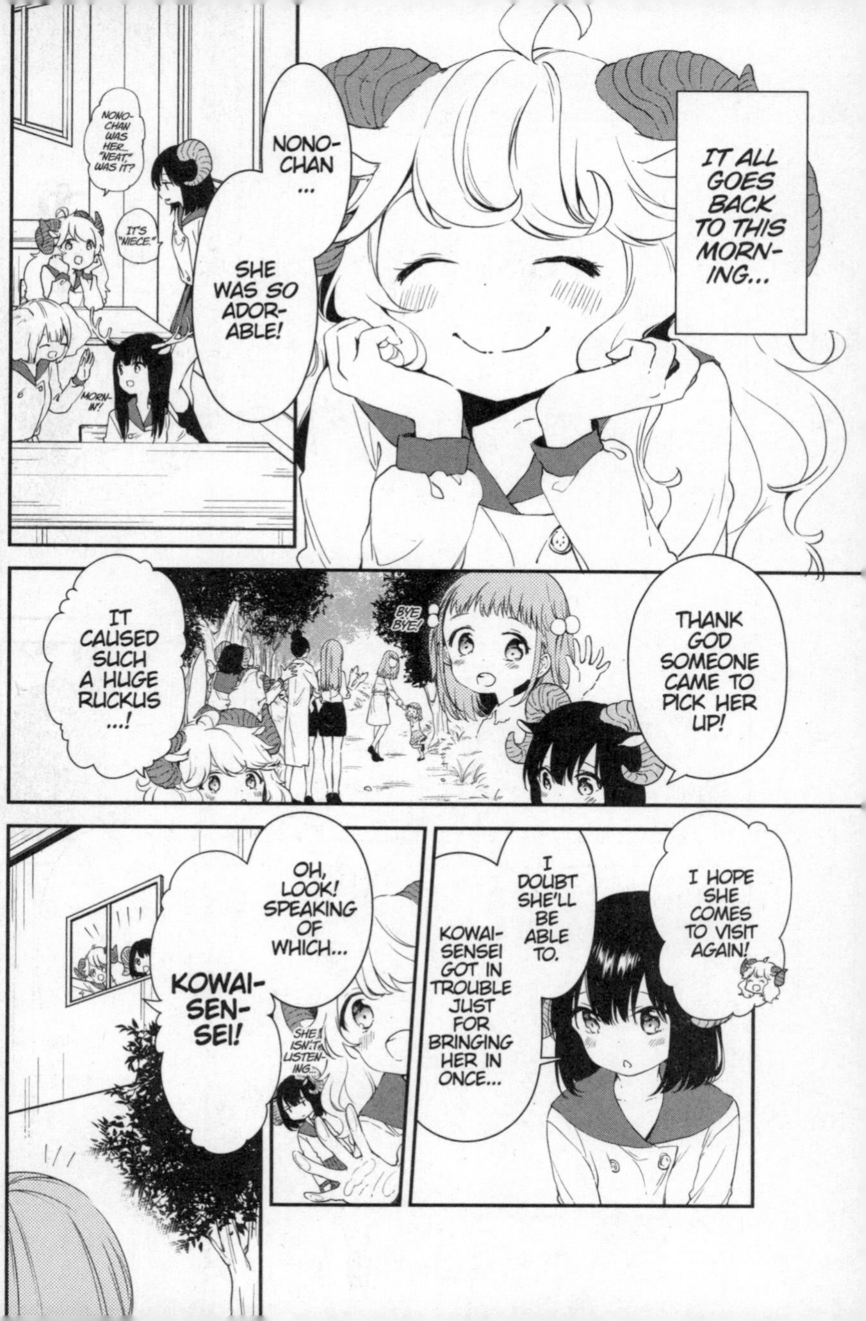
IT ALL GOES BACK TO THIS MORNING...
NONO-CHAN...
SHE WAS SO ADORABLE!
NONO-CHAN WAS HER... "NEAT," WAS IT?
IT'S "NIECE."
MORNIN'!
THANK GOD SOMEONE CAME TO PICK HER UP!
BYE BYE!
IT CAUSED SUCH A HUGE RUCKUS...!
I HOPE SHE COMES TO VISIT AGAIN!
I DOUBT SHE'LL BE ABLE TO.
KOWAI-SENSEI GOT IN TROUBLE JUST FOR BRINGING HER IN ONCE...
OH, LOOK! SPEAKING OF WHICH...
KOWAI-SENSEI!
SHE ISN'T LISTENING...

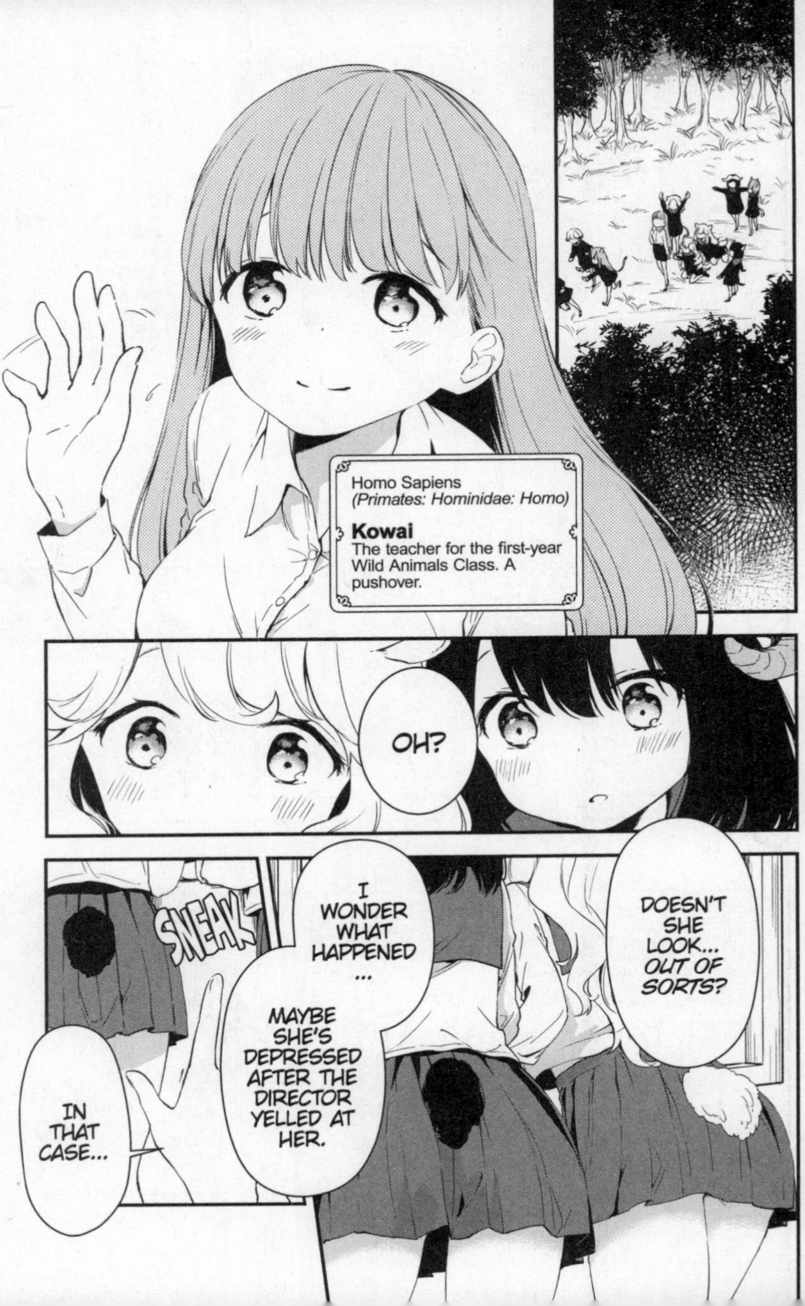
Homo Sapiens
(Primates: Hominidae: Homo)
Kowai
The teacher for the first-year Wild Animals Class. A pushover.
OH?
DOESN'T SHE LOOK... OUT OF SORTS?
I WONDER WHAT HAPPENED ...
SNEAK
MAYBE SHE'S DEPRESSED AFTER THE DIRECTOR YELLED AT HER.
IN THAT CASE...

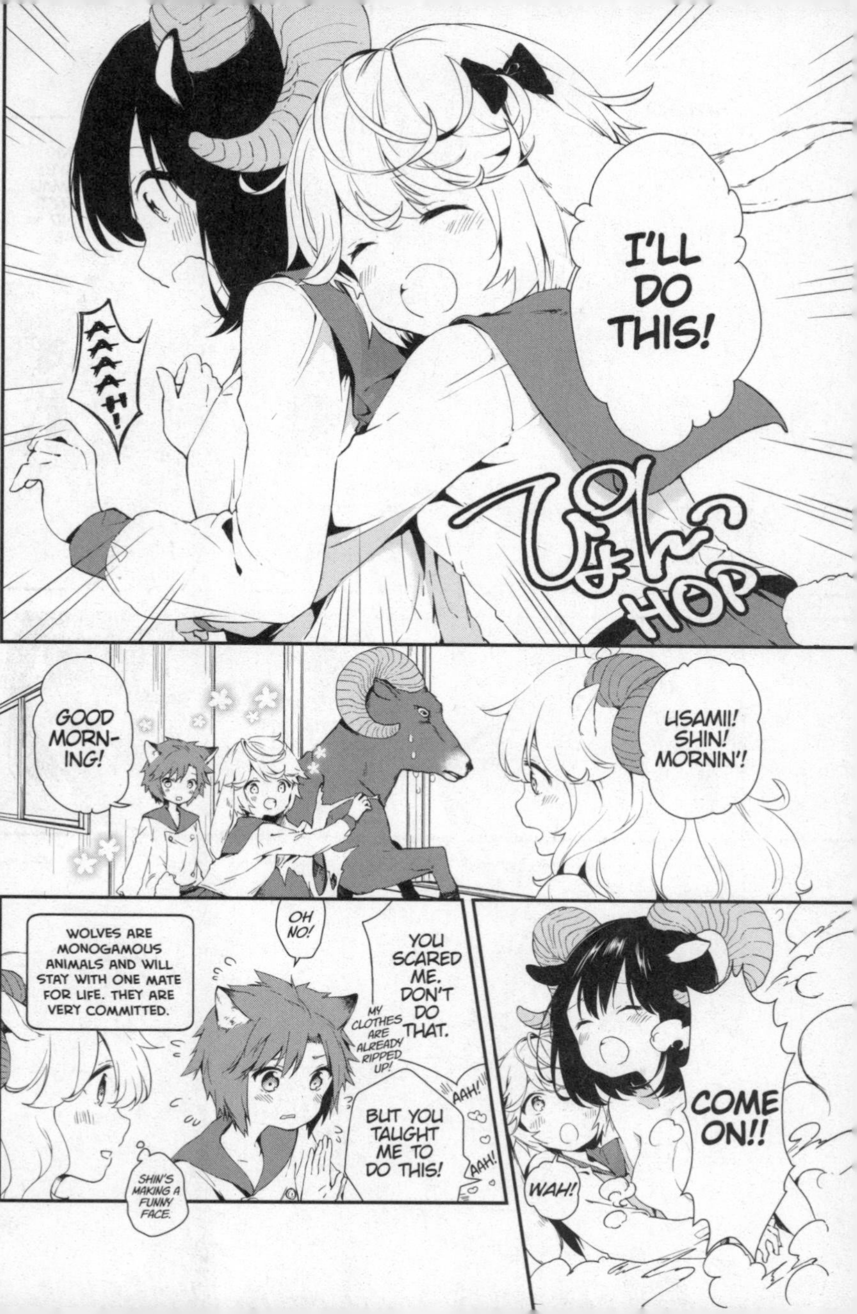

I'LL DO THIS!
ぴょん
HOP
AAAAH!
USAMII! SHIN! MORNIN'!
GOOD MORNING!
COME ON!!
WAH!
YOU SCARED ME. DON'T DO THAT.
OH NO!
MY CLOTHES ARE ALREADY RIPPED UP!
BUT YOU TAUGHT ME TO DO THIS!
AAH!
AAH!
WOLVES ARE MONOGAMOUS ANIMALS AND WILL STAY WITH ONE MATE FOR LIFE. THEY ARE VERY COMMITTED.
SHIN'S MAKING A FUNNY FACE.

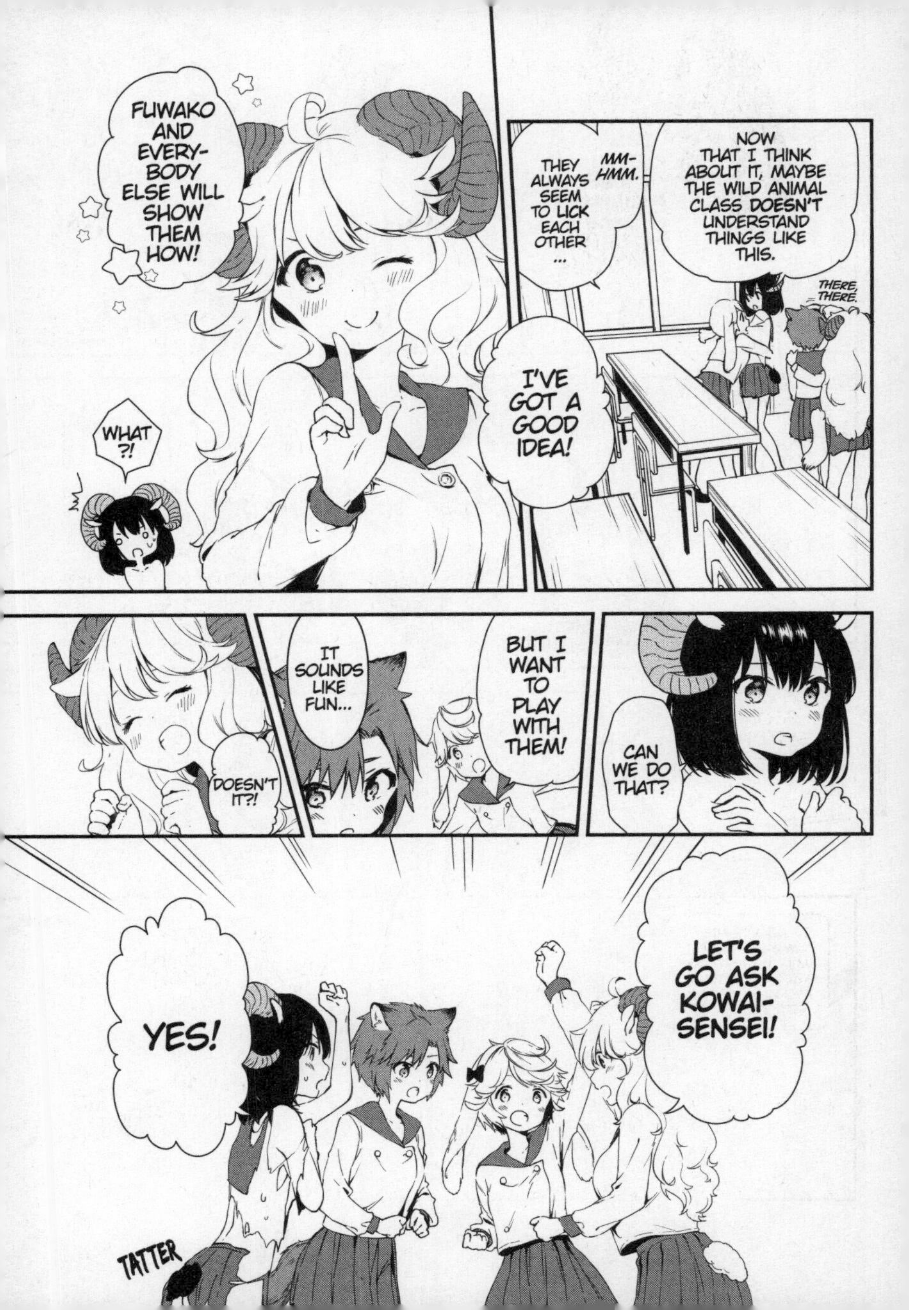
NOW THAT I THINK ABOUT IT, MAYBE THE WILD ANIMAL CLASS DOESN'T UNDERSTAND THINGS LIKE THIS.
MM-HMM.
THEY ALWAYS SEEM TO LICK EACH OTHER ...
THERE, THERE.
I'VE GOT A GOOD IDEA!
FUWAKO AND EVERY-BODY ELSE WILL SHOW THEM HOW!
WHAT ?!
CAN WE DO THAT?
BUT I WANT TO PLAY WITH THEM!
IT SOUNDS LIKE FUN...
DOESN'T IT?!
LET'S GO ASK KOWAI-SENSEI!
YES!
TATTER

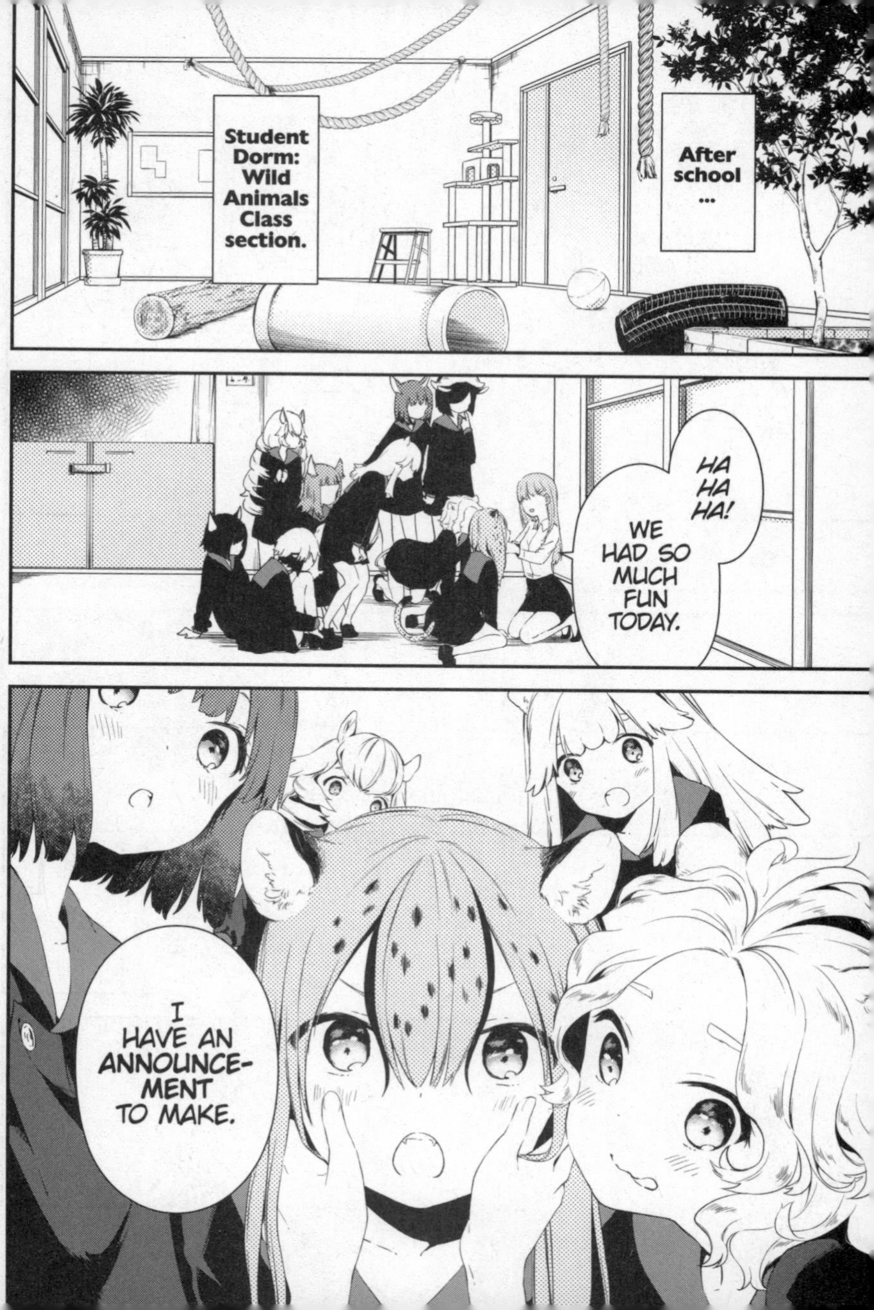
After school ...
Student Dorm: Wild Animals Class section.
HA HA HA! WE HAD SO MUCH FUN TODAY.
I HAVE AN ANNOUNCE-MENT TO MAKE.

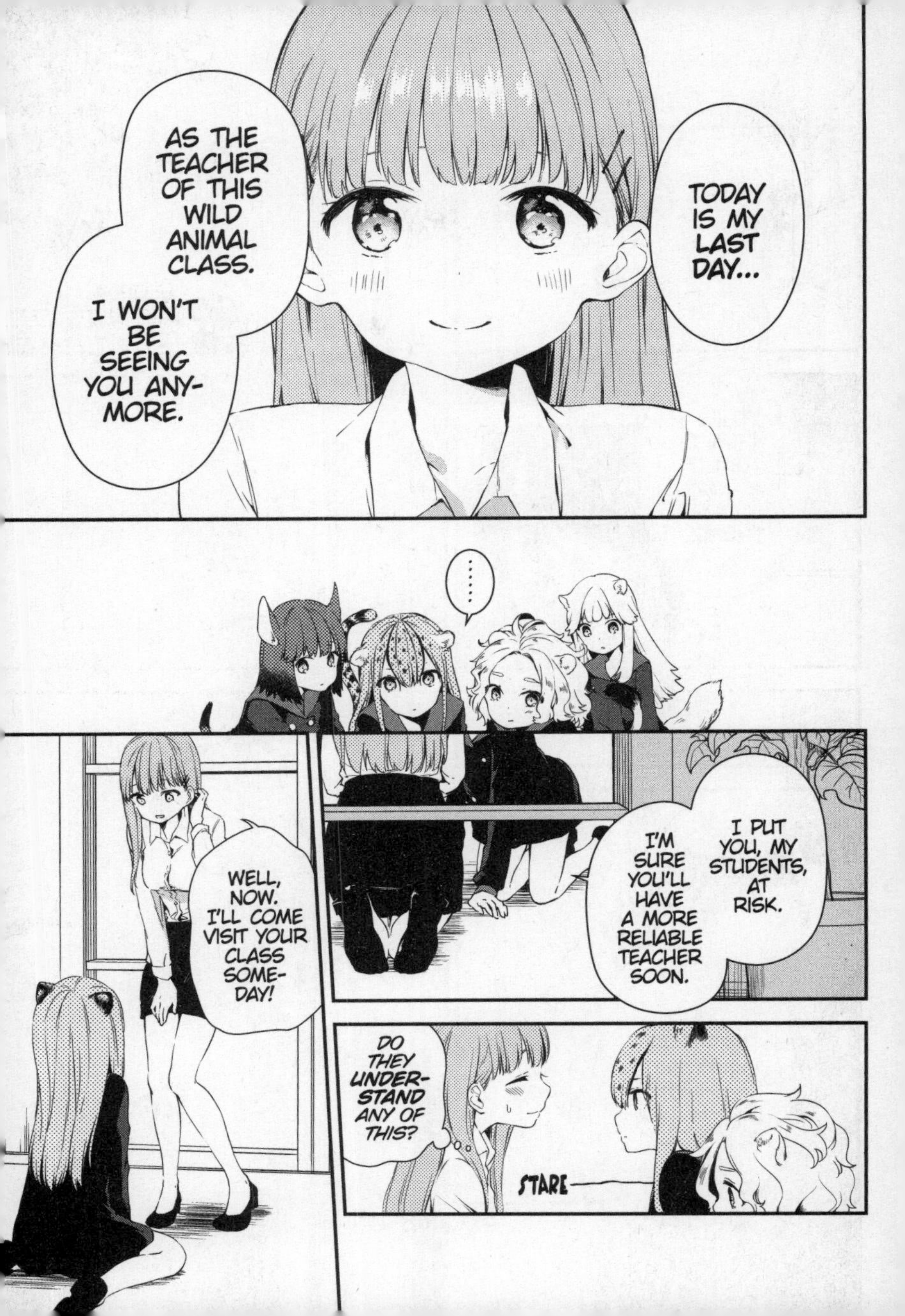
TODAY IS MY LAST DAY...
AS THE TEACHER OF THIS WILD ANIMAL CLASS.
I WON'T BE SEEING YOU ANY-MORE.
......
I PUT YOU, MY STUDENTS, AT RISK.
I'M SURE YOU'LL HAVE A MORE RELIABLE TEACHER SOON.
STARE
DO THEY UNDER-STAND ANY OF THIS?
WELL, NOW. I'LL COME VISIT YOUR CLASS SOME-DAY!

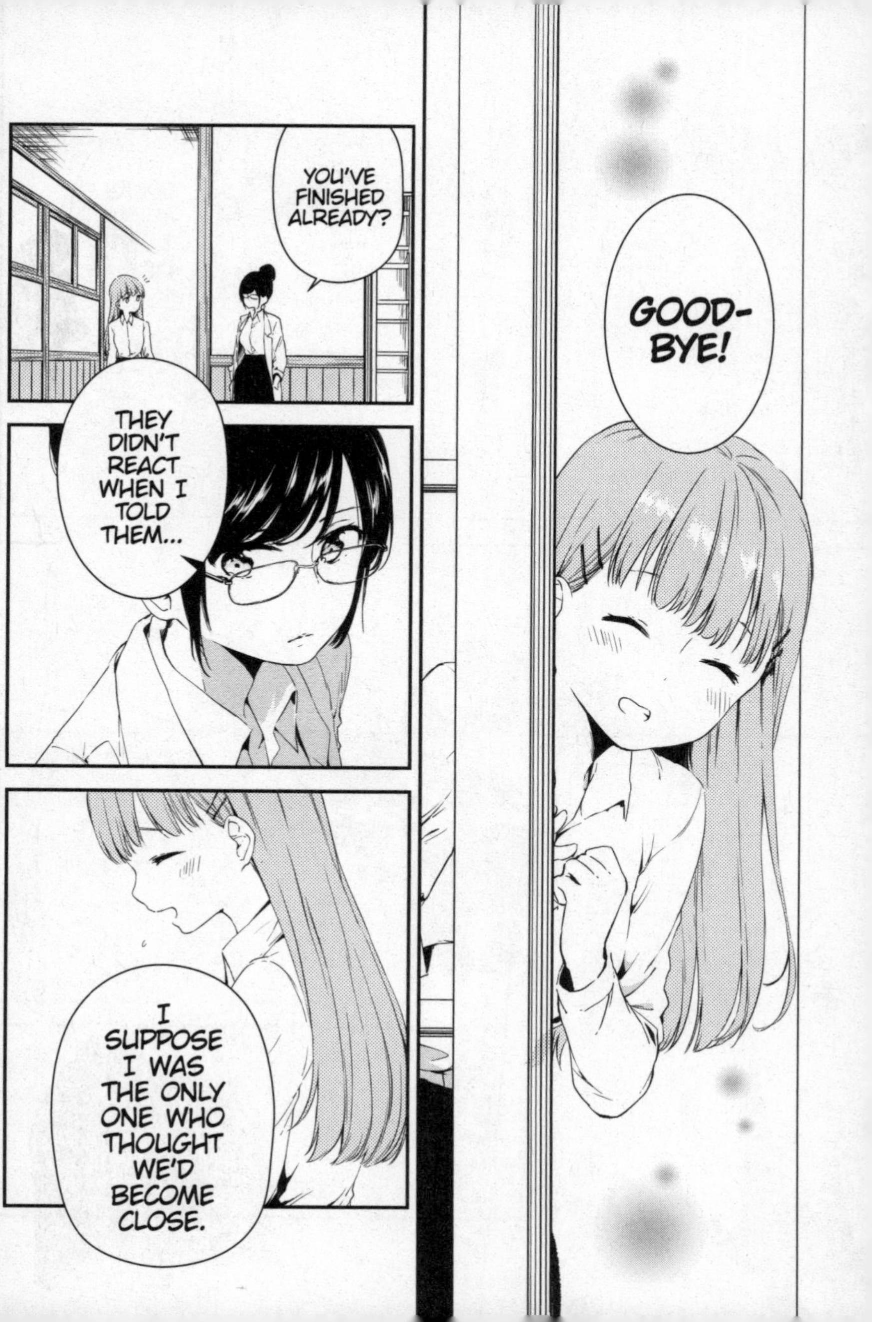
GOOD-BYE!
YOU'VE FINISHED ALREADY?
THEY DIDN'T REACT WHEN I TOLD THEM...
I SUPPOSE I WAS THE ONLY ONE WHO THOUGHT WE'D BECOME CLOSE.

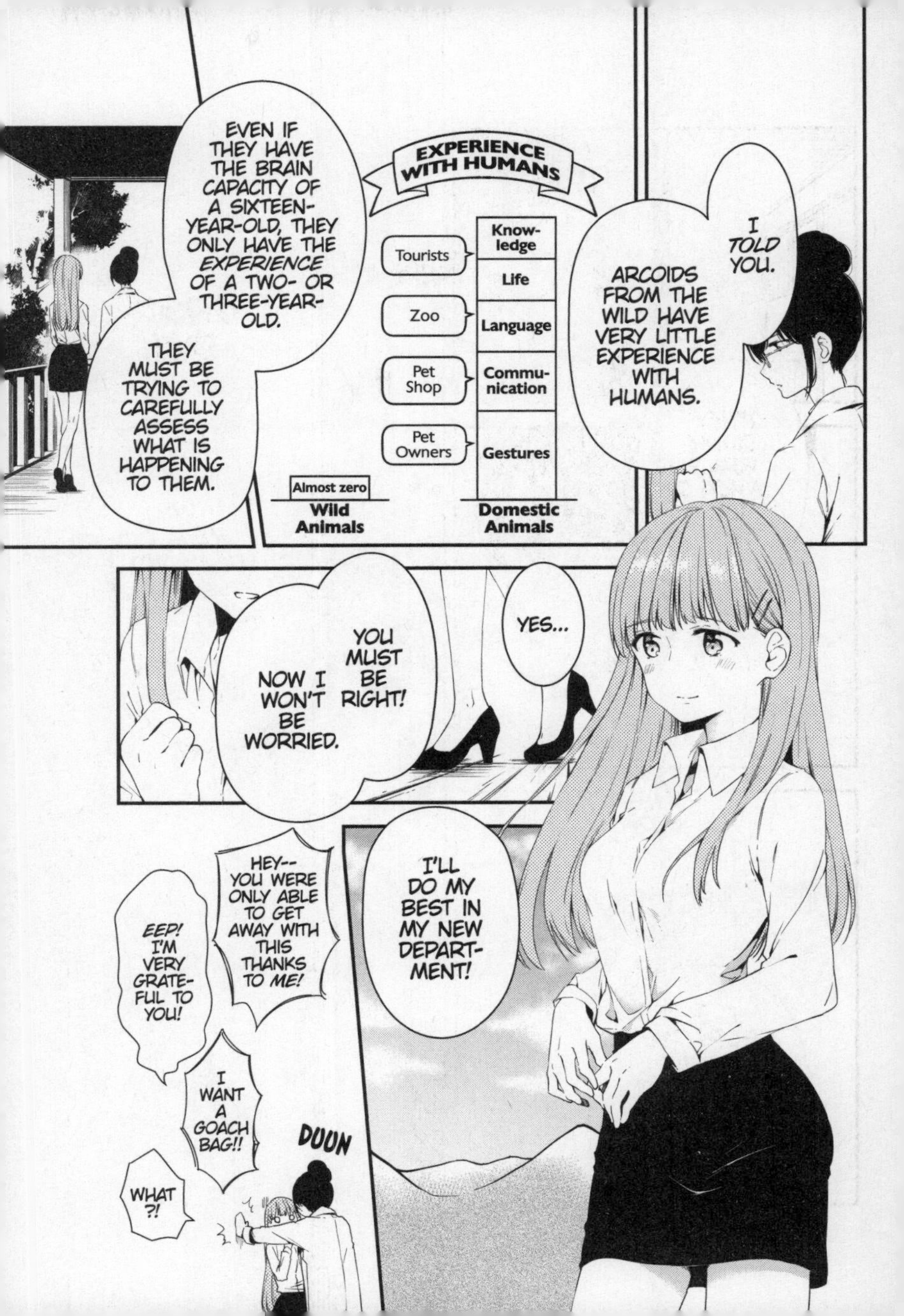

I TOLD YOU.
ARCOIDS FROM THE WILD HAVE VERY LITTLE EXPERIENCE WITH HUMANS.
EXPERIENCE WITH HUMANS
Knowledge
Life
Language
Communication
Gestures
Tourists
Zoo
Pet Shop
Pet Owners
Almost zero
Wild Animals
Domestic Animals
EVEN IF THEY HAVE THE BRAIN CAPACITY OF A SIXTEEN-YEAR-OLD, THEY ONLY HAVE THE *EXPERIENCE* OF A TWO- OR THREE-YEAR-OLD.
THEY MUST BE TRYING TO CAREFULLY ASSESS WHAT IS HAPPENING TO THEM.
YES...
YOU MUST BE RIGHT!
NOW I WON'T BE WORRIED.
I'LL DO MY BEST IN MY NEW DEPARTMENT!
HEY-- YOU WERE ONLY ABLE TO GET AWAY WITH THIS THANKS TO *ME!*
EEP! I'M VERY GRATEFUL TO YOU!
I WANT A GOACH BAG!!
DUUN
WHAT?!

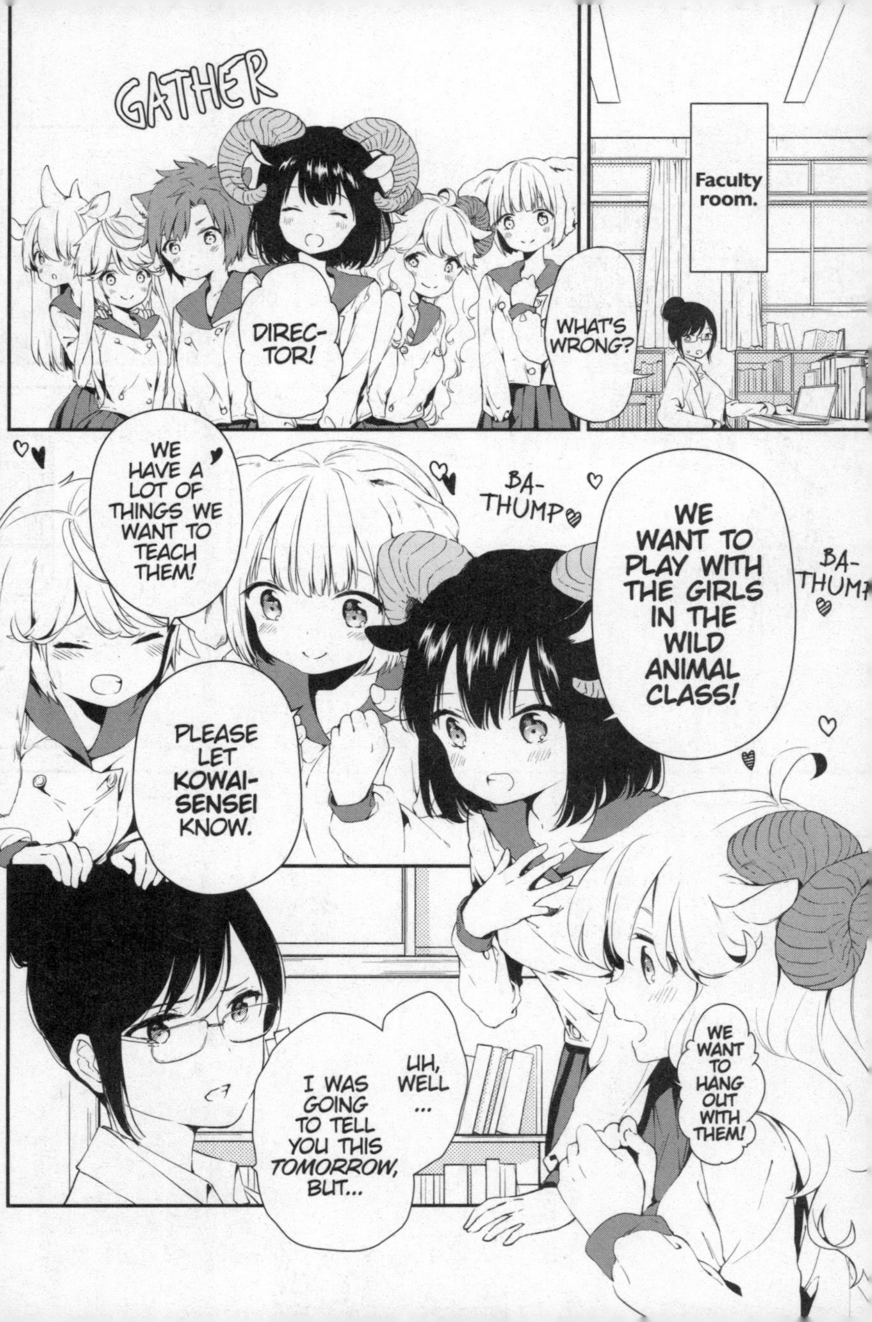
Faculty room.
GATHER
DIRECTOR!
WHAT'S WRONG?
BA-THUMP
WE WANT TO PLAY WITH THE GIRLS IN THE WILD ANIMAL CLASS!
BA-THUMP
WE HAVE A LOT OF THINGS WE WANT TO TEACH THEM!
PLEASE LET KOWAI-SENSEI KNOW.
WE WANT TO HANG OUT WITH THEM!
UH, WELL...
I WAS GOING TO TELL YOU THIS *TOMORROW*, BUT...

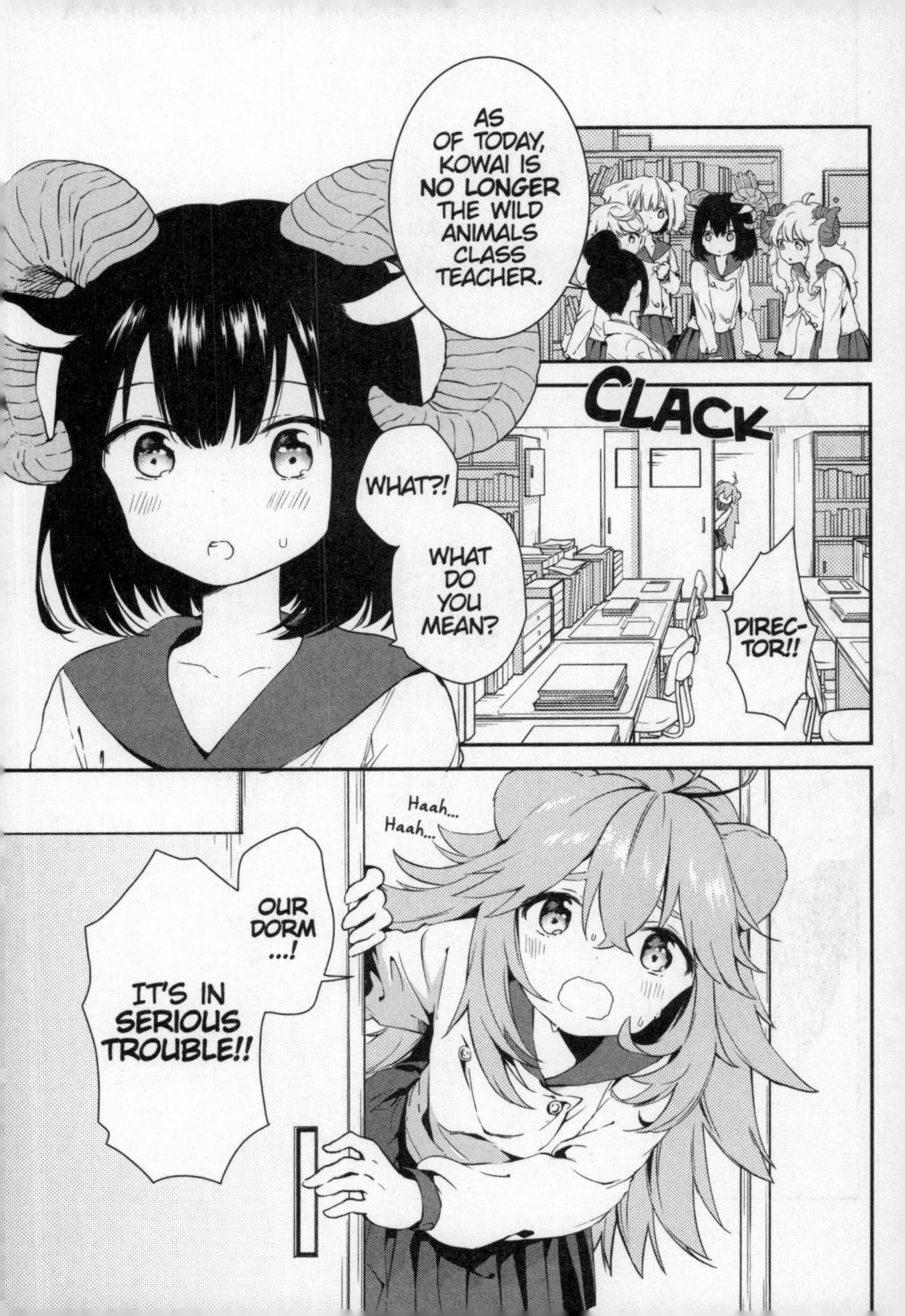

AS OF TODAY, KOWAI IS NO LONGER THE WILD ANIMALS CLASS TEACHER.
CLACK
DIRECTOR!!
WHAT?!
WHAT DO YOU MEAN?
Haah... Haah...
OUR DORM ...!
IT'S IN SERIOUS TROUBLE!!

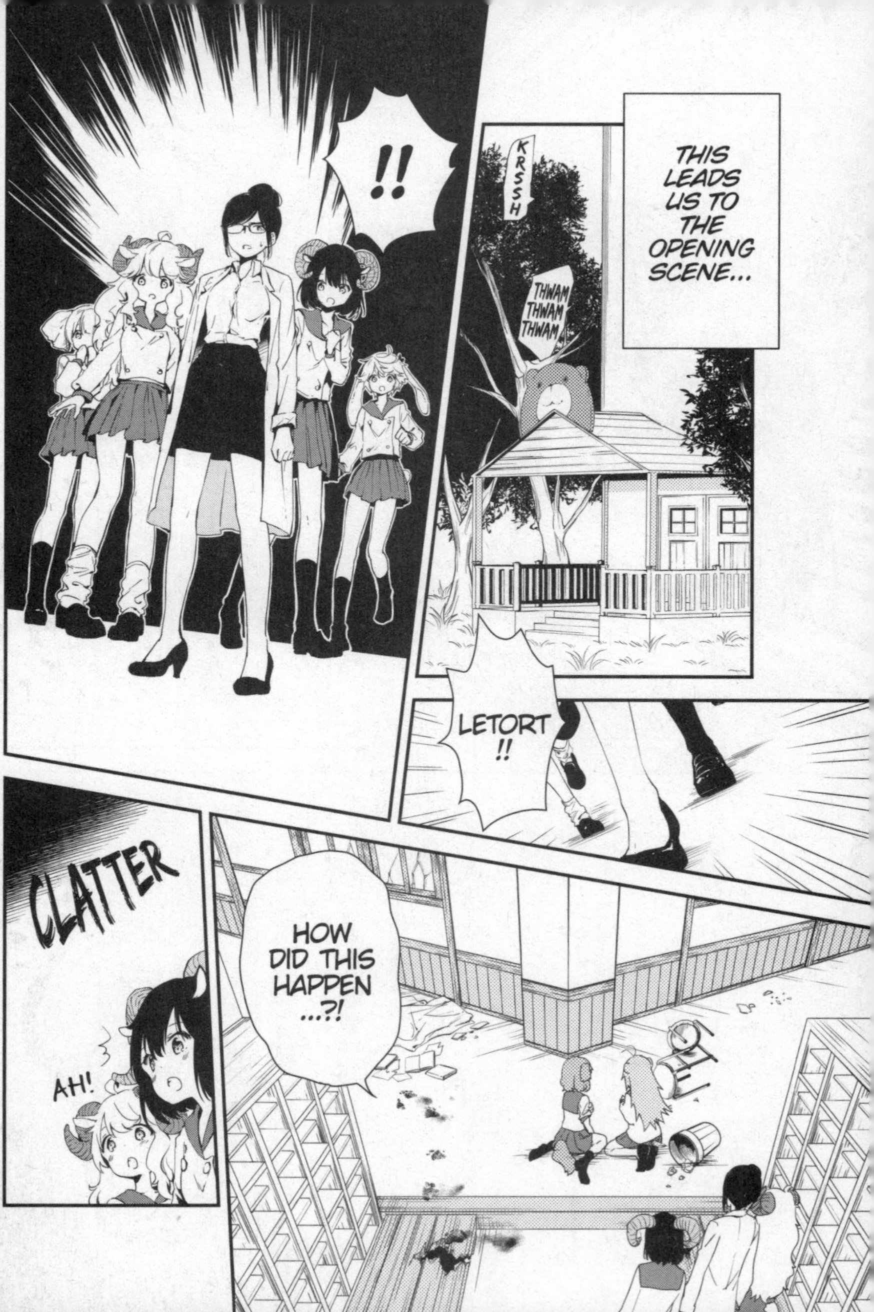
THIS LEADS US TO THE OPENING SCENE...
KRSSH
THWAM THWAM THWAM
!!
LETORT !!
HOW DID THIS HAPPEN ...?!
CLATTER
AH!

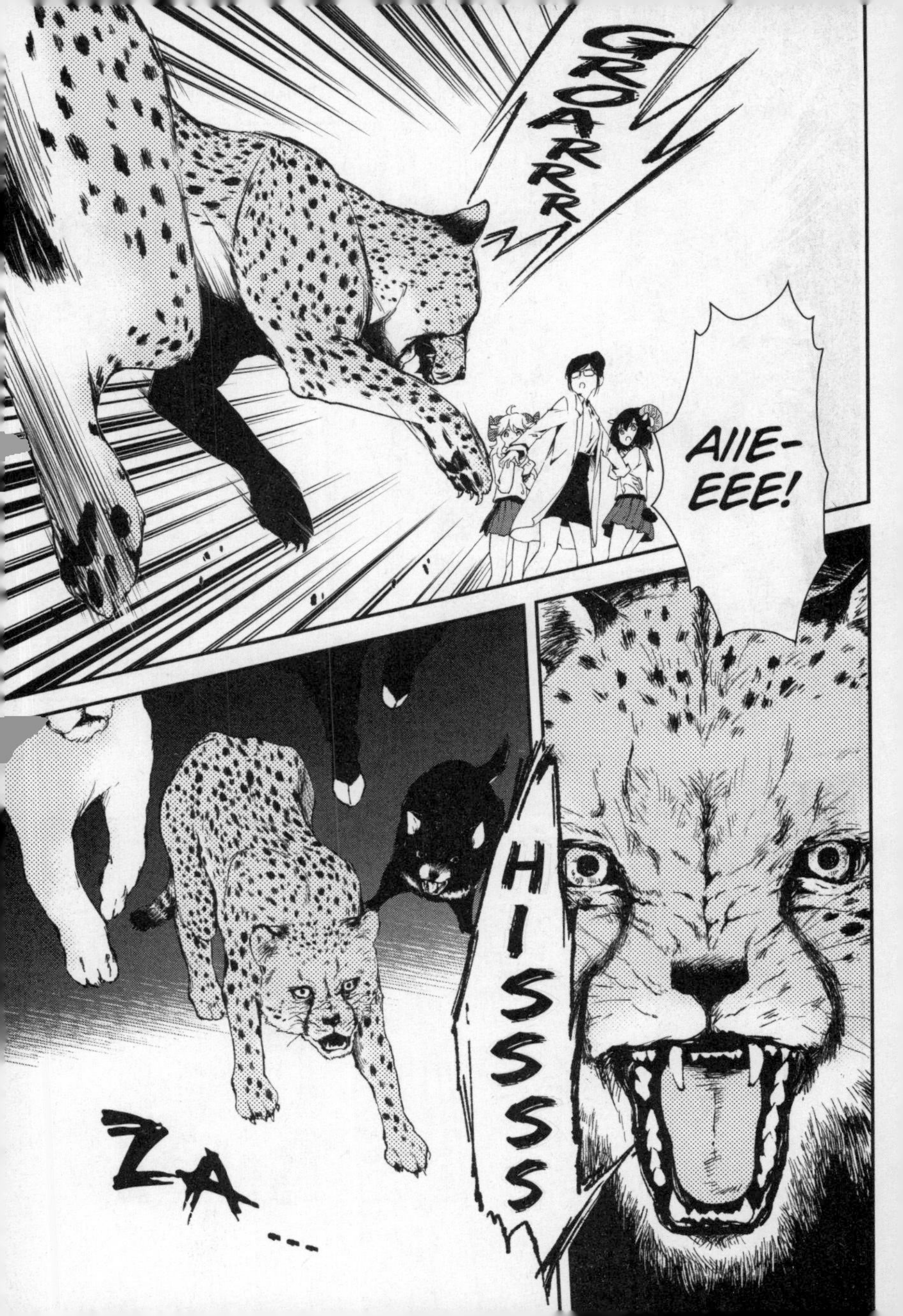
GROWL
GROARRR
AIIE-EEE!
HISSS
ZA...

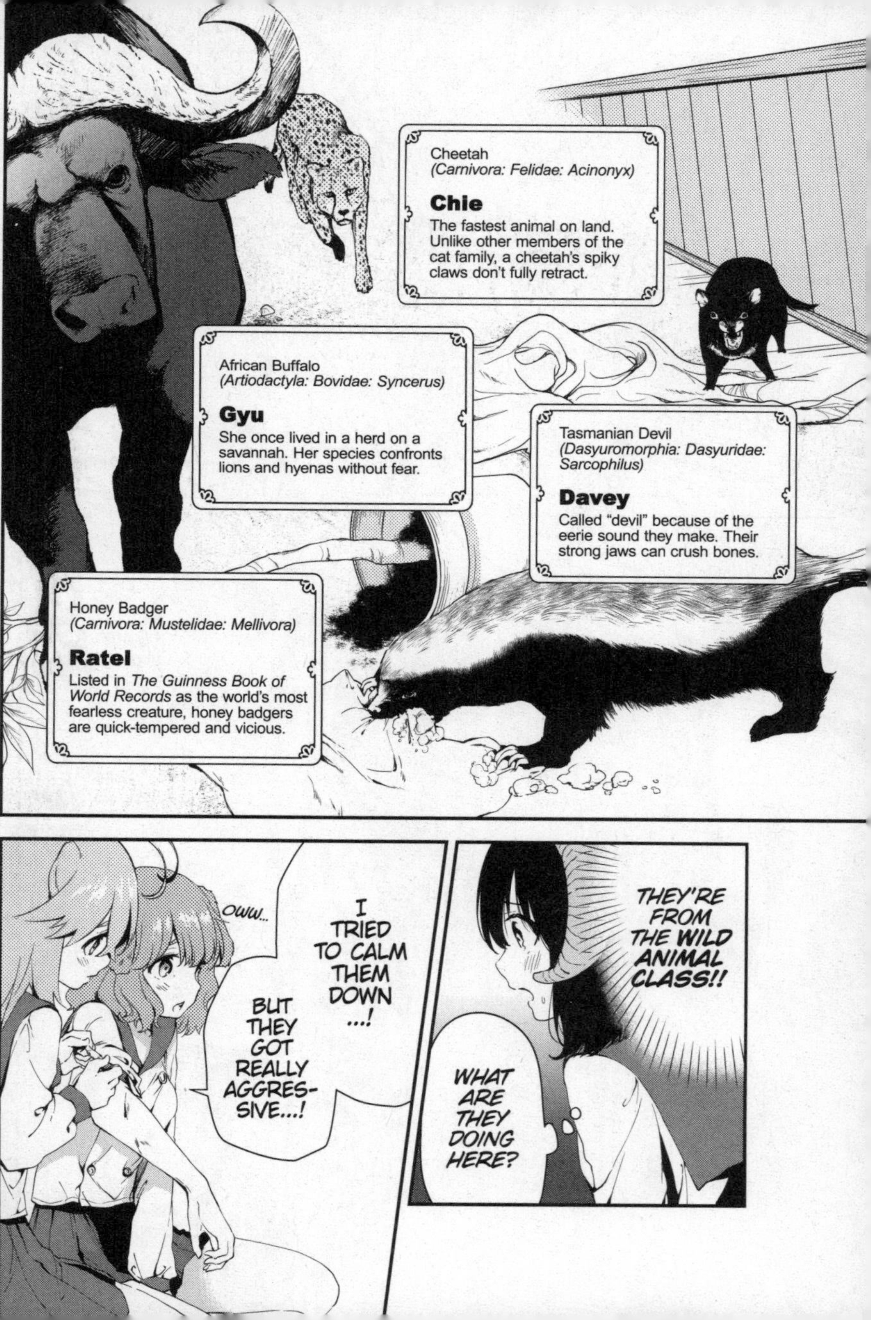
Cheetah
(Carnivora: Felidae: Acinonyx)
Chie
The fastest animal on land. Unlike other members of the cat family, a cheetah's spiky claws don't fully retract.
African Buffalo
(Artiodactyla: Bovidae: Syncerus)
Gyu
She once lived in a herd on a savannah. Her species confronts lions and hyenas without fear.
Tasmanian Devil
(Dasyuromorphia: Dasyuridae: Sarcophilus)
Davey
Called "devil" because of the eerie sound they make. Their strong jaws can crush bones.
Honey Badger
(Carnivora: Mustelidae: Mellivora)
Ratel
Listed in The Guinness Book of World Records as the world's most fearless creature, honey badgers are quick-tempered and vicious.
THEY'RE FROM THE WILD ANIMAL CLASS!!
WHAT ARE THEY DOING HERE?
OWW...
I TRIED TO CALM THEM DOWN...!
BUT THEY GOT REALLY AGGRES-SIVE...!

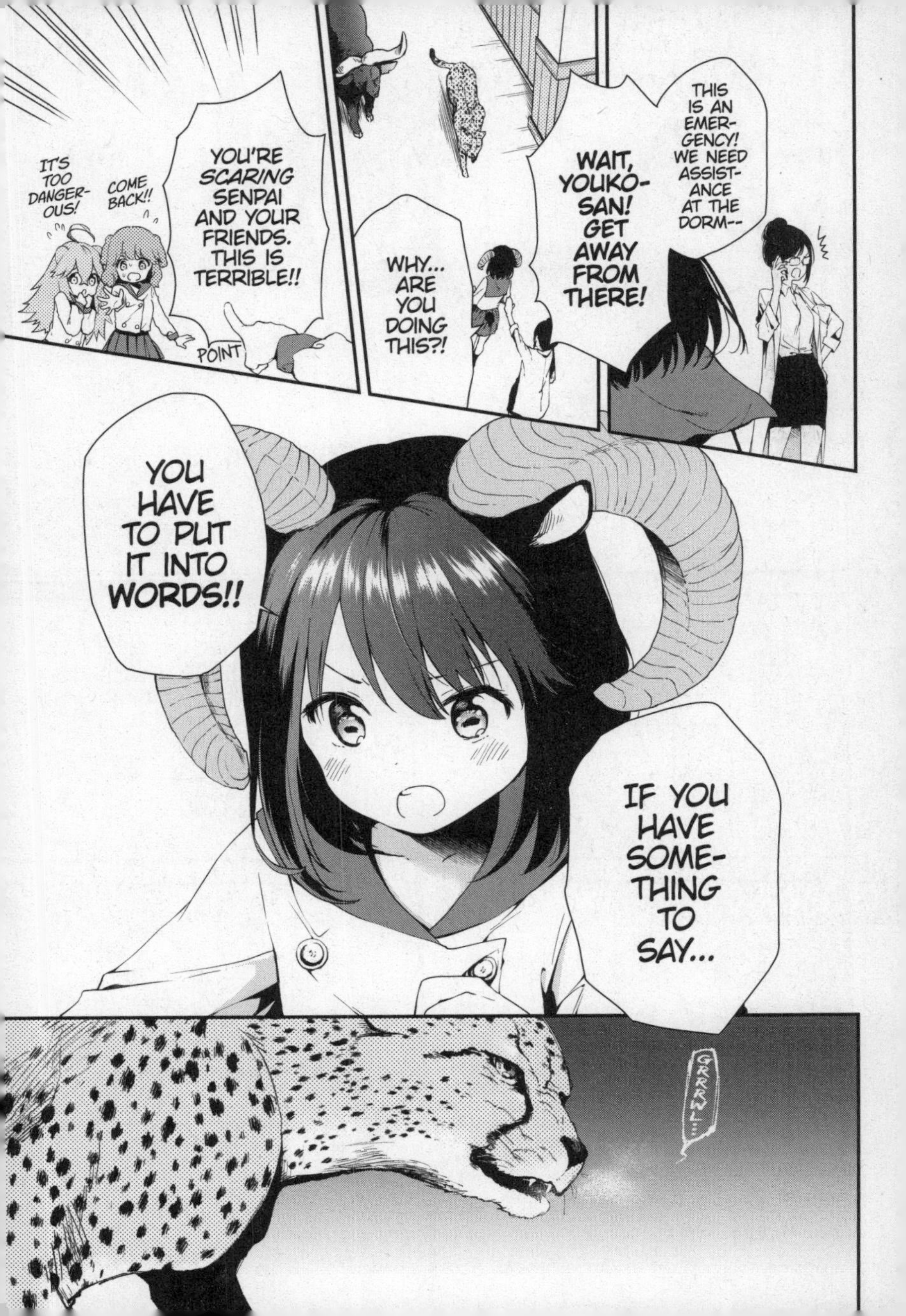

THIS IS AN EMERGENCY! WE NEED ASSISTANCE AT THE DORM--
WAIT, YOUKO-SAN! GET AWAY FROM THERE!
WHY... ARE YOU DOING THIS?!
YOU'RE SCARING SENPAI AND YOUR FRIENDS. THIS IS TERRIBLE!!
COME BACK!!
IT'S TOO DANGEROUS!
POINT
IF YOU HAVE SOMETHING TO SAY...
YOU HAVE TO PUT IT INTO WORDS!!
GRRRWL...

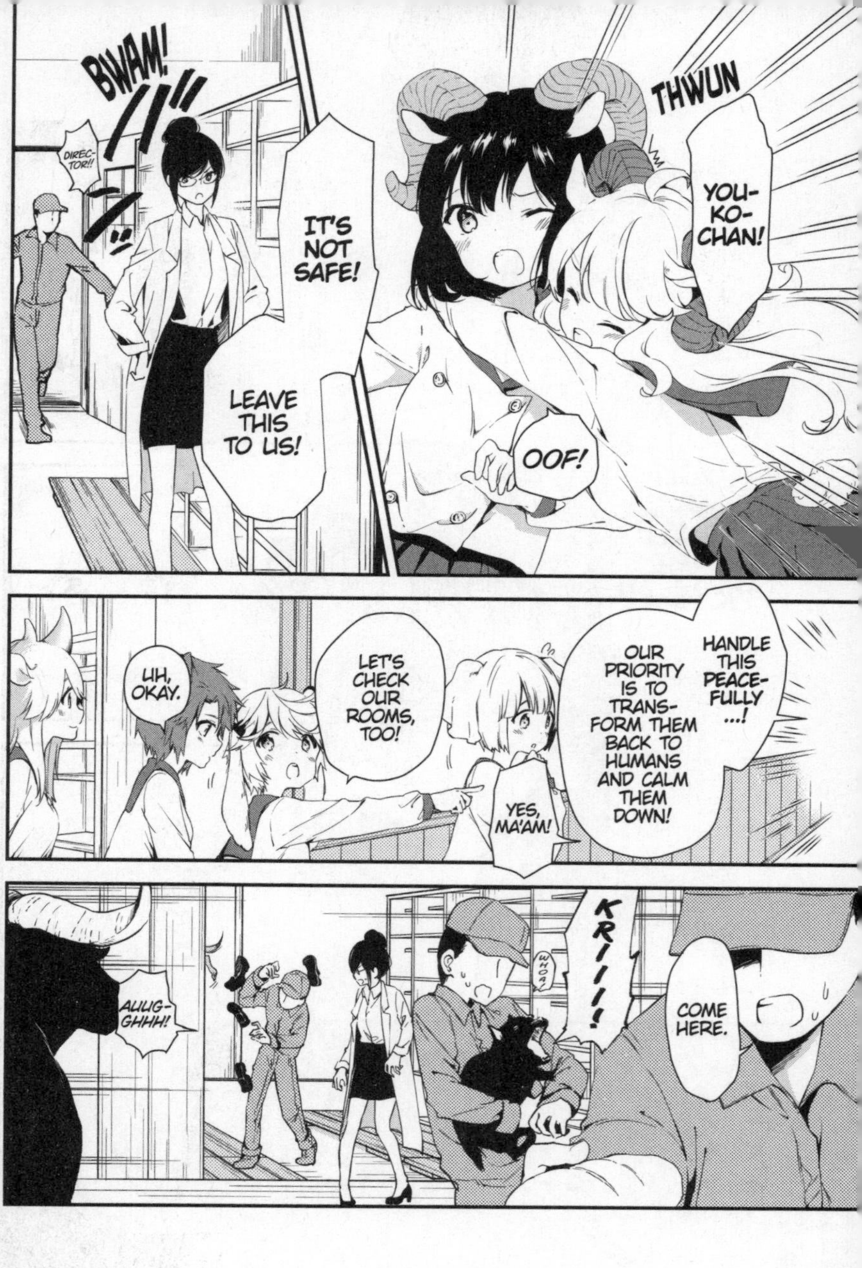
THWUN
YOU-KO-CHAN!
OOF!
IT'S NOT SAFE!
LEAVE THIS TO US!
BWAM!
DIREC-TOR!!
HANDLE THIS PEACE-FULLY ...!
OUR PRIORITY IS TO TRANS-FORM THEM BACK TO HUMANS AND CALM THEM DOWN!
YES, MA'AM!
LET'S CHECK OUR ROOMS, TOO!
UH, OKAY.
COME HERE.
KRIIII!
WHOA!
AUUG-GHHH!

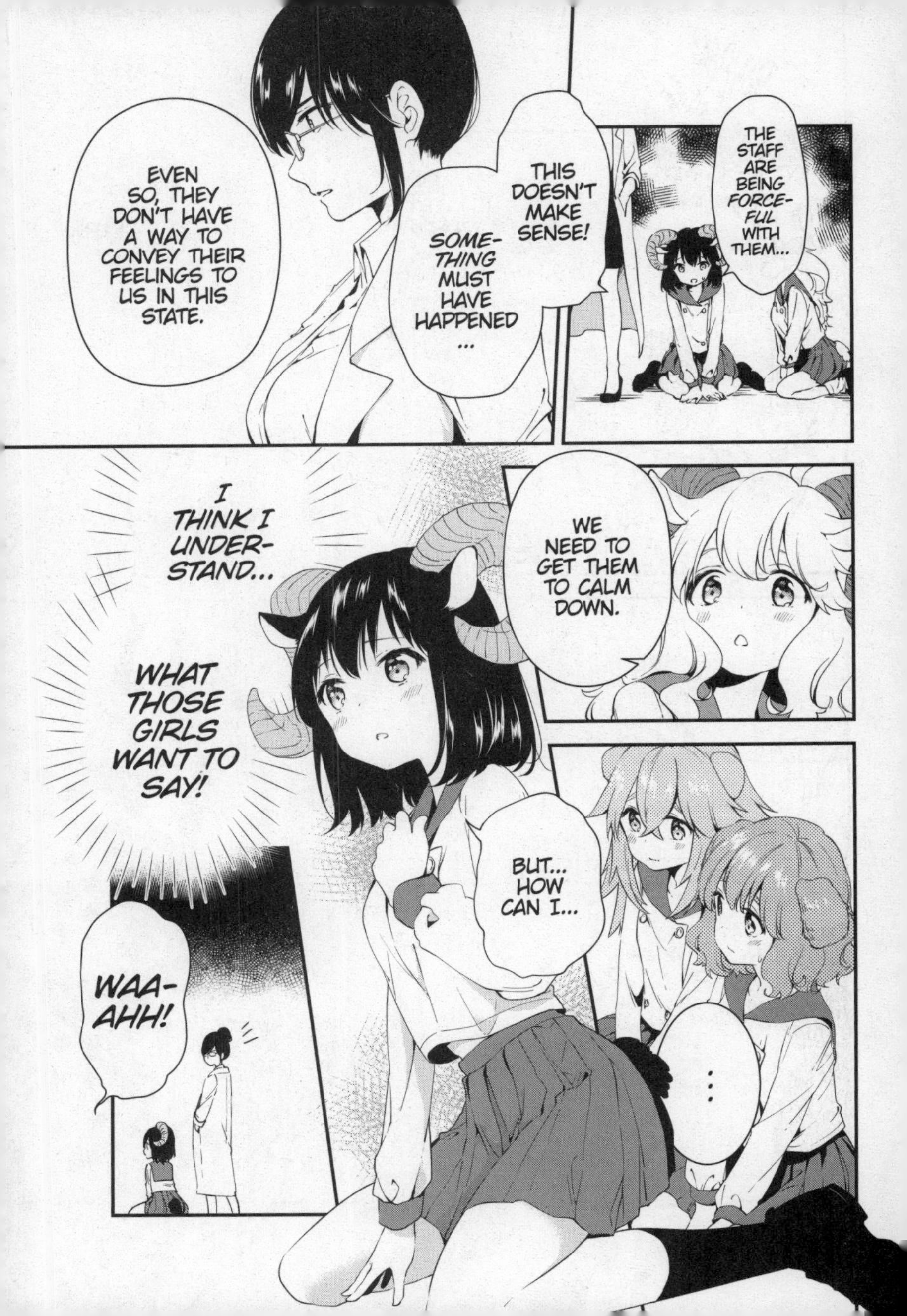
THE STAFF ARE BEING FORCE-FUL WITH THEM...
THIS DOESN'T MAKE SENSE!
SOME-THING MUST HAVE HAPPENED...
EVEN SO, THEY DON'T HAVE A WAY TO CONVEY THEIR FEELINGS TO US IN THIS STATE.
WE NEED TO GET THEM TO CALM DOWN.
I THINK I UNDER-STAND...
WHAT THOSE GIRLS WANT TO SAY!
BUT... HOW CAN I...
...
WAA-AHH!

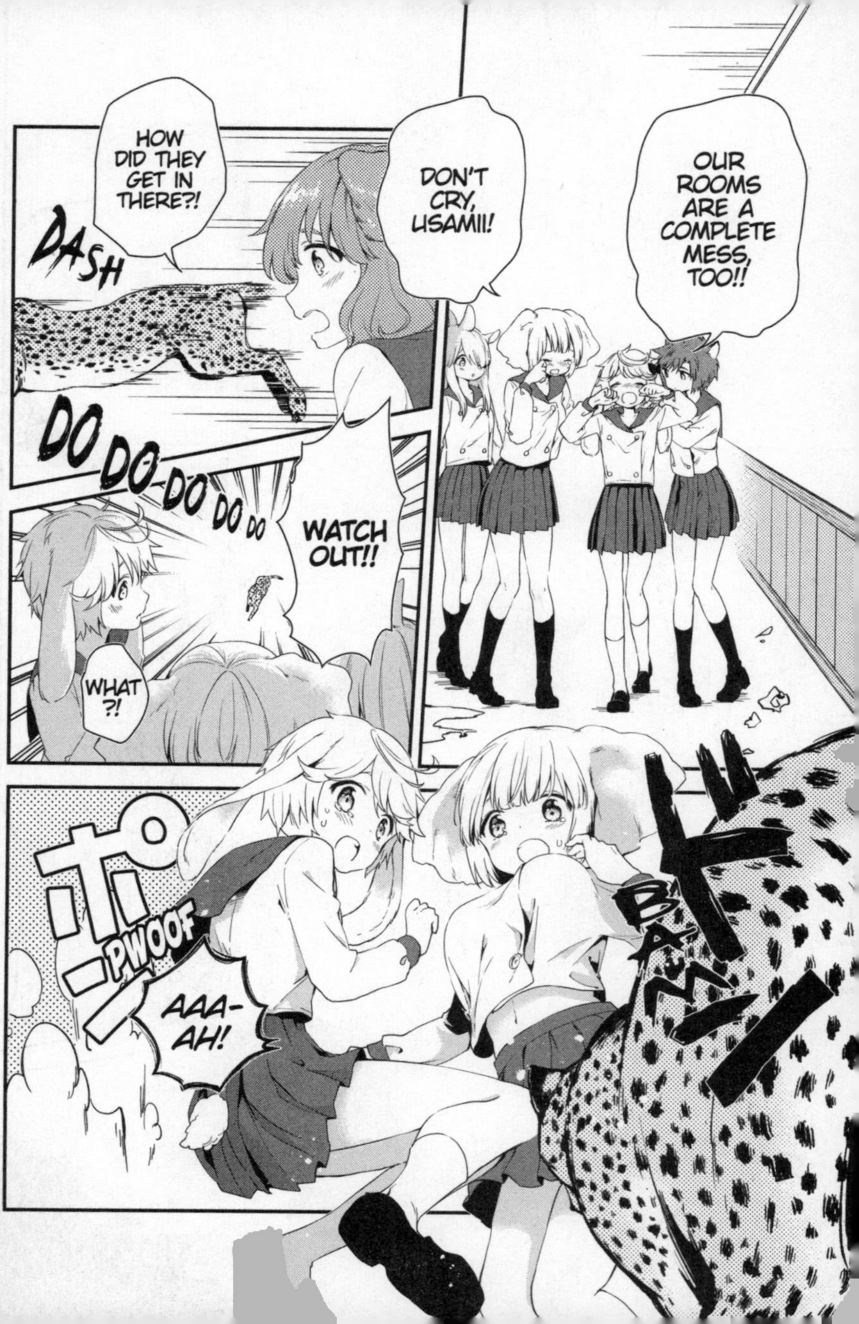
OUR ROOMS ARE A COMPLETE MESS, TOO!!
DON'T CRY, USAMI!!
HOW DID THEY GET IN THERE?!
DASH
DO DO-DO-DO DO DO
WATCH OUT!!
WHAT?!
BAM
AAA-AH!
PWOOF

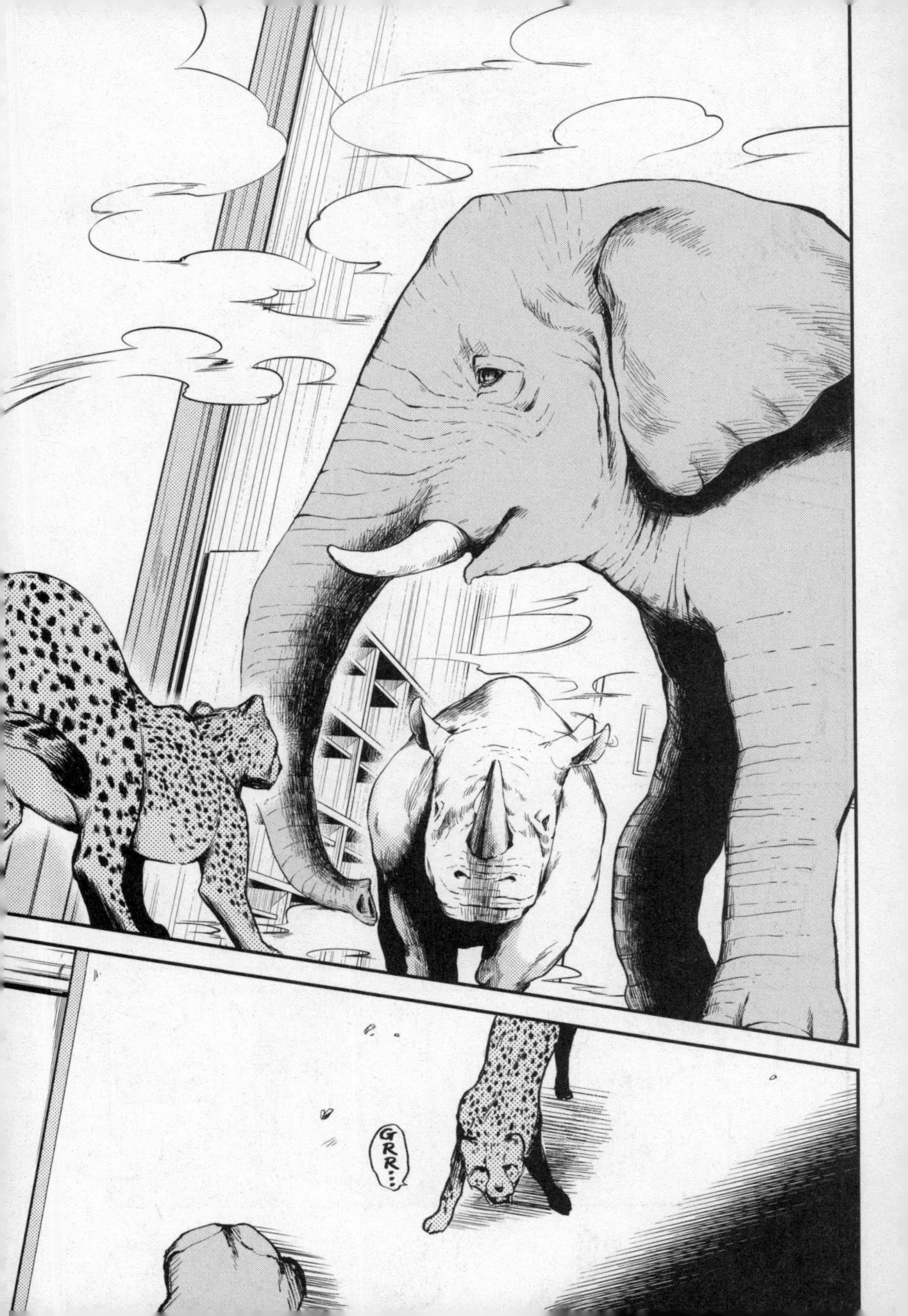
GRR...

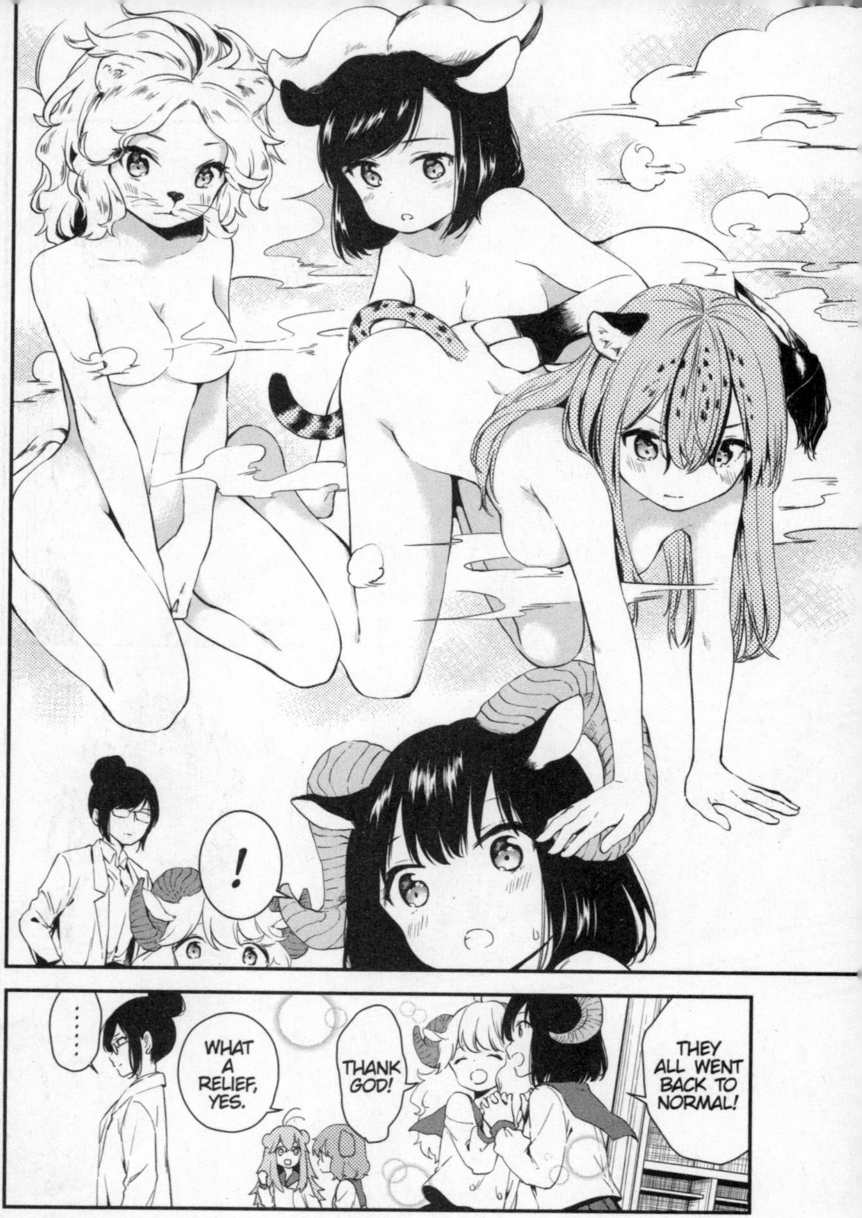
!
THEY ALL WENT BACK TO NORMAL!
THANK GOD!
WHAT A RELIEF, YES.
......

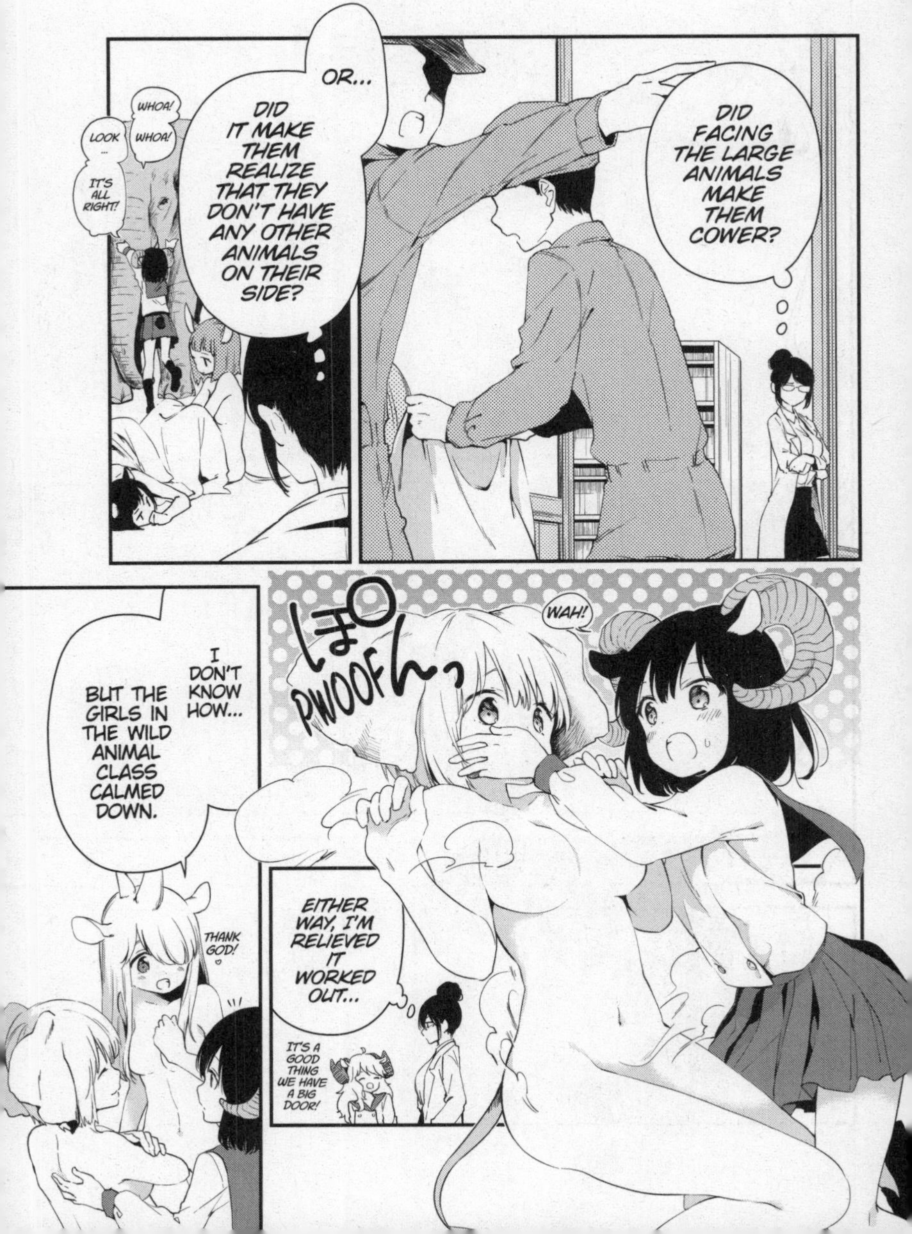
DID FACING THE LARGE ANIMALS MAKE THEM COWER?
OR...
DID IT MAKE THEM REALIZE THAT THEY DON'T HAVE ANY OTHER ANIMALS ON THEIR SIDE?
WHOA!
WHOA!
LOOK ... IT'S ALL RIGHT!
WAH!
ぽ PWOOFん
I DON'T KNOW HOW...
BUT THE GIRLS IN THE WILD ANIMAL CLASS CALMED DOWN.
EITHER WAY, I'M RELIEVED IT WORKED OUT...
IT'S A GOOD THING WE HAVE A BIG DOOR!
THANK GOD!

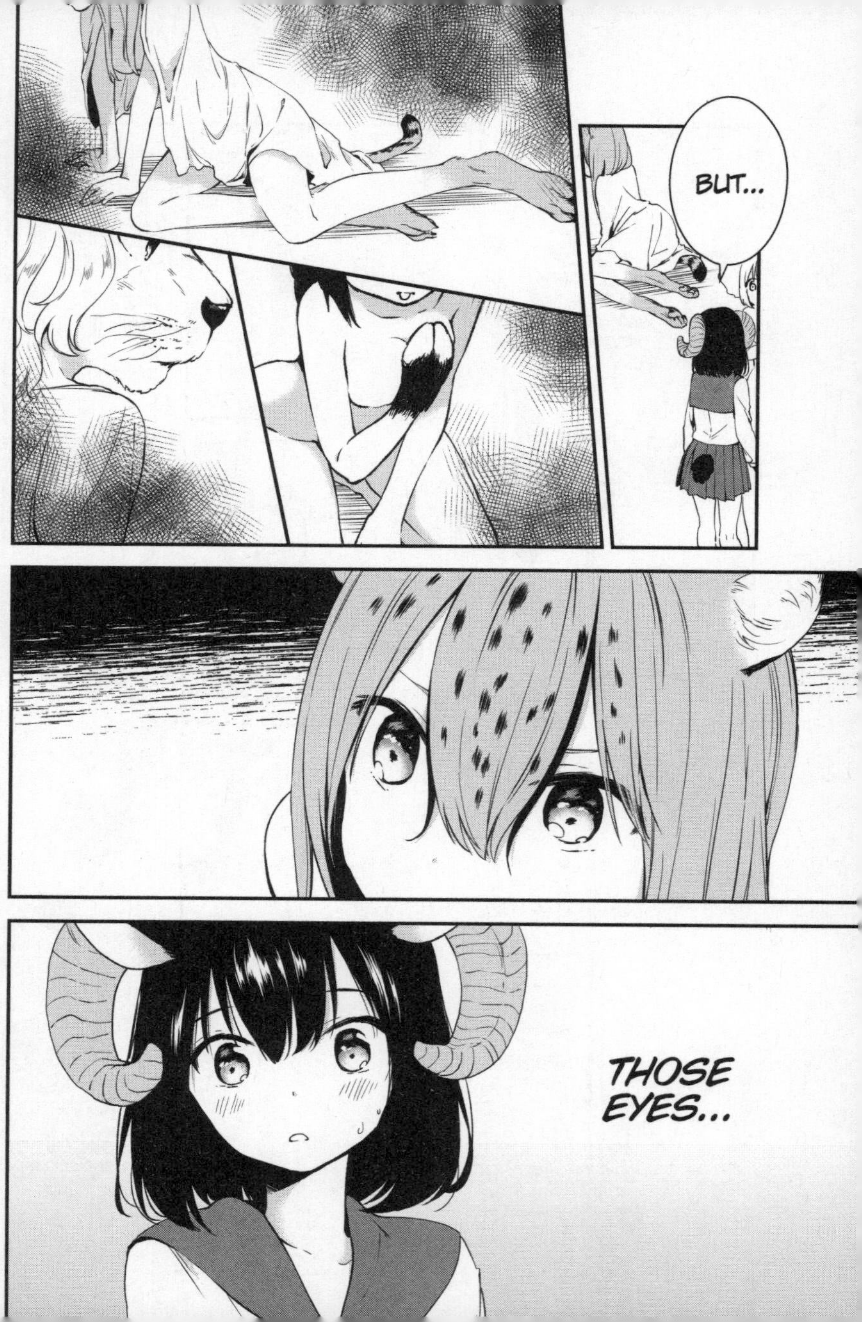
BUT...
THOSE EYES...

Life in the Wild Animal Class

...
Huh?!
!
TP
TP
VORO VORO VORO VORO VORO VORO VORO
SHUUUN
Stop it!!
RAHH!

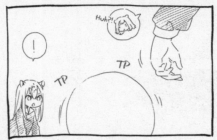

DNAは教えてくれない

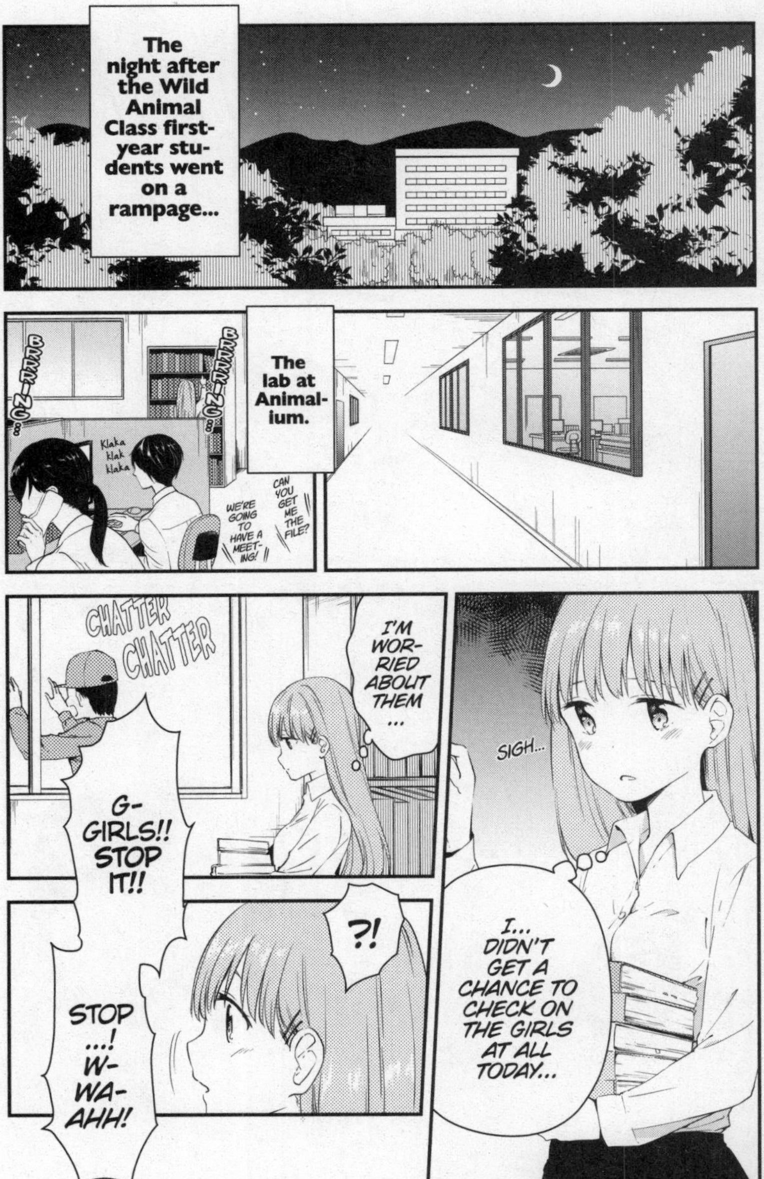
The night after the Wild Animal Class first-year students went on a rampage...
The lab at Animalium.
CAN YOU GET ME THE FILE?
WE'RE GOING TO HAVE A MEETING!
BRRRING...
BRRRING...
Klaka klak klaka
SIGH...
I... DIDN'T GET A CHANCE TO CHECK ON THE GIRLS AT ALL TODAY...
I'M WORRIED ABOUT THEM...
CHATTER CHATTER
G-GIRLS!! STOP IT!!
?!
STOP...! W-WA-AHH!

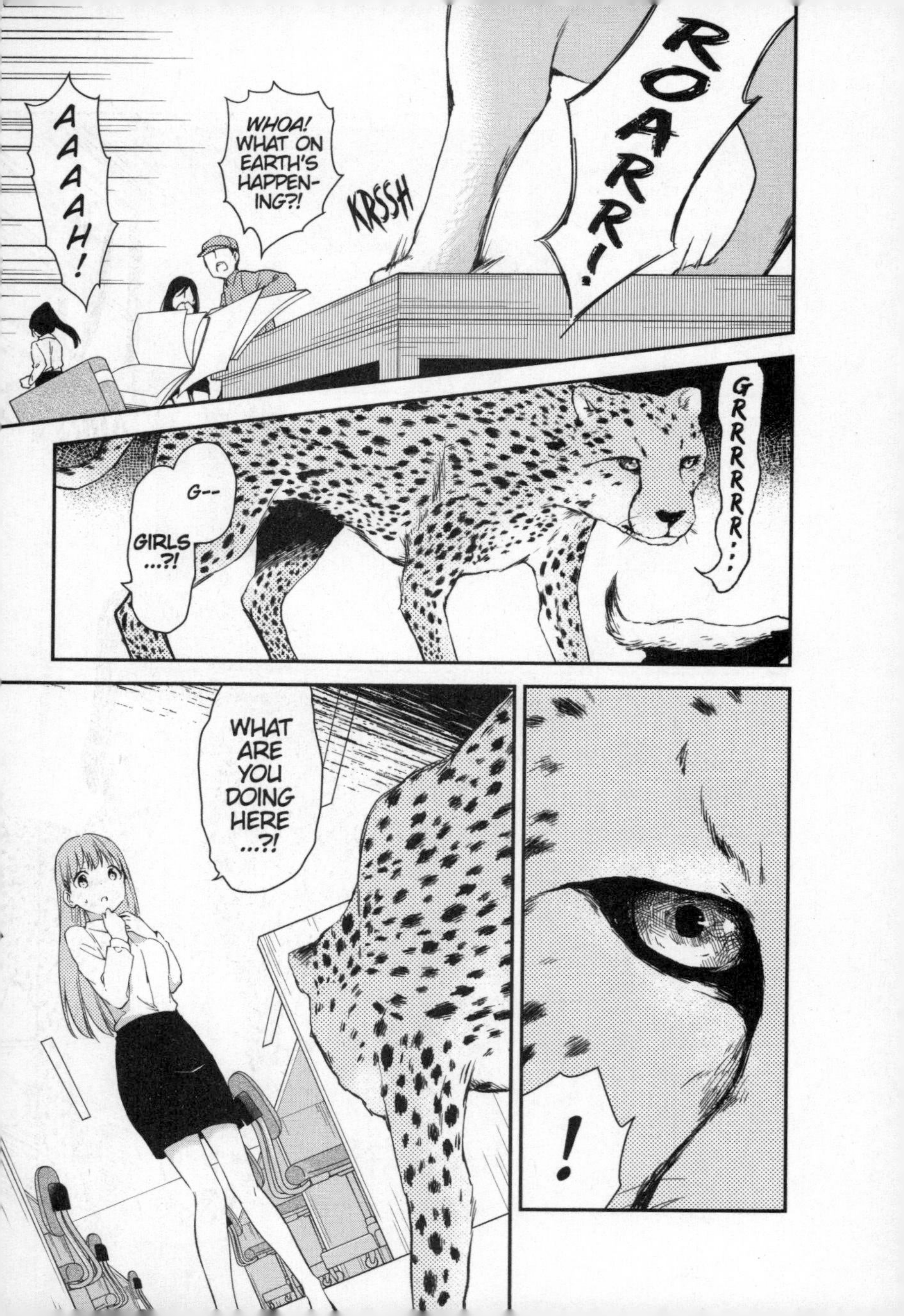
ROARR!
KRSSH
WHOA! WHAT ON EARTH'S HAPPENING?!
AAAAAH!
GRRRRRR...
G-- GIRLS...?!
!
WHAT ARE YOU DOING HERE...?!

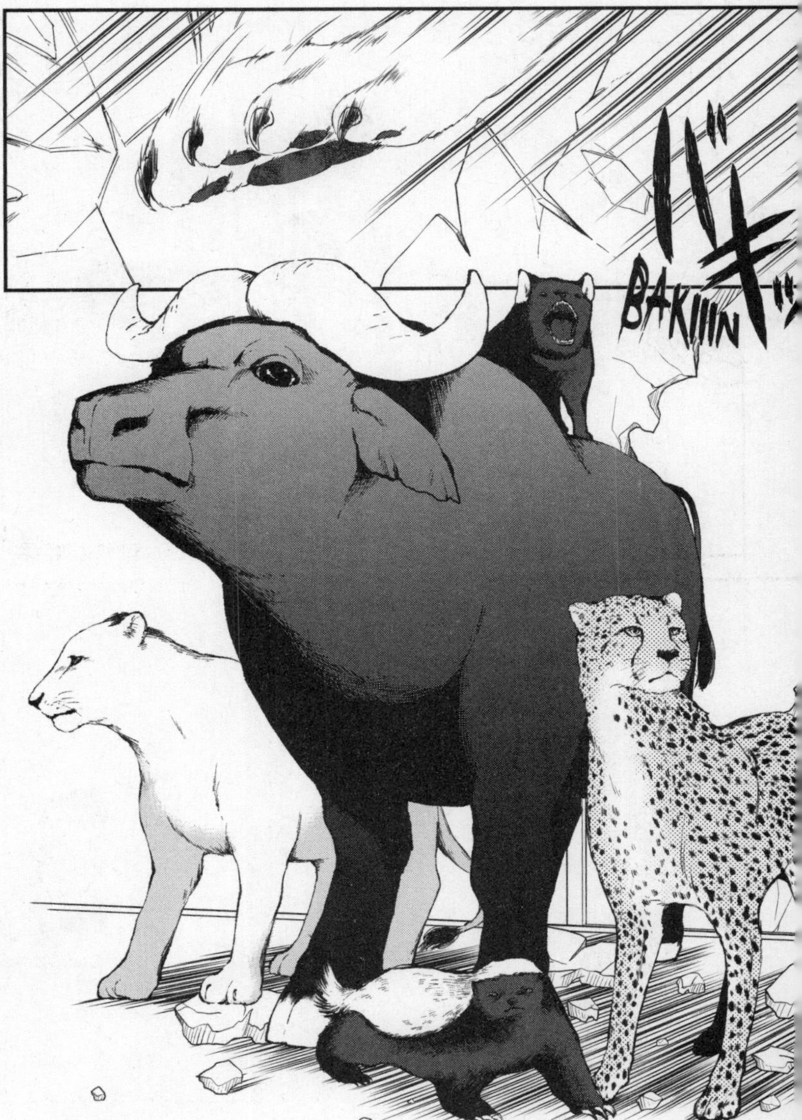
バキッ
BAKIIIN

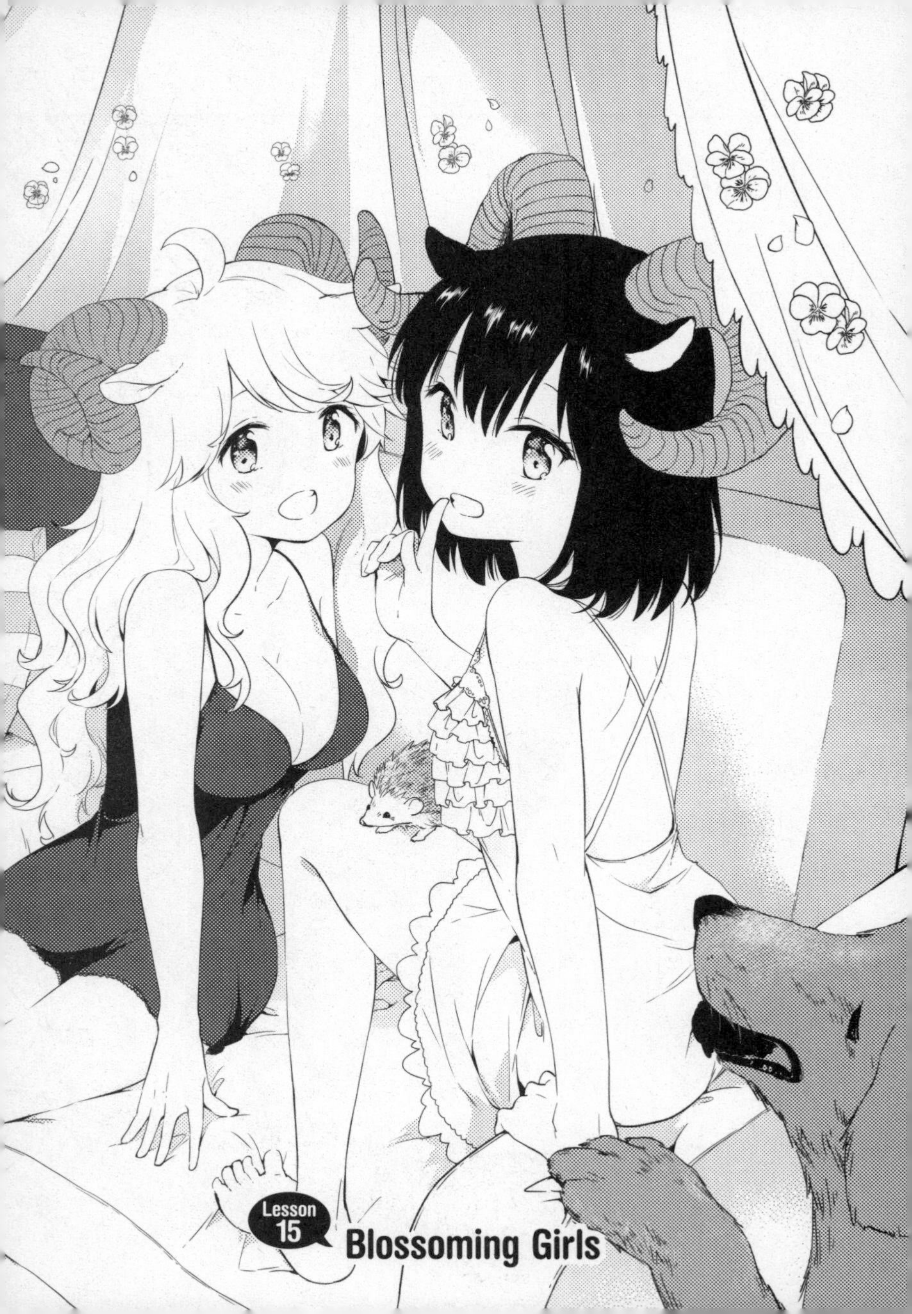
Lesson
15
Blossoming Girls

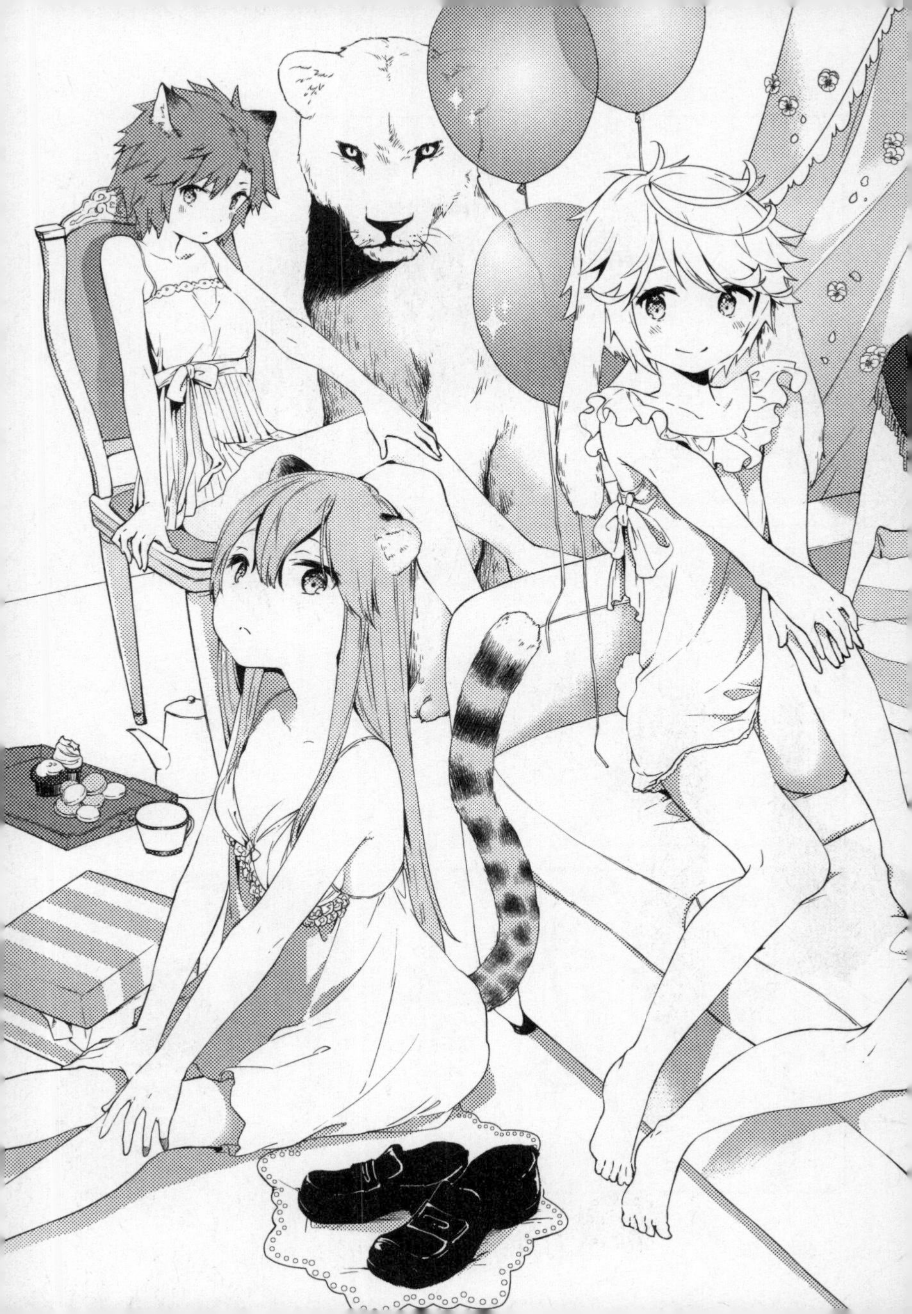

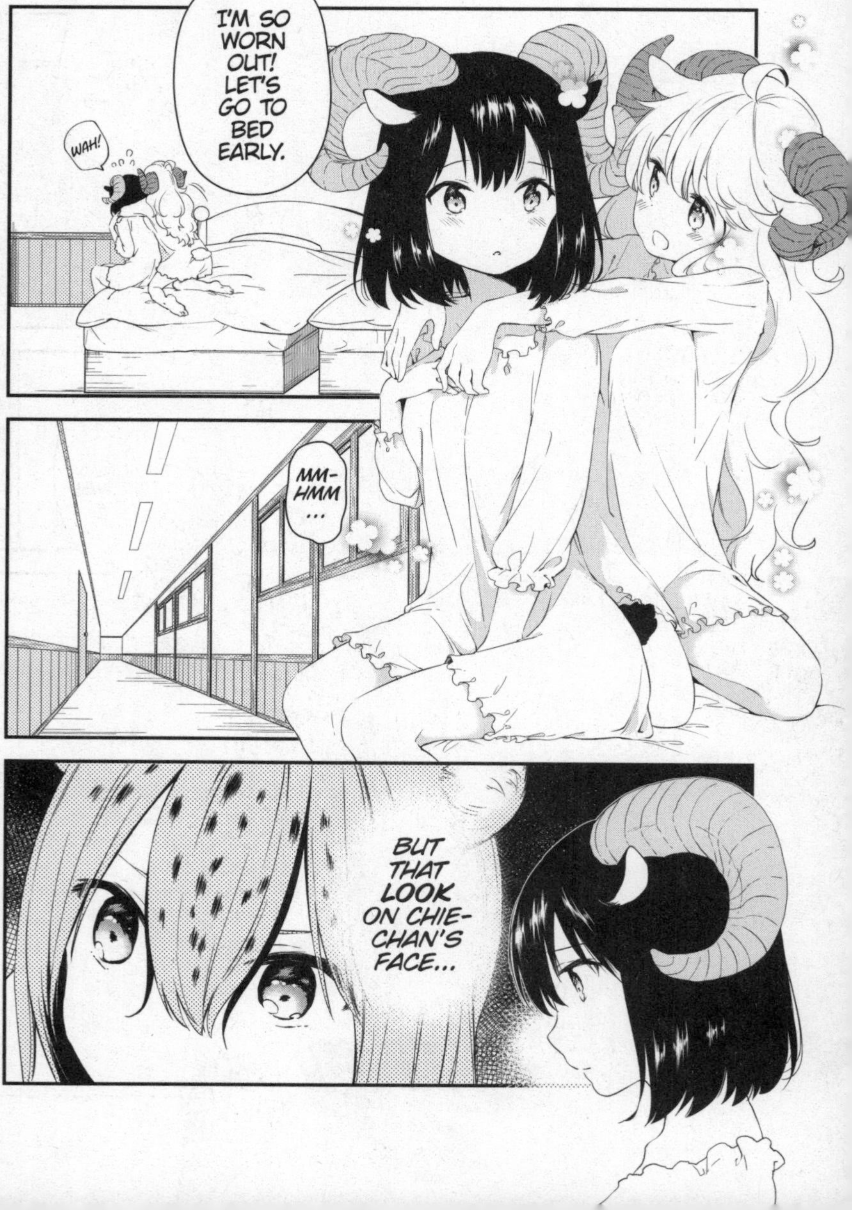
I'M SO WORN OUT! LET'S GO TO BED EARLY.
WAH!
MM-HMM...
BUT THAT LOOK ON CHIE-CHAN'S FACE...

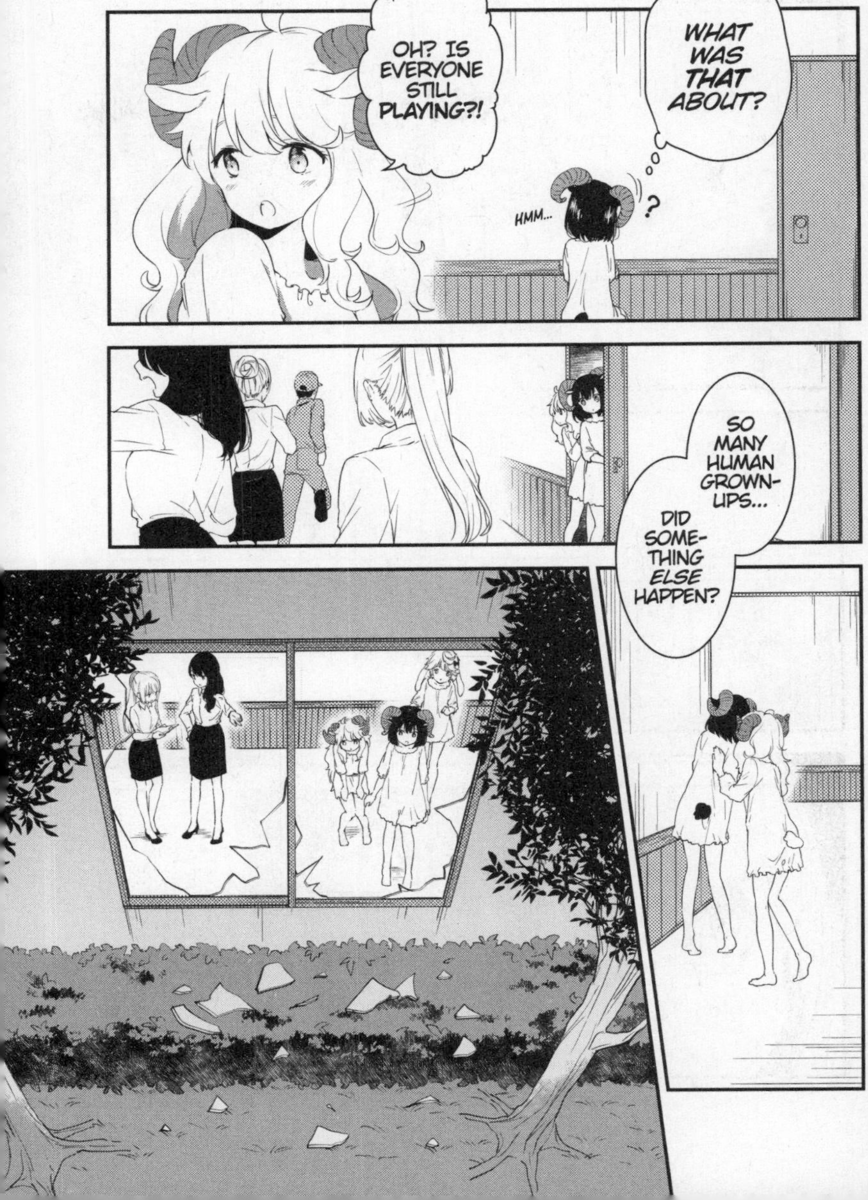
WHAT WAS THAT ABOUT?
?
HMM...
OH? IS EVERYONE STILL PLAYING?!
SO MANY HUMAN GROWN-UPS...
DID SOME-THING *ELSE* HAPPEN?

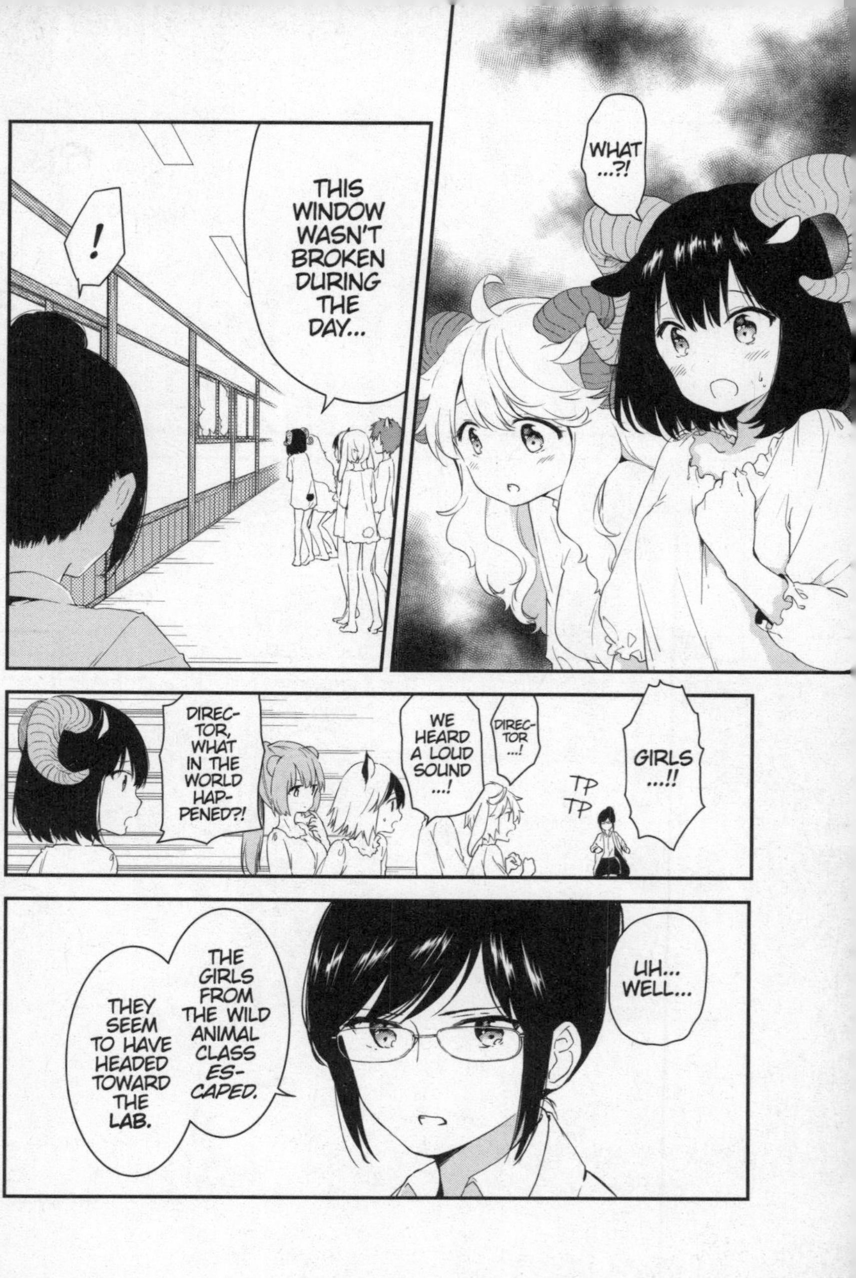
WHAT ...?!
THIS WINDOW WASN'T BROKEN DURING THE DAY...
!
GIRLS ...!!
TP TP
DIREC-TOR ...!
WE HEARD A LOUD SOUND ...!
DIREC-TOR, WHAT IN THE WORLD HAP-PENED?!
UH... WELL...
THE GIRLS FROM THE WILD ANIMAL CLASS ES-CAPED.
THEY SEEM TO HAVE HEADED TOWARD THE LAB.

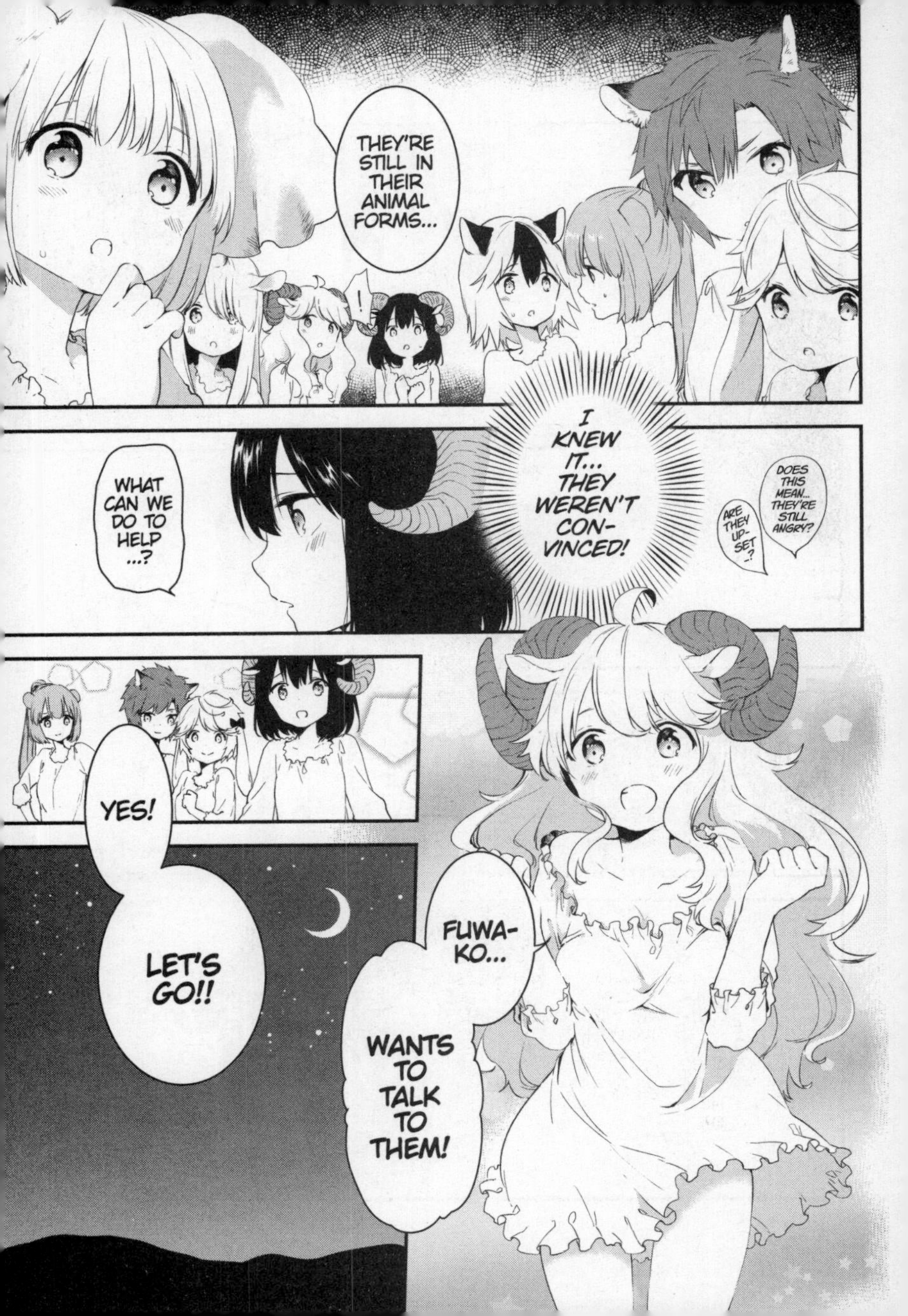
THEY'RE STILL IN THEIR ANIMAL FORMS...
!
DOES THIS MEAN... THEY'RE STILL ANGRY?
ARE THEY UP-SET...?
I KNEW IT... THEY WEREN'T CON-VINCED!
WHAT CAN WE DO TO HELP...?
FUWA-KO... WANTS TO TALK TO THEM!
YES!
LET'S GO!!

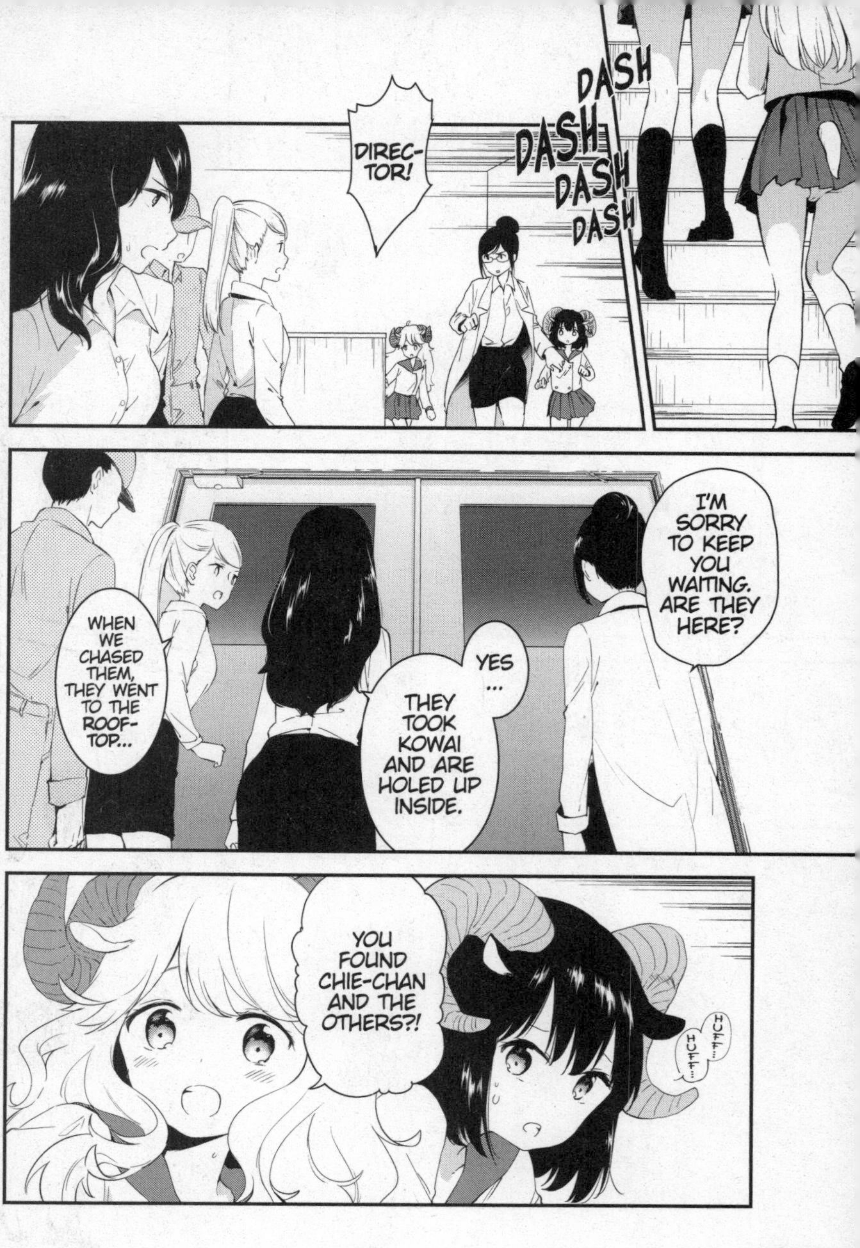
DASH DASH DASH DASH
DIRECTOR!
I'M SORRY TO KEEP YOU WAITING. ARE THEY HERE?
YES...
THEY TOOK KOWAI AND ARE HOLED UP INSIDE.
WHEN WE CHASED THEM, THEY WENT TO THE ROOFTOP...
YOU FOUND CHIE-CHAN AND THE OTHERS?!
HUFF... HUFF...

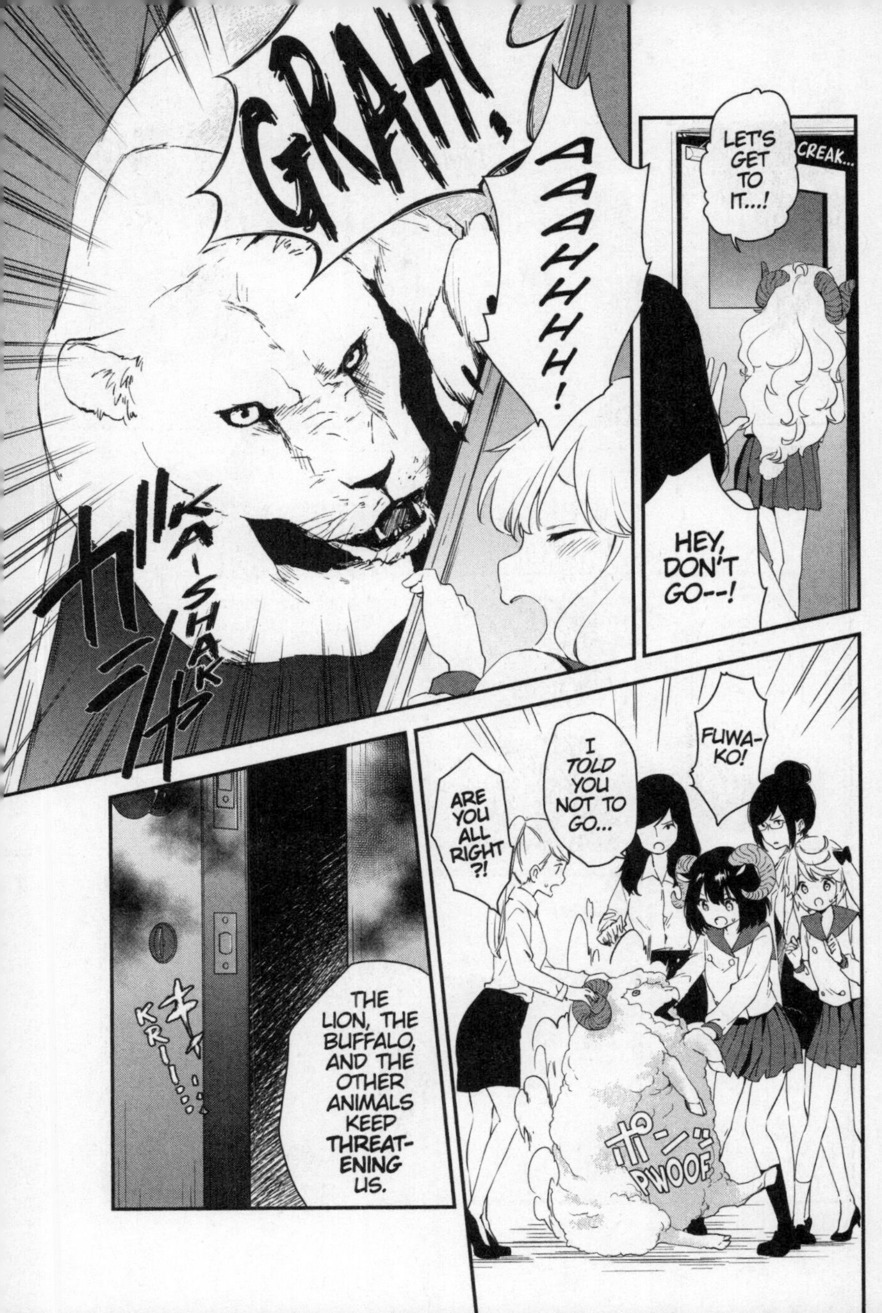

LET'S GET TO IT...!
CREAK...
HEY, DON'T GO--!
GRAH!
AAAAHHHHH!
KA-SHAK
FUWAKO!
I TOLD YOU NOT TO GO...
ARE YOU ALL RIGHT?!
PWOOF
KRI-I-I...
THE LION, THE BUFFALO, AND THE OTHER ANIMALS KEEP THREATENING US.

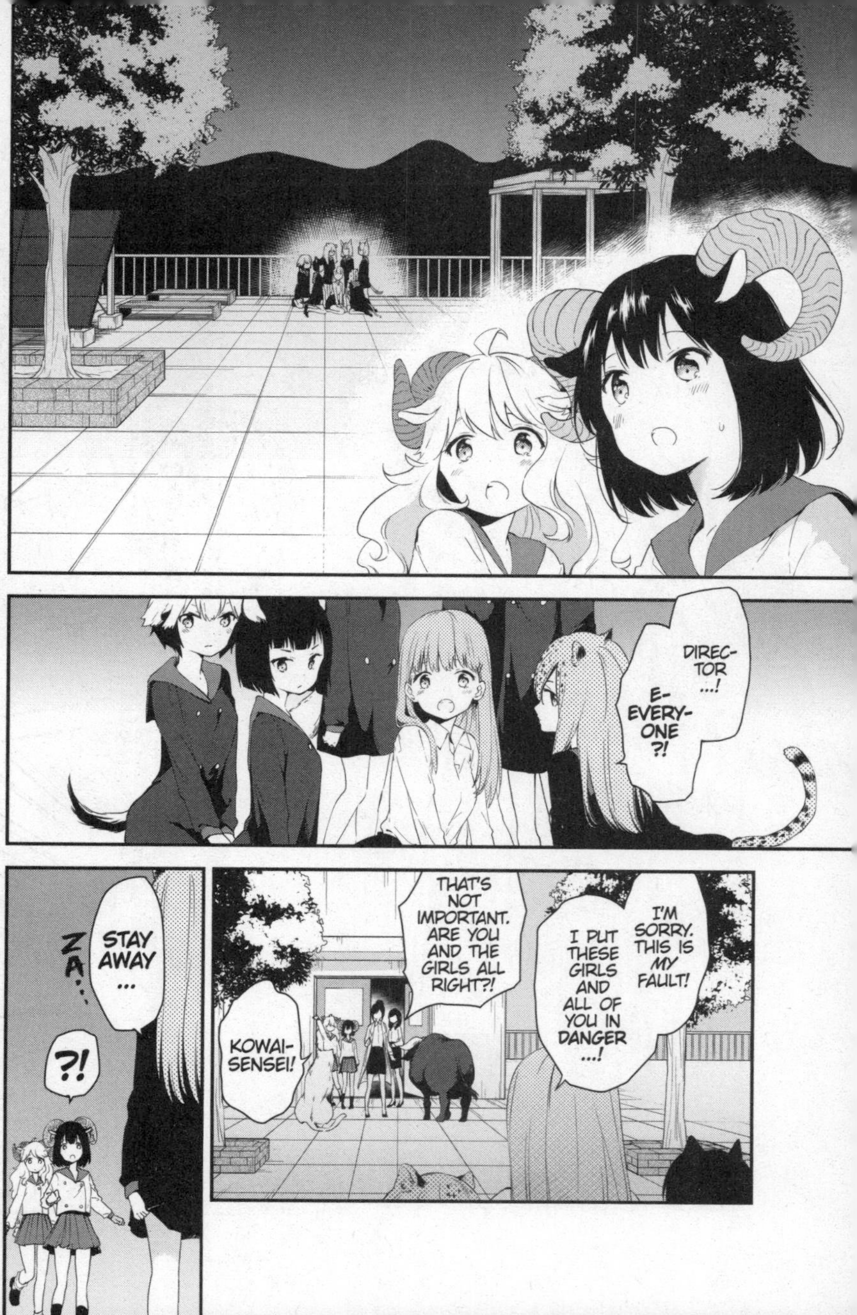
DIREC-TOR ...!
E-EVERY-ONE ?!
I'M SORRY. THIS IS MY FAULT!
I PUT THESE GIRLS AND ALL OF YOU IN DANGER ...!
THAT'S NOT IMPORTANT. ARE YOU AND THE GIRLS ALL RIGHT?!
KOWAI-SENSEI!
STAY AWAY ...
ZA...
?!

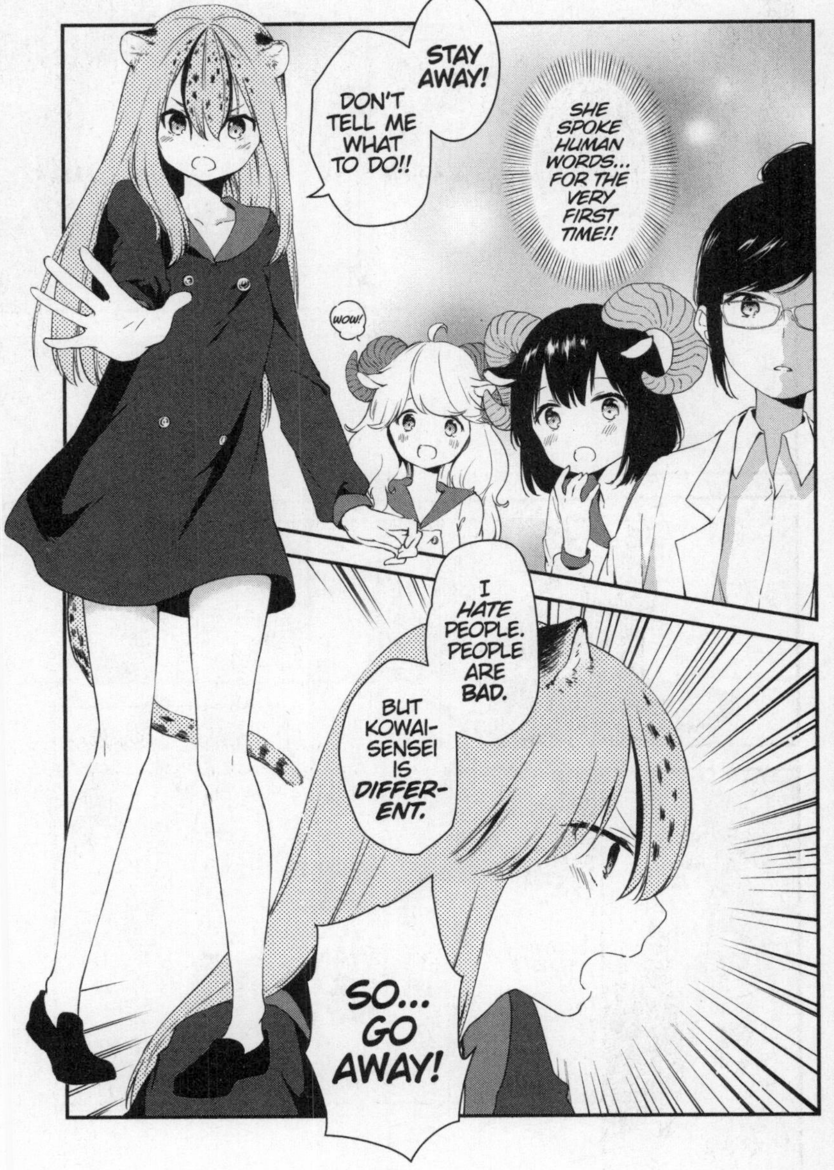
SHE SPOKE HUMAN WORDS... FOR THE VERY FIRST TIME!!
STAY AWAY!
DON'T TELL ME WHAT TO DO!!
WOW!
I HATE PEOPLE. PEOPLE ARE BAD.
BUT KOWAI-SENSEI IS DIFFER-ENT.
SO... GO AWAY!

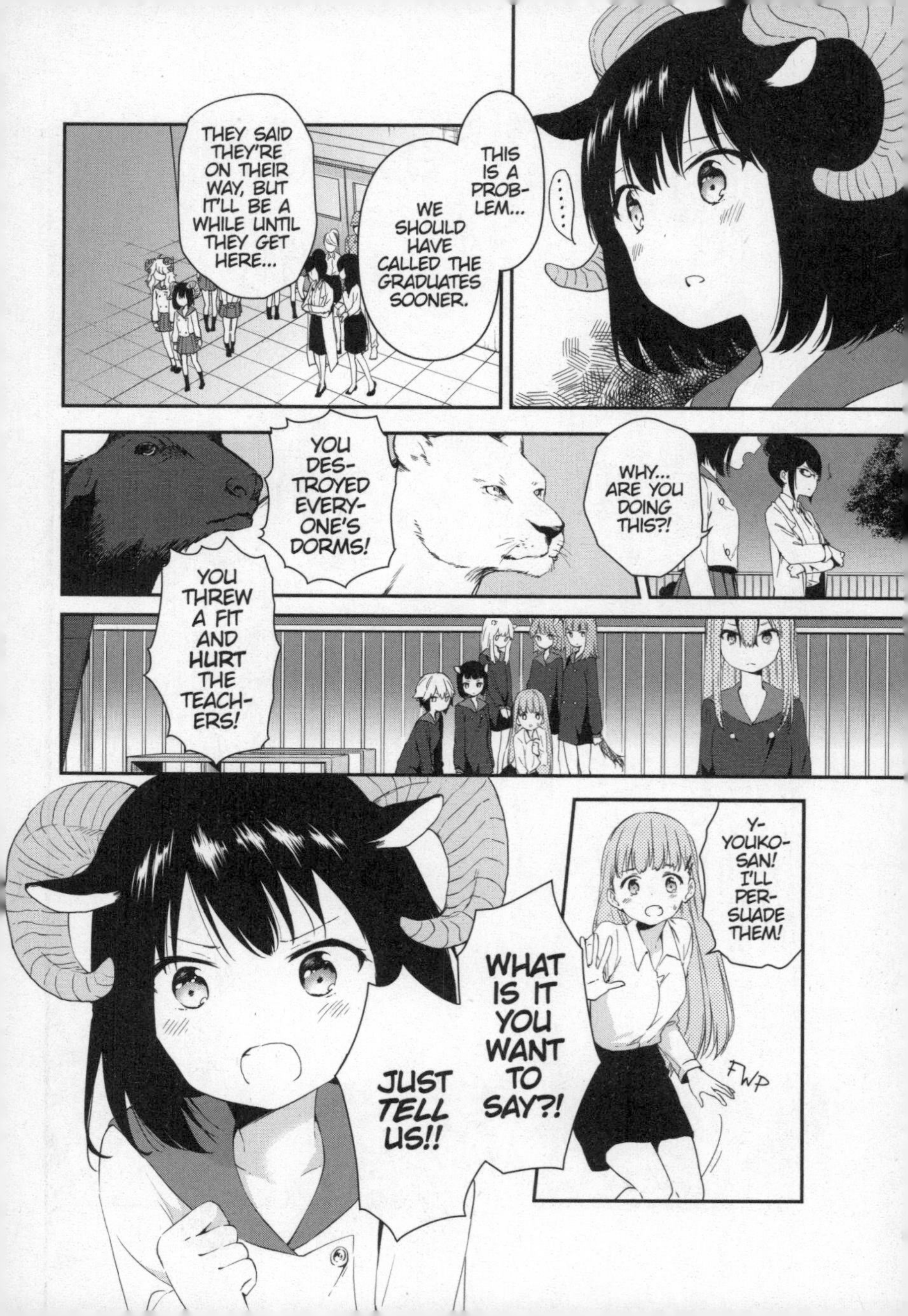

......
THIS IS A PROBLEM... WE SHOULD HAVE CALLED THE GRADUATES SOONER.
THEY SAID THEY'RE ON THEIR WAY, BUT IT'LL BE A WHILE UNTIL THEY GET HERE...
WHY... ARE YOU DOING THIS?!
YOU DESTROYED EVERYONE'S DORMS!
YOU THREW A FIT AND HURT THE TEACHERS!
Y-YOUKO-SAN! I'LL PERSUADE THEM!
FWP
WHAT IS IT YOU WANT TO SAY?!
JUST TELL US!!

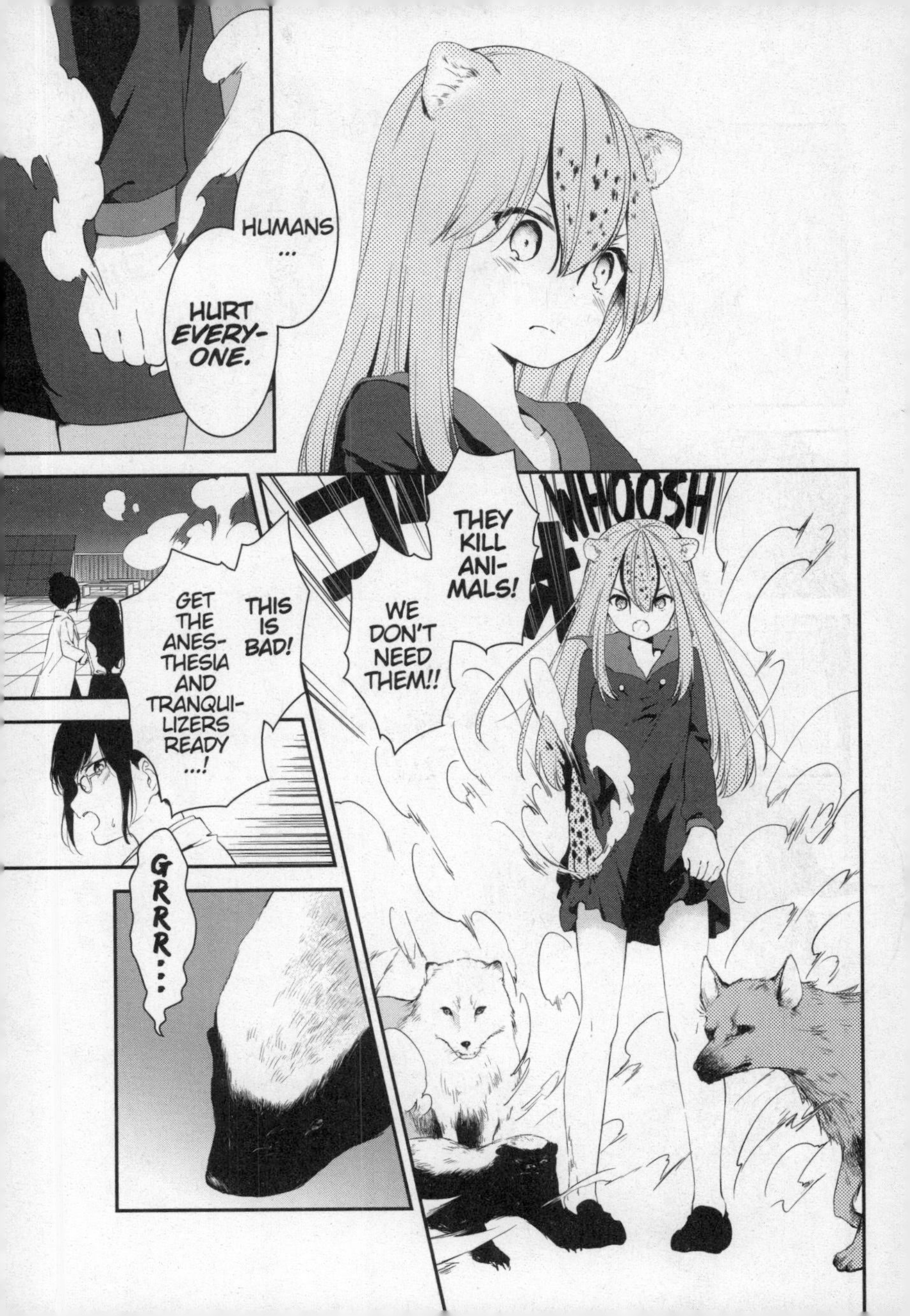
HUMANS ...
HURT EVERYONE.
WHOOSH
THEY KILL ANIMALS!
WE DON'T NEED THEM!!
THIS IS BAD!
GET THE ANESTHESIA AND TRANQUILIZERS READY ...!
GRRR...

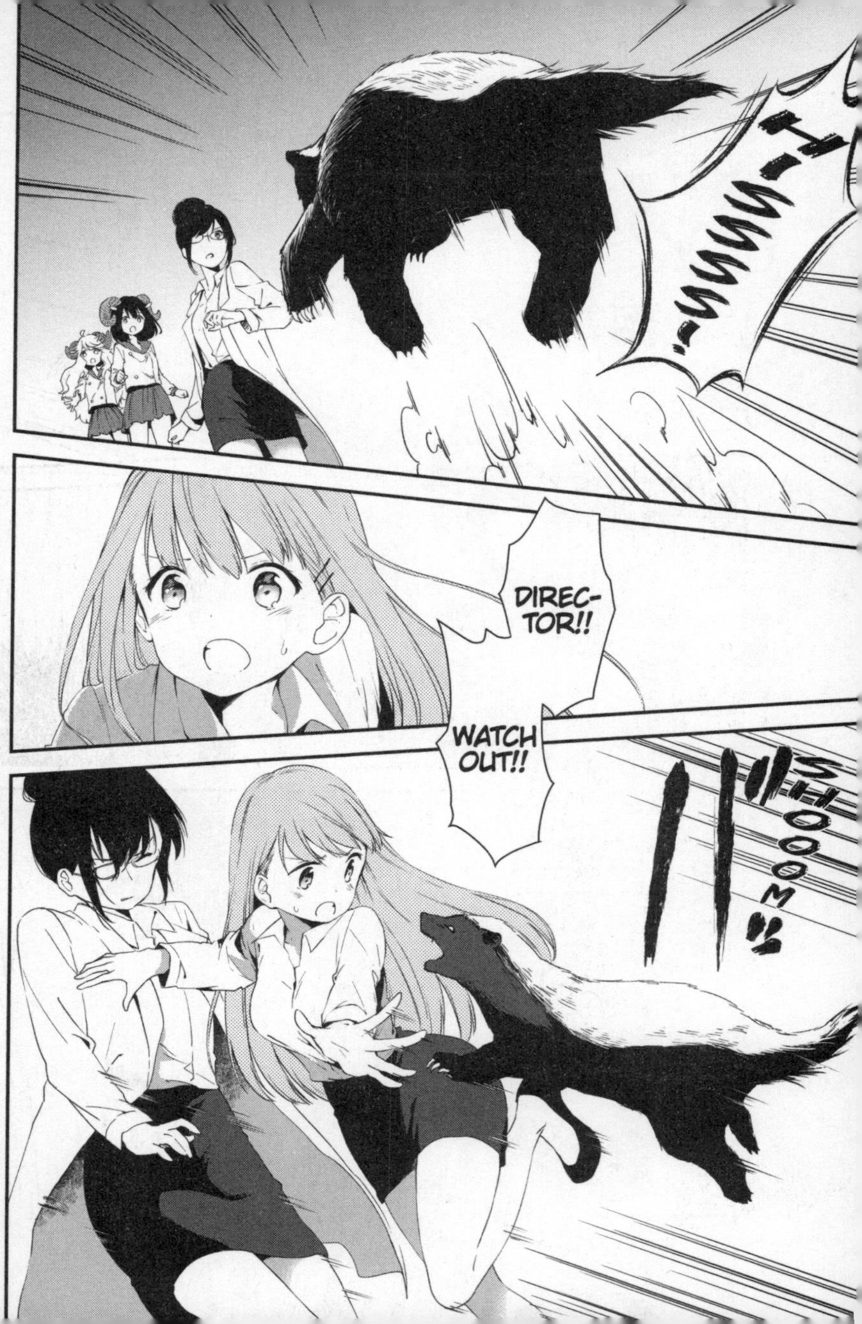
HISSSS!
DIREC-TOR!!
WATCH OUT!!
SHOOOOM!!

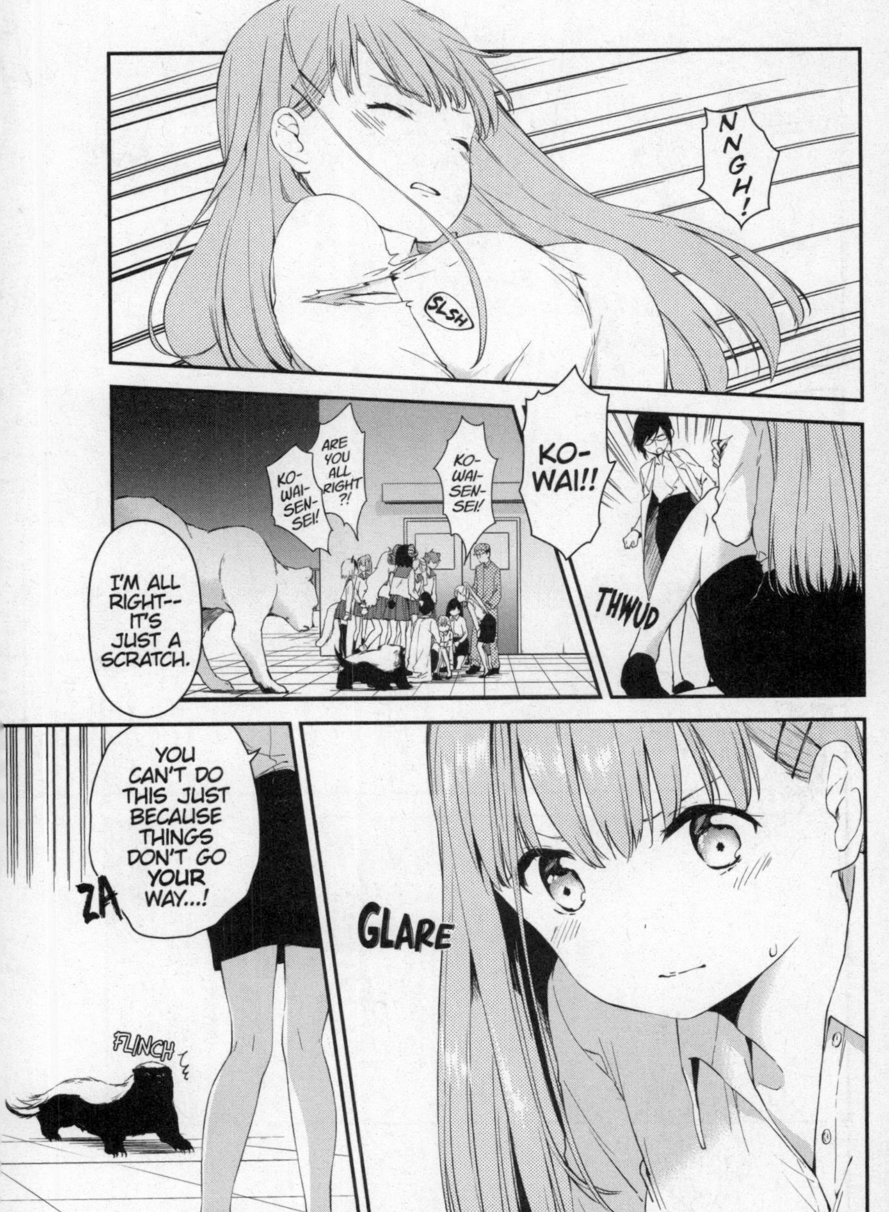

NNGH!
SLSH
KO-WAI!!
THWUD
KO-WAI-SEN-SEI!
ARE YOU ALL RIGHT?!
KO-WAI-SEN-SEI!
I'M ALL RIGHT-- IT'S JUST A SCRATCH.
GLARE
YOU CAN'T DO THIS JUST BECAUSE THINGS DON'T GO YOUR WAY...!
ZA
FLINCH

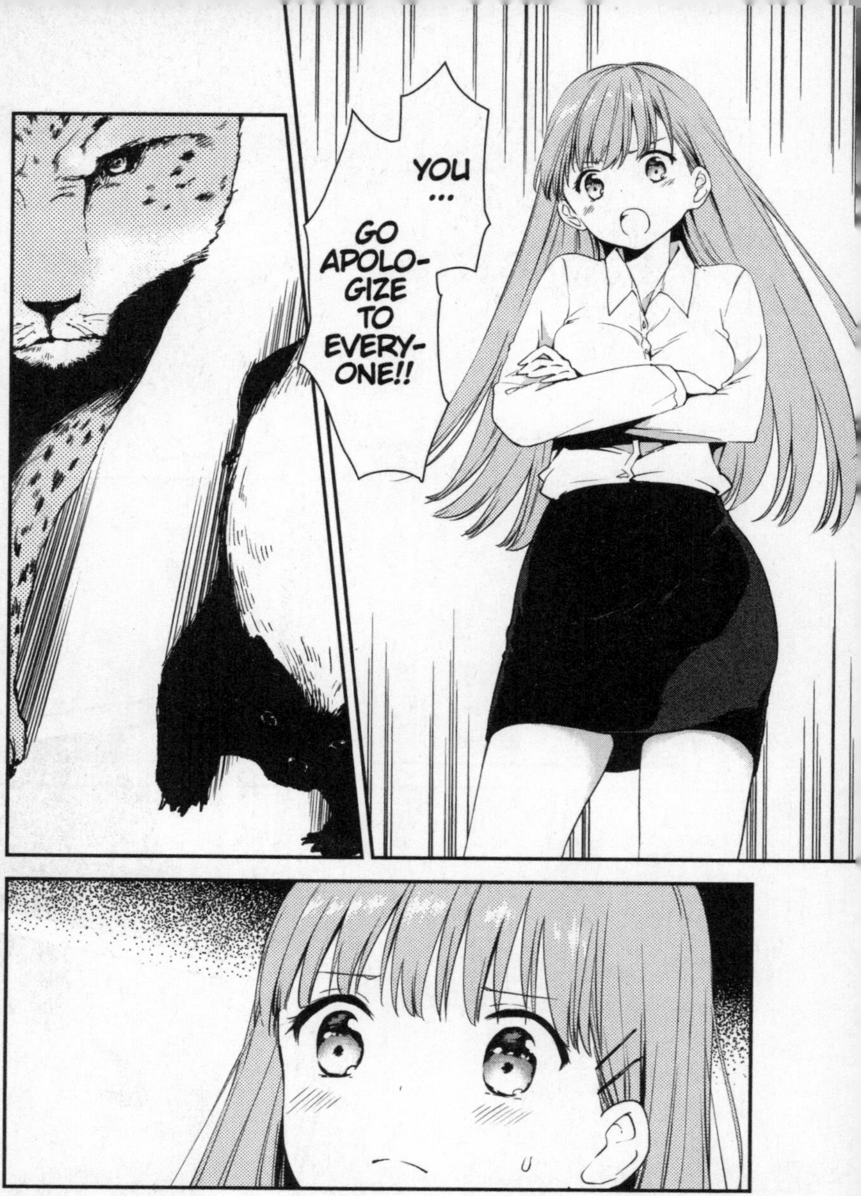
YOU ... GO APOLOGIZE TO EVERYONE!!

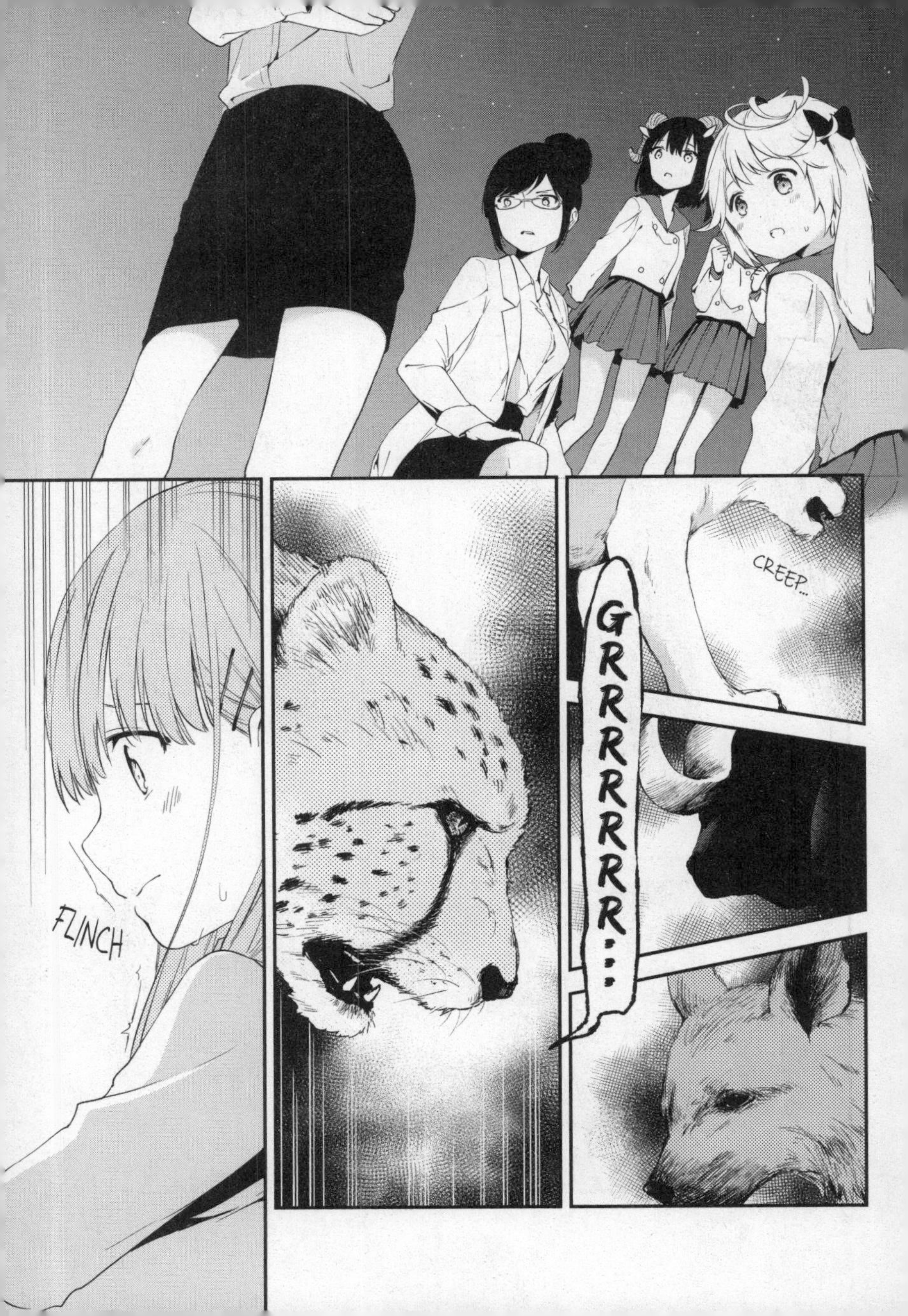
CREEP...
GRRRRRRR...
FLINCH

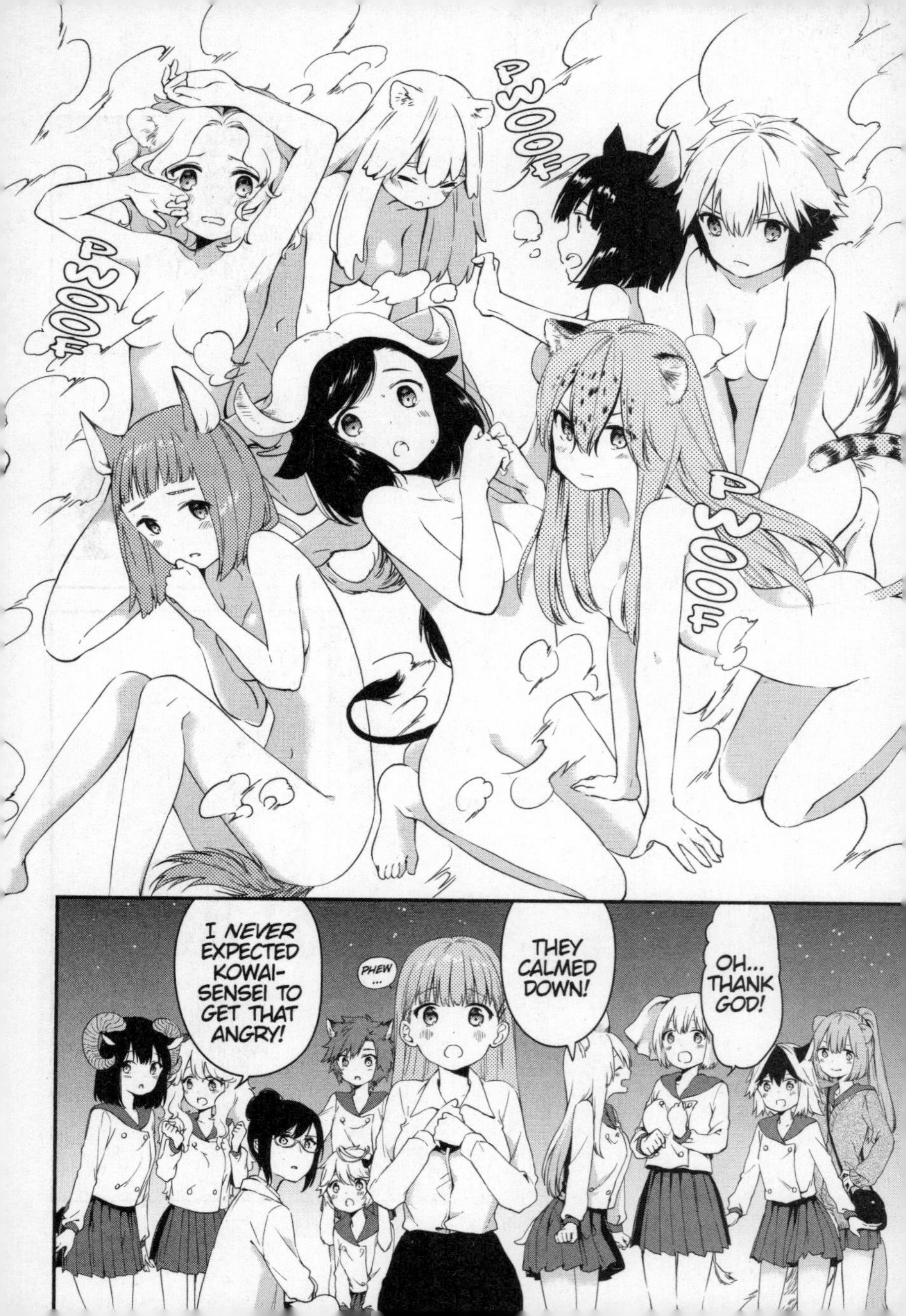
PWOOF
PWOOF
PWOOF
OH... THANK GOD!
THEY CALMED DOWN!
PHEW ...
I *NEVER* EXPECTED KOWAI-SENSEI TO GET THAT ANGRY!

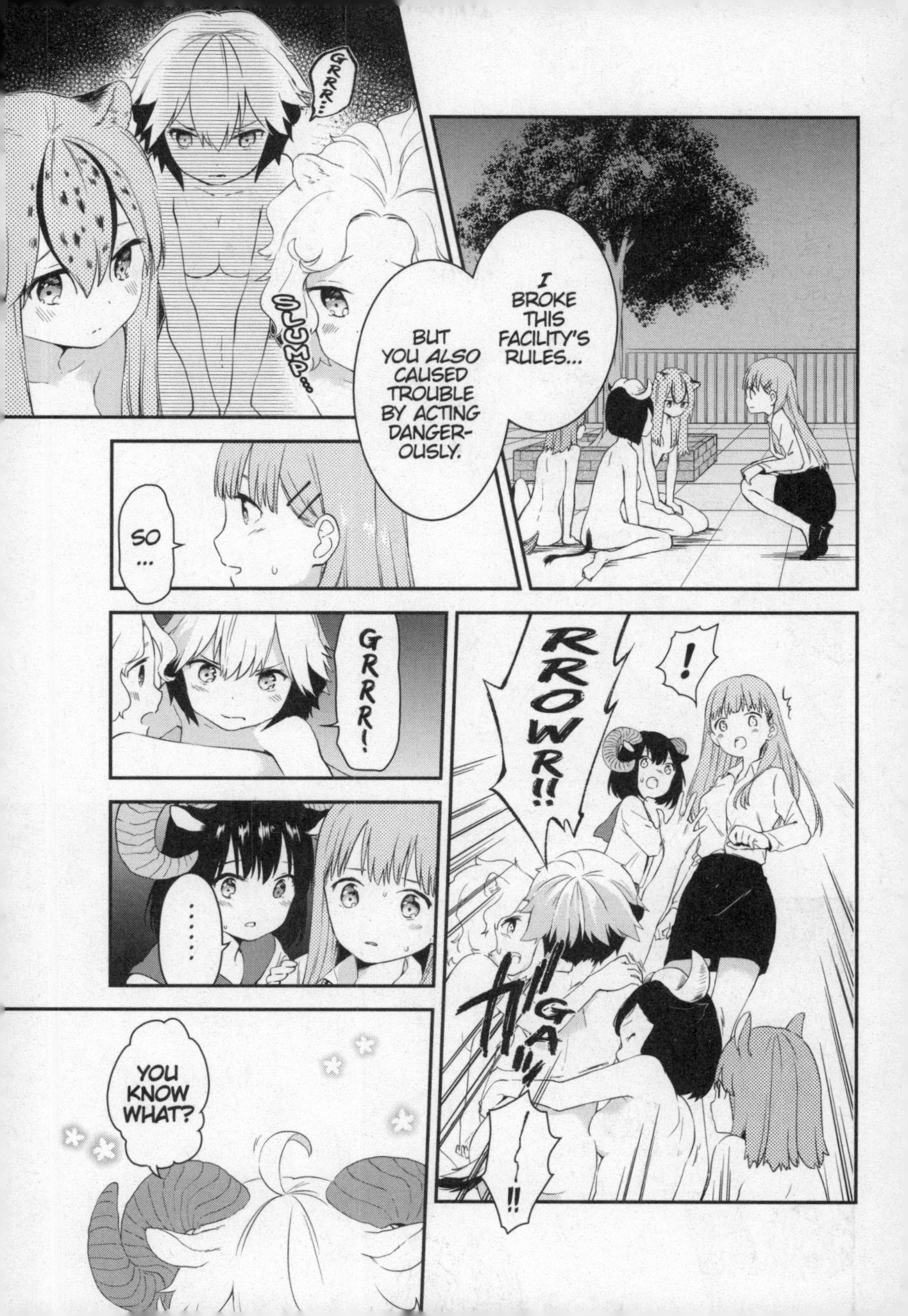

I BROKE THIS FACILITY'S RULES...
BUT YOU ALSO CAUSED TROUBLE BY ACTING DANGEROUSLY.
GRRR...
SLUMP..
SO ...
GRRR!
RROWR!!
!
......
HAGA!!!
!!
YOU KNOW WHAT?

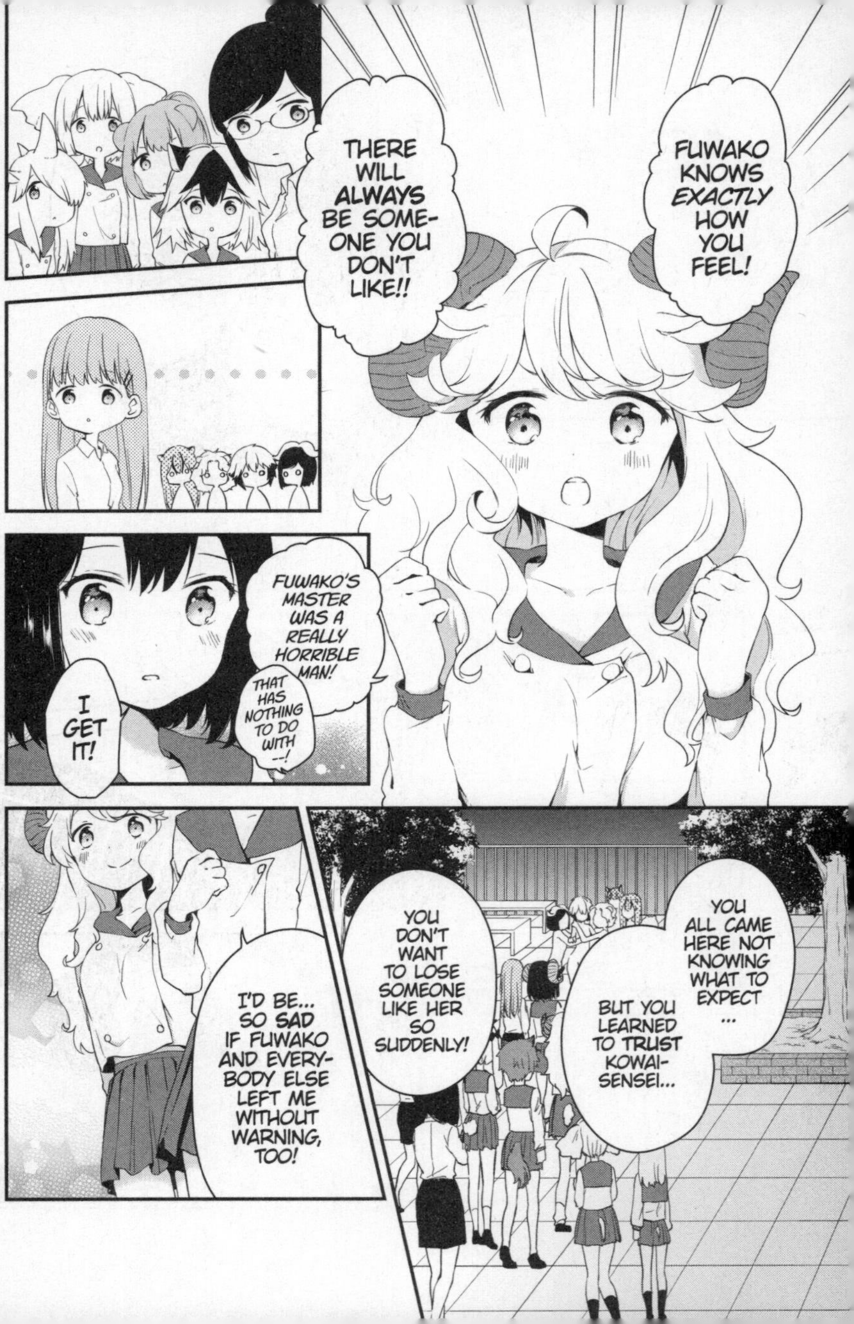
FUWAKO KNOWS *EXACTLY* HOW YOU FEEL!
THERE WILL ALWAYS BE SOMEONE YOU DON'T LIKE!!
FUWAKO'S MASTER WAS A REALLY HORRIBLE MAN!
THAT HAS NOTHING TO DO WITH --!
I GET IT!
YOU ALL CAME HERE NOT KNOWING WHAT TO EXPECT ...
BUT YOU LEARNED TO TRUST KOWAI-SENSEI...
YOU DON'T WANT TO LOSE SOMEONE LIKE HER SO SUDDENLY!
I'D BE... SO SAD IF FUWAKO AND EVERYBODY ELSE LEFT ME WITHOUT WARNING, TOO!

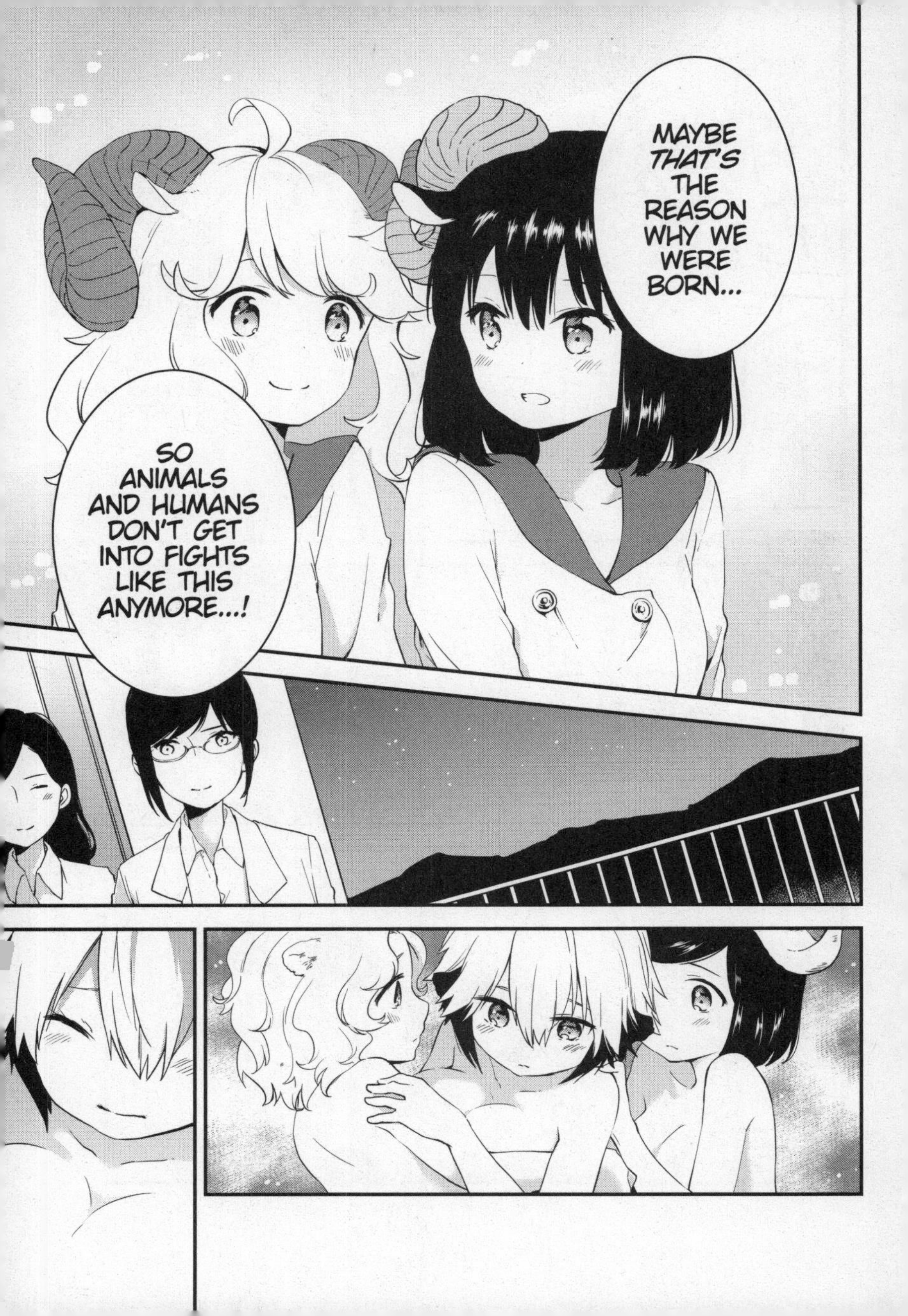
MAYBE *THAT'S* THE REASON WHY WE WERE BORN...
SO ANIMALS AND HUMANS DON'T GET INTO FIGHTS LIKE THIS ANYMORE...!

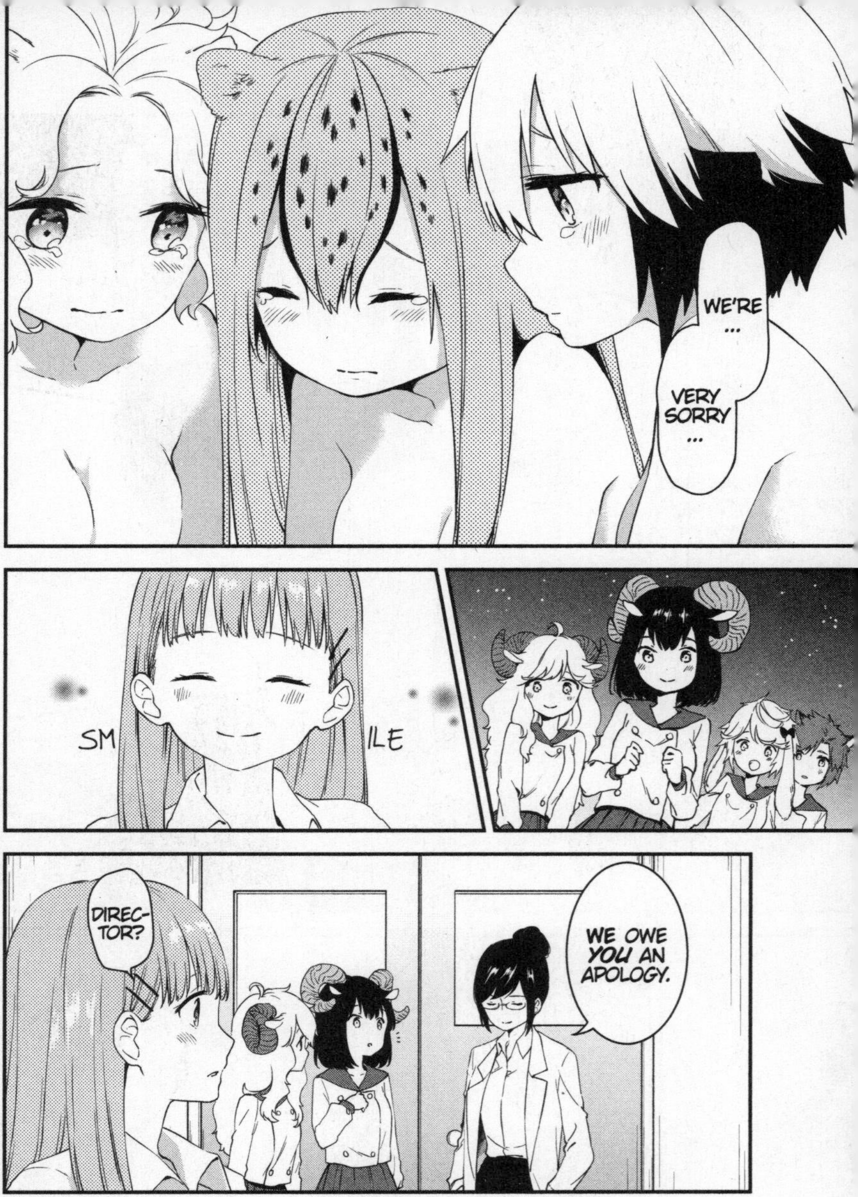
WE'RE ...
VERY SORRY ...
SM ILE
WE OWE YOU AN APOLOGY.
DIRECTOR?

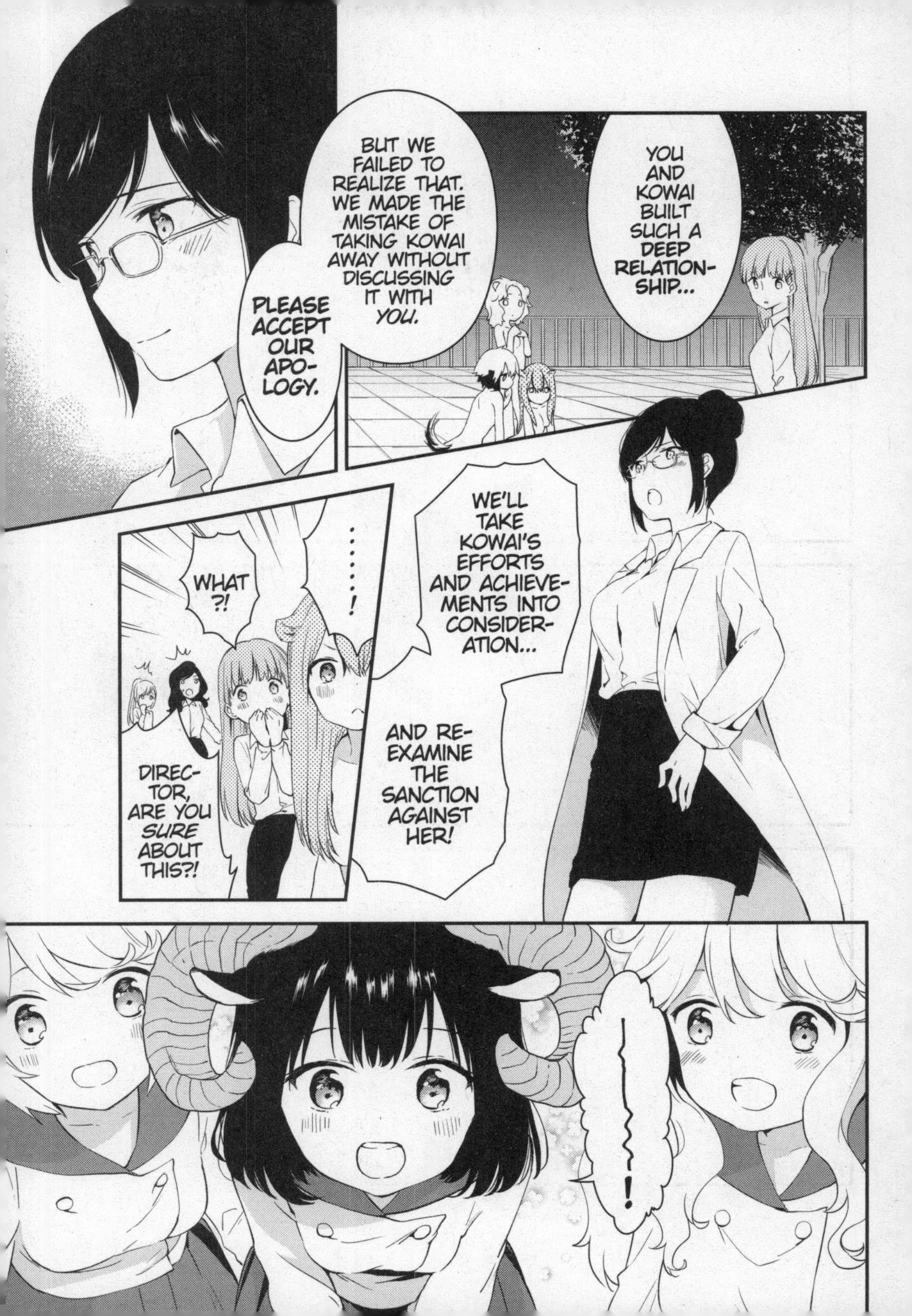
YOU AND KOWAI BUILT SUCH A DEEP RELATIONSHIP...
BUT WE FAILED TO REALIZE THAT. WE MADE THE MISTAKE OF TAKING KOWAI AWAY WITHOUT DISCUSSING IT WITH YOU.
PLEASE ACCEPT OUR APOLOGY.
WE'LL TAKE KOWAI'S EFFORTS AND ACHIEVEMENTS INTO CONSIDERATION...
AND RE-EXAMINE THE SANCTION AGAINST HER!
......!
WHAT?!
DIRECTOR, ARE YOU SURE ABOUT THIS?!

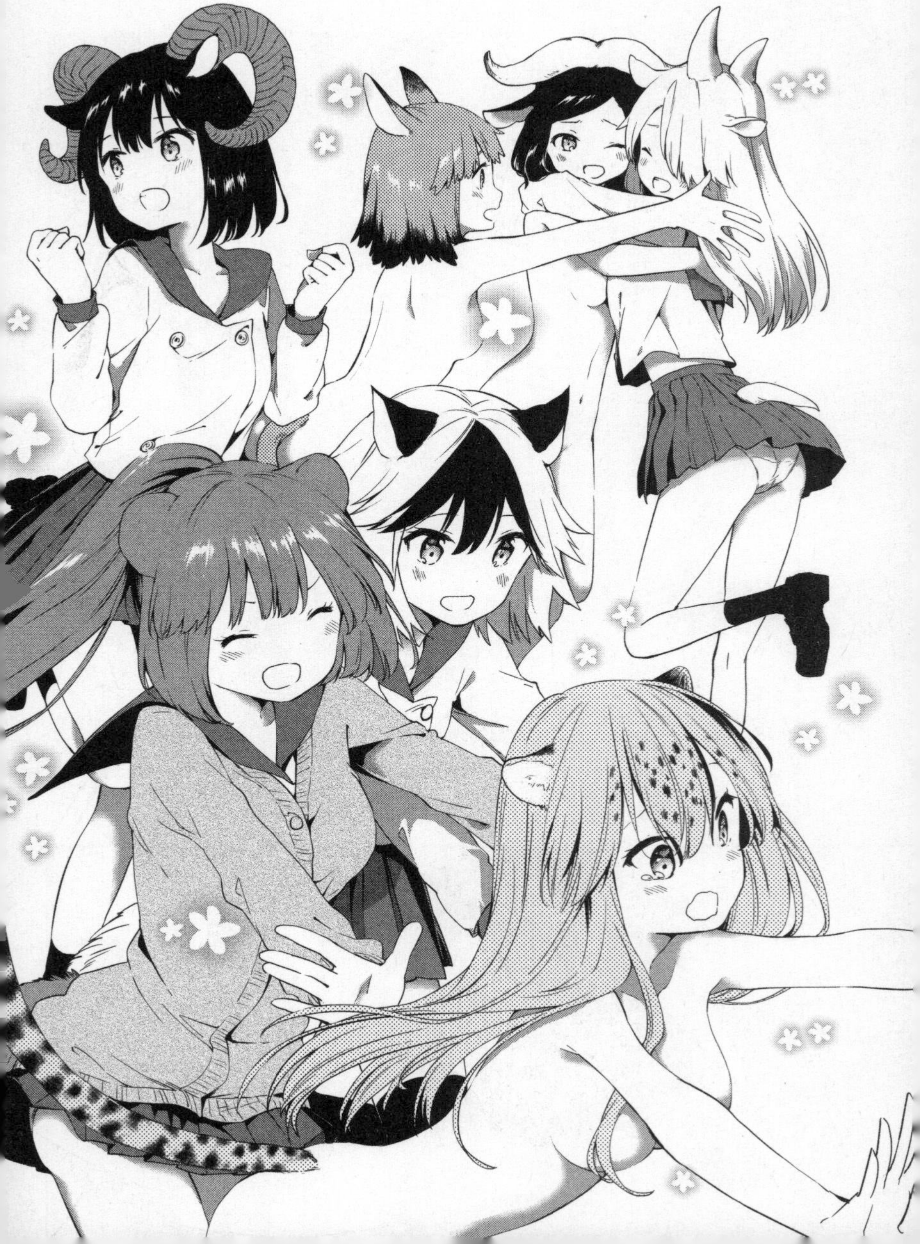

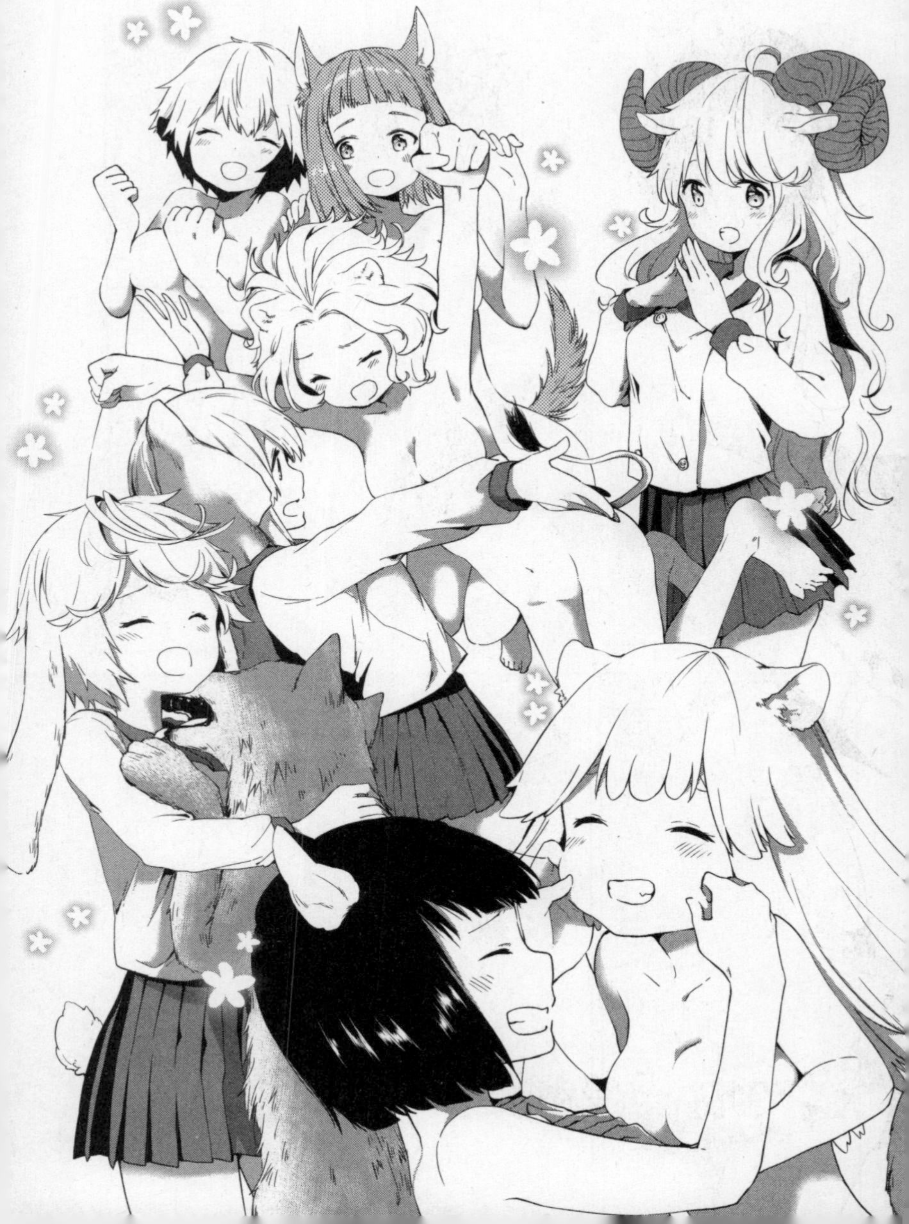

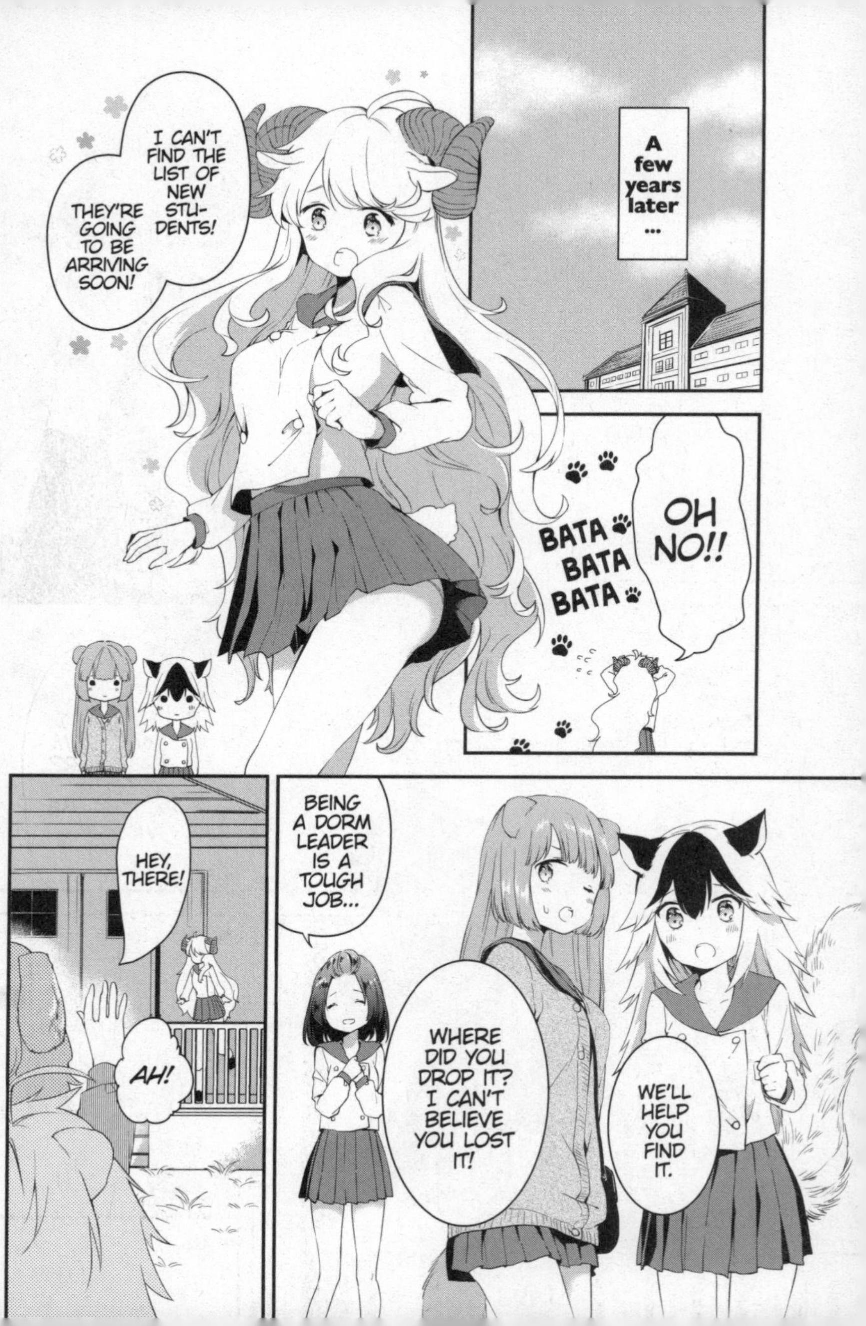

A few years later...
I CAN'T FIND THE LIST OF NEW STU-DENTS!
THEY'RE GOING TO BE ARRIVING SOON!
OH NO!!
BATA BATA BATA
BEING A DORM LEADER IS A TOUGH JOB...
WE'LL HELP YOU FIND IT.
WHERE DID YOU DROP IT? I CAN'T BELIEVE YOU LOST IT!
HEY, THERE!
AH!

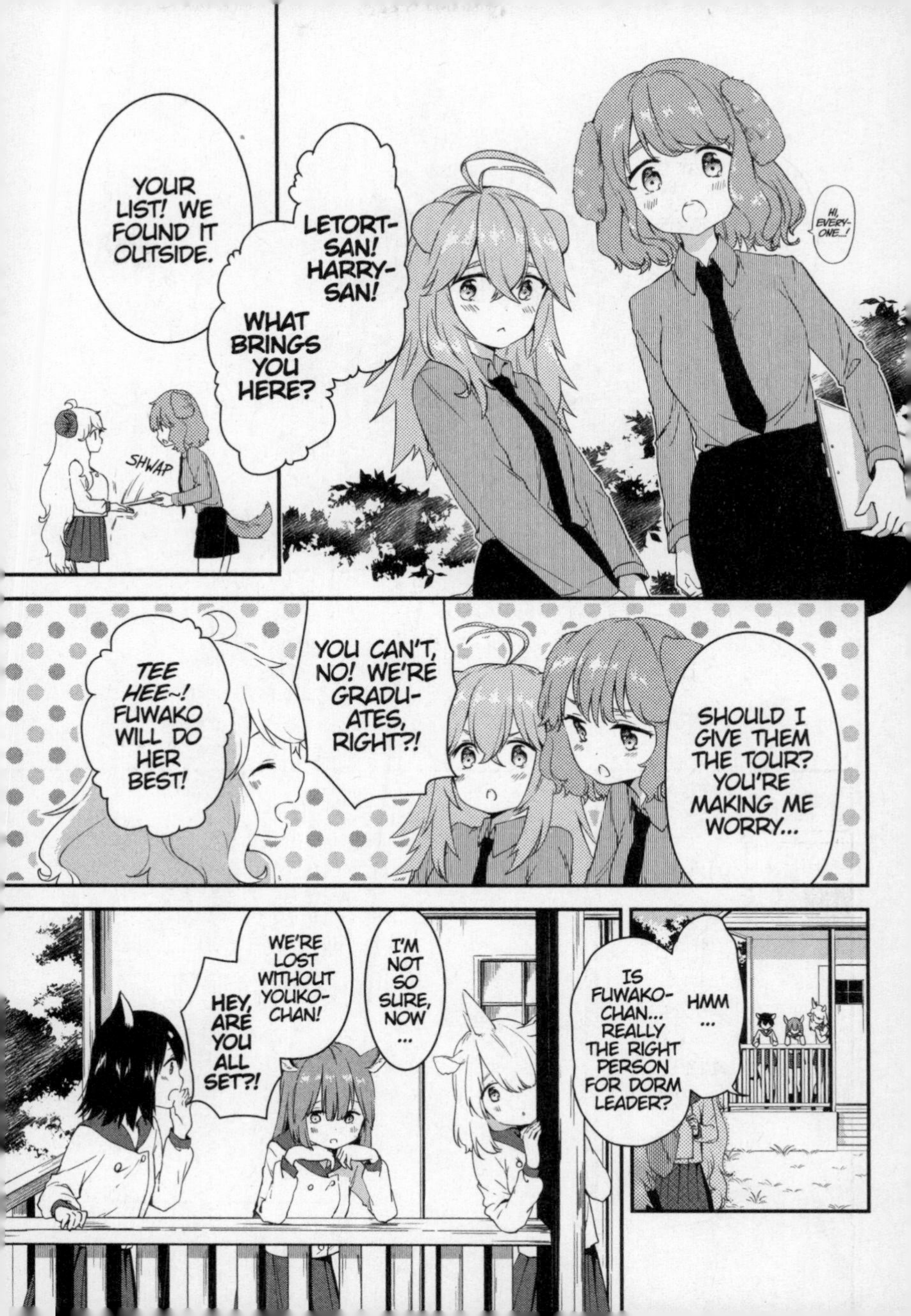
HI, EVERY-ONE...!
LETORT-SAN! HARRY-SAN!
WHAT BRINGS YOU HERE?
YOUR LIST! WE FOUND IT OUTSIDE.
SHWAP
SHOULD I GIVE THEM THE TOUR? YOU'RE MAKING ME WORRY...
YOU CAN'T, NO! WE'RE GRADU-ATES, RIGHT?!
TEE HEE~! FUWAKO WILL DO HER BEST!
HMM ...
IS FUWAKO-CHAN... REALLY THE RIGHT PERSON FOR DORM LEADER?
I'M NOT SO SURE, NOW ...
WE'RE LOST WITHOUT YOUKO-CHAN!
HEY, ARE YOU ALL SET?!

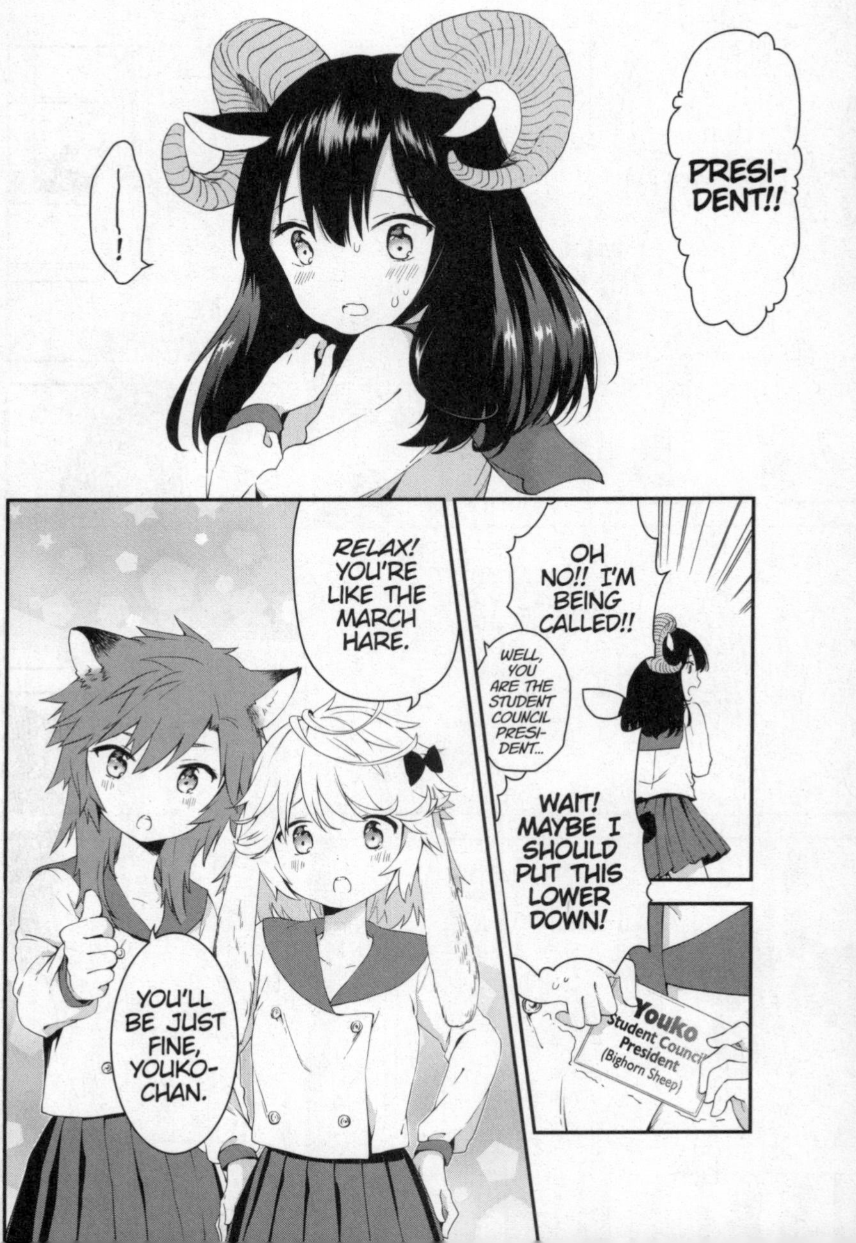
PRESIDENT!!
!!
OH NO!! I'M BEING CALLED!!
WELL, YOU ARE THE STUDENT COUNCIL PRESIDENT...
WAIT! MAYBE I SHOULD PUT THIS LOWER DOWN!
Youko Student Council President (Bighorn Sheep)
RELAX! YOU'RE LIKE THE MARCH HARE.
YOU'LL BE JUST FINE, YOUKO-CHAN.

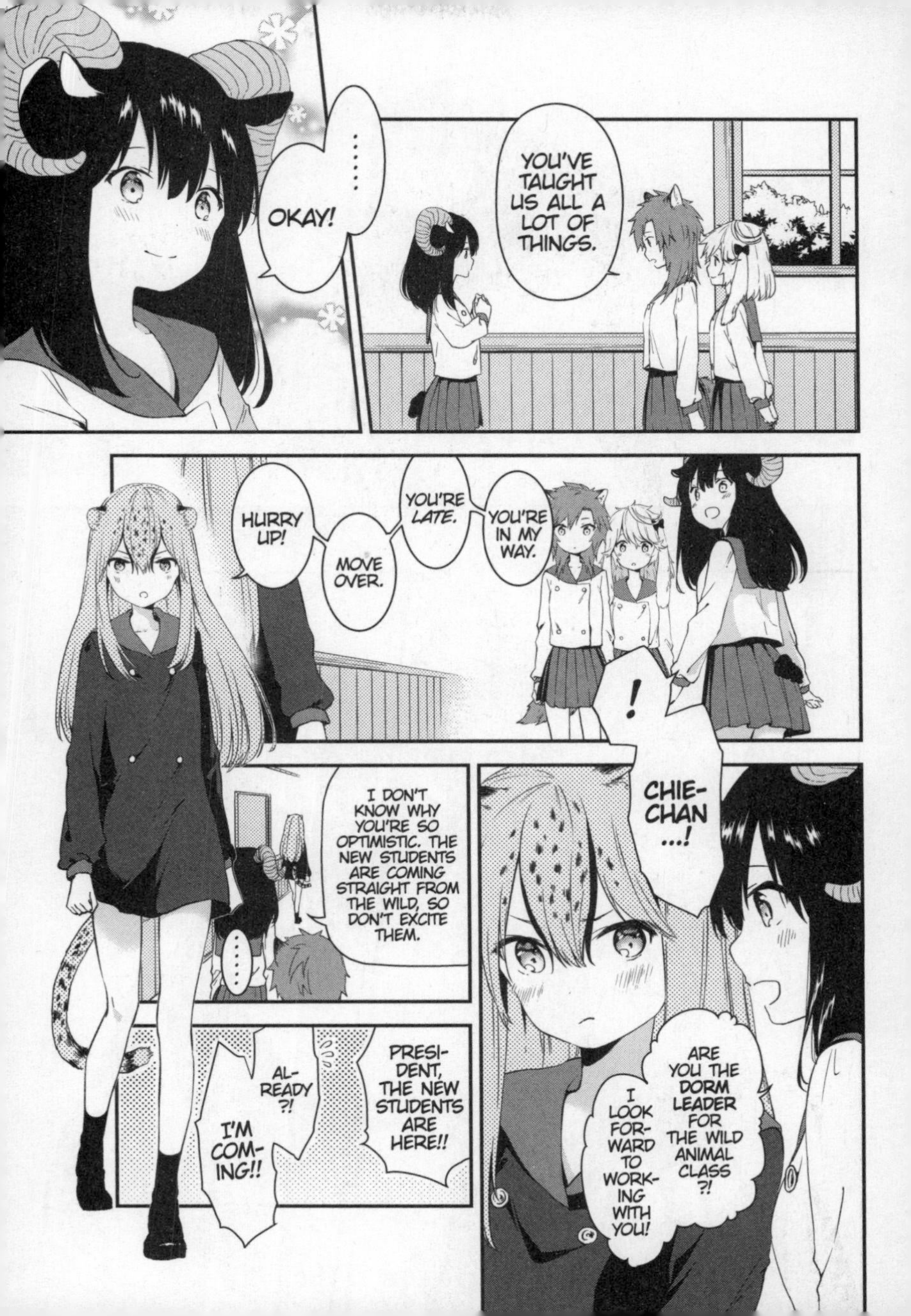
YOU'VE TAUGHT US ALL A LOT OF THINGS.
......
OKAY!
YOU'RE IN MY WAY.
YOU'RE LATE.
MOVE OVER.
HURRY UP!
!
CHIE-CHAN ...!
ARE YOU THE DORM LEADER FOR THE WILD ANIMAL CLASS?!
I LOOK FORWARD TO WORKING WITH YOU!
I DON'T KNOW WHY YOU'RE SO OPTIMISTIC. THE NEW STUDENTS ARE COMING STRAIGHT FROM THE WILD, SO DON'T EXCITE THEM.
......
PRESIDENT, THE NEW STUDENTS ARE HERE!!
ALREADY?!
I'M COMING!!

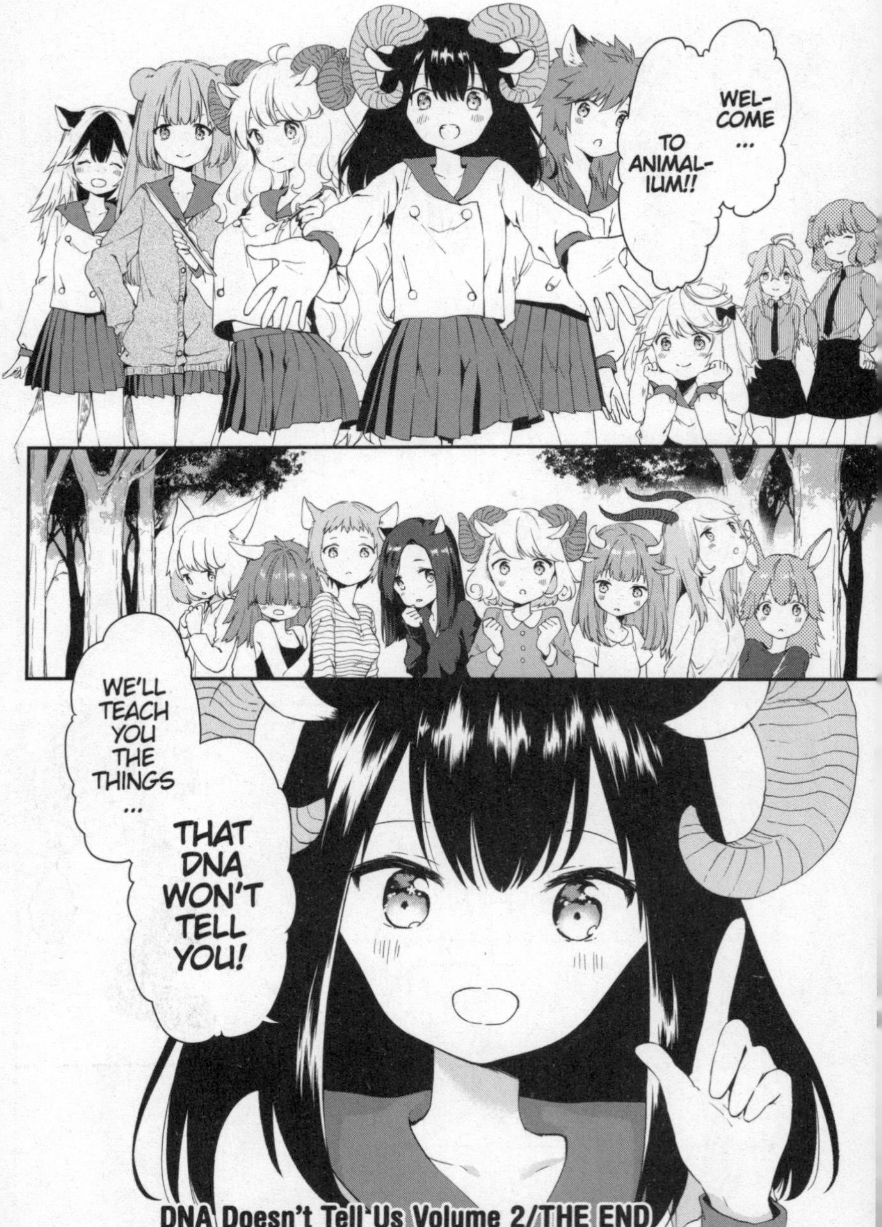
WEL-COME ... TO ANIMAL-IUM!!
WE'LL TEACH YOU THE THINGS ...
THAT DNA WON'T TELL YOU!

DNA Doesn't Tell Us Volume 2/THE END

There are lots of charming things about animals that I didn't get to show you. If you came across any animals you're still curious about, keep researching them. Thank you to the readers and to everyone who has given me support!

Mintarou

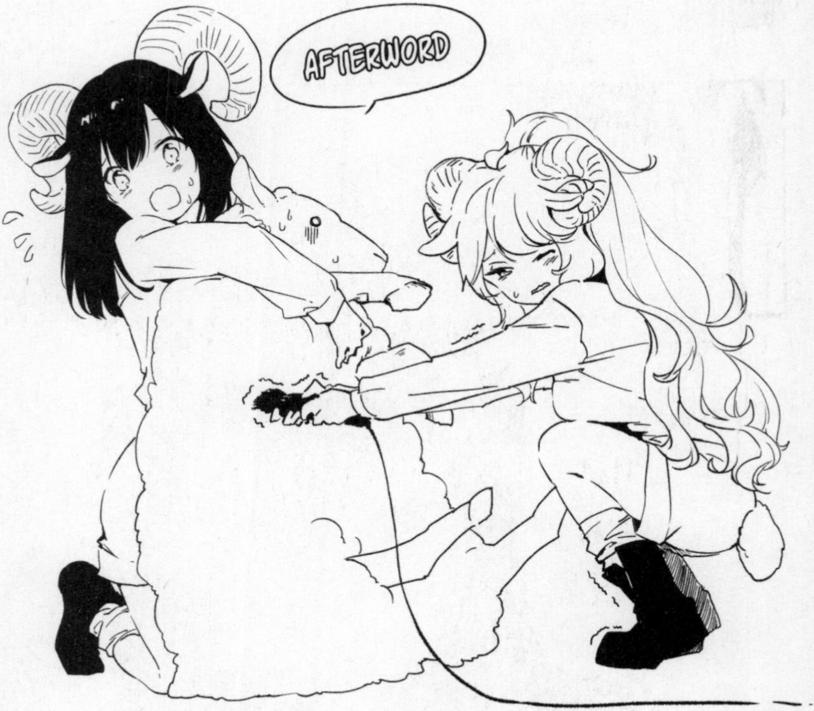
AFTERWORD

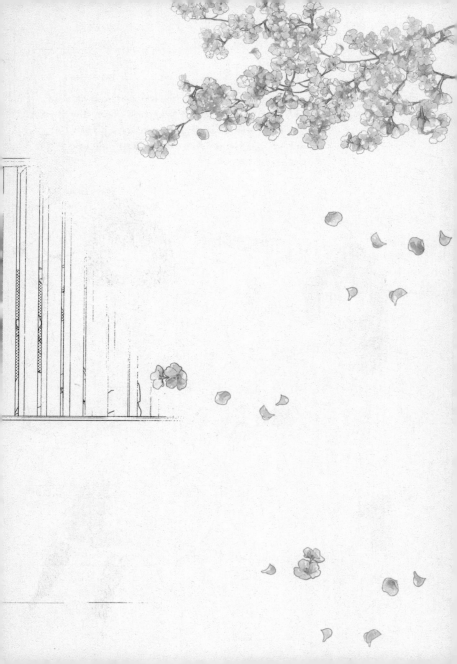

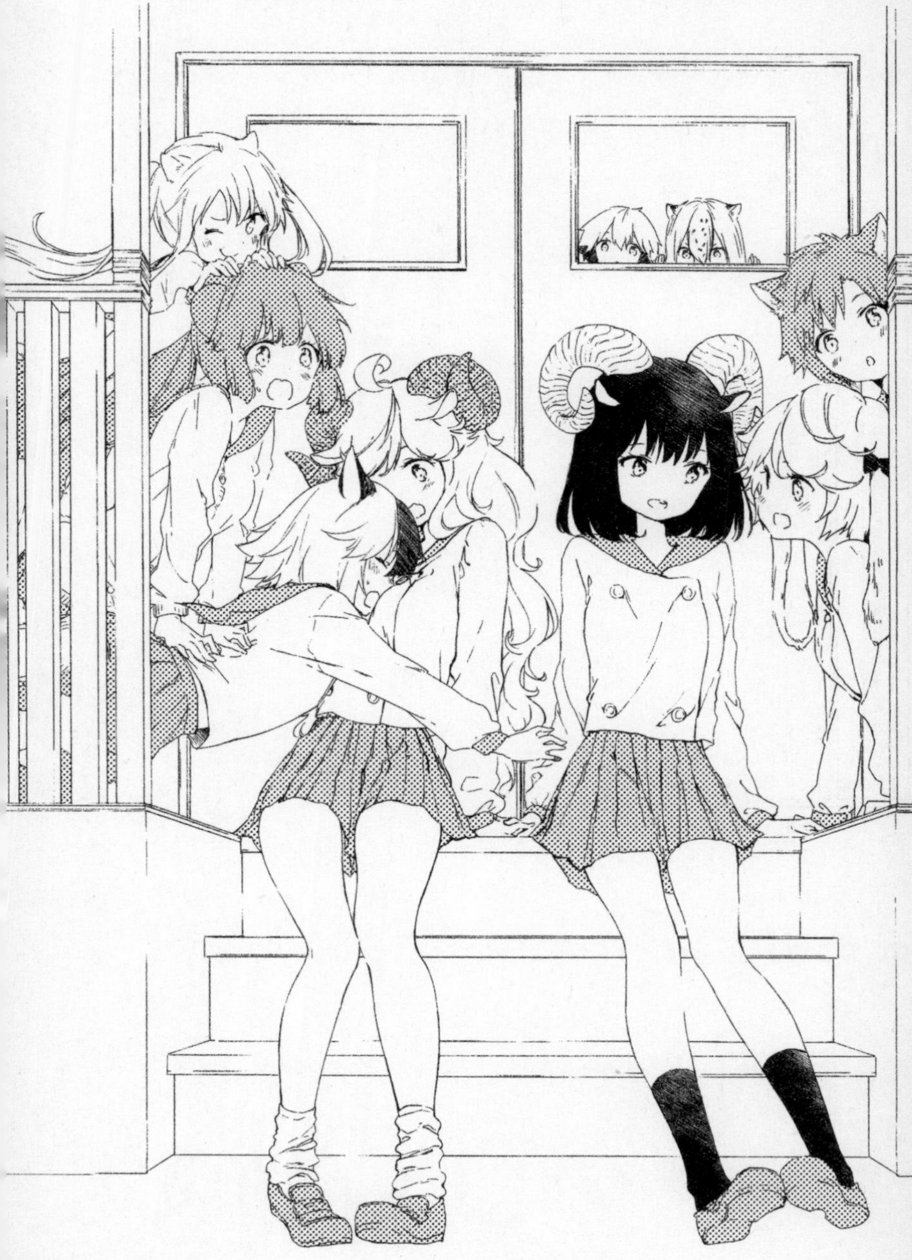

DNA Doesn't Tell Us

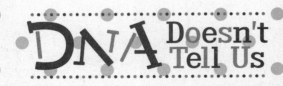